ABBREVIATIONS AND REFERENCES

The abbreviated titles of Shakespeare's works are those in C. T. Onions, *A Shakespeare Glossary*, 2nd edn, 1919. Passages quoted or cited are from the volumes of the new Arden Shakespeare or, in the case of *Hamlet* and the Sonnets, from the complete Tudor Shakespeare, ed. Peter Alexander (Collins, 1951).

I. EDITIONS

Q	*The Historie of Troylus and Cresseida . . .* Written by William Shakespeare . . . Imprinted by *G. Eld* for *R. Bonian* and *H. Walley . . .* 1609 [First State]. *The Famous Historie of Troylus and Cresseida . . .* 1609 [Second State].
F	*Mr. William Shakespeares Comedies, Histories, & Tragedies,* 1623 [First Folio].
F2	*Mr. William Shakespeares Comedies, Histories & Tragedies,* 1632 [Second Folio].
F3	*Mr. William Shakespear's Comedies, Histories, and Tragedies . . . The third Impression,* 1664 [Third Folio].
F4	*Mr. William Shakespear's Comedies, Histories, and Tragedies . . . The fourth Edition,* 1685 [Fourth Folio].
Rowe	*The Works of Mr. William Shakespear . . . Revis'd and Corrected By N. Rowe Esq.,* 1709 [Rowe², a 2nd edn, 1709].
Rowe³	*The Works of Mr. William Shakespear . . . Revis'd and Corrected by N. Rowe Esq.,* 1714.
Pope	*The Works of Shakespear . . . Collected and Corrected . . . by Mr. Pope,* 1723.
Pope²	*The Works of Shakespear . . . Collected and Corrected . . . by Mr. Pope,* 1728.
Theobald	*The Works of Shakespeare . . . Collated with the Oldest Copies, and Corrected; with Notes . . . By Mr. Theobald,* 1733.
Theobald²	*The Works of Shakespeare . . . Collated . . . and Corrected: With Notes . . . By Mr. Theobald. The Second Edition,* 1740.
Hanmer	*The Works of Shakespear . . . Carefully Revised and Corrected by the former Editions,* ed. Thomas Hanmer, 1744.
Warburton	*The Works of Shakespear. The Genuine Text . . . settled . . . By Mr. Pope and Mr. Warburton,* 1747.
Johnson	*The Plays of William Shakespeare . . . To which are added Notes by Sam. Johnson,* 1765.
Capell	*Mr. William Shapeskeare his Comedies, Histories, and Tragedies,* ed. Edward Capell, 1768.
Steevens	*The Plays of William Shakespeare . . . To which are added*

	notes by Samuel Johnson and George Steevens, 1773 [Variorum '73].
Var. '78	The Plays of William Shakespeare . . . The Second Edition, Revised and Augmented, 1778 [Steevens[2]].
Var. '85	The Plays of William Shakespeare . . . The Third Edition, 1785 [Steevens[4]].
Rann	The Dramatic Works of Shakespeare . . . with notes by Joseph Rann. 1789.
Malone	The Plays and Poems of William Shakespeare . . . with . . . notes by Edmond Malone, 1790.
Var. '93	The Plays of William Shakespeare . . . The Fourth Edition. 1793 [Steevens[4]].
Var. '03	The Plays of William Shakespeare . . . The Fifth Edition. Revised and augmented by Isaac Reed, 1803.
Var. '13	The Plays of William Shakespeare . . . Revised and augmented by Isaac Reed. . . . The Sixth Edition, 1813.
Var. '21	The Plays and Poems of William Shakespeare . . . [with] a life of the poet . . . by the late E. Malone . . . [ed. J. Boswell] 1821 ['Boswell's Malone'].
Singer	The Dramatic Works of William Shakespeare with Notes . . . by Samuel Weller Singer, 1826.
Knight	The Pictorial Edition of the Works of Shakespeare, ed. Charles Knight, 1838–43.
Collier	The Works of William Shakespeare . . . with the various readings, and notes . . . by J. Payne Collier, Vols 2 and 9, 1842.
Collier[2]	The Plays of Shakespeare: The text regulated by the old copies, and by the recently discovered Folio of 1632, containing early manuscript emendations. Edited by J. Payne Collier, 1853.
Delius	Shakesperes Werke. Herausgegeben und erklärt von N. Delius, 1854–60.
Singer[2]	The Dramatic Works of William Shakespeare . . . revised by Samuel Weller Singer, 1856.
Dyce	The Works of William Shakespeare. The Text revised by the Rev. Alexander Dyce, 1857.
Grant White	The Works of William Shakespeare, ed. Richard Grant White, 1857–65.
Collier[3]	Shakespeare's Comedies, Histories, Tragedies, and poems. Edited by J. Payne Collier, 1858.
Staunton	The Plays of Shakespeare, ed. Howard Staunton, 1860.
Camb.	The Works of William Shakespeare, ed. William George Clark and W. Aldis Wright (The Cambridge Shakespeare), 1863–6.
Keightley	The Plays of William Shakespeare. Carefully edited by Thomas Keightley, 1864.
Dyce[2]	The Works of William Shakespeare . . . Second Edition, 1865.
Hudson	The Complete Works of William Shakespeare, ed. H. N. Hudson, 1881.
Verity	The Pitt Press Shakespeare, ed. A. W. Verity, 1890–1905.
Craig	The Complete Works of Shakespeare, ed. W. J. Craig, 1891.
Deighton	Troilus and Cressida, ed. K. Deighton (Arden Shakespeare) 1906.

Lee	*The Works of Shakespeare*, ed. S. Lee (Caxton edition), 1910.
Tatlock	*The Works of Shakespeare*, ed. J. S. P. Tatlock, 1912.
Kittredge	*The Works of Shakespeare*, ed. G. L. Kittredge, 1936.
Alexander	*William Shakespeare, The Complete Works*, ed. Peter Alexander, 1951.
Variorum	*Troilus and Cressida*, ed. H. N. Hillebrand (supplemented by T. W. Baldwin) (New Variorum Shakespeare), 1953.
Sisson	*William Shakespeare, The Complete Works*, ed. C. J. Sisson, 1954.
NCS	*Troilus and Cressida*, ed. Alice Walker (New Cambridge Shakespeare), 1957.
Munro	*The London Shakespeare*, ed. John Munro, 1958.
Whitaker	*The History of Troilus and Cressida*, ed. Virgil K. Whitaker, (Pelican Shakespeare), 1958.
Seltzer	*The History of Troilus and Cressida*, ed. Daniel Seltzer (Signet Classic Shakespeare), 1963.
Riverside	*The Riverside Shakespeare*, textual ed. G. Blakemore Evans, 1974.

2. OTHER WORKS

Abbott	E. A. Abbott, *A Shakespearean Grammar*, 1869, etc.
Alexander, '*Troilus*'	Peter Alexander, '*Troilus and Cressida*, 1609', *Library*, IX, 1928–9.
Aquinas	St Thomas Aquinas, *Summa Theologiae*, ed. P. Caramello, 1962.
Aristotle	Aristotle, *Nicomachean Ethics*, trans. J. A. K. Thomson (as *The Ethics of Aristotle*), 1955.
Ascham	Roger Ascham, *The Scholemaster*, 1570.
Bayley	John Bayley, *The Uses of Division*, 1976.
Bradbrook	M. C. Bradbrook, 'What Shakespeare did to Chaucer's *Troilus and Criseyde*', *SQ*, IX, 1958.
Bullough	Geoffrey Bullough, *Narrative and Dramatic Sources of Shakespeare*, Vol. VI, 1966.
Campbell	O. J. Campbell, *Comicall Satyre and Shakespeare's Troilus and Cressida*, 1938.
Caxton	William Caxton, *The Recuyell of the Historyes of Troye. Written in French by Raoul Lefevre. Translated and Printed by William Caxton*, ed. H. Oskar Sommer, 1894.
Chambers	E. K. Chambers, *William Shakespeare*, 2 vols, 1930.
Chapman	George Chapman, *Chapman's Homer*, ed. Allardyce Nicoll, 1957.
Chaucer	Geoffrey Chaucer, *Works*, ed. F. N. Robinson, 2nd edn, 1957.
E.E.T.S., e.s.	Early English Text Society, extra series.
Franz	Wilhelm Franz, *Shakespeare-Grammatik*, 1939.
Gerard	John Gerard, *The herball, or generall historie of plantes*, 1597.
Golding	*Shakespeare's Ovid, being Arthur Golding's translation of the Metamorphoses*, ed. W. H. D. Rouse, 1904.
Greg	W. W. Greg, Introductory Note to *Troilus and Cressida*,

	Shakespeare Quartos in Collotype Facsimile, 8, 1952.
Greg, 'Printing'	W. W. Greg, 'The Printing of Shakespeare's *Troilus and Cressida* in the First Folio', *PBSA*, XLV, 1951.
Greg, *SFF*	W. W. Greg, *The Shakespeare First Folio*, 1955.
Henryson	Robert Henryson, *Works*, ed. Denton Fox, 1981.
Hinman	Charlton Hinman, *The Printing and Proof-Reading of the First Folio of Shakespeare*, 1963.
Hodges	C. Walter Hodges, *The Globe Restored*, 1953.
Hotson	Leslie Hotson, *Shakespeare's Sonnets Dated*, 1949.
Hulme	Hilda Hulme, *Explorations in Shakespeare's Language*, 1962
Hunter	G. K. Hunter, '*Troilus and Cressida*: a tragic satire', *Shakespeare Studies* (Tokyo), 1977.
Iliad	Homer, *The Iliad*, trans. E. V. Rieu, 1950.
Jonson	Ben Jonson, *Works*, ed. C. H. Herford and Percy Simpson 1925–52.
Kimbrough	Robert Kimbrough, *Shakespeare's* Troilus and Cressida *and its Setting*, 1964.
Kökeritz	Helge Kökeritz, *Shakespeare's Pronunciation*, 1953.
Langland	William Langland, *Piers Plowman, The B Version*, ed. George Kane and E. Talbot Donaldson, 1975.
Leishman	J. B. Leishman (ed.), *The Three Parnassus Plays*, 1949.
Lydgate	John Lydgate, *Lydgate's Troy Book*, ed. Henry Bergen, *E.E.T.S.*, 1906–35 (e.s. 97, 103, 106, 126).
Mackenzie	D. F. Mackenzie, 'Printers of the Mind', *SB*, XXII, 1969.
MSR	Malone Society Reprints.
Mucedorus	ed. C. F. Tucker Brooke, in *The Shakespeare Apocrypha*, 1908.
Muir	Kenneth Muir, '*Troilus and Cressida*', *Sh.S.*, 8, 1955.
Nashe	Thomas Nashe, *Works*, ed. R. B. McKerrow, revised F. P. Wilson, 1966.
Noble	Richmond Noble, *Shakespeare's Biblical Knowledge*, 1935.
Nowottny	W. M. T. Nowottny, ' "Opinion" and "Value" in *Troilus and Cressida*', *EC*, 4, 1954.
OED	*Oxford English Dictionary*.
Onions	C. T. Onions, *A Shakespeare Glossary*, 2nd edn, revised, 1919.
Ovid	See Golding.
Pollard	A. W. Pollard and others, *Shakespeare's Hand in the Play of Sir Thomas More*, 1923.
Presson	Robert K. Presson, *Shakespeare's* Troilus and Cressida *and the Legends of Troy*, 1953.
Schmidt	Alexander Schmidt, *Shakespeare Lexicon*, 1874 (Vol. I), 1875 (Vol. II).
Sidney	Sir Philip Sidney, *The Countesse of Pembroke's Arcadia* (1590/3), ed. Albert Feuillerat, 1965 reprint of 1912 edn.
Sidney, *Apologie*	Sir Philip Sidney, *An Apologie for Poesie*, ed. Geoffrey Shepherd, 1973.
Sisson	C. J. Sisson, *New Readings in Shakespeare*, 1956.
Spenser	Edmund Spenser, *Minor Poems*, ed. E. de Selincourt, 1970.

Spenser, *Faerie Queene*	Edmund Spenser, *The Faerie Queene*, ed. J. C. Smith, 1972.
Spurgeon	Caroline Spurgeon, *Keats's Shakespeare*, 1928.
Sternfeld	F. W. Sternfeld, '*Troilus and Cressida*: Music for the Play', *English Institute Essays*, 1952.
Thersytes	Anon., Tudor Facsimile Texts, 1912.
Thompson	Patricia Thompson, 'Rant and Cant in *Troilus and Cressida*', *Essays and Studies*, 1969.
Tilley	M. P. Tilley, *A Dictionary of Proverbs in England in the Sixteenth and Seventeenth Centuries*, 1950.
Traversi	Derek Traversi, *An Approach to Shakespeare*, Vol. 2, 1969.
Walker	Alice Walker, 'The Textual Problem of *Troilus and Cressida*', *MLR*, XLV, 1950.
Walker, *Textual Problems*	Alice Walker, *Textual Problems of the First Folio*, 1953.
Watson	C. B. Watson, *Shakespeare and the Renaissance Concept of Honour*, 1960.
Whiter	Walter Whiter, *Specimen of a Commentary on Shakespeare* (1794), ed. Alan Over and Mary Bell, 1967.
Williams, Charles	Charles Williams, *The English Poetic Mind*, 1932.
Williams, Philip	Philip Williams, 'The "Second Issue" of *Troilus and Cressida*, 1609', *SB*, II, 1949–50.
Williams, Philip, 'Q and F'	Philip Williams, 'Shakespeare's *Troilus and Cressida*: the Relationship of Q and F', *SB*, III, 1950–1.
Wilson	F. P. Wilson (ed.), *Oxford Dictionary of English Proverbs*, 3rd edn, 1970.
Wordsworth	William Wordsworth, *Lyrical Ballads* (Preface), 1800.

4. PERIODICALS

EC	*Essays in Criticism*
E&St	*Essays and Studies*
ES	*Englische Studien*
MLN	*Modern Language Notes*
MLR	*Modern Language Review*
N&Q	*Notes and Queries*
NSST	*New Shakespeare Society Transactions*
PBSA	*Papers of the Bibliographical Society of America*
PMLA	*Publications of the Modern Language Association*
SB	*Studies in Bibliography*
Sh.S.	*Shakespeare Survey*
SQ	*Shakespeare Quarterly*
TRSL	*Transactions of the Royal Society of Literature*

INTRODUCTION

I. THE TEXT

There are two substantive texts of *Troilus and Cressida*, the Quarto of 1609 (Q) and the Folio of 1623 (F); and because of the complex nature, both of their relationships and its consequences for the dating of the play, it will be best to sketch first what may be generally agreed about them, and then to proceed to a more detailed account of the problems that they give rise to.

On 7 February 1602/3, there appeared in the *Stationers' Register* a conditional entry:

> Ent^{r}ed for his copie in Full Court holden this day.
> M^r to print when he hath gotten sufficient aucthority
> Robertes. for yt. The booke of Troilus and Cresseda as yt
> is acted by my lo: Chamberlens Men vj^d

It is not clear whose authority might have been required, and hence we cannot be sure whether Roberts intended to publish, or whether this was a 'blocking' entry by the Lord Chamberlain's Men to prevent unauthorized printing. Since it is unlikely that the Company (later the King's Men) should have had two plays called *Troilus and Cressida*, it is probable that the play entered by Roberts was Shakespeare's, although, as Greg observed,[1] 'it may not, of course, have already assumed the exact form in which it has been preserved'.

On 28 January 1608/9 there was a further entry in the *Register*:

> Ri. Bonion Entred for their Copy vnder thandes of m^r Segar
> Henry deputy to Sr Geo. Bucke and m^r wa^{r}d. Lownes a
> Walleys booke called. The history of Troylus and Cressida.
>   vj^d

This entry was followed during the year by the Quarto, printed for Bonian and Walley by George Eld. The Quarto exists in two states (Collation A—L⁴ M² (M2 blank) [first state]; ¶² A2—4 B—L⁴ M¹ [second state]). The first calls the play, both on the title-page and in the head-title and running-title, 'The Historie

---

1. Introductory note to *Troilus and Cressida*, Shakespeare Quartos in Collotype Facsimile, 8 (1952).

of Troylus and Cresseida' (thus agreeing with the entry in the *Register*) and says that the play is 'As it was acted by the Kings Maiesties seruants at the Globe'. The second cancels the first title-page, and substitutes a new half-sheet signed ¶, containing a new title-page (first leaf) and an Epistle to the reader (second leaf). The new title-page is different only in its upper half (i.e. the lower half, from 'Written by William Shakespeare' to the end of the imprint, is from the same setting of type as the first); it reads

> The / Famous Historie of / Troylus and Cresseid. / Excellently expressing the beginning / of their loues, with the conceited wooing / of Pandarus Prince of Licia.

There is no mention of a company or of a theatre; and indeed the Epistle strongly implies that the play had never been acted in a public theatre, and (in order to appear in print) had made some kind of 'escape', since the 'grand possessors' would have prevented publication of it (together with other comedies [sic] by the same author) had they been able.

There are some press-corrections in the Quarto: one in sheet A (two, if one should count an error in the running-title); one in E; fourteen in F; and two in K, of which one is well-known (Ariathna's/Ariachna's) and represents a conflation of Ariadne and Arachne.[1]

On the evidence of the running-titles, the Quarto was printed with two skeletons (X and Y) as far as sheet E; sheet F was printed with a third skeleton (Z) (as one can see from the absence of -*us* ligatures in *Troylus*), and the sequence then proceeded thus:[2]

Sheet	A	B	C	D	E	F	G	H	I	K	L	M
Skeleton	X	Y	X	Y	X	Z	Y	X	Y	Z	X+Y	X+Y

Since sheets L and M were printed in this rather unexpected way, it is usually supposed[3] that M, which is only a half-sheet (with the second leaf blank), must have been printed with the half-sheet containing the new title-page and Epistle. From this it

1. Two compositors were employed to set most of the Quarto, but a third was introduced to set sheet F. Details are given in Appendix I.
2. This account of the printing is substantially that given by the late Philip Williams, Jr (conveniently summarized in Hillebrand, *Variorum*). I do not wholly accept Dr Williams's subsequent theory of text.
3. The argument was advanced by Philip Williams ('The "Second Issue" of *Troilus and Cressida*, 1609', *SB*, II, 1949–50, pp. 29–33), basing himself on the theory of F. Bowers (*SB*, I, 1948–9, pp. 199–202).

should follow that the new title-page represents an alteration during the course of printing, and not subsequent to it. Three of the fifteen known copies of the Quarto are in the first state, with the original (cancellandum) title-page (but, of course, containing the complete text of M); one (the Daniel-Huth copy) has both the original title-page and the new half-sheet cancellans (as well as the complete half-sheet of M, with M2 blank); and all the rest are in the second state, with the cancellans half-sheet. Of the three copies in the first state, the Martin Bodmer copy (formerly Rosenbach) is uncut.

The Folio text of *Troilus* stands at the beginning of the Tragedies. Had Jaggard been able to follow his original intention, it would have succeeded *Romeo and Juliet* in the Tragedies; and three pages were set before policy was changed. It is generally assumed[1] that there were difficulties of copyright: that Walley, the surviving partner of the two who had published the Quarto, refused permission for the Quarto text to be used; and that Jaggard laid *Troilus* aside in the hope of reaching agreement with Walley in the near future. At any rate, it is certain (from the survival of one example of the original gg3) that *Romeo* at first ended on gg3^r, and that *Troilus*, without a Prologue, started on gg3^v. The full story of the printing of F *Troilus* may be read in Hinman: what matters at present is that, at a very late stage in the printing of the Folio, Jaggard seems to have resolved his problems over copyright, and *Troilus* was printed between the Histories and the Tragedies (i.e. after *Henry VIII* and before *Coriolanus*). It was too late for inclusion in the Catalogue of plays at the beginning of the Folio. And since it was necessarily printed on a new quire (beginning, therefore, on the recto of a leaf, whereas the original setting had begun on the verso of gg3), Jaggard acquired, from what source we do not know, the text of the Prologue, and set it in a new large type, to fill the whole recto of his first leaf. The verso, containing the first page of text, was then re-set from the original leaf (gg3^v), and varies from it only by minor accidents. The next two pages are all that is left (except for the chance survival of the rejected gg3^v) of the original setting of the opening of *Troilus*: that is, Jaggard saved the original leaf (paginated 79–80) from what was otherwise the imperfect quire gg, and inserted it between the re-set first page and the bulk of the play (which was, of course, freshly set). As a

1. E.g. by W. W. Greg, *The Shakespeare First Folio* (1955), p. 445, and by Charlton Hinman, *The Printing and Proof-Reading of the First Folio of Shakespeare* (1963), Vol. I, pp. 27–8; Vol. II, p. 261.

result, the first two leaves of F *Troilus* are separate leaves (non-conjugate) and belong to two different periods of printing of F, although they derive ultimately from the same copy. Neither leaf bears a signature, though they are conventionally denominated χ1 and χ2.

I remarked above that Jaggard contrived to resolve his problems over copyright. What actually happened can only be surmised, but it is plausible surmise: unfortunately, final proof is wanting.[1] Jaggard, in acquiring copy for the Folio, was content to use Quarto copy (and sometimes even 'bad Quarto' copy) if he could get it. In four cases he met difficulty. Matthew Law held the title of three plays (*Richard II*, *1 Henry IV* and *Richard III*), and since there is irregularity (that is to say, delay) in the printing of all three in the Folio,[2] it is most likely that Law was obstructive, and that although printing was delayed, agreement was reached in time for the three plays to appear in their proper positions and to be included in the Catalogue. Since *Troilus* was delayed far longer than were the three Histories, the natural inference is that Walley was more recalcitrant than Law.[3] But one can go further. The first three pages of the Folio text are a simple reprint of the Quarto: the remainder of the Folio text is printed from the Quarto, but with reference to some other text (presumably MS),[4] and it is clear that Jaggard must, at a late stage, have got access to something which, being different from Walley's Quarto, made him free of any legal stay imposed by Walley. What the text was, one cannot be sure, and the question need not be investigated for the moment; but since Jaggard had bought Roberts's business in 1608 or thereabouts, it seems possible that (whatever the nature of the MS he acquired) he claimed independent title to *Troilus* on the strength of Roberts's entry of 1602/3.[5]

A preference for printed copy would be reasonable—such copy holds few difficulties for the compositor, and it makes casting-off easy—so that we need not be surprised if Jaggard were to have used an altered Quarto as copy for *Troilus*.[6] Differences

1. Substantially, I follow Hinman and Greg.

2. Hinman, Vol. II, p. 523.

3. Hinman, Vol. I, pp. 27–8; Vol. II, p. 523.

4. W. W. Greg, 'The Printing of Shakespeare's *Troilus and Cressida* in the First Folio', *PBSA*, XLV (1951), pp. 273–82; Alice Walker, *Textual Problems of the First Folio* (1953), pp. 68–93.

5. Greg, ibid.

6. Peter Alexander proposed this theory in 1928–9 ('*Troilus and Cressida*, 1609', *Library*, IX, pp. 267–86).

between Q and F, though numerous, are seldom large: the major alterations in F concern less than a line at a time; and the chief value of F lies in supplying lines which were omitted, sometimes by accident, from Q. None of the passages peculiar to F exceeds six lines in length; and an uncut or untrimmed copy of Q should have given plenty of room for MS additions to be made in the margin. (The Bodmer copy, uncut, with its width of 6 in., as against the 4¾ in. of most shorn Quartos, suggests how much room a collator may have had to work with if, indeed, he did not find it as easy to insert omitted passages on paper slips, flown-in to a margin.)

Two variant passages combine to give some indication of the nature of the F text. At iv.v.95, Q reads

Vlisses: what Troyan is that same that lookes so heauy?
Vlis.   The yongest sonne of *Priam*, a true knight,

and continues the 'character' for several lines; by l. 108 comes

They call him Troylus

Now, plainly, the speech of Ulysses is, as a whole, correct, and the identification of Troilus comes properly as a climax, when he is formally called a second Hector; equally plainly, there is something wrong with the first line of the passage. F clears up this error: Q has dropped a short speech of Ulysses' ('They are oppos'd already'), while retaining the speech-heading; the speech-heading has then been expanded into a vocative (*Vlisses*:) and the speech-heading for this one-line question of Agamemnon's ('what Troyan is that same that lookes so heauy?') has also been omitted. But having set this out properly, F commits what appears to be an error of its own: it begins Ulysses's speech thus:

The yongest Sonne of Priam;
A true Knight; they call him *Troylus;*
Not yet mature

and then runs correctly, repeating

They call him *Troylus.*

at the proper place. There is no need, I think, to postulate authorial *alteration* in Q: its error is really an eye-slip, falsely 'corrected' (speech-heading made into vocative). Hence, F's insertion of the half-line

they call him *Troylus;*

must be one of two things: either it represents an attempt to cut the speech by half (which would have been inept, since the speech would have lost much of its point, and the lineation would have been twice erroneous), or—and this is much more likely—Shakespeare at some stage wrote

> The youngest sonne of *Priam*, a true knight,
> They call him *Troylus*

and then cut the last four words, reserving them for the end of the speech. If that be so, then Q must derive from what Greg calls 'a properly edited manuscript';[1] and F must have had access to a MS which was either itself foul papers or else an imperfectly corrected copy of them.

The other variant passage is connected with the lines v.x. 32-4. Both texts read (substantially)

> *Pan.*   But here you, here you.
> *Troy.*   Hence broker, lacky, ignomyny, shame,
>   Pursue thy life, and liue aye with thy name.

F inserts the passage, altering the first speech to

> Why, but heare you?

at the end of v.iii, which is an appropriate place (for Pandarus has no business on a battlefield). Clearly, Shakespeare used the exchange first at v.iii, and then, having decided to let Pandarus speak the Epilogue, he adapted it and transferred it to v.x. F has recovered the original arrangements (as it did in iv.v) and again has failed to see that the recovery was not needed. The dismissal at v.iii (before the final battle) must represent Shakespeare's first design: it is plausible, since it gives Pandarus an excuse (by delivering a letter) for intruding into a scene of warriors about to fight; and it allows the pander (with all his associations of debased sexuality, derived from the rest of the play) to be rejected simultaneously with the last message from the faithless mistress. The dismissal at the end of the play (as both texts have it) loses something by reducing the force of the end of v.iii: it is more dramatically effective to curse Pandarus than to criticize a dishonest letter; but it gains much, by allowing Pandarus (despite the implausibility involved) to enjoy the last bitter word at the expense of the audience. Thematically, the end-of-the-play position is better; but as craftsmanship it looks like patchwork.

A number of passages which occur in F only may be mentioned here in order to be dismissed, for they are simple omissions which tell us nothing of the nature of either text. Three of them

---

1. *SFF*, p. 347.

are lengthy (I.iii.70–4; II.iii.60–4;[1] and IV.v.164–9); one (v.x.21–2) is needed to complete a couplet; none of the remainder exceeds one line in length, and most are intended to explain minor movements on stage (I.iii.314; II.iii.94; III.i.107; IV.v.94; IV.v.131; IV.v.205; v.ii.67; v.iii.58).

Other passages peculiar to F may represent matter cut from Q, as being thought too wordy, or otherwise inept. Consider, for example, the following passages:

(a)

> Which entertain'd, Limbes are in his instruments,
> In no lesse working, then are Swords and Bowes
> Directiue by the Limbes.   (I.iii.354–6)

This fits the argument, but is not absolutely necessary to it: Nestor has already foreseen one good consequence for the army of the victorious duellist; the present passage offers a second. In l. 354 'in' is superfluous (perhaps anticipating l. 358, perhaps merely the next word but two). In l. 355, 'In' = 'in', not 'E'en' (*pace* Dr Walker): 'working' means 'operation'.

(b)

> Now the dry Suppeago on the Subiect, and Warre
> and Lecherie confound all.   (II.iii.76–7)

Little is lost or gained by including or omitting this kind of thing. Thersites is copious, and could well be abbreviated (although not so lamely as at v.i.22–6—for which F substitutes 'and the like'); and nothing in context allows one to judge what is gained, either way.

(c)

> Or like a gallant Horse falne in first rank,
> Lye there for pauement to the abiect, neere
> Ore-run and trampled on   (III.iii.161–3)

Neither Q nor F is metrical: Q halts in l. 160, and F in l. 163 (besides leaving l. 160 halved). The sense of F's addition is sound, if one should take *Lye* as imperative; 'neere' is obviously an error for 'rear' ('reere'). F may make the passage long-winded (Ulysses' account of competition and pursuit has run from l. 155); perhaps F's addition was meant to follow l. 155 ('Keepe then the path, / Or like a gallant Horse . . . / Lye there . . .')

---

1. Easily accounted for: the words 'Patroclus is a fool' occur twice, at the ends of ll. 59 and 64.

(d)
> Their louing well compos'd, with guift of nature   (IV.iv.79)

Probably simple omission in Q, but the eye of the compositor (or scribe) may have been misled by an attempt to emend l. 80 (perhaps 'flowing' [F 'Flawing'] for Q 'swelling'). Yet all might be kept: 'flowing' could stand after 'nature' (as Sisson suggested) so that Greek graces, powerful by nature, are enhanced by art.

(e)
> [*Deiph.*]   Let vs make ready straight.
> *Æneas.*   Yea, with a Bridegroomes fresh alacritie
>   Let vs addresse to tend on *Hectors* heeles:
>   The glory of our *Troy* doth this day lye
>   On his faire worth, and single Chiualrie.
>   (IV.iv.142–6)

An inept passage, wordy, and wrong in tone (see Commentary), and therefore rightly excised in Q.

(f)
>   To hurt by being iust; it is as lawfull:
>   For we would count giue much to as violent thefts
>   And rob in the behalfe of charitie.   (V.iii.20–2)

This looks like the result of hasty editing in MS (Q): Cassandra's preceding remark ('do not count it holy') lacks an antecedent for 'it'. Perhaps 'To hurt by being iust' should have stood in Q, as a separate half-line. (In l. 21, 'count' is a false start, and 'as' is usually emended to 'use'.) Again, this may be a first shot, properly (but imperfectly) excised.

Of all these omissions from Q, the simple oversights may be neglected. The rest (i.e. (a) to (f)) tell us, what we surmised already, that MS (F) was close to foul papers. About Q, we can only conclude that its MS was edited in some way (which again we had surmised), but we do not know how close was MS (Q) to MS (F). We ought to notice, however, that on the whole there was something to be said for both Q and F in the readings cited above; and while I have occasionally postulated 'editing' (see the remarks on V.iii.20–2), it is hardly possible to say what agent performed it, or for what purpose. In fact, as far as our enquiry has gone, it is possible to say how F produced some of its readings (and hence, from what it derives), but not what lies behind Q.

One passage needs discussion here, as showing what may be a further instance of first and second shots (although without any omission), and that is the tangle at I.iii.357, in which each text

is wrong. Indeed, there is complicated variation beginning at
l. 352:

   Q What heart receiues from hence a conquering part
   F What heart from hence receyues the conquering part

Either version might stand (in Q, Nestor is alluding to the Greek
dismay, should Achilles lose; in F, to the encouragement to the
Trojans, should Hector win). What matters is that F immediately
supplies two and a half lines, which must plainly have given
trouble at some point (e.g. 'are *in* his instruments, | *In* no lesse
working': see above, p. 7) and may represent a first shot by
Shakespeare, which he repented of, and deleted. It is not hard,
at any rate, to see further attempts at revision (or, should one say,
first and second drafts?) in ll. 357–62. Each text might be
faulted in terms of point and economy:

  Q 357 Giue pardon to my speech? therefore tis meete
          Achilles meete not *Hector*, let vs like Marchants
    359 First shew foule wares, and thinke perchance theile
          sell;
          If not; the luster of the better shall exceed,
    361 By shewing the worse first: do not consent,
          That euer *Hector* and *Achilles* meet,

  F 357 Giue pardon to my speech:
          Therefore 'tis meet, *Achilles* meet not *Hector:*
    359 Let vs (like Merchants) shew our fowlest Wares,
          And thinke perchance they'l sell: If not,
    361 The luster of the better yet to shew,
          Shall shew the better. Do not consent
    363 That euer *Hector* and *Achilles* meete:

The main difference here is that F has divided l. 357 at the
caesura, and gone on, in effect, to add a line. In words alone, the
beginnings and ends of the two passages are alike ('Giue ...
Hector', 'do not ... meet'), and one line or other is therefore
redundant: Ulysses says *twice* that the two should not meet, and
can hardly be said to have reached the kind of rhetorical climax
that might justify iteration. But, metrically, almost any line
could be omitted, and without much loss: it would be easy (and
metrical) to go from

               Giue pardon to my speech?

directly to

                  do not consent,
          That euer *Hector* and *Achilles* meet, . . .

It looks very much as if Shakespeare, having allowed Ulysses to object to Nestor's proposal, wishes to give him a brief opportunity to offer reasons. (The *consequences*—

> For both our honour and our shame in this
> Are dog'd with two strange followers

—must always have stood in the text: Nestor alludes to them directly in both Q and F.) Each text, therefore, offers an alternative draft (with 'Therefore tis meet . . . *Hector*' promoted in the order of argument), and each shows signs of word-play and parallelism inadequately considered (in Q, 'meete . . . meete'; in F, 'meet . . . meet': 'better . . . better': 'shew . . . shew . . . shew'). On the whole, Q is preferable; but it is not clear that F shows *corruption*— rather, a groping for formulae which proved inadequate.[1]

In general, variants between Q and F do not show any obvious or consistent pattern. Many are indifferent. Some encourage an editor to give a preference on graphical grounds. In other cases, he may prefer a text (as Dr Walker sometimes prefers F) because of what appears to be a better preservation of rhetorical schemes. In theory, since F seems to be printed from a copy of Q collated with an authoritative MS, its readings ought to be superior, except in cases of simple mechanical error, or where (in passages for which F is the only text) there seems to have been difficulty in deciphering copy (e.g. at III.iii.161–3). What is much more disturbing is that occasionally the F reading, in a part of the text which *ex hypothesi* is set from Q, displays a graphic error of the kind normally to be expected in setting from MS: for example,

F	the rude breuitie and discharge of our Iniurious time;	
Q	the rude breuity, and discharge of one, Iniurious time	(IV.iv.40–1)

F	the almighty Fenne	
Q	the almighty sunne	(V.ii.172)

F	Coole statues	
Q	Could statues	(V.x.20)

From such evidence (and there is not a great deal of it) one cannot usefully begin to determine (or modify) one's notion of how F dealt with its copy; but there is enough there to suggest that F's variants need not be given that respect which might, in theory, have been their due.

1. I doubt whether Dr Walker is right in blaming the F readings on Jaggard's Compositor B (*Textual Problems*, p. 83).

But as far as connections with the playhouse may go, F is more useful than Q, for its stage directions are more complete. Greg's analysis is useful: 'F reproduces, with few and presumably accidental exceptions, the stage-directions of Q, but it sometimes modifies them, and it adds a considerable number of its own'. He then lists these two groups,[1] and adds

> The common base with Q is obvious, and no less obvious is the revision there has been for the stage . . . Many, but by no means all necessary entrances and exits have been supplied, but that at [iv.iv.104] is misleading, and there are other signs of carelessness. Additional noises are provided. Some of the defects that remain may be due to imperfect collation, some may be oversights of the compositor. The additional notes might have been made on the foul papers, but they are frequent enough to suggest an intention to provide complete directions for performance.

What then can we say of the copy for Q? The dialogue is obviously incomplete by comparison with F, although there are few instances in which the sense goes halting. To that extent, MS (Q) *might* have been theatre copy, but only to that extent; for the stage directions are wholly inadequate for performance, since some thirty entrances and exits are wanting.[2] Greg thought that what directions are provided 'bear on the whole the impress of the author rather than the theatre'.[3] Certainly, there is a measure of imprecision, which is usually taken to imply an author, confident that the book-keeper will tidy things up for him: 'Agamemnon . . . with others' (i.iii.1) or 'Flowrish enter all of Troy' (iv.v.63) are certainly insufficient for getting actors 'on', and might indeed be authorial. What may be more significant still is the tendency in Q to confuse or omit speech-headings—most especially at ii.i.39ff. One would have to suppose two things in order to explain these as authorial error: first, that the dialogue was written first, and the names added later; and secondly, that short speeches were written on the same line (since at ii.i.40 Q reads

Ther. Thou shouldst strike him. *Aiax Coblofe.*

where *Aiax* is plainly the speaker's name). There can be no proof that dialogue was ever written out without speakers' names by the playwright when first composing, although there is no

1. *SFF*, pp. 343–4.
2. ibid., p. 341.
3. ibid.

inherent probability against it if the writer were making a fair copy.[1] But it is quite likely that MS (Q) had two short speeches to the line, since the Q shows precisely such an arrangement in several places: in the present scene (II.i) it occurs at ll. 4, 6, 24, 54, 61, 78, 80, 84, 91 and 95; it is frequent in I.ii (twice, in verse passages), and in v.ii as well; and it may account for a disputed reading at III.i.55, and confusion at II.iii.221–2.

If Q's stage directions suggest an author rather than a book-keeper, that does not of itself mean that MS (Q) was autograph; for the stage directions and the text might imply different things. But an author might be as liable to eye-slip as a scribe (II.iii.59–65), and an author, in making a transcript, might well introduce deliberate or accidental variants. Certainly, an author might alter a text for the worse as he copied: the Q version of IV.ii.74

> the secrets of neighbor *Pandar*

is, I think, inferior to F's

> the secrets of nature

but it might be genuine, even so.[2] What is more difficult to believe is that Shakespeare should apparently have been unable to decipher his own handwriting, and in place of F's

> euery graine of Plutoes gold;

should write

> euery thing.   (III.iii.196)

I doubt whether anyone (scribe, compositor or author) would deliberately alter the F version to 'euery thing' (although somebody, in abbreviating F at v.i.19–22, was willing to write 'and the like' as the climax for a vehement curse). It is *just* possible that the MS was illegible at this point, and that therefore the compositor improvised; but the compositor was Eld B (who set title-page and Epistle, and was probably the better workman). It seems best to leave the problem of this variant unresolved: a decision on inadequate evidence would falsify any theory of the origin of Q; and such a variant could never result from the same process as did F's recoveries at IV.v.164 ff. and v.iii.20–2; so that to leave it is not to proceed dishonestly.

---

1. I do not therefore suppose that he was.
2. Two objections may be made to Q's reading. It is vulgarized (see Commentary) and below Æneas' dignity; and it refers to something (namely, Pandarus' discretion) of which Æneas knows little, and Troilus nothing at all, since he was not on the stage during ll. 43–59.

What occasional literal error in Q might tell us about the copy is ambiguous, since error might be caused by a compositor misreading a Shakespeare MS or by a compositor misreading a scribal transcript, or by a scribe misreading a Shakespeare MS. Hillebrand (*Variorum*, pp. 343–4) collected examples of error and characteristic spelling, of which the most useful are: Q 'lad', F 'Lord' (III.i.102); Q 'day', F 'drop' (IV.v.132); Q 'day', F 'dogge' (V.i.60); Q 'push', F 'pash' (II.iii.204); Q 'distruction', F 'distraction' (V.ii.41); Q 'Court', F 'coact' (V.ii.117).[1] One might also notice Q 'loue', F 'come', (III.iii.4); Q 'louer' F 'crowne' (III.ii.91); and Q 'Lul'd', F 'But' (IV.i.17). Q reads 'beains' (F 'braines') at II.i.103, which implies a misreading of copy[2] the reverse of what one finds in *Othello* I.iii.327 (where Q reads 'brain' for '[beam]'). The interesting spellings in Thersites' speech at v.i.60 ('Moyle . . . Fichooke', for F's 'Mule . . . Fitchew') could perhaps be authorial (and follow immediately upon an o/a misreading—'day' for 'dog').[3]

If one turns to such variants as that at II.i.14 (Q 'vnsaltcd': F 'whinid'st') there is no certainty to be got. F's reading is the harder, and therefore to be preferred: it is also more insulting (= mouldiest). Q of course makes good sense (which is why the alteration was made); leaven is not only yeast, but yeasted dough, and unsalted dough is tasteless and repulsive enough. The choice here is not really between genuine alternatives, although perhaps 'unsalted' was easier to pronounce.[4] The real difficulty lies in variants like

F   my heart will be blowne vp by the root.
Q   my heart wilbe blowne vp by my throate.   (IV.iv.53)

Dr Walker sees F as correct, and Q as an attempt to make sense of 'th'roote', misunderstood. She is almost certainly right; and yet Q's 'by my throate' might perhaps be defended (since the phrase suggests the 'mother' or *hysterica passio*).

I hesitate to pass judgement, the evidence is so contradictory; and yet, while it is hardly possible to say for certain what *must* lie behind Q, it is not necessary therefore to conclude that no opinion can be held. Since the choice is essentially a simple one—author,

1. Perhaps one might add 'at' (F 'out') at II.i.103.
2. It is possible that 'beains' is merely foul case.
3. See also E. A. J. Honigmann's remark on 'Shrike'/'shriking' (II.ii.98, III.iii.141) as possible Shakespearean spellings, in *The Stability of Shakespeare's Text* (1965), pp. 88–9.
4. One may compare this with Gloucester's phrase 'In his anointed flesh rash boarish fangs' (*Lr* III.vii.57) where 'rash' is altered to 'stick' in F.

or scribe—we can at any rate say that the author *might* have produced much of the copy for Q. In the muddle at i.iii.354–65, the readings of Q, though imperfect, are decidedly to be preferred; and many minor misreadings in other places could easily derive from a Secretary hand of the kind that we believe that Shakespeare wrote. The evidence of the stage directions is neutral: it might indicate authorial copy, although it might equally indicate transcription from such copy. But a few readings seem to point another way. Thersites' 'moyle' and 'fichooke', being dialect forms (of 'mule' and 'fitchew') could well be authorial, and perhaps would not show through a transcript (though, self-evidently, they showed through the setting of type), but such dialect forms are absent from the rest of the play. The readings 'loue' (for 'come', at iii.iii.4) and 'louer' (for 'crowne', at iii.ii.97; but I think that Delius's 'cover' ('couer') was right) look like the errors of a man used to Secretary hand, and trying to copy from a script which contained Italian letter-forms. Yet 'shrike' (= shriek) (for 'strike', at ii.ii.211) appears to be a case of the opposite kind. Here, the majority of editors follow F ('strike'); and if F is right, then 'shrike' must represent a misreading of 't' as Italian 'h' (for the Secretary 'h' could never be mistaken for 't'). But, were that true, it tells us only that with the earlier examples ('loue' and 'louer') the copy appears to have been in a hand which included Italian letter-forms; whereas with 'shrike' we cannot judge what the *handwriting* was at all (since the letter 't' is much alike in both alphabets). We can only estimate the habits of the compositor who wanted to read 't' (Italian or Secretary) as 'h' (Italian)—which seems to imply that, in *part* of the copy, some Italian letter-forms were used, but we cannot be sure where.

It seems to me, on balance, that where there are such possibilities of error, there is probably more than merely compositor and author to cause it, and one cannot reject the idea that Q's copy was a transcript.[1]

One may, I think, ignore (since they tell us so little about the nature of copy for Q or F) the following three classes of variant:

(a)   There are seven omissions from F itself, of which two are two lines long, and the rest vary from one line to one word in length. The cut from Thersites' curse (v.i. 19–22) must be

1. One might, of course, take note of the contradictory evidence, and postulate mixed copy—perhaps, a transcript for most of the text, supplemented by passages in a different hand, which represented later, and minor, revisions or additions. But at that point one applies Occam's razor.

deliberate; the two lines from iii.iii.105–6 are caused by eye-skip (three lines successively end in 'selfe';) and the rest are almost certainly accidental. None, barring perhaps the damaged rhyming couplet at iv.v.29, seriously affects the sense.

(b) Next is that group of readings, scattered through the text, in which words or phrases are transposed; they vary from 'say so' Q (ii.iii.86; F 'so say'), or 'till now not' Q (iii.ii.119; F 'not till now'), to the more complex shift at iii.ii.148–9:

Q   I would be gone:
Where is my wit? I know not what I speake.
F   Where is my wit?
I would be gone: I speake I know not what.

(The transposition of two lines in F at ii.ii.45–6 is obviously wrong, and probably derives from clumsiness in moving type from the galley to the bed of the press.)

(c) The third group is that large class of variants, consisting of single words or phrases (and omitting those, like 'smile / smite' at v.x.7, which are merely literal error) where the variation is either between near-synonyms or else between words of graphic similarity. Near-synonyms include such readings as i.iii.149 ('sillie': 'aukward'); ii.ii.59 ('attributiue': 'inclineable'); i.iii.19 ('call them shames': 'thinke them shame'); iv.i.57 ('soyle': 'soylure'); i.iii.164 ('right': 'iust'); v.ii.159 ('giuen': 'bound'); iv.i.54 ('deserues': 'merits'); ii.iii.195 ('Shall': 'Must'). Graphic siblings include i.iii.262 ('restie': 'rusty'); v.ii.133 ('spoile': 'soyle'); iv.v.13 ('yond': 'yong'—but that is perhaps a mere literal); i.iii.275 ('couple': 'compasse').

One more point may be noticed about Q, which affects less its origin than its immediate provenance: it sets in italic type
(a) words and phrases of learned origin;
(b) words and phrases which may have been thought to be of learned origin;
(c) parentheses;
(d) moral gnomes or apophthegms (which are more often distinguished by quotation marks).
Parentheses are so marked at i.ii.94 and i.iii.328–9; moral observations at i.ii.292, 294, 298, and i.iii.117 (which should perhaps be reckoned merely a parenthesis), and v.ii.111. Words or phrases (of both kinds) may be found at: i.ii.128 (*Autumne*), i.ii.297 (*maxim*), i.iii.125 (*chaos*), i.iii.343 (*indexes*), ii.i.39

(*Coblofe*), ɪɪ.i.47 (*Asinico*), ɪɪ.i.70 (*modicums*), ɪɪ.i.73 (*pia mater*), ɪɪ.i.119 (*Cl[o]tpoles*), ɪɪ.ii.28 (*Compters*), ɪɪ.ii.168 (*Morrall Philosophie*), ɪɪ.iii.35 (*Amen*), ɪv.ii.31 (*chipochia*), ɪv.v.178 (*quond[a]m*), v.i.43 (*maior*), v.ii.48 (*Greeke*), v.ii.75 (*Whetstone*).

Such erratic use of italic type is often assumed to be due to copy rather than to printer's habits; and scholars sometimes suppose that MS (Q) was marked—whether by a scribe, or by a reader, can hardly be determined—and that the marking, or underlining, was taken by the compositor to indicate italic.[1] This is plausible, but not certain, and as a theory it carries with it the dangerous corollary that if someone other than author or scribe were to have marked a MS in any way, he might not confine himself to underlining.[2] But in any case, certain other plays printed by Eld display a tendency to use italic unexpectedly,[3] and it is likely that at least one of Eld's compositors had such a habit. We should also notice that, while the individual words or phrases listed occur through the play, the italicized (or otherwise distinguished) lines and parentheses are confined to the first three scenes (ending on C3; indeed, all occur in the *outer* formes of A, B and C). The exception, Cressida's farewell, is found on the inner forme (K3ᵛ) of K.

To sum up, then: the variants in the Q show many of the more common types of scribal error (some of which, of course, might equally well be caused by a compositor); but few of those which might be taken to indicate copy of a specific kind are consistent with one another. Most errors (as opposed to synonym variants) might point indifferently to author, scribe or compositor.

The consequences for an editor are simple. Where we cannot identify the nature of copy with certainty, then the nature of the copy can have no effect on an editor's method, except in so far as agnosticism gives him more freedom of choice. Since we know only that F was (largely) printed from Q, we are left with Q as copy-text. Where F is sole authority, we must follow F, while being prepared to amend when F is evidently wrong. Where Q and F differ, we must decide each reading on its merits. This edition is, therefore, eclectic, with a bias towards Q.

There is evidence in Q that disturbance to the process of printing extended further than to the resetting of the title-page

1. This apparently occurred when a marked Quarto was used as copy when E. Blount reprinted *Endymion*: see Walker, *Textual Problems*, p. 84.

2. This possibility is raised by Walker, ibid.

3. E.g. *Northward Hoe* (1607) has *Englishman*, *Welshman*, *Dutchman*, *Frenchman*, *Aqua-vitae*, *Baboune*, and *Sulpher*.

and the addition of the Epistle. In short, it is possible that some material may have been added to the text—perhaps in III.i, almost certainly in III.ii—and that this upset the calculation made in casting-off, and caused delay in setting sheet F (which runs from III.i.110 to III.iii.50), as well as entailing the use of a third compositor. But while one may demonstrate the facts of disturbance, nothing emerges from an analysis of the text which requires any change in editorial method; and although it is tempting to see a connection between disturbed text in III.ii (the wooing scene) and what the second title-page calls 'the conceited wooing of Pandarus Prince of Lycia', yet no connection can be demonstrated beyond any doubt. Because of that, I have confined my notes on the disturbance to an Appendix.

Note

In conformity with modern English practice, and for the sake of consistency within the New Arden series, I have read *Trojan* throughout. It should, however, be noted that the spellings of both Quarto and Folio (*Troian* or *Troyan*) imply that *Troyan* was the pronunciation intended (see OED entry under *Trojan*). *Troia* was the name of the city, in the Latin texts that Shakespeare would have known, and *Troy, Troyan, Troylus* represent the sounds that he expected his audience to hear.

2. THE DATE

If we assume, as scholars almost unanimously do, that the *Troilus* which was entered by Roberts in February 1603 was indeed Shakespeare's play, then we may assume further that the play was probably completed during the later months of 1602. The *Stationers' Register* says that the play had been acted by the Lord Chamberlain's Men;[1] and in that case, if the entry were a 'blocking entry', to prevent unauthorized printing, then it would be natural to infer that the play was new, and had been acted in late 1602 or early 1603.

1. 'as yt is acted' is ambiguous. The natural sense of the words would imply performance on several occasions: that is, *Troilus* was in the repertory. On the other hand, if Alexander was right in positing a private performance, and if the Epistle in the Quarto was right in implying that no performance in a public theatre had taken place, then the phrase 'as yt is acted' means only 'as it has been [privately] acted', and tells us nothing about the number of performances. We do not know how far the Q text represents the play acted in 1602/3 (as Greg remarked: Introductory note to Quarto facsimile, p. 1 n).

It is unlikely that the play can be dated much earlier. It is not mentioned by Meres in *Palladis Tamia* (1598), unless one were to accept the theory of Leslie Hotson[1] that *Troilus* was formerly called *Love's Labour's Won*—a theory that, Helen notwithstanding, implies a forced interpretation of the play. References to *Troilus* in other works are difficult to demonstrate. A speech by Dryfat, in Middleton's *The Family of Love* (*c.* 1602), has sometimes been seen as a parody of Ulysses' oration on Degree; but the fact of parody has not been proven, and the date of *The Family of Love* is not certain. It is also possible that *Saint Marie Magdalens Conversion*, by I.C. (1603) alludes to *Troilus*. The poet wrote, with uncommon bathos,

> Of Helens rape and Troyes beseiged Towne,
> Of Troylus faith, and Cressids falsitie,
> Of Rychards stratagems for the English crowne,
> Of Tarquins lust, and Lucrece chastitie,
> Of these, of none of these my muse nowe treates.

These lines touch on two themes of *Troilus*, on the subject of another play of Shakespeare's, and on the subject of one of his poems. To that extent, they look like an allusion to *Troilus* as a well-known play: as far as we know, nobody else at the time had written on all three subjects (Lucrece, Richard, the Trojan War). But since we need not suppose that all three are *meant* to be connected with one another, the allusion is not well attested; and unless we suppose that the play entered by Roberts was *not* Shakespeare's then I.C. only confirms what we know already—that *Troilus* existed by 1603.

The most likely remark that may refer to *Troilus* occurs in the anonymous *2 Return from Parnassus* (IV. v). In that play, Will Kemp says that Shakespeare has given Jonson a 'purge' that made him 'beray his credit' (= befoul his reputation). This, on the face of it, seems to suggest something in a Shakespeare play analogous to the emetic administered to Crispinus in *Poetaster*. In literal terms, nothing of the kind remains in the canon, although we know (from Jonson's testimony) that an absurd hyperbole once stood in the text of *Julius Caesar*, of which we now find no trace, and we might therefore suppose that a purge of Jonson had been excised. Of the extant plays, *Twelfth Night* offers the incident nearest to a purge (in the gulling of Malvolio), but the parallel is hardly exact enough. If we interpret 'purge' more liberally (as a kind of 'derision medicinable'), such an incident of course occurs

---

1. Leslie Hotson, *Shakespeare's Sonnets Dated* (1949), pp. 37–43.

in *Troilus* III.iii; but Achilles in his supine insolence has little in common with Jonson. If 'purge' means *any* satirical attack or portrait, then the picture of Ajax, in *Troilus* I.ii, might serve,[1] but as a portrait—even a satirical portrait—of Jonson, the picture is so poor a likeness as to lose its point.[2] Besides, the account of Ajax hardly corresponds to what Kemp seems to have implied. *2 Return* is later than *Satiromastix* (*c.* August 1601).

There are few references in *Troilus* itself which can help in dating. Agamemnon's use of the word *mastic* (I.iii.73) has sometimes been seen as an allusion to the War of the Theatres, by way of paronomasia (*Histriomastix, Satiromastix*), but Shakespeare almost certainly derived the word from Sidney's *Arcadia*. The line 'The fool slides o'er the ice that you should break' was thought by Collier to refer to an incident reported in Robert Armin's *Nest of Ninnies* (otherwise *Foole upon Foole* (1600)), but the allusion is not certain. The Prologue of *Troilus* calls himself 'A Prologue arm'd, but not in confidence / Of Authors pen, or Actors voyce'; and this is usually taken to be a reference to the Prologue of Jonson's *Poetaster* (who *was* armed): it would make the date of *Troilus* later than mid-1601 (the usual date for *Poetaster*). Both Q, and F in its first state, lacked the Prologue, which is, in respect of any argument about date, an independent thing; but the Prologue, being detachable, might easily have been removed from the text once it had lost its topical point. In that case, the *absence* of the Prologue from Q strengthens the argument for dating *Troilus* soon after *Poetaster*.

Stylistic considerations, notoriously subjective and unreliable, have suggested both early and late dating for *Troilus*. The wide variety of styles in the play, and especially the mannered rhetoric of Troilus, and the rhymes of Cressida, persuaded some critics that the play had been begun as early as *Romeo* (presumably as a love story) and developed later as a Trojan War play. Such an argument ignores Shakespeare's constant use of the full range of linguistic devices available to him, and especially his delight in the

---

1. M. Castelain, *Revue germanique*, III (1907), pp. 146–55, saw Jonson as Ajax both here and at II.iii.86 ff. Any notion of Jonson as being Ajax throughout derives from F. G. Fleay, *Life of Shakespeare* (1886), and, ultimately, from Robert Cartwright, *Shakespeare and Jonson* (1864): see Hillebrand, *Variorum*, pp. 375–7.

2. But no actor, and no producer, needs to be told that the best means of parody on stage—mime, dress, mimicry of speech—need never appear in the prompt-book. (The censor who reads a play but does not watch a performance does only half his work.) In any case, slight changes in timing can make the most innocent text either seditious or uproariously ribald and obscene.

juxtaposition of strongly contrasted modes of speech and action.
It ignores, too, the possibility that such a character as Troilus
might at times be subjected to mild parody. Besides, as E. K.
Chambers pointed out,[1] it is hard to date a text by such devices
as rhyme: rhymed couplets are frequent as late as *Macbeth*.
In any case, an attempt, both tentative and conservative, to date
Troilus by a combination of evidence from metrical formulae
placed the play in about 1602.[2]

Greg[3] was inclined to think that the *Troilus and Cressida* written
for the Admiral's Men by Chettle and Dekker (1599) might have
prompted Shakespeare to think of a play on the subject. Certainly,
if a rival company possessed a Troy play, then the Lord Chamberlain's Men might have found it expedient to possess one too; but
even if we suppose that Shakespeare always followed fashions set
by other writers, and initiated nothing himself, this would only
place *Troilus* in 1600 or so.

Late 1602, therefore, seems to be the date of composition of the
play, for want of better evidence; yet the text was not printed until
1609, and it is possible that some alterations were made during
those seven years. The writer of the Epistle in Q, who seems to
have been an interested party, insisted that *Troilus* was 'a new
play', but while he may have been right in implying that the play
had not hitherto been widely known, it does not follow that he
thought, or meant, that it had only recently been written. Some
second thoughts show through in both Q and F: the two different
places for the rejection of Pandarus (in F) indicate clearly that at
one stage Shakespeare meant the play to end with Troilus'

But march away.
Hector is dead, there is no more to say.

Pandarus' epilogue is therefore a substantial addition to the
original design; and there may have been some thirty-eight lines
added to the wooing scene (III.ii) (a matter which I discuss in
detail in Appendix I). But even such material alteration might
have occurred early: many play-texts undergo violent alteration
in the process of preparation for performance; and there is no

1. *William Shakespeare* (1930), I.446.
2. H. D. Gray, *MLN* XLVI (1931), pp. 147–50. In terms of the referent of its
imagery, *Troilus* has sometimes been linked with *Hamlet* (especially by Caroline
Spurgeon, *Shakespeare's Imagery* (1935)), and, on those grounds, a further
connection might be made with 2 *Henry IV*. To that extent, *Troilus* could
certainly be dated in 1601–2, or a little earlier.
3. *SFF*, p. 347 n.

necessity to see here any evidence for revision later than 1602–3.

Greg, in arguing (as Alexander did) that *Troilus* might have been written for private performance before lawyers, suggested as an example of the occasion 'the habitual All Saints or Candlemas festivities of the Inner Temple'[1] (although he goes on to admit that 'there is no shred of external evidence with which the conjecture[2] can be supported'). By page 347, however, Greg had sketched his own 'plausible outline', and proposed a performance at Christmas. I wish to propose, in my turn, that (if we assume a performance during the twelve days of Christmas) there might be *internal* evidence to support the notion, and that this might allow us to enquire into the later limit for dating the play.

It is clear that in the Epilogue Pandarus is teasing the audience. They may or may not be mocked as the 'traitors and bawds' of l. 37, since those belong to a formal apostrophe: they are no more necessarily present than the 'world, world' of l. 36. 'Good traders in the flesh' and 'Brethren and sisters of the hold-door trade' (ll. 46, 52) are, however, addressed directly to the audience. (Presumably, the young lawyers did not mind being called bawds. Are we to assume that there were also women in the audience?) But the direct address is there to make a point: in two months' time, in this same place, Pandarus will make his will. The usual comment on the lines is that the lawyers are being mocked, Pandarus is comically dying (Lechery eats itself), and there is just enough legal reference to support Alexander's theory. This is reasonable: Pandarus might well make his will at an Inn of Court. But why should he do it in two months?

I consider this small puzzle to be of a piece with the evidence of the new title-page and the Epistle. For the writer of those two (who may well have been a lawyer), the play was a comedy, and Pandarus was Prince of Licia—in context, an Homeric Cupid (cf. p. 27, n. 3). Grant then the theory (which Greg proposed) of a Christmas performance, and Pandarus becomes instead a Lord of Misrule, whose reign would end with Twelfth Night. Pandarus is not perhaps the perfect candidate for the role; but he, like Misrule, represents the delights of the flesh, and like Misrule, he is abdicating from his function. In two months, more or less, Pandarus will make his will, and die. Two months from Epiphany (6 January) brings us to the beginning of March, and (in certain years) to Ash Wednesday.

1. ibid., p. 340.
2. That is, the whole theory of a special text, prepared for private performance, according to Alexander's theory.

This is all very tenuous. It assumes a performance during the Christmas season, and it assumes that Pandarus is to be equated with Misrule. And finally, it assumes a connection between the play and the Church calendar. Yet consider: Pandarus' remark must have had *some* point; and why should he not 'make his will' at a lawyers' Shrove Tuesday feast, being ready to die—to the flesh, at least—next day? If he did, then we should be able to find the year in which 'some two months' is the period from Epiphany to Shrove Tuesday. It is unfortunate that no precision is possible. Two months from Epiphany to Lent can be found in 1598, 1603 (the year of the Roberts entry), 1606 and 1609, thus giving one a choice of two years (in effect), since 1598 is too early, and 1606 is not significant. It would be tempting to suppose that the Epilogue at least might be dated to 1609 (just before publication of Q), but it is a supposition with nothing certain to support it, and for want of other evidence, the Epilogue —and therefore the rest of the copy for Q—may be dated to 1602.

3. SOURCES

It is always difficult to demonstrate with finality what must have been the source of a play, and the difficulty increases in geometrical proportion when the subject of that play is something as well known and as widely disseminated as the Trojan War or the story of Troilus and Cressida. Robert Kimbrough[1] showed how far the two stories had become matter for ambivalent treatment by about 1600; nobody can tell how much has been lost of the plays and popular ballads which treated of them;[2] and even if we could be sure that we had all the relevant texts on our shelves, yet we could not identify sources with assurance. We may not so circumscribe the freedom of an author to handle matters as he chooses; and to say, because one earlier writer treats a topic thus, that therefore Shakespeare (who did likewise) follows him, is to fly in the face of reason. I shall therefore offer a conservative account of the problem, remembering always that, even if we knew all the books that Shakespeare read, we cannot know anything of his conversations.

For the Trojan War material—that is, for the action which derives ultimately from Homer—Shakespeare is likely to have drawn upon Homer himself (in a Latin or a French or an English

1. *Shakespeare's* Troilus and Cressida *and its Setting* (1964).
2. ibid., pp. 27–39.

translation), upon Ovid, Caxton, and perhaps Lydgate. For the Troilus story—the great medieval addition to the matter of Troy—he almost certainly drew upon Chaucer (although the assumption is sometimes disputed). I shall deal first with the medieval sources.

(a) CHAUCER

We can be fairly sure that Shakespeare read Robert Henryson's *Testament of Cresseid*, in which Cressida is afflicted with leprosy as a punishment for her unfaithfulness, and is given alms, all unknowingly, by Troilus. Feste, in *Twelfth Night*, recalls the incident ('Cressida was a beggar': III. i. 56); and Pistol too knows of it ('Fetch forth the lazar kite of Cressid's kind': *Henry V* II. i. 76). And, since Henryson's poem was printed with Chaucer's works between 1532 (Thynne's edition) and 1721, being usually regarded as part of the Chaucer canon, there is an *a priori* case for supposing that Shakespeare had read Chaucer's *Troilus* as well. (He seems to have recalled v. 666–79—where Troilus watches the Greek tents from the walls of Troy—in *The Merchant of Venice* v. i. 3–6.) There are other references to *Troilus and Criseyde* in the plays: Petruchio's spaniel is called Troilus (*The Taming of the Shrew* IV. i. 134); Benedick remembers that Troilus was 'the first employer of panders'; Rosalind thinks of him, half-mockingly, as 'one of the patterns of love'; Pistol, proud to bear a sword, is unwilling to disgrace himself by acting as a go-between for Falstaff ('Shall I Sir Pandarus of Troy become, / And by my side wear steel?': *The Merry Wives of Windsor* I. iii. 71–2). But, except for the allusion in *The Merchant of Venice*, these are all references to type-figures, and prove nothing but familiarity with the tradition, in which both Cressida and Pandarus had declined into types of infamy, and Troilus was almost culpably gullible. Yet, ultimately, even if not directly, Chaucer's poem must have been Shakespeare's chief source for the love story: Lydgate offers only brief allusions, referring his reader back to Chaucer; and Caxton confines himself to a mere skeleton of narrative, in which Troilus' mistress is called Briseyde.

In determining the debt to Chaucer, we face several difficulties:

(i) Chaucer, Caxton and Lydgate draw on a common source for much incidental detail: e.g. Antenor is to be exchanged for both Cressida and King Thoas—something which comes ultimately from Guido or Benoît; and Troilus is constantly referred to as a second Hector by all three;

(ii) differences in the modes of narrative and of drama may conceal the influence of Chaucer's poem upon the play: the dramatic need for speed and economy of means may radically alter single incidents;

(iii) similarly, the more detached and sceptical tone of the play may disguise an influence;

(iv) the translation of material from a fourteenth-century poem to a seventeenth-century play may itself involve changes (cf. what happened in turning *The Knight's Tale* into *Two Noble Kinsmen*); and finally,

(v) granted the general form of the action, some details already in Chaucer might have occurred independently to Shakespeare.

Yet one might argue that what Shakespeare is doing seems to be designed for an audience which was familiar with Chaucer, and which appreciated the shift in tone and the partial degradation of characters (especially the greater triviality and vulgar fussiness of Pandarus).[1]

In terms of action, Chaucer's Book i corresponds to i.i of Shakespeare's play, with Pandarus, full of proverb lore, consoling Troilus (624–721), and praising Criseyde at great length (880–9, 981–7). Book ii determines i.ii, although again the leisurely narrative is compressed: Pandarus breaks in on Criseyde, asking what she reads, and making a long comparison of Hector and Troilus; Criseyde hears and sees Troilus returning from the field (612 ff.) and subsequently watches in company with Pandarus as Troilus passes her window (1247–74). (The letter of ll. 1002–204 may perhaps be the 'token from Troilus' that Pandarus promises at i.ii.285). The general resemblance of Book iii to iii.ii is obscured by the devices used by Chaucer's Pandarus to conceal the lovers' meetings: his fiction of the persecution of Cressida has no more place on the stage than has the 'grete reyne', or the bedding of the lovers; but their shyness at first meeting is certainly in the poem, together with their mutual vows of truth and fidelity (1485 ff.). Their aubade, cursing the dawning, together with Pandarus' facetious greeting of Cressida, belongs to iv.ii.8ff., 23 ff (cf. iii.1422ff., 1557ff.).

Chaucer, like Shakespeare, puts Calchas' plea for the exchange straight after the celebration of the lovers' union (iv.64–133); Criseyde, on hearing the ill news, rejects her father (666–8) and tears her hair (736ff.); Troilus and Criseyde meet in great sorrow to lament their ill fortune (1128ff.); Troilus fears the

1. See especially M. C. Bradbrook in *SQ*, ix (1958), pp. 311–19.

Greeks as possible suitors (1485–91), and is rebuked by Criseyde
for doubting her faith (1604–10); and Criseyde formally curses
herself, should she prove untrue. Little in the action of Book v
corresponds to that of the play: Troilus rides out with Criseyde
for the exchange (though he says no word to Diomede), and
fights furiously when he knows for certain of Criseyde's infidelity; but most resemblances here are verbal merely, or
concern some other part of the play (e.g. Troilus' contempt for
Cassandra and her account of his dream may perhaps have
helped to form ii.ii.99, 123, as well as v.iii.78–9).

Verbal connections are hard to prove, though easy to collect,
but are sometimes persuasive. The general loquacity of Pandarus,
and his readiness with proverbs and 'olde ensaumples' is common
to poem and play: in that respect, Shakespeare's Pandarus
derives directly from Chaucer's;[1] but the resemblance can be
closer; e.g. with

> Were it for my suster, al thy sorwe,
> By my wit she sholde al be thyn tomorwe   (i.860–1)

compare

> Had I a sister were a grace, or a daughter a
> goddess, he should take his choice.   (i.ii.239–41)

or, with

> Ech for his vertu holden is for deere,
> Both heroner and faucon for ryvere.   (iv.412–13)

compare

> . . . the falcon as the tercel, for all the ducks i'th' river—. . .
> (iii.ii.52)

Other verbal resemblances are less obvious, and of themselves
may carry no weight, but in a context of this kind (where the

---

1. Chaucer's Pandarus, although 'Cressid's uncle' (*All's W.* ii.i.96–7)—
which need not make him elderly—is always thought of as relatively young, and
a fit companion for Troilus in point of age (though he might well be senior).
In this, Chaucer follows Boccaccio. But Shakespeare goes out of his way to
make his Pandarus verge upon senility. He does not merely watch over the
lovers as if they were children: his language is that of an elderly man, full of
rhetorical questions, repetition of phrases, wordy anecdote—all the characteristics, indeed, of a semi-literate gossip. He constantly 'produces' the scene in
which he appears, suggesting movements, commenting on action; and his
conversation, when not mere word-spinning, is full of promptings and nudgings.
The whole effect is to trivialize and vulgarize; and it may be no accident that
when the lovers are to part, Pandarus seems to act the Bawd, with Cressida as
Prostitute; he addresses her as 'wench', and complains of her effect on his client
('Oh poor gentleman!').

action of the poem has clearly influenced the play) not only words and phrases but also images and ideas may perhaps be properly derived from Chaucer. Of this kind are I.71 ('Now was this Ector pitous of nature'), I.631 ('A wheston is no keruyng instrument': cf. v.ii.75), I.743-9 (concealing love by affecting contraries), I.415-16, 969, II.1-5 (all images associating the lovers with boats, and making harbour), II.638 ('His helm to-hewen was in twenty places'), III.540-6 (Troilus prays to Apollo: cf. I.i.98), III.1716-25 (Troilus, to disguise his strong feelings of love, makes great entertainments, and is praised for honour and largesse), IV.85-8 (Calchas enumerates what he has lost in going over to the Greeks), v.131-2 (Diomede offers service to Criseyde—'I pray you, day and nyght, Comaundeth me'), and v.1718-19 ('Myn owen deth in armes wol I seche / I recche nat how soone be the day').

We may conclude that Shakespeare could have drawn directly upon Chaucer for the love-action. What is not quite so clear is what he did (or meant to do) with what he took. I noticed above some of the factors which make derivation hard to demonstrate (pp. 22-4); and these same factors are they which make it hard to judge what was being done in the play. In *Two Noble Kinsmen* much was altered, merely in translating from one mode to the other: Theseus became more fierce and rigorous than in *The Knight's Tale*: and the *Tale* was developed into five Acts. In *Troilus*, the long poem yields the action of a third of the play at the most; and there is no space (even had Shakespeare wished for it) to make clear the Chaucerian springs of action. Some of what happens in the play, therefore, happens by default; an action is given out of its context; and although we may agree that the lovers, like the heroes, are treated in a way that is not wholly respectful, we need not therefore read too much into the details of Shakespeare's handling of them. Cressida was bound to fall at once in the play: only in the poem could she have three years of delight with Troilus, and many days to yield to the persuasions of Diomede.

(b) CAXTON AND LYDGATE

As possible sources, Caxton, Lydgate and Chaucer may be considered together, in any account of the Troy legend in the Middle Ages, and separately, in their influence on Shakespeare. The forms of the Trojan War story familiar to most medieval readers derived ultimately from Dares Phrygius (= Trojan) and Dictys Cretensis (= of Crete, and hence pro-Greek). The

Ephemeris Belli Troiani of Dictys is of the fourth century AD: the *De Excidio Troiae Historia* of Dares is sixth century: both were claimed to be the work of eye-witnesses of the war,[1] and were therefore necessarily held to be superior to Homer, although Dares was naturally preferred by the English and those other peoples of western Europe who traced their ancestry back to the Trojans.[2] Dares' work was translated into Latin verse by Joseph of Exeter (twelfth century) and into French by Benoît de Sainte-Maure (*Roman de Troie*, twelfth century). Benoît was in turn translated into Latin prose by Guido delle Colonne (*Historia Troiana*, 1287), and it is the *Historia* which is the chief medieval source for the story of Troilus. On the other hand, because Benoît had first developed the theme of rivalry between Troilus and Diomede for the hand of Briseida (and especially because he had treated it at greater length than Guido had done), it was to Benoît that Boccaccio turned for his *Filostrato,* a poem which made the Troilus-Cressida story far more important than the Trojan War, and which first laid emphasis on the character of Pandarus (Pandaro), cousin to Griseida and friend of Troilo.[3] The process by which Troilo falls in love Boccaccio took obliquely from Benoît, adapting the story in which, long after the death of Hector, Achilles visits Troy during a truce, and seeing Priam's daughter Polyxena in the temple, suddenly loves her. Boccaccio (and perhaps Joseph of Exeter) was the principal source for Chaucer's *Troilus and Criseyde*. Guido's *Historia* was translated by (amongst others) Raoul Lefèvre, chaplain to Duke Philip of Burgundy; and this fifteenth-century *Recueil* in French prose was translated by William Caxton as *The Recuyell of the Historyes of Troye* (translated by 1471; probably published in 1474, and thereafter in 1502, 1503, 1553, 1596 and 1607: the versions of 1596 and 1607 were 'newly corrected, and the English much

1. Dictys was said to have fought under Idomeneus (who occurs in *Iliad* II). Dares was a priest of Hephaestus (*Iliad* v), and (according to Homer) lost a son at the hands of Diomedes. The works attributed to them were edited by F. Meister, 1872–3.

2. The story of how Brute, great-grandson of Æneas, founded London (New Troy) was told by Geoffrey of Monmouth (*Historia Regum Britanniae, c.* 1139). 'Greek' and 'merry greek' were for long pejorative terms: 'Trojan' was (on the whole) complimentary.

3. Cressida derives ultimately from Briseis, awarded in the *Iliad* to Achilles as a prize. Pandarus is in Homer a Lycian archer, son of Lycaon, killed by Diomede; he is treacherous and rash, but wholly unconnected with any love relationships. To Homer, Troilus is merely a son of Priam, a 'happy charioteer', and dead by the time Priam prepares to recover the body of Hector (*Iliad* XXIV). Virgil briefly alludes to his death (*Aeneid,* I. 474–8).

amended, by William Fiston'). John Lydgate's *Troy Book* (begun in 1412, printed in 1512 and 1555) is based directly upon Guido, but his English verse story is much longer than its model, moralizes freely, and develops the chivalric aspects of the material. Books III and IV deal with the siege, and the final capture and burning of Troy.

Clearly, Caxton (at second-hand) and Lydgate (directly) derive from the same source, and indeed, like most other versions of the Troy story, theirs differ only in detail, proportion and emphasis: the battles and truces in which they deal are necessarily much the same; and on the whole, Shakespeare seems to have drawn rather upon Caxton than upon Lydgate. From Caxton he got the names of the gates of Troy, the form 'sagittary' for the Centaur, and perhaps the name Polyxena (who is 'Pollicene' to Lydgate, although Shakespeare may have known the name from Ovid).[1] If the word 'orgulous' came into *Troilus* from Caxton, then Shakespeare read him in an edition earlier than that of 1596 (which gives 'proud' instead of 'orguyllous'). In Caxton (but not in Lydgate) Cressida is greeted by many of the Greeks, and receives gifts from them (cf. IV.v.17 ff.); Hector embraces Ajax, calling him 'cousin-german' (cf. IV.v.120), though this occurs during the battle, and not after their duel. Helenus (according to Troilus in the Trojan council scene) is a 'coward preste' (cf. II.ii.37–40); Troilus is compared to Hector, being 'seconde after hym of prowesse'; Hector in battle almost loses 'Galathee his hors' (cf. V.v.20); Hector is reproached at some length for showing mercy, and not taking victory when he can get it (cf. IV.v.118, V.iii.37–48; but Caxton relates this to the battle in which Hector and Ajax meet by chance, and Ajax successfully dissuades his cousin[2] from consolidating his victory); Hector and Achilles meet during a truce, at Achilles' desire (cf. III.iii.236–40; but in Caxton, Patroclus is already dead); Achilles, on the same occasion, is vexed by Hector's brag, and 'achauffid hym sore' (cf. IV.v, and especially Ajax's 'Do not chafe thee, cousin; / And you, Achilles, let these threats alone'[3]); Diomede captures Troilus' horse and sends it to Cressida (cf. V.v.1–4); one of Priam's bastard sons is given a name (Margareton: cf. V.v.7, Margarelon); Hector strips rich armour from a Greek, and is slain 'pryvely' by Achilles (cf. V.viii); Achilles, in preparing to slay Troilus, instructs his Myrmidons to encircle him

---

1. See below, p. 32.
2. Caxton explicitly calls Ajax the son of Telamon and 'Exione'.
3. The word 'chafed' is found also in the Prologue, l. 2.

(cf. the killing of Hector, v.viii. 1–7); and Achilles negotiates with Hecuba for the hand of Polyxena (cf. iii.iii. 193–4 and v.i. 36–43). Many of the names in the battles of Act v seem to be grouped in Caxton as in Shakespeare; and the impression is strong that Shakespeare absorbed a good deal of Caxton, while transposing incidents, chronology and persons, as he found it convenient.[1] Against this may be set the forms of proper names in Caxton (Ylyon, Pryant, Exyone, Andromeda [-etha] for Andromache), and the fact that, for Caxton, Antenor not only was 'a ryght wyse man' but also 'spacke moche'; in Shakespeare, he is mute—a contradiction only apparently ironic, for how could an audience have known of it?[2]

Much of Lydgate's account, in précis, seems very like Caxton's. Troilus is to be surrounded by the Myrmidons, Ajax Telamon is son to Exyon, Troilus is 'The seconde Ector . . . Ector the seconde', and so on; and in point of detail Caxton is often nearer to what we find in *Troilus*. Often; but not invariably. Caxton offers a short list of 'characters' of Greeks and Trojans, sometimes[3] combining contradictory matter from both Dares and Dictys; but his comments are brief and of little value, for who can distinguish two heroes because one lisps?[4] Lydgate, on the other hand, gives longer and more coherent descriptions. His Diomede is both 'lecherous of complexyon' and 'decyvable of what ever he hyghte' (cf. v.i.87–96); his Cressida explicitly follows Chaucer's; and he makes clear the difference of Ajax Telamon and Ajax Oileus (whom Shakespeare effactually conflates, so that it is Ajax Telamon who unexpectedly predominates in iv.v). His Troilus may also have reminded Shakespeare of the character's traditional virtues: he is 'faythfull, juste and stable' and in love 'trewe as any stele'.[5] Other details may tell either way. The Greek king whom Hector pursues and kills has an embroidered cote armour (not rich armour, as in Caxton and Shakespeare), and Diomede brings Cressida directly to her father, so that she is never welcomed by the Greeks; yet Lydgate

1. E.g. Hector meeting Achilles after the death of Patroclus; Achilles loving Polyxena after the death of Hector; the details of Hector's death borrowed from the death of Troilus.

2. But see my remarks on Peter Alexander's Inns of Court theory (Appendix II, pp. 307–10).

3. See Kimbrough, p. 32.

4. E.g. (of Hector) 'He was grete and had hard membres and myght souffre moche payne, and was moche heery and crispe and lisped'.

5. Cf. iii.ii. 175 (but the phrase was proverbial for a true lover, and had been so throughout the Middle English period).

suggests that Cressida yielded to Diomede almost at once[1] (cf. the chronology of IV.v, v.i, v.ii); and when Hector is to be dissuaded from fighting, Lydgate's account is nearer to that in *Troilus* (first Andromache, then Priam and Hecuba, with support from Cassandra: cf. v.iii). It is Lydgate who refers to the sun as 'Tytan', and especially so on the day of Hector's death ('whan Tytan went downe': cf. v.x.25, 'Let Titan rise as early as he dare').[2] It may be accident that he describes Achilles in love as 'walowynge' (cf. *Troilus* at III.ii.11): and the term is probably a mere Chaucerism;[3] it is much more significant that Troilus' successful slaughter of the Myrmidons is set out in formal parallelisms that recall the elaborate figures applied to Hector (IV. 2726–31: cf. v.v.19–29). And finally, it is Lydgate who explicitly condemns Achilles for his barbarous behaviour (and reproaches Homer for having made so much of him). In sum, Lydgate may have helped to produce the conflated and contradictory Shakespearean Ajax: he may have influenced occasional phrasing, and the ordering of one incident (v.iii); and he seems to have suggested how far set 'character' pieces might have been useful.

(c) OVID[4]

The debt of Shakespeare to Ovid needs to be treated with some discrimination. In terms of frequency of allusion, Ovid (and especially the Ovid of the *Metamorphoses*) is one of his favourite authors, as a glance at the Commentary will show; so that in a sense it is irrelevant to point to most of his allusions in *Troilus*.[5] Indeed, one ought really to confine comment to Book XIII (the contest of Ajax and Ulysses for Achilles' armour)—a passage which Shakespeare certainly knew, for he had used it in *Lucrece* when describing the painting which Lucrece moralizes (ll. 1394–400). That contest gave Shakespeare the model for shrewd, politic Ulysses and bold, impatient and simple-minded Ajax. In Ovid, Ajax boasts his descent (perhaps remembered in the burlesque treatment of his parentage and upbringing at

1. '. . . longe or it was nyght . . . gave hir herte vnto Dyomede' (III. 4435, 4437).

2. Perhaps the point is irrelevant, for Chaucer uses the word too (III. 1464) and so does Henryson in the *Testament of Cresseid* (l. 9).

3. Cf. *Troilus and Criseyde*, v. 211.

4. In quoting from Ovid in this section I use Arthur Golding's translation.

5. E.g. Daphne and Apollo, Argus (Book I); the raven and Coronis, the crow's warning, Mercury stealing Apollo's cattle (Book II); the Gorgon's blood in Libya (Book IV); Arachne (Book VI); Medea's dragons (Book VII); Ariadne (Book VIII).

II.iii.241–7); he recalls his strength in overthrowing Hector (cf. I.ii.34–5); and he is contemptuous of Ulysses as a man who works covertly, and not in the open field. Ulysses, by contrast, opens his reply with modest eloquence (cf. I.iii.54ff.); he distinguishes honour inherited and honour won by courage (perhaps cf. III.iii.112ff.); he alludes to Achilles' mother (cf. III.iii.94), to his own embassy to Troy (cf. IV.v.216–17), and to a lottery (cf. I.iii.374); and he makes the climax of his argument the antithesis of brawn and brain—the need for intelligence and direction, the steersman superior to the rower (I.iii.197–210). So much is well-known. But it is worth noticing also that Ovid's allusions to the Trojan War extend further than that: Books XI and XII also contain a good deal of material that Shakespeare seems to have drawn upon for this play. I would not wish to suggest that Ovid is a major source—there are fuller accounts of Troy elsewhere, and we can be fairly sure that Shakespeare used them—but a number of incidents and topics and persons are found in Books XI and XII that also occur in *Troilus* or that help to explain an association of ideas or a turn of phrase. As Dr Walker rightly insisted,[1] 'what had always fired [Shakespeare's] imagination was Troy, not Troilus', and what Ovid provided was a cobweb of Trojan legend, of which any part might vibrate with the touch of another.

Book XI, then, gives the contest between Pan and Apollo ('the fiddler Apollo' of Thersites, at III.iii.301–2, rather than the lover of Daphne from Book I, whom Troilus invokes at I.i.98). Then follows the building of Troy's walls by Laomedon, with Apollo to help him; the first conquest of Troy by Hercules, aided by Telamon, and Hesione given to Telamon as a reward (perhaps the basis of Shakespeare's assumption that Hesione was Ajax' mother: cf. II.ii.78, 81, IV.v.119 n., IV.v.132–3); and the love of Peleus for Thetis, and the conception of Achilles (cf. III.iii.94). Book XII begins with the start of the Trojan War, combined with an account of the House of Rumour (which must have influenced not only Chaucer, but also Shakespeare when he wrote *2 Henry IV*). Nestor, invited by the courteous request of Achilles, narrates the fight of the Lapiths and Centaurs, and recalls his own youthful vigour as equal to Hector's (cf.IV.v.201–9, where Hector's courteous 'good old Chronicle' is like Achilles' compliment, and where Nestor regrets that age prevents him from fighting Hector now). The Lapith-Centaur battle itself may have guided Shakespeare to another detail: most of the

1. NCS, p. xxiii.

Homeric battles are fought with orthodox weapons or with great rocks, but in Ovid, trees and furniture (and even altars) are made to serve as clubs, and heroes die by having their heads and brains battered and beaten to pulp (cf. II.i.102–3, 'knock out either of your brains'; III.iii.247, 'prophetically proud of an heroical cudgelling'; III.iii.300, 'when Hector has knocked out his brains').[1] Neptune, at the end of the book, urges the death of Achilles to Apollo, calling the hero 'barbarian', and remembering how Hector's corpse had been dragged round his own city[2]—a collocation which may have been enough to remind Shakespeare that it was Hector and not Troilus who suffered thus, though Ovid does not say explicitly that Achilles did it. And (by way of postscript) in Book XIII itself, when the arms have been allotted to Ulysses, and Ajax is dead, there is an unexpected incident (ultimately from the *Trojan Women*); for the ghost of Achilles demands Polyxena as a sacrifice, and the killing is to be performed by Neoptolemus—an ironic situation for 'Neoptolemus so mirable' (IV.v.141) and for the Achilles who is kept from battle by his love for Polyxena.

Ovid also gave Shakespeare many concepts that seem to underlie Ulysses' speech on Degree. Commentators frequently appeal to Ovid's description of Chaos and Creation as a text which gave a hint to Shakespeare, but it might be better to refer to the gradual decline of society from the Golden Age, in the same first book of *Metamorphoses*, as a source for the pattern of Ulysses' argument. Envy, Pride and Lust are three vices of the Iron Age (l. 148), closely associated with ships and discoveries:

> And shippes that erst in toppes of hilles and mountaines had
>   ygrowe
> Did leap and daunce on uncouth waves.   (ll. 150–1)

Violence leads to deceit and malice: guest and host, fathers and sons-in-law are mutually dangerous (ll. 162–4); murder occurs between wife and husband, stepmothers and children; and children lament the survival of their parents (ll. 166–8), until at last justice (which in *Troilus* loses its name) leaves the 'earth in slaughter drownèd'. There is also in the same book plenty of detail that seems to have influenced Nestor's first speech in the debate: seas and ships, storms and winds (even 'blustering

---

1. This last passage is followed at once by the reference to 'fiddler Apollo', which I also trace to Ovid: (see above, p. 31).

2. This derives from the beginning of *Iliad* XXIV, where Apollo rates the Gods for supporting 'the brutal Achilles . . . who has no decent feelings in him and never listens to the voice of mercy'. See also my notes on Lydgate above.

Boreas'—recall Nestor's 'ruffian Boreas'); and the herd and the
tiger are mingled in Deucalion's flood (ll. 355–6). Agamemnon's
search for a remedy for disorder is matched by Jove's (ll. 208–9)

> I never was in greater care nor more perplexitie
> How to maintaine my soveraigne state and Princelie royaltie . . .

Ulysses seems also to have remembered the story of Lycaon, who
so offended Jove, murdered and ate a man (in order to test
Jove's divine power), and for his crime was turned to 'a ravening
Woolf' (l. 276)—a pattern which may underlie the declination
into 'appetite, an universal wolf'. And finally, one ought not to
forget how, in Ovid's version of the founding of Troy, disastrous
floods are linked with treason, as if the disorders of the Greek
debate were to be linked in Shakespeare's mind with the un-
remitting pattern of betrayal, within and without Troy.

(d) HOMER

One's opinion on the nature of Shakespeare's debt to Homer is
affected in great measure by one's view of the translation which
he is likely to have used. According to Tatlock,[1] Shakespeare
might have used any of eight translations of the whole or part of
the poem (five giving Latin verse, or Latin prose, or literal Latin
with the Greek; either of two in French; and Arthur Hall's
translation from the French of Books I–X).[2] It is also likely that
he knew Chapman's *Seauen Bookes of the Iliades* (1598), which
afforded him Books I, II, VII–XI, although one need not therefore
follow Bullough, in seeing Shakespeare's play as a mock for
Chapman's hero-worship of the Greeks.[3] Those who argue for
the use of Chapman point out[4] that matter from Chapman's
Books corresponds to what we find in the play in Acts I–IV (the
Greek council, Hector's challenge, Ajax as Hector's opponent),
and that what Chapman omits (the duel of Paris and Menelaus,[5]

1. J. S. P. Tatlock, *PMLA*, xxx (1915), p. 742.
2. Tatlock argued that Shakespeare must have known a Latin or French
translation, to account for 'Pandarus Prince of Licia' on the title-page of Q
(second state); but the title-page was almost certainly composed by the
publishers or by their agent.
3. Geoffrey Bullough, *Narrative and Dramatic Sources of Shakespeare*, Vol. VI
(1966), p. 87. Bullough sees a connection between the adulation shown by
Chapman, and the 'high-sounding language' of parts of *Troilus*. He need not
be wrong. Yet elevation of language might be seriously intended; and 'satiric
treatment of the Greeks' could derive from many sources.
4. Following J. F. Palmer, *TRSL*, 2nd series, xv (1893), pp. 64 ff.
5. Yet this duel may be alluded to in I.i. 112–13 and I.ii. 217–18; and something of Homer's account of the sequel (the end of Book III) may have coloured
the only appearance of Helen with Paris in the play (III.i).

Pandarus' breaking the truce, Diomede's fight with the Gods, Hector consoling Andromache and frightening his son) is also omitted by Shakespeare. The argument is persuasive, and the better for not depending on minor agreements in point of language. But even so, it may not demonstrate indebtedness. Grant that, in a play, Shakespeare would find it better to deal with what was peripheral to, or contingent upon, the fighting: that he dealt with action thwarted: and that he kept the fighting in *Troilus* until the end of Act v; and it is clear that much of the material in the play is bound to be either non-Homeric or else what is not central in Homer.

Some details in *Troilus* may derive from those parts of the *Iliad* not yet translated by Chapman. Ulysses' taunt (iii.iii.189–90) that Achilles' deeds

> Made emulous missions 'mongst the gods themselves,
> And drave great Mars to faction

may refer to *Iliad* xx (where the Gods are drawn up for battle in two camps) or to *Iliad* xxi (in which Mars (Ares) fights with Pallas Athene): in both books it is the acts of Achilles that are the cause.[1] In Books xviii–xix it is the death of Patroclus that brings Achilles back into the battle (cf. v.iii), although Shakespeare also links this with Hector's slaughter of the Myrmidons. Hector's fatal desire for the splendid armour of a nameless Greek comes direct from Caxton, but may also be a reminiscence of the occasion of the death of Patroclus; for Patroclus (*Iliad* xvi) wears the armour of Achilles, and after his death at Hector's hand (*Iliad* xvii) Hector takes the armour, whereupon Zeus at once determines that Hector shall die. When the dead Hector is dragged round the field, it is (*Iliad* xxii) behind Achilles' chariot: Shakespeare follows Lydgate's phrasing ('At the tayle of his hors') for Troilus' report of the action (v.x.4–5), and that of Caxton when Achilles determines on the ignoble deed:

> Come: tie his body to my horse's tail;   (v.viii.21)

(cf. Caxton: 'and toke the body and bonde hit to the taylle of his horse'). Shakespeare, that is to say, draws in such a detail upon three sources: on Caxton and Lydgate (since he follows the phrasing of each) and perhaps on Homer (since he applies the

---

1. Mars tries to join in during Book xv, to avenge the death of his son Ascalaphus, and he engages briefly with Diomedes in Book v. He also stirs up the Trojans in Book v (although there his function is more nearly allegorical), and he accompanies Hector to the field, whereupon the victorious Diomedes prudently withdraws.

details to the death of Hector, whereas Caxton and Lydgate are writing of the death of Troilus).[1]

It is probable that the foul-mouthed Thersites came directly from Chapman's translation.[2] Shakespeare never allows him to speak to the Greek generals in council, as Homer does (*Iliad* II), although he there makes Nestor refer to him; but hints of what his Thersites says, and is, may be found in Chapman. For example

(a)

> ... against the state
> Of *Agamemnon* he would rayle ...
> ... rashly and beyond al rule usde to oppugne the Lords ...

Cf.

> ... Thersites,
> A slave whose gall coins slanders like a mint,
> To match us in comparison with dirt ...
>
> > (1.iii. 192–4)

(b)

> ... whose rauen-like voice a tuneles iarring kept

Cf. I would croak like a raven: I would bode, I would bode.

> > (v.ii. 188–9)

(c)

> The filthiest Greeke that came to Troy[3]

Cf. No, no: I am a rascal, a scurvy railing knave: a very filthy rogue. (v.iv. 28–9)

(d)

> Who in his ranke minde coppy had of vnregarded wordes

Cf. ... rank Thersites ... (1.iii. 73)

It should be clear, even from such evidence, that Shakespeare probably knew something of Homer (and it is *a priori* likely that he would at any rate have glanced at Chapman's *Seauen Bookes*).[4]

1. On the other hand, Shakespeare might easily have recalled the allusion in *Aeneid* II, when the mutilated Hector appears to Æneas in a dream.

2. Ovid, *Metamorphoses* XIII, mentions him in passing. Erasmus, *Adagia* ('Thersitae facies') translates a phrase from Homer about him ('hunc omnium qui ad Troiam venisset, foedissimum fuisse'). He goes on: 'Ac totum hominem a capite, quod aiunt, usque ad pedes ita graphice depingit et corporis vitia et animi morbos, ut dicas pessimum ingenium in domicilio se digno habitasse'. Thersites also appeared in a sixteenth-century interlude as a boastful coward.

3. See citation from Erasmus in previous note.

4. G. K. Hunter ('*Troilus and Cressida*: a tragic satire', *Shakespeare Studies* (Tokyo), 1977, pp. 1–23) makes a strong case for Shakespeare's familiarity with the *Seauen Bookes*, and argues that the 'shock' of meeting Homer, after knowing

It is equally clear that little can be unequivocally traced to Homer, since much of what Shakespeare may have taken from him was already available to him in some form in his medieval sources.[1] And (apart from a dramatic action that seems to correspond to the *Seauen Bookes*) what might otherwise be traced to Chapman in particular is a handful of minor verbal resemblances. In Chapman's address *To the Understander* occurs the word 'impair' ('nor is it more impair to an honest and absolute man's sufficiency'), which occurs also at IV.v.103 ('Nor dignifies an impare thought with breath') and not elsewhere in Shakespeare. At 1.224, 'this broad language' *may* have affected 'broad Achilles' (1.iii.190); and at 1.272, 'giue not Stream / To all thy power' may be reflected in two *Troilus* images ('stream of this commencement', II.iii.133 (Q): ('stream of his dispose', II.iii.165 (Q,F)). The word 'swinge', otherwise only a verb in Shakespeare (= whip, beat) and always with contemptuous or low associations, is found as a noun at 1.iii.207 ('For the great swinge and rudeness of his poise'), and is used at least twice as a noun in the *Seauen Bookes*:[2]

plain fierce swinge of strength	(III.173)
giue mine anger swinge	(IX.617)

It is just possible, too, that the marginal note at III.181 ('Ajax armed, and his dreadful manner of approach to the combat') may have helped produce

> Give with thy trumpet a loud note to Troy,
> Thou dreadful Ajax, . . .   (IV.v.3–4)

Too much weight ought not to be given to individual minor resemblances, in word or matter. Yet in Chapman's translation (as in Golding's Ovid), many details come together, which weigh in the gross, though not individually, and which weigh all the more for occurring in the *Seauen Bookes*. I shall list them briefly, for the reader's consideration.

(a)
[The simile of the bees swarming, compared with the Greeks gathering to hear Agamemnon (II.71ff.).]

---

only medieval versions of the Troy story, led Shakespeare to dramatize 'the gross discontinuity between the languages we use and the facts "as they are" '.
  1. Apart from the death of Hector, consider the Trojan council (brief, in *Iliad* VII; at length, in Caxton, pp. 515ff).
  2. Jonson, however, also uses the noun (*Poetaster*, v.ii.40).

Cf.   When that the general is not like the hive
             To whom the foragers shall all repair,
             What honey is expected?   (I. iii. 81–3)

(b)
We must not all be kings. The rule is most irregularre
Where many rule.   (II. 172–3)

Cf.   The specialty of rule hath been neglected, . . .
                                               (I. iii. 78)

(c)
O that my youth were now as fresh and all my powers as sound!
Soon should bold Hector be impugned!   (VII. 139–40)

[Cf. Nestor, wishing to meet Hector's challenge (I. iii. 290 ff.).]

(d)
             Alas, my forces are not now as in my younger life.
                                               (XI. 579)

             O si praeteritos referat mihi Iupiter annos,
             Qualis eram.   (VII. 112, margin)

[Cf. Nestor to Aeneas (I. iii. 290–300); Nestor to Hector (IV. v.
204–8).]

(e)
                   Hector strooke on his knees.
                                               (VII. 239, margin)

Cf. They say he yesterday coped Hector in the battle and struck
    him down. (I. ii. 34–5).

(f)
[Nestor promptly dealing with an alarm at night (X. 66 ff.).]

Cf.   . . . now play him me, Patroclus,
             Arming to answer in a night alarm.
                                               (I. iii. 170–1)

(g)
Hector everywhere among the Greeks: the simile of reaping
(XI. 58 ff.).

Cf.   There is a thousand Hectors in the field;
             Now here he fights on Galathe his horse
             And here lacks work: anon he's there afoot,
             And there they fly, or die, like scaled sculls
             Before the belching whale; then is he yonder,
             And there the strawy Greeks, ripe for his edge,
             Fall down before him like a mower's swath.
                                               (V. v. 19–25)

(e) GREENE

A minor source for *Troilus* may also be found in Robert Greene's *Euphues his Censure to Philautus* (1587).[1] Greene's work consists of four discussions between certain Greeks and Trojans during a truce, and it raises a number of topics for moral debate which produce some similarities to Shakespeare's play. Sometimes resemblances are verbal, as when Helen is called 'pearl' and 'piece' (cf. i.i. 100, iv.i.63); or when 'tickled' and 'tickling' are connected with Cressida and change (cf. iv.v.61). Others suggest questions raised in the play: Helenus justifies wise and deep insight in a captain, against mere strength: Ulysses is critical of women: Trojans are called ignorant of moral philosophy: Hector says that Nature teaches one to maintain Paris' deeds by force of arms; and indeed the rights and wrongs of the war are discussed in a way that suggests something of Shakespeare's Trojan council, considering Justice as well as the *Lex Talionis*, and noting that Trojans 'measure all their passions by will' (cf. ii.ii. 54, 59, 63, 66, 180). In that there is no other known source or model for Shakespeare's council scene, Greene may have provided one, and his effect has been to extend what was already available to the dramatist: that is, the possibilities for moral debate inherent in whether Helen should be returned or not.

4. THE PLAY

Any detailed discussion of the play must, I think, be controlled by certain general observations about its shaping and about the most obvious of its methods of proceeding. I shall begin with the first of these.

Of those plays of Shakespeare which take their titles from persons, several show some disproportion between the play as a whole and the part played by the eponymous person or persons within it. The Histories may perhaps form a class on their own: nobody expects, say, Henry IV to be omnipresent in *Henry IV*; but the notion of a *reign* means that the King's influence is implied throughout a play, though his body may be absent. Caesar, notoriously, dies halfway through *Julius Caesar*, but is known later by his effects, in a form of 'revenge' action. Tragic heroes usually appear throughout, with brief absences. *Cymbeline* is, of

---

1. The possible connections were first discussed by C. H. Herford in *NSST*, II (1888), pp. 186–90, and subsequently by Kenneth Muir in *N&Q*(1955), pp. 141–2, and by Virgil Whitaker in *English Renaissance Drama* (1976).

course, an anomaly. But *Troilus and Cressida* is an anomaly as well; and if we compare it with *Romeo and Juliet* and *Antony and Cleopatra*, those other plays in which two lovers share a title, then the degree of anomaly becomes apparent. In *Romeo*, for example, the proportion to the whole play of those scenes in which one lover (or both) appears is roughly 9:10 (91 per cent), and in that play Romeo or Juliet are seen primarily as lovers, and have no other effectual function. In *Antony*, the proportions are much closer to those of *Troilus* (57 per cent and 58 per cent respectively), but one ought to distinguish. Whatever is done by Antony or Cleopatra, whether as lovers or as political figures, is significant, because there is one main action to the play; and throughout the play, when any other politician deals with Antony or Cleopatra, he acknowledges in effect that their liaison (or marriage) is itself a political and public matter, and he acts accordingly. In *Troilus*, this is not so. Not until Act IV does anybody but Pandarus deal with the lovers as lovers; and only in Act V does Troilus act publicly in a way which other men (in effect, only Diomedes) know to be related to his love for Cressida. There are two long scenes in which Troilus appears as other than as the lover of Cressida. In II.ii he supports Paris in the Trojan debate, and in IV.v he is present (and spoken of) but not active. If, therefore, one should exclude II.ii, and all of IV.v but the last sixteen lines,[1] the proportion changes; and indeed, if we count lines instead of scenes, the figures are significantly different: namely, 39 per cent. To count those scenes from the whole play in which Troilus and Cressida appear *as lovers* would change the proportion radically: the 'love' plot occupies exactly 33 per cent of the play, whether counting by lines or scenes.[2]

The second point (that is, the methods of proceeding) concerns means towards an end. In terms of source material, what Shakespeare dealt with in *Troilus* was history or, at any rate, history shading over through 'story' towards useful myth, which is to say much the same thing. And if that material, in either war-plot or love-plot, were to be of use to a dramatist, then it had to deal, as much of Caxton and Lydgate did deal, with other

1. At the end of the scene, Troilus briefly asks for Ulysses' assistance in finding Calchas' tent, and tactfully puts by Ulysses' ironic questions.
2. In a two-plot play such figures are significant; and one ought to be cautious about putting too much emphasis on the Troilus-Cressida plot. On the other hand, any such judgement should not—and, of course, cannot—ignore that criticism which has seen the different actions of the play as closely inter-related both in language and theme.

matters than violent action. War in itself is not dramatic;[1] the kind of action which it entails can best be made into drama in terms of cinema; and a Shakespearean play must deal, not with war, but with the tensions of war, attitudes to war, consequences of war and interludes in war. What concerns Shakespeare, therefore, is what happens 'during all question of the gentle truce'; and his Trojan War play is necessarily concerned with these moments when men, taking breath, look backwards or forwards—to causes and effects, to tactical error and ultimate victory, to past heroes and to their own future reputation, to reasons (in any context) for past and future actions. But *Troilus* differs from plays such as *Antony* or *Coriolanus*, in which the reasons for those actions belong to *both* the private and the public life of a man. Antony, in preferring Cleopatra before Octavia, is performing an action with political and military consequences: Coriolanus performs a similar act when he places respect of family before politics or common prudence; and in each case, the development of the whole man within the play is involved in the act of choice. In *Troilus*, that is hardly so. The acts which provoked the war—the capture of Hesione and the rape of Helen—are far in the past; and the chief actors are either dead (Hercules and Laomedon) or present as mere nonentities (Helen and Paris). The kind of judgement that justifies the rape is proffered by Paris in the Trojan debate (II. ii) and Troilus subscribes to it, and acts upon it in his own affairs; but there is little *causal* connection between Troilus' behaviour towards Cressida and that other, perhaps major, action of the play. War-plot and love-plot, if one must so call them, are related by analogy, and form an action which is complete by any standard but that of the chronicle play; but it is an action in which separate acts are largely ineffectual. Indeed, most of the play deals with inaction. Agamemnon says so; Troilus opens the play by unarming (and then changing his mind); Hector argues for an end to action (II. ii); the 'policy' of Ulysses in I. iii has grown into an ill opinion by V. iv, by which time the idle Achilles had been twinned with the idle Ajax; Paris (by his past action, the cause of the war) would have armed (III. i) had not Helen wished it otherwise; Troilus can hardly come to Cressida even by Pandarus until III. ii, and is then kept at a distance from her by the bargaining of Greeks and Trojans (what Troilus calls 'injury of chance')

---

1. I do not mean that Shakespeare never presented fighting on stage: plainly he did, and as far as one can tell, battle-scenes were much relished. The real drama, however, lies elsewhere in the plays.

(IV.iv), and by the prudence of Ulysses (V.ii). It is the coincidence of successful days for both Hector and Troilus that, by pure accident, kills Patroclus, provokes Achilles, and causes the death of Hector and the imminent doom of Troy.

In such a dramatic situation—and it is what makes up nine parts of *Troilus*—men wait, and while they wait, they question, argue and play. And it is the forms of those questions, and that play, which gives to *Troilus* its peculiar dramatic idiom. There is no other play in the canon that asks quite so often 'who was that?' or 'what is the value of this?' and tries, moreover, to give a full answer to the question. No other play tries so obviously to argue the general case and then to present exemplary images upon the stage. No other play asks so many riddles, or plays so many logical games, or insists so firmly upon logical distinctions, or acts out so many characters, whether at the level of mime or of language alone. Few plays contrive such a degree of symmetry, and stylization, or use more often such merely formal devices as 'passing over the stage'; few have employed so much the brief 'character', on the Theophrastan model. No other play seems to find its persons so isolated that they must be continually writing letters or sending messengers or ambassadors to one another. It will therefore be appropriate to deal with the play first in terms of its crucial scenes of argument and demonstration, and then, in a little more detail, in terms of the characteristics that I have mentioned above.

(a) CRUCIAL SCENES

There are five or six scenes that seem to me to be crucial to any discussion of *Troilus*, in the sense that one's response to them determines very largely one's response to the whole play; and of these, two are made deliberately to reflect one another. To say that they are symmetrical is not wholly accurate; yet the Greek council scene (I.iii) and the Trojan council scene (II.ii) are built to a similar pattern, namely, discussion/interruption/resumption or fresh topic/change of course by a major speaker—and in what follows here this near-symmetry should be remembered. These two scenes establish the conceptual terms in which, in a general sense, the rest of the play's inaction is to be determined, but they do not, with one exception, exemplify the dramatic means to be used. The remainder of those scenes which I have called crucial differ from these two, in that they combine argument with some form of demonstrative or exemplary action.

The Greek debate in I.iii is, properly speaking, no debate at all, and what is usually referred to as the debate occupies the first half of the scene. It is no debate, because there is no real meeting of minds. Agamemnon offers consolation and moral encouragement to a general staff that has become disheartened. Nestor 'applies' what his leader has said: that is, he glosses and develops the latter part of Agamemnon's speech. Ulysses, with extreme deference and elaborate compliment—it takes him fourteen lines—offers to comment; and it is only when he is encouraged to proceed that there is propounded a thesis of any relevance to the Greeks. Ulysses now speaks thrice: two long speeches (63 lines and 43 lines), followed by a coda of 14 lines; and when he has done, the so-called debate is over. What follows it has nothing to do with it.

How we are meant to take the opening of the scene (ll. 1–54) is not wholly clear. Critics have sometimes argued[1] that Agamemnon is digressive and redundant, and have pointed to the frequency of unusual Latinate words that both define and (effectually) represent the obstructions to thought and action which the speech seems to convey. Certainly, it is hard to feel that the Greeks are able to state their problem in terms which will allow them to solve it. To some extent, therefore, the style of Ulysses' first tentative speech is almost a parody of what his superiors have described and enacted, for he is elaborate and long-winded, and his syntax is nothing if not 'tortive and errant'. But when he launches himself, he is brisk and confident; and his oration, a diagnosis by a skilled physician, is none the worse for being built on commonplaces.

His argument is, briefly, this. The Greeks are disorderly and factious, and since difference of rank is disregarded, no further order can be apparent: once allow disorder at all, and you decline into chaos. That chaos he illustrates from the effects of planetary disorder, proceeding to a vision of ultimate anarchy, in which 'degree' is lost, and the growing evil of individual licence proves self-destructive. What he means by 'degree' is fundamental. In one sense it is hierarchy in the state or the army ('specialty of rule'): in another, order itself—which would, of course, imply some measure of hierarchy. (Homer's Ulysses says much the same, when trying to prevent the Greeks from abandoning the

---

1. E.g. Charles Williams, *The English Poetic Mind* (1932), pp. 54–5. Derek Traversi (*An Approach to Shakespeare*, Vol. 2, 1969, p. 38), is even less sympathetic: 'there is no recognisable development of thought to justify the complexity'.

siege, in *Iliad* II.) All order and all distinction of individuals—all possibility, indeed, of recognizing one man from another—is gone, if degree is 'visarded';[1] and this, Ulysses calls a sickness, an 'envious fever', which has infected the whole Greek host.[2]

Nestor approves the diagnosis; Agamemnon asks the remedy; and at that point, Ulysses appears to abandon his argument. His obvious course should be to accuse Achilles of fomenting dissension, and to predict that, in restoring the hero to his proper place and function, Agamemnon and his generals will restore order to the Greeks at large. That, indeed, is what Nestor says, when he 'applies' Ulysses' second speech ('And in the imitation of these twain . . . many are infect'). But Ulysses does not do so: instead, in a speech of venomous precision, he describes the burlesque acting of Patroclus. The situation is piquant, for what Patroclus had satirically enacted was Agamemnon as an actor playing a 'conqueror' part, with Nestor as a senile and arthritic fool; and Ulysses, in his turn, verges upon miming the original satire for the two objects of it.[3] How far his speech requires (or receives) action is uncertain; but the language at least, though decorous, hovers on the edge of ambiguity; so that Agamemnon is liable to carry with him henceforth a hint of that 'to-be-pitied and o'er-wrested seeming' that belonged in truth to the acting of Patroclus. Ulysses is demonstrating here what he will recommend subsequently for the treatment of Achilles: if men cannot understand an explanation, they must be shown an example instead; and if what they cannot understand is within themselves (and that may be implied in the unwieldy language of Agamemnon's opening speech), then such a demonstration is doubly necessary. Achilles will be shown pride in others as it affects himself; and here, Agamemnon must be shown, in its most influential form, the growing anarchy that he has so far ignored—that is, in the playing of a parody of himself and Nestor at their most vulnerable, by Achilles' 'male varlet'. The very language of Ulysses comes near to stage action;[4] and we have therefore language-as-gesture (by Ulysses) which presents to us burlesque action (by Patroclus),

1. This possibility is worked out in detail elsewhere in the play, in theatrical enactments of the problems of identification.

2. Fever it may be; but what Ulysses really complains of is the loss of logical distinctions, categories and relationships.

3. The hint is sometimes taken (rather crudely) by producers: Tyrone Guthrie, in 1956, had his Agamemnon look like Kaiser Wilhelm II, and his Nestor strongly resembled—in speech at least—the aged Sir Winston Churchill.

4. One may recall the mimetic language of Thersites: III.iii.250–69.

which in its turn is a travesty of what we have already seen and heard (Nestor and Agamemnon at their most formal).

At this point Ulysses begins a brief analysis of the Greeks' preference for brute force and direct action (rather than judgement, timing and intelligence work), and the Greek generals might almost be moving towards effective action when the scene is halted by the entry of the herald Æneas,[1] and all opportunity for debate is at an end.

This interruption, like the irruption of Cassandra into the Trojan council, radically alters the whole situation. Ulysses was, in effect, lucky in the timing of it, for not 40 lines after his medicine has been administered to Agamemnon, Æneas offers a further dose: he proves, by failing to know the Greek general from among his staff, that Ulysses' thesis is sound, and that degree has indeed been visarded. Yet that is not the primary function of the entry. The effect of Æneas' appearance is to change the course of an action which was already uncertain in its development, and to change the tone of it more radically still— more even than Ulysses had done, for Æneas speaks with a proud and playful arrogance, of something a world away from Greek fears of disorder and collapse. The challenge he brings is not wholly serious; but its effect is other than Hector has proposed (as we learn from II.ii): the original purpose was to stir up Agamemnon; but the real consequence is the scheming of Ulysses. It is ironical that not only should a plan go awry, but that Ulysses, who has spoken so eloquently of the need for order and degree, should now propose a complete 'neglection of degree' in order to cure Achilles. One need not, perhaps, be surprised in the end to learn that the cur Ajax is now 'prouder than the cur Achilles': it is a proof that one cannot always employ disorder to cure disorder.[2]

Two minor points about the scene may be noted. Of Agamemnon's speech, it is to be remarked that his chief point—

1. It is possible to see Æneas here as representing fighting as a chivalric game, and it is true that he does so (cf. I.i.113: 'Hark what good sport is out of town today'), as does Hector, whom he represents. But Æneas is in one way *realistic*—men can treat fighting as a game without thinking war either trivial or entertaining—and there can be no doubt that the arbitrary rules and conventions of his challenge are far more efficient than the rumination of the Greeks.

2. One may agree that 'pride hath no other glass/To show itself but pride' (III.iii.47–8) but the cure of like by like does not necessarily work with all vices: the analogy with homeopathic medicine (*pace* Aristotle in the *Poetics*) is not sound.

the encouraging notion that worth is proved by hardship—is for the moment irrelevant; but his observation that aims and ends seldom agree is almost always borne out by the action of the play. Of Æneas' manner, and the way in which the whole scene alters from the point at which he enters, it is worth noting that the effect is purely localized; and when we reach the scene of the Trojan council, we do not find that Æneas was characteristic of Ilium.

But more important by far is the way in which the scene changes gradually from start to finish, and that what began as a serious diagnosis of ills and their cure has declined by the end into mere chicanery, which proposes that two major warriors should be treated like simple-minded children. Still, the council *does* correspond to the serious council of *Iliad* II, and the Greeks *do* enquire into the means towards an end proposed. What we may not observe—and perhaps Shakespeare's audience was not meant to observe it—is that they take their end for granted. When the war is to be discussed, it is the Trojans who enquire whether or not Helen is worth keeping; the Greeks, with right on their side, never ask whether she is worth the effort of recovery. And in looking at the Greek discussion of means rather than ends, we may observe that Ulysses in his great defence of degree is doing something that later is shown to be characteristic of him: he is using a sledgehammer to crack a nut. There is no reason to question the seriousness with which his argument is advanced; but the eloquent sermon does not quite correspond to its text. What Ulysses is really attacking is the widespread dislike, within the Greek army, of staff officers and strategy:

> The still and mental parts,
> That do contrive how many hands shall strike
> When fitness calls them on and know by measure
> Of their observant toil the enemy's weight—
> Why, this hath not a finger's dignity.
> They call this bed-work, mapp'ry, closet-war; . . .
>
> (I. iii. 200–5)

The true assumption which underlies his speeches is that one should not divorce action from reasoned consideration. Granted, he has a specific application for that; but for the play as a whole, his speech on degree is chiefly important for its general account of disorder in society. Ulysses' speech is strictly coordinate with the speeches of Hector in the Trojan council. Ulysses considers the *political* consequences of pride and passion, as they issue in disorder; Hector, the moral and personal consequences of judgement involved with passion, in place of objective 'election'. Both appeal to principles of law, Hector citing the laws of nature and of nations, and Ulysses the law (about which Hooker writes so tellingly) by which the universe maintains itself in order. From the dramatist's point of view, both Ulysses and Hector establish clearly those principles by which each side ought to conduct itself. The statesman in each party speaks with clarity and persuasive eloquence. Neither, in the end, manages to live up to the principles which he enunciates; but the audience at any rate is in no doubt about the canons that apply.

The Trojan debate in II.ii, which is the second crucial scene, corresponds in form and in function to the Greek council of I.iii, but the matter of it is different. The Greek council derives its matter from the *Iliad* (and there from a moment of crucial decision), in which immediate advantage and not ultimate justification was in question. The Trojan council scene derives instead from what had become, by Shakespeare's time, a standard topic for academic dispute: namely, was it better that Helen should be kept, or that she should be returned? As a result, the Trojans produce a true debate, not too far in form from a disputation, with Priam as moderator.[1] The shape of the scene is, in general terms, that of the Greek council scene:[2] the conclusion of it is determined by Hector's decision to follow a lesser good than that for which he had argued—rather as, in I.iii, the conclusion is determined by Ulysses' decision to apply good principles to inferior ends.

The similarities in form, then, are obvious; the differences are at least as important, for the Trojans discuss the two possible bases for action, and Cassandra's brief appearance is wholly germane to their argument.

The first part of the scene, although it is partly animated by being a family dispute, raises a major question of the play: Hector assumes a value for Helen, and judges her unworthy as a motive for action; Troilus enquires how far, on the contrary, an objective valuation is possible in any conditions. And, as far as this part of the scene is concerned, Troilus is not quite as rash as he is sometimes said to be. His point is that the intrinsic value of any object must be first determined, and that the determination

---

1. It is not fair to call Priam, as critics have sometimes done, an ineffectual chairman of debate. His function is to oversee the *method* of argument: hence his rebuke to Paris at ll. 143–6. 2. See p. 41 above.

is itself a matter of uncertainty. His error consists in using an example where the intrinsic and the attributed values must necessarily be inextricably confused: 'I take today a wife' is the perfect hypothesis for a man defending passional judgements, but it has only a distant connection with the case of Helen. The more the emotions are involved, the more is the whole man concerned in the act of choice; and that is proper to the risk involved in marrying, even though time might subsequently alter one's feelings. But the only man passionally concerned in keeping Helen is Paris (who does not yet speak). Troilus invokes honour to help justify his argument, and is right as far as his example goes: one cannot pledge oneself to a woman in marriage and then renegue—to do so is dishonourable. But honour in that sense has nothing to do with Helen: the only 'honour' which there involves the Trojans is the honour of keeping her by force of arms: as Paris says later, he would have

> the soil of her fair rape
> Wip'd off in honourable keeping her. (II.ii. 149–50)

This is question-begging. Troilus' first notion of honour was justifiable: you act (by marrying) and maintain the justice of your act because you were involved in an *anterior* judgement. But the next sense of honour is different: you act (in stealing Helen as a quid pro quo) and justify your act subsequently; you attribute honour to the act afterwards by fighting in the field—where honour may indeed be gained, and defended, but where fighting cannot change wrong into right. You may eventually argue that, in doing such deeds, you acquire reputation— a third sense of honour—and by the end of the scene, that is what Troilus has done (II.ii. 200). He is wrong, then, in the method of his argument: he has shifted his ground without admitting it (or perhaps without noticing it). But there was nothing fundamentally wrong in his *first* position, and we ought not to transfer our disapproval of his judgement on Helen to his judgement on Cressida.[1]

Hector, of course, is right in insisting on the primacy of intrinsic value but he has no time to develop his argument, for Cassandra interrupts him.[2] She also is right: she deals in funda-

---

1. The design of *Troilus*, by which parallel and analogy invite us to pass judgement on things apparently similar, does not therefore require that we should judge *all* similars in the same way. The play also invites us to make distinctions.

2. As Professor Brooks reminds me, Hector has no need to develop his argument. The appeal to the *ius naturale* and the *ius gentium* was unanswerable:

mentals;[1] but Troilus mocks her 'brain-sick raptures' and rejects
Hector's notion that justice depends on the effects of time:
justice, he says, (in ironic riposte to Hector's earlier argument)
is absolute, and not subject to circumstances.[2] His assertion, and
that of Paris, who supports him, are rebutted by Hector on the
ground (implicit in Troilus' first argument) that passionate
involvement has here no place. Hector's argument deserves
some attention.[3]

Hector argues, first, that Paris and Troilus are too young and
too impetuous to judge rightly, and, secondly, that the return of
Helen is required by justice. (He has shifted his ground: hitherto,
he based his argument on prudence.) This first point derives
ultimately (as commentators have noted) from Aristotle's
Nicomachean Ethics, I.3:

> Political science is not a proper study for the young. The
> young man is not versed in the practical business of life from
> which politics draws its premises and its data.

And indeed Aristotle himself observes a further reason for this
incapacity:

> He [the young man] is, besides, swayed by his feelings, with
> the result that he will make no headway and derive no benefit
> from a study the end of which is not knowing but doing. It
> makes no difference whether the immaturity is in age or in
> character. The defect is not due to lack of years, but to *living*

---

no appeal could be made to any other principles of right in international affairs.
To refuse to acknowledge their supremacy was the same as to refuse to acknowledge degree; anarchy followed in each case. It is highly significant that in
Chapman's translation of *Iliad* XXII (not published until 1611), the dying
Hector, faced by the inflexible vengeance of Achilles, says 'I (knowing thee
well) foresaw/Thy now tried tyrranie, nor hop't for any other law,/Of nature, or
of nations . . .' (ll. 307–9). There is nothing that corresponds to the phrase in
the Greek text.

1. Cassandra, of course, does not argue: she asserts the truth with all the
force of inspired prophecy; but it is her doom never to be believed. Twice
she interrupts the action of the play; and each time she is disregarded and
disaster follows.

2. 'Justice' is too complex a concept to be subsumed in any one formula;
one may note, however, that Ulysses (I.iii.116–17) agrees with Aristotle that
distributive justice, at least, consists in restoring a balance—'right and wrong,/
Between whose endless jar justice resides, . . .' (cf. *Ethics*, v. 4). All citations
from Aristotle are from the Penguin Classics edn (trs. J.A.K. Thomson).

3. The sources of Hector's argument are only touched on here; but I have
dealt with them at greater length in Appendix III, pp. 311–13.

the kind of life which is a succession of unrelated emotional experiences [my italics].

This is a reason which, whether or not it applies to Paris, fits Troilus like a glove. 'Firm of word' he may be; but throughout the play he oscillates violently from one emotional extreme to another; his arguments here are passional in basis; and he suffers perpetually from excessive depression, excessive delight and excessive wrath, despite his repeated claim (i.i.27–8, v.ii.63–4) that he is more patient than Patience herself. (Hector, we may recall, is also patient: his 'patience / Is as a virtue fix'd', i.ii.4–5, and he fails in it only when felled by Ajax.)

Hector argues that a passionate nature is incompatible with justice or prudence, since it seeks some form of self-gratification (and hence, further passion), and he compares the man seeking pleasure or revenge to the deaf adder of Psalm lviii. Indeed, he goes further (still basing himself on Aristotle): justice, he says, is natural; the most natural form of justice (that is, of due debt properly paid) is wife to husband; and each civilized country has laws to control those passionate men who resist such justice. The application is made clear: a universal law condemns the policy of Paris; for Helen is indeed wife to Sparta's king, and both natural law and the laws made by man require that she be returned. The debate ought now to conclude, for the thesis is climactic and unanswerable. But at that point, Hector hesitates: he inclines in one respect, he says, to his younger brothers, in so far as fighting for Helen is 'a cause that hath no mean dependence / Upon our joint and several dignities'. And this hesitation is between absolute and relative good. The relative good is personal honour: something which the *Ethics* relegates to a lower plane (i.5). And when Hector finally turns about, and admits to having sent a challenge to the Greeks, we may find the cause again analysed by Aristotle: he compares the occasional irrational or unpredictable act to the uncontrolled movement of a limb; and in so far as a man performs such an act, so far is he, in Aristotle's view, incontinent: that is, he is swayed by impulse, and not by reason. (As Thersites remarks, 'All incontinent varlets'.)

The coming together of Troilus and Cressida in iii.ii is a curious scene. In the first place, it opens, as the play did, with Troilus frustrated, and wholly dependent on Pandarus: with Troilus, moreover, given much to elaborate verse rhetoric, in strong contrast to the chatty prosiness of Pandarus. Secondly,

when the lovers are brought together, they greet with a kiss but
say little, and the incident, for the moment, lives chiefly in the
comments of Pandarus, as the Presenter.[1] Thirdly (the lovers
being at last alone), there is a prose 'wooing'. Pandarus re-enters,
and the lovers then enact a verse 'wooing'. And fourthly, the
scene ends with a formal statement, by the lovers and Pandarus,
of their function as seen by history and tradition—faithful
Troilus, faithless Cressida, and Pandarus the go-between.

In one sense, the scene belongs to Pandarus. Perhaps it is
what the second title-page refers to as the 'conceited wooing of
Pandarus Prince of Licia': certainly, although Pandarus is not
always 'on', he opens and closes the scene, and it is his deflating,
prosaic speech which reduces the rhetoric of Troilus, and may
make the first kiss less serious than it might be. He it is, too, who
comments on the action in legal terms. He fusses over the two
lovers like an old nurse, and his advice and his urging makes him
sound like an aunt producing a children's charade—a trait
which he manifests again when Troilus and Cressida are to part.
Most of this, critics have already noticed, and discussed. But it is
easy when acknowledging the ambiguous nature of the scene to
overrate Pandarus: the lovers are not always subject to his
vitiating comments and what they say is of consequence.

It is difficult, however, to know how to judge the scene. I have
said elsewhere[2] that there may be revision, and perhaps duplication, at this point: certainly, whatever hesitation Cressida may
display, she hardly needs to express it, and be talked out of it,
twice over (ll. 72–97, 137–68). But it is even more obvious that
the style of the prose wooing, at least, is difficult to place. Nowhere else in the play do the lovers speak prose to one another;
and the prose here is sometimes awkward and strained, attempting
a wit and an hyperbole that is, perhaps, courtly, but may, rather,
be old-fashioned, and fit for deflation by Pandarus' prose.
Stylized it certainly is: the Troilus who at the moment of achieving
his desire can speak as simply as Bassanio did ('You have bereft
me of all words, lady': cf. *Mer. V.* III.ii.176), can shift quite
suddenly to

1. This is the essence of Shakespeare's technique with Pandarus: he
comments, insinuates, obtrudes; and while his style is usually 'low' and
without much substance of argument, he makes his effect by contrast with
context. His intrusiveness is predominant, extending even to action (cf. IV.iv.13–
14: 'Let me embrace, too'), but most frequent in speech, as when (in the same
scene) he answers a question posed *to Troilus* (*Cress.* 'Have the gods envy?'
Pand. 'Ay, ay, ay, ay, 'tis too plain a case.').

2. See the discussion of the text, pp. 16–17, and in Appendix I, pp. 304–6.

What makes this pretty abruption? What too curious dreg
espies my sweet lady in the fountain of our love?

(III. ii. 63–5)

where the obtrusive fullness of the metaphor, and the formal
word-order, draw attention to the artifice. Yet under such
formality, which develops by way of shows and pageants and
small allegories (blind fear, seeing reason), there lies a serious
argument. For Cressida, characteristically, the protestations of a
lover may be allowed to glance at his sexual vitality: she is a
true niece to Pandarus, in lowering the tone of a conversation:

They say all lovers swear more performance than they are able,
and yet reserve an ability that they never perform: . . .

(III. ii. 83–5)

But that is not what Troilus means. His dismissal of a lover's
Petrarchan protestations is not merely the rejection of a style of
rhetoric, but also of a mode of negotiation: he dislikes the
merchant's language of love, which makes excessive claims (and
in that he picks up a theme touched on elsewhere—by Ulysses,
by Pandarus, by Paris).[1] He plays briefly with courtly exaggeration, in order to reject it. Like the lover in the Sonnets, he would
be known, and loved, for what he truly is, and the language of
advertising in the world of lovers is for him a deceit. ('Promise,
large promise, is the soul of an advertisement', said Samuel
Johnson [*Idler*, no. 40].) But the problem implicit in the language
used by lovers takes Troilus at once to the nature of love itself,
and he touches for a moment on the truth that underlies hyperbole: that love inhabits a dimension greater than lover or
beloved, and that mere measure cannot correspond to the desire.
There's beggary in the love that can be reckoned. And hence,
since hyperbole only exaggerates the discrepancy between
love and its language, Troilus will use only the simplest of
language, related only to the truest of deeds. He wants to be
judged by what he is and does, and not by what he says. ('Few
words to fair faith.') He wants nothing of past reputation, or of
future hope and promise, to interpose between what he is and
what he loves: 'No perfection in reversion shall have a praise in
present'.[2] What he is rejecting, therefore, is what belongs, in the
next scene, to the torpid Achilles (who rests on 'good deeds past')
or to the conceited Ajax, who dwells already in the glory that

1. By Ulysses, at I. iii. 358; by Paris, at IV. i. 76–9; and by Pandarus, at V. x. 46.
2. Troilus here concentrates upon what *is* (as opposed to what *may be*, and
how that may change his opinion). His 'simplicity' (the right metaphysical
term) has brought him to a position which resembles that of Agamemnon,

should come to him if he defeats Hector next day. Troilus is consistent. He may sometimes speak like the fashionable lover when he is at leisure merely to contemplate his condition; but in any crisis he is 'as true as Troilus'. Ulysses says so, in IV.v: Troilus is

> Speaking in deeds, and deedless in his tongue;

and when he speaks, he is straightforward:

> what [he] thinks he shows, . . .

So much for the prose wooing. With Pandarus' return the lovers turn to verse, and to a different topic. Hitherto, Troilus has spoken of the gap between promise and performance; now, Cressida speaks of the gap between her behaviour in the past and her true feelings, and moves on to regret the double self that she finds in herself: the one that is at her command, and can withdraw from Troilus; and the other that, having divided her, would stay in order to be deceived by her lover's promises. (If Troilus briefly recalls Bassanio, then Cressida here a little resembles Portia:

> Beshrew your eyes!
> They have o'erlook'd me and divided me;
> One half of me is yours, the other half yours—
> Mine own, I would say, but if mine, then yours,
> And so all yours.   (III.ii.14–18)

But 'shudd'ring fear' leaves Portia (l. 110) as perhaps it does not leave Cressida.)

The discussion is brief; and the lovers take up the stances which establish them as types. Troilus affirms his faith that Cressida will indeed prove to be what he believes she is: a woman not subject to time and change, whose constancy is of another order than the physical decline of her bodily beauty, and who will answer him with a love as pure and simple as his own. And having said it, he prophesies, and turns himself into a proverbial comparison for good faith. Cressida likewise prophesies; but her vision is of future obloquy. What she sees, beyond the wrack of cities and the death of history, is a time when (should she now prove untrue) she will be still the archetype of all unfaithful women. Troilus' prophecy was simple, and his own

---

greeting Hector. In the context of battle, past and to come, Agamemnon's feelings must necessarily be in contradiction (welcome/enemy). But 'in this extant moment' faith and troth can operate 'with most divine integrity' (IV.v. 167–9).

name a climax to all fidelity; but Cressida's is conditional, and the curse which she utters is prophecy as well. The 'hand-fasting' which Pandarus then performs becomes itself an irony. It looks like a legal betrothal; it looks like a wedding; but it sounds, in context, as if its power as a contract derived from the prophecies just spoken; so that the truth in Cressida's vision (which we know for truth) asserts the truth of Pandarus' own prophecy—he will be the first pander, if either lover proves untrue. It is an odd situation. Elsewhere in the play, men look forward to future fame, or (like Ulysses) mock others with the want of it, but the case remains hypothetical. Even Ajax, liable to break his neck in vainglory, is presented to us only in the words—not wholly reliable—of Thersites. But here, Time stops, and three people, pronouncing a doom upon themselves, become for the moment the visible images of what they *shall* be. It is for the moment only; and Pandarus hurries to complete his function.

But the important scene in Act III is III.iii, in which Calchas successfully pleads for the exchange of Antenor and Cressida, and in which Achilles is mocked by Ulysses. Like IV.v, to which it corresponds, it has analogies with the great Eastcheap scene in *I Henry IV* (II.iv): it is constructed of several separate 'actions'; it proceeds to a climax in a significant debate (between Achilles and Ulysses); and it contains within itself lesser *mimetic* actions (the scorning of Achilles by the Greek generals near the beginning, and the pageant of Ajax to conclude).

The first thirty-seven lines dispatch an important piece of business, in which leave is granted for the exchange of Cressida and Antenor: an ironic touch, which undercuts the wooing scene that immediately precedes, and looks forward to the disastrous collapse of Troilus' faith in v.ii. Yet the significance of this passage does not lie in its function as pivot to the Troilus action: it lies also in what Calchas says about himself. For in his opening speech, Calchas strips himself categorically naked, in a way that no other Shakespearean character had done before this, save perhaps Richard II at his deposition. He has lost everything: made himself no more than a traitor; deprived himself of all that 'time, acquaintance, custom, and condition' can make of a man; and has become as one new-born, or wholly foreign—a man without name, nature, attributes, or relationship. Unaccommodated man, for the moment, stands on the stage: a figure with nothing but a momentary dramatic function, a being defined largely by negatives; and, in the logic of the play's games with language and dramaturgy, it is by comparison with Calchas that we must judge the natures of those other figures who are defined, or who define themselves, before us. He is the lay-figure, upon whom the logical categories can be disposed: the naked entity, that invites attributes.

The second incident—the scorning of Achilles—is brief. Its function is to offer pride a reflection of itself—to allow the eye to see itself, as Ulysses later implies. Its method is reminiscent of I. ii, for what we have here is another instance of characters 'passing over the stage'; at the same time, there is a connection with that former visit of the Greeks to Achilles (in II. iii). But here the processes are reversed. In II. iii, Achilles proudly withdrew: Patroclus was his spokesman: Agamemnon had laid by his 'appertainments' to make the visit; and the result was no more than a mock-praise of Ajax. In III. iii, it is Achilles who finds his appertainments withdrawn: the Greek generals go off haughtily: Agamemnon speaks with Achilles at one remove (by way of Nestor); and the result is a prolonged analysis of the ways in which man and his attributes may be related.

That analysis represents the Greek view of reputation and value, and it is meant to stand with the Trojan debate, wherein Hector distinguished the intrinsic and the attributed virtues of Helen. But in that debate, the value of Helen was nevertheless a secondary matter, and inferior to the problem of whether or not the war should continue. Helen, besides, *did* nothing: what she *was* alone was the question; and attribution of qualities derived from the words and deeds of others. Trojans or Greeks daily 'painted' her in their blood, to assert her beauty (I. i): Paris' servant defined her by her attributes, without naming her, in order to tease Pandarus (III. i). Achilles is another matter, for he is not a goal of action, but an actor; men have attributed qualities to him, on the strength of his former deeds, and now he attributes those qualities to himself, and ceases to act. He has become static, in a world in which value (according to Ulysses) is constantly changing. He is isolated from men by his own choice, and (like so many people in this play) needs messengers and ambassadors in order to communicate with his own kind. Like Calchas, he has suddenly become a lay-figure, from whom the qualities by which he was known are slowly being removed.[1] As Ulysses

---

1. Calchas, however, knew quite well the consequences of his act and needed no prophetic power to foresee them. Achilles not only does not foresee but hardly recognizes what has already happened (e.g. III. iii. 88: 'Fortune and I are friends').

reminds him, 'perseverance . . . keeps honour bright'; reputation depends upon constant activity, irrespective of the *inherent* worth of the man. The Red Queen puts it best: 'Now *here*, you see, it takes all the running you can do, to keep in the same place. If you want to get somewhere else, you must run at least twice as fast as that' (*Through the Looking-Glass*, Ch. 2). It is Ajax, 'a very horse', a man who is, by implication, without intelligence or moral being,[1] who will become renowned through the chance of a momentary success against Hector.

One may be tempted to look a little askance at this doctrine of Ulysses. Certainly, it appears at first sight to be a plea for the ambitious and thrusting man—for emulation, in fact—and to that extent, it might not be congruent with his argument in the Greek debate, when he pleaded for degree and order, and deplored emulation. But one ought to distinguish. Ulysses is wise and ironical throughout the play: his judgements are sensible; and if he sometimes lapses from wisdom to mere policy and shrewd plotting, that is because no other Greek has the wit to be as adaptable to circumstance as he is. His pronouncements have often enough the force of a tradition behind them, but his purpose is to *use* his eloquent commonplaces: as Aristotle said (in a passage which is a good gloss on Ulysses' function in I.iii), 'A doctor does not deliberate whether or not he will cure his patients, nor an orator whether or not he is to win over his audience, nor a statesman whether or not he is to produce law and order' (*Ethics*, III.3). Men debate only about means in such cases; and the business of Ulysses is always to use such arguments as come readily to hand, in order to persuade men as he wishes. In the Greek council scene he used eloquence and oblique mockery in a sermon on order: here, he disputes shrewdly with Achilles on the effects of Time upon reputation. He argues as Agamemnon did in II.iii, although the tropes are different: the 'fair fruit in an unwholesome dish' has become 'alms for oblivion'; but the purpose and the argument are the same. Achilles must learn that, as Sidney remarked (borrowing also from Aristotle) 'it is not *Gnosis* but *Praxis* must be the fruit' (p. 112). It is useless, from Ulysses' point of view, to have Achilles sulking in his tent, because Achilles must fight if the Greeks are to profit by him. The 'engine not portable' is not even a potential threat. Achilles must act effectively if he is to serve the cause of those 'honours that are without him'; and if that is to be achieved, then Ulysses

1. Cf. *Ethics*, I.9: 'We do not naturally speak of . . . a horse or other beast as happy, for none of the brute creation can take part in moral activities.'

must in his turn act effectively—which means that he must use all his tactical skills, even though in the end it means threatening Achilles with what is known to the Greek intelligence service.

When teasing Agamemnon and Nestor, in I.iii, Ulysses showed himself master of mimetic speech: the account of Patroclus' play-acting in Achilles' tent becomes, shrewdly, a piece of direct play-acting by Ulysses in the tent of Agamemnon. The same skill appears briefly in this dispute with Achilles: the

> fashionable host,
> That slightly shakes his parting guest by th'hand,
> And with his arms out-stretch'd, as he would fly,
> Grasps in the comer. (III.iii.165–8)

is a figure that must for the moment appear on stage. And such half-mime, briefly introduced in the debate of these two, develops rapidly into full-scale mime as soon as Ulysses has left and Thersites enters; for (although Thersites could hardly have known Ulysses' purpose)[1] the process of letting pride find a glass to show itself is not confined to the scornful passage of the Greek generals. The scene closes with a piece of professional mime by the fool Thersites, with Patroclus as his 'feed'.

The passage concerned is brief (ll. 243–297) but it sums up several of the play's techniques. It begins with Thersites' paradox—

> Ajax goes up and down the field, asking for himself

—a remark which may indeed pun on 'a Jakes', but which nevertheless attributes even to Ajax that multiplicity of selves which several of the characters are granted, and which Cressida in particular deplores (III.ii.146–9) though she exemplifies it in effect (v.ii). Yet Ajax's two 'selves' are a consequence of his pride: in II.iii he had described himself *without recognizing himself* (ll. 160–1, 209–19), and now he knows neither himself nor anybody else. For a man who cannot distinguish Thersites from Agamemnon, the world outside himself is as isolated and distant as it is for Achilles (II.iii.185–91, and cf. p. 54 above). And the alienated Ajax is now so perfect a figure of Pride that he can think of nothing but playing his part perfectly: so perfect a figure of Pride that Achilles can recognize him for what he plays, but almost fails to make the application of the sin to himself. As a consequence, the isolated Achilles and the isolated Ajax stand far

---

1. Cf. the effect (useful to his purpose, but quite unpredictable by Ulysses) of the entry of Æneas in I.iii.

removed, each the perfect mirror for the other; and all that
Achilles can do, from the full distance of his self-induced isolation,
is to send Ajax a letter.

The scene in the next act which corresponds to III.iii is IV.v.
It is, that is to say, another long, demonstrative scene, of compound structure; but whereas one can draw simple parallels in
structure between the scenes of the Greek and Trojan debates,
there is little to compare in the shaping of these later scenes. The
differences follow from the difference of function: III.iii was to
demonstrate the psychological and theatrical attributes of Pride,
while hinting at the limited and relative nature of reputation;
but IV.v is to show the integrity of both Hectors (Troilus, described, and Hector, demonstrated), together with the dual nature
of Ajax, and the further frustrations that attend on human action.
For this scene finds its climax in the frustrated plot of Ulysses: its
centre is a duel which comes to nothing but embracement, as if

> a brother should a brother dare
> To gentle exercise and proof of arms. (*1H4* v.ii. 53–4)

At the same time, much of its dramatic force comes from a variety
of demonstrations of the nature of a man or woman, as Cressida is
kissed, Achilles grows surly or malign, Hector is magnificent or
wrathful, and Ajax behaves with unexpected courtesy.

The very opening of the scene is an anti-climax, as Ajax adopts
an inflatedly heroic stance, the trumpet sounds, and nothing
follows at all. Ulysses' dry comment, however, leads to the brief
enquiry

> Is not yond Diomed, with Calchas' daughter?

which is answered in a manner characteristic of this play, as
Ulysses explains (and moralizes) the individual nature of
Diomedes' walk. What follows from that is, at one level, the
metamorphosis of Cressida: the divided girl of III.ii has left part of
herself behind, and is transformed as she enters the Greek camp.
At a second, we are presented with a variation on another of the
play's devices—a round game, with Cressida kissed in turn,
sometimes by the true man, sometimes by his surrogate (Patroclus
for Paris, for Menelaus), and sometimes not at all, as Ulysses
contrives to snub Cressida, insult Menelaus, and avoid demeaning
himself by kissing a whore. But the kissing is a momentary
interlude: what failed to happen in answer to Ajax and his
trumpet, and what we almost forgot in the round game, now

occurs, as the Trojans enter, announced by a full flourish, and
Æneas sets the tone of the ensuing exchange, at a level which
nicely avoids both the heroic burlesque and the unheroic charade
of the Greeks. Shakespeare, moreover, loses no opportunities in
this play; the dexterity which takes us directly from Ulysses'
mordant 'character' of Cressida to the normal ritual of combat is
that which opened the play on Troilus' contempt for war, or
moved straight from the Greek war council to the salon of the
vapid Helen.

The symmetry of the scene is manifest in the patterning whereby the formal kissing, early on, is balanced against the formal
introductions of heroes, near the end, as Hector is greeted by the
Greek generals, in much the same order as that in which they
kissed Cressida.[1] Similarly, the hybrid nature of Ajax, and hence
the divided motives of Hector, are the preliminary to the duel, as
Æneas contrives both to explain the problem, and to put Achilles
in his place: just so, after the duel, Hector himself develops more
elaborately the double nature of Ajax (although he waits until
after he has met all the Greeks, before putting down Achilles in
his turn.)[2] This formal figuring, by which a scene becomes almost
dance-like, about a highly formal combat, has its stylized counter-
parts in other details. Few scenes in the canon, even in comedy,
can have depended so much upon recognition, introduction,
characterizing and identification. For consider: at l. 13 we have
the identity of Diomedes established; Cressida is named (l. 17);
Nestor (effectually) introduces Agamemnon; Nestor then names
himself (in the third person); Achilles follows, in the same mode;
Patroclus identifies himself and Menelaus by acting the part of
each in turn; and Ulysses, who is nameless, as far as Cressida is
concerned, translates both Menelaus and Helen into the realm of
impossibility. That movement completed, we have Ulysses'
pointed 'character' of Cressida-as-whore. The Trojan entry
provokes a tart comment from Achilles: in his eyes, secure pride,
and contempt for an opponent, are enough to confirm that the
challenger is Hector. Æneas at once tries the gambit that was so
successful when he announced the challenge, except that this
time he employs a logical syllogism:

1. Here, as with the two visits to Achilles' tent, the *visual* repetition would be
clear to an audience. It is the reader who misses something of the pattern of
iteration.
2. For an audience that knows the story, this incident is a painful irony, for
it is Achilles who kills him, and not he Achilles. Similar irony operates when
Hector courteously rejects Ulysses' prophecy ('I must not believe you').

Æneas.   If not Achilles, sir,
        What is your name?
Achill.   If not Achilles, nothing.
Æneas.   Therefore Achilles,   (IV. v. 75–7)

and proceeds to distinguish the virtues in which Hector excels—those virtues of generosity and courtesy, in fact, which forbid him to slaughter his cousin. The cousin is then put, with Hector, into a formal pattern of syntax and rhyme—

> Half heart, half hand, half Hector comes to seek
> This blended knight, half Trojan and half Greek;
>   (IV. v. 85–6)

and, while the marshals determine 'the order of the fight', Ulysses proceeds to a *second* 'character'.

This sketch is more complimentary: the details derive in part from tradition, in that Troilus is 'Hector the secounde', as all the medieval sources had said; but the qualities that are attributed to Troilus come out of Aristotle: Ulysses, citing the report of Æneas, defines the Liberal Man.[1] Once the fighting is over, Hector produces his own stylized account of his cousin, in which Ajax is divided vertically into Greek and Trojan, as if he were an heraldic blazon. (Just so, Æneas, in his polite fencing with Diomedes in IV. i, saw himself as an heraldic lion *passant regardant*.) A polite exchange follows: then the Greek generals arrive in sequence, and in sequence greet Hector. Agamemnon, all generosity, contrives that his warmth of welcome shall be placed in a context which effectually excludes the Trojan War, as he isolates 'this extant moment' from the 'formless ruin of oblivion' which stretches before and after. Hector's mock for Menelaus depends on two facetious oaths and a jest from the *Metamorphoses*: Menelaus becomes lame Vulcan, scorned by both Venus (=Helen) the faithless wife and Mars (=Paris) the cuckold-maker. Nestor translates Hector, in his turn, into a god, with his Jovial generosity;[2] and then places himself and Hector in the perspective of history, as he recalls his own fight with Laomedon, founder of Troy, and judges Hector his superior. Hector retorts by translating Nestor into History itself:

1. The Liberal Man has his proper place in a play so much given to the consideration of justice: cf. Aquinas, *Summa Theologiae*, 11a–11ae.117.5, 'Respondeo . . . quod liberalitas non est species iustitiae . . . Habet tamen quandam convenientiam cum iustitia . . . liberalitas a quibusdam ponitur pars iustitiae, sicut virtus ei annexa ut principali.'

2. Hector, throughout the scene, displays the characteristics of Aristotle's Magnanimous Man: see the discussion in Appendix III, pp. 314–16.

Let me embrace thee, good old chronicle,
That hast so long walk'd hand in hand with Time;
Most reverend Nestor, I am glad to clasp thee.
                                    (IV. V. 201-3)

Hector and Ulysses put the 'extant moment' back into the course
of the war, and become, on the one hand, the hope of Troy, and
the other, the prophet of Troy's fall. And the sequence ends with
the direct confrontation of Hector by the man who is to preside
over his slaughtering, in which Achilles, invoking the gods, that
they may foretell the manner of Hector's death, contrives to see
Hector as a beast of the chase. It is an astonishing series, running
from common-sense observation and logic to metaphor and
myth; from history, to the timeless; from heraldry, through
ethical theory, to the latest fashion in Theophrastan sketch; and it
gathers up into itself, before the action of the play suddenly
accelerates in the fifth act, much of what Shakespeare has been
saying about the Trojans and Greeks, and the odd variety of
dramatic modes by which he has said it.

The last scene, in this series in which the topics of the play are
argued and then exemplified, is v. ii. It is a scene much discussed,
and much moralized, by critics, as if it were the focus of the whole
play: the point at which, for one hero at least, the dire events
can be seen to spring from their amorous causes. But one ought
perhaps to modify the traditional view slightly. Troilus is not the
type of all those, Greek or Trojan, who have been mistaken in
their notions of love or war: he is the only person whom we are
allowed to watch as he involves himself emotionally both in the
act of judgement and the consequences of the act. In doing that,
he becomes, by the standards of his play, not indeed a complex
character but a developed character—the only one who can be
seen to change in any significant way—and in some measure he is
therefore the kind of character whom Shakespeare will use
subsequently in tragedy. This does not make him a tragic
character now, and it does not turn *Troilus and Cressida* into a
tragedy; but it shows something, perhaps, of Shakespeare's
methods.

By a little, v. ii is the shortest of the key-scenes, and it bears
small resemblance to the others in the shaping of its material:
perhaps III. iii comes nearest to it, with the enacted scorn for
Achilles, which is then analysed by Achilles himself. What
distinguishes v. ii is its unusual staging (often noticed) in which
Diomedes and Cressida are watched by Troilus and Ulysses, and

all four are observed by Thersites. How one should visualize that staging it is hard to say. On the stage of a public theatre, one would expect the lovers to be upstage, by an entry—perhaps a curtain, perhaps one of the doors, (and possibly with a cresset: see note to v. ii. 5), while Troilus and Ulysses stood downstage on one side, and Thersites downstage on the other, having followed those two on. (At such a private performance as Alexander suggested, all this might be much more compressed, although some great halls were close, in the dimensions of the staging that they would permit, to the public theatres, and certainly had doors in the hallscreen.) What is fairly plain, at all events, is the general effect. The *writing* of the scene does nothing to suggest any major contrast in mode between the speech of the lovers and that of the comment upon it—there is not, that is to say, any hint of a play within a play at that level—but the marked formalism of the staging emphasizes the 'exemplary' nature of the wooing action, while allowing it to remain naturalistic—naturalistic, that is, until Cressida takes her farewell, in rhyming, emblematic fashion. At the same time, Troilus has none of the advantages normally enjoyed by Shakespeare's eavesdroppers, since he has not arranged the eavesdropping (as Claudius or the Duke of Vienna or Sir Toby had done) and he could do nothing to intrude upon it even if he wished to ('This place is dangerous,/The time right deadly'); moreover, he is himself the subject of satiric comment by Thersites. (Ulysses attracts no satire but serves as a further commentator upon Troilus, though one of whose presence Troilus is aware.) The audience, therefore, enjoys the advantage of two wholly opposite ways of apprehending: it can respond as fully as it chooses to the emotional and metaphysical tensions of Troilus' experience, while seeing constantly before it the visible evidence for the structured artifice of an argument.[1] It has, further, the advantage of knowing that, while (for one part of the mind) there is something to be said for Thersites' opinions, yet sanity lies much closer to the judicious, dispassionate utterances of Ulysses.

But to say all this is not to write Troilus down: he is not—as Paris might more fairly be called—'that same young Trojan ass that loves the whore there'. As Charles Williams points out,[2] he is a young man in a situation very like that of Hamlet, and his reaction to it is not far from Hamlet's. He has received a

1. Logically considered, the dramatic construction here resembles the working of mock-heroic language.
2. *English Poetic Mind*, pp. 59–60, 68.

profound shock to his moral being; his metaphysical world is questioned; and like Hamlet, he wants to determine first the nature of the shock—

> To make a recordation to my soul
> Of every syllable that here was spoke.[1]
>
> (v. ii. 115–16)

Unlike Hamlet, he *ends* by unpacking his heart with words: unlike Hamlet, he proceeds at once to effect his revenge if he can. But all of that belongs with the nature of each man's play, and not with his dilemma. Troilus' triumph in this scene is to work out in linguistic terms something that corresponds to the moral interlude that he has seen, in which the devil Luxury defeated Humanum Genus, and in which what the spectator had thought to be love was shown to be nothing but a lust of the blood and a permission of the will. His reaction is not to be dismissed in a phrase from Thersites, for Troilus is not trying to 'swagger himself out on's own eyes'. Rather, he is saying 'Look here upon this picture and on this'; and his difficulty lies in one point—that he is moralist and metaphysician to himself, and not to another. It is not easy to oppose two images of Cressida in lucid terms while suffering from the effects of shock—of knowing within one's being 'the spacious breadth of this division'. Troilus, in such circumstances, may be allowed his paradoxes.[2] For his problem is profound; he knows within himself what it is to be at once nominalist and realist. Williams compares him to the Wordsworth of the 1790s, and indeed Wordsworth offers a comment on what Troilus suffers: writing in the 1800 *Preface*, he speaks thus of poetry:

> its object is truth, not individual and local, but general and operative; not standing upon external testimony, but carried alive into the heart by passion; truth which is its own testimony . . . .

This is precisely the dilemma of Troilus, who knows suddenly this opposition of 'external testimony' and the truth which is borne

---

1. Hamlet likewise wants to record what he believes he has seen and heard: not only 'My tables—meet it is I set it down' but also 'From the table of my memory/I'll wipe away all trivial fond records/ . . . And thy commandment all alone shall live/Within the book and volume of my brain/Unmix'd with baser matter' (*Ham.* i. v. 107, 98–104).

2. If we are to find Troilus merely comic, or even ludicrous, in this scene, then we must be prepared to laugh at the Shakespeare who wrote Sonnets 93, 137 and 138.

into the heart 'by passion': a dilemma which makes him a puzzle both to the sceptical Thersites and the dispassionate Ulysses. For Troilus, no decision is *merely* an act of the unimpassioned intelligence; he would sympathize entirely with Wordsworth's rejection of all who treat only with the superficies: who indulge in 'a taste for Poetry . . . as if it were a thing as indifferent as a taste for rope-dancing, or Frontiniac or sherry'. Troilus is one of those who refuse to think merely in terms of 'taste' or inclination, or even of prudence and what Hector called 'modest doubt'. He is prepared to stand by his judgement, because that judgement has been the act of the whole man and not of the prudential intellect. In comedy, such an act makes a man ridiculous, but largely because the man turns suddenly from one kind of action to another, and (frequently) does not see with any completeness the figure he cuts. In tragedy, such an act isolates a man, but he is seldom in doubt about what he has done, or what he now is. In either case, the man is vulnerable because of his act, and is allowed to live out the consequences. Because *Troilus* is such a schematized play, and because Troilus himself is not really at the centre of its affairs, he is not permitted to live out the consequences, but has in effect only this scene in which to find his balance.

(b) TIME AND TIME'S SUBJECTS

Time occupies a peculiar place in the world of *Troilus*. The play is (primarily, I think) a Trojan War play, and to that extent we are taken up into one of the great Matters of Western Europe. We ought to be involved in a sense of origins, and to take sides with the Trojans against the Greeks; but although Shakespeare makes his Trojans, by a little, the more attractive party, and although the Troilus story belongs with Troy, one finds oneself nevertheless outside the world of the play. In one of the most sympathetic essays to be written about *Troilus*, John Bayley[1] made the point that this play, alone in the canon, takes place only in play time, without any sense of what he calls 'novel time'. One might cavil at details of his argument, but what he points to is undoubtedly true of the play and of our response to it. These persons are *acting*, no more; and it is natural enough, in the world of *Troilus*, that they should act not only for us, but for one another (as indeed I have tried to show). If the play deals with a moment from an illustrious sequence, then the parts played will derive from that. But they will be *parts*, however complex, and behind them there is nothing

1. *The Uses of Division* (1976), pp. 185–210.

really there at all:[1] the *part* is continuous, but not the personality. 'Everything takes place in, and ends in, the present'.[2] With the exceptions of Calchas and Cassandra—and what other Shakespearean play was afforded two prophets?[3]—nobody can speak of what will be (although Ulysses comes close to it); but many speak of what might well be, though often enough the reference is merely for the sake of an argument. There is a structure of allusion, forwards and backwards, without much sense that past or future have come alive for the speaker. (Ulysses and Cressida are both eloquent on the passage of Time, but one is in effect cursing herself, and the other pointing out to Achilles the destruction wrought by Time upon Fame.) Much more characteristic is the effect, most obvious at the end of iii.ii, in which men and women step wholly out of the play's action, and present themselves as typical figures in what to them is an hypothetical tradition, belonging to the future: the True Lover, the False Mistress, the Pander. And for those who do not do that, there is the opportunity to stand back for the moment and sum up the situation—the 'advantage of the time' that prompts Calchas; the just-appearing 'baby-figure' of 'things to come at large' that takes the eye of Nestor. It is 'this extant moment'—a moment out of the action of war or war's surrogate—that allows Agamemnon to speak with pure sincerity to Hector. Troilus, assured of Cressida at last, assimilates her to his wish that there might somewhere be one woman not subject to the corrupting and decaying influences of Time. Ulysses, on the other hand, urges constant action, for only so will one's present honour be maintained even as it now is.

And if it be true that the persons merely play a part, and have no 'life' implied for them beyond that part, then the persons will be discontinuous, because the play is so. That is not to call the characters ill-drawn, for they are not; but a character without any inner continuity will be, in effect, continually trying-on roles, and that is what we find. Indeed, Bayley remarks of Troilus that his love 'consists only in moments: the moment when he is giddy with desire . . . the moment when he sees Cressida together with Diomedes.'[4]

Time is, however, significant in a further way in *Troilus*. None of the characters develops (with the possible exception of Troilus

1. ibid., p. 189.
2. ibid., p. 188.
3. And each prophet, in a different way, discredited (as Professor Jenkins reminds me).
4. Bayley, p. 204; cf. *Ethics*, 1.3, quoted above, pp. 48–9.

himself), but what each one values had once a beginning, or will have an end, or will come to be, if he is patient enough. Agamemnon promises that Troy will fall at last (with the advantage that those who waited in patience for the fall will be proved worthy of gaining by it); Pandarus also preaches patience to Troilus; and Cressida foresees that early success is self-defeating: 'Men prize the thing ungain'd more than it is'. The Trojan debate turns on the prospect of 'promis'd glory'; Achilles is warned of glory promised for Ajax, at the cost to himself and his son. Indeed, 'emulation', the word that echoes through the play, seems to involve even the Olympians, for Achilles had formerly provoked 'emulous missions 'mongst the gods themselves'. Time calumniates, and is envious, and injurious (III.iii)—not least, because it can turn a protestation of good faith into a curse on infidelity (IV.ii.102–8). And all men, according to Ulysses, are alike in preferring the new (and slight) to the old-fashioned. All this has to be made explicit in a play in which (since no-one changes in essentials but lives in a kind of stasis) all things prized must be given a form of postulated existence for the future. If men, or concepts, may be played with, so that Ajax becomes the equal of Nestor for wisdom and of Achilles for valour, then one may go further than dressing up in voices: one may extend the dimensions to include hypothetical time. Ajax becomes the historical slayer of Hector, and Achilles the successful lover of Polixena, whereas Cressida grows into a woman whose moral worth enjoys an immortality denied to her body.[1] Time itself grows old and doting (but also a thief and an arbitrator), yet it also appears as Nestor, aiding the gestation of Ulysses' notions, or as Nestor's companion, for whom the aged Nestor is Chronicle. Time, in effect, grows a body, whereas men and women are transformed to metaphysical entities. Metamorphosis is the word: how many beasts are invoked in the course of the play? And change may come to the man who waits for Time to prove that worth does not change. Troilus refuses to turn back the silks upon the merchant, for that would be to make experience the test of value; yet in his protestation to Cressida he will say 'Praise us as we are tasted, allow us as we prove'.

(c) TIME, TREASON AND PROPHECY

Time brings to birth, and kills; it endows, and deprives. With the passage of time, Nestor is no longer a great warrior. In the end, as

---

1. III.iii.246 ff.; v.i.38–45; III.ii.156–66.

Ovid points out, Milo weeps to see his once-Herculean arms 'hang flapping downe, and nought but empty skin' (*Metamorphoses*, xv. 254). And Helen weeps likewise, to see her wrinkles in the glass, and wonders that she should twice have been ravished for her beauty.[1] Time, indeed, betrays us. Time's is the fundamental note of betrayal from which the overtones of all other treasons are derived. Stay the passage of time, and Cressida is true, Antenor still the faithful 'alye' of Priam.[2] The play achieves its essential stasis for more than four acts because only one betrayal is committed in the course of them, and that affects three people, and not the Siege of Troy. For most of the dramatic action, it is *trivial* things that are done—games, rituals, mere paradigms of serious act. Greeks and Trojans alike are contemplating immediate past and immediate future, but (until Time's accidents betray their expectations) they themselves perform no actions of weight. Once they begin to perform such actions, then they themselves may also become active traitors, as well as the victims of treachery: Cressida is not alone in infidelity. Because the play truly opened (as the Prologue pointed out) *in medias res* it is pregnant with irony throughout, and that irony is seldom comic. During the whole period of inaction, the irony is potential, for no act is complete: one knows tension, but no release. Once action begins, then change occurs, in men and in situation, and what was ironic pregnancy becomes actual fulfilment (or frustration) of design or expectation.

Even in purely verbal terms, it is not difficult to find traitors in the text. Troilus calls himself a traitor within thirty-five lines of the play's beginning, for he has moved, within his own mind, from the position of continual contemplation that he desires. Pandarus, at the play's end, invokes traitors (or should it be traders?) and bawds in the audience. Troilus abuses Diomedes, calling him traitor in an attempt to bring him to battle, but well knowing also that Diomedes is an accessory to betrayal. Thersites refers to the traitor Calchas; and Calchas himself admits that he has incurred a traitor's name. Indeed, if one turns to real treasons, one may begin with Calchas (who changed sides). Cressida has abandoned Troilus. Helen has abandoned Menelaus. Æneas (according to one tradition)[3] and Antenor (certainly) will betray Troy. And finally, Achilles is doubly a traitor, for he has corres-

---

1. Her situation is much like that of La Belle Heaulmière, and is likewise tragically ironic ('Time that gave does now his gift confound').

2. The word is Golding's: *Metamorphoses*, xiii. 248.

3. Cf. p. 70 n.

ponded with Troy in order to betray the Greek cause;[1] and he betrays the principles by which he has hitherto acted, for his killing of Hector is mere butchery, at second-hand, and yet he claims the credit for it, and aggravates his evil-doing by his abuse of the dead body.

One might even push the metaphor (or analogy) further, and say that Ulysses and Hector are also guilty of betraying their principles, in that what they first propose is other than, and superior to, what they finally attempt: Ulysses stoops to rig a lottery; Hector drops his argument in order to issue a challenge. It looks a little like forcing the word beyond its proper sense; and yet the *structure* of their acts conforms to the play's pattern, as laid down by Agamemnon: that hope's designs are less in deed than in promise; that by their very nature all 'actions highest rear'd' develop 'checks and disasters' of themselves; and that all recorded actions have gone awry,

> not answering the aim
> And that unbodied figure of the thought
> That gave't surmised shape. (I.iii. 15–17)

For some men, it is possible to act as if Time held no secrets, and as if no action were ever modified by circumstances. These are the prophets, and they do not necessarily foresee as a consequence of deduction from the patterning of things in general: their foresight and prophecy is from a vision, as Priam explains:

> Thy wife hath dreamt; thy mother hath had visions:
> Cassandra doth foresee; and I myself
> Am, like a prophet, suddenly enrapt. (v.iii.63–5)

If the play has effectually *stayed* Time: if the moment has been 'frozen': then the prophets are those who move outside this state of immobility; and our list of them may begin with Priam, Hecuba and Andromache. Cassandra was always known as a prophet: the curse upon her ensured that she was never to be believed; but for an *audience* her prophecies are both profound and a form of tragic irony.

Ulysses likewise prophesies the fall of Troy—he has done so on his embassy, he repeats himself to Hector—and, like Cassandra, he is not believed.[2] Troilus is hailed as a prophet by Cressida

1. Betrayal of the Greeks was to win him Polyxena.

2. But Ulysses is not infallible. His prophecy is really the fruit of wisdom and prudence. In his own affairs—in policy—he can err; and 'policy grows into an ill opinion'.

when he propounds his own constancy and faith. Ulysses, at his interview with Achilles, foretells the imminent glory coming to Ajax; but that is perhaps shrewdness rather than insight: besides, Ulysses is hardly upon oath. Calchas prophesies: indeed, the Greeks believe that his gift may be of continual strategic use to them; and Calchas himself uses his 'sight . . . in things to come' as a bargaining counter when he pleads for possession of his daughter.[1]

Time therefore is the most powerful of Shakespeare's dramatis personae, dominating the plays, and changing his nature according to the decorum of the scene. In comedy (which has its own ways of dealing with Time, and, within its proper limits, controlling him) Time is the main factor which controls the plotting, for comedy frequently requires exact timetables, even when (as in *As You Like It*) there is 'no clock in the forest'. On the other hand, Time exists in comedy as an enemy to be defeated, and love and happy marriage are the means by which, if he cannot be destroyed, he can be kept from destroying: all lovers in comedy know 'a mightier way' than a poet's to 'Make war upon this bloody tyrant'; so that, despite the controlling hand of Time in the action of the play, the comic characters in some measure dominate Time. In tragedy, Time predominates, controlling action and persons by showing inescapable change, revealing what was hidden, threatening worse ages to come. What Time emphasizes in tragedy is not maturation but ageing: Time represents the public part of life, the part in which one is caught and forced to make decisions. No man rules a state by a subjective sense of time.

But to remember the 'bloody tyrant Time' is to recall the degree to which Time dominates the Sonnets as well. The Sonnets are preoccupied repeatedly with the action of Time and the ways in which he may be defeated: like *Troilus*, they express this in those images of change and flux which Shakespeare learned from Ovid's *Metamorphoses*, and Time can only be defeated by the art of the poet (who like Ovid himself can rear imperishable monuments),[2] or by a love which is not subject to accident and change. The Sonnets, that is to say, oscillate between two positions: that in which Time and change threaten to be victorious, and that in

1. It is not clear whether or not Shakespeare believed that Calchas knew how Antenor would betray Troy.

2. Nevertheless, the sonnet which seems to me to be closest to what possessed Shakespeare's imagination in *Troilus*—setting aside those which deal with the knowledge of being betrayed—is Sonnet 64, especially ll. 9–10: 'When I have seen such interchange of state,/Or state itself confounded to decay . . .'

which they may be met and defeated; or (to put it in another way) that in which Shakespeare contemplates the unchanging, while fearful of change, and that in which, standing outside the process of growth and decay, he can observe the flux of Time. Effectually, these positions determine much of what happens in *Troilus*.

For, in *Troilus*, we find two things which inevitably require a constant emphasis upon Time. The characters, largely unchanging, are fixed in their virtues or vices, and given already to contemplating their fellows and subsequently themselves; and as soon as they think not of what they are but what in future they will be, they step outside the stream of Time. They prophesy, or they affirm their determined fame, or they look back over Time past (which has ceased to move).

Nestor becomes a chronicle (IV. v. 201) or a typical old man[1] or even the figure of Time himself.[2] Troilus, Cressida and Pandarus, in a moment when Time is stayed, all predict their future reputations. Agamemnon greets Hector with a generosity and courtesy that can exist, at their ease, only in a moment outside the steady progression towards the fall of Troy. Calchas, Cassandra, Ulysses and Achilles—even Pandarus and Hecuba and Andromache—all prophesy and are therefore, while they do so, not subject to Time. Time, for all these people, is the means by which they see themselves and others. But we must combine with that our knowledge of an action already determined. Time for the audience or reader of this play is the perspective in which the *known* action proceeds. Hector threatens Achilles, but we know that Achilles will kill him. Ulysses predicts the final fall of the city, and—despite Hector's modest rebuttal—we know that he is right. We know, as Troilus cannot know, that Cressida will be unfaithful. We know that the son of Thetis will die an early and unworthy death (although Homer asserts Achilles' knowledge, and Shakespeare refuses to mention that he might know). We know, as Shakespeare certainly knew from Ovid, that Polyxena would be sacrificed by 'Neoptolemus so mirable' to appease the angry ghost of Achilles.[3] Most ironic of all, we know, when

1. Homer, like Chapman, notes the characteristic habit of discussing past rather than present, as well as the recurrent regret that one is no longer what one was.

2. A man who was visibly old enough to have fought with Laomedon was almost necessarily the emblem of Chronos.

3. Shakespeare is careful to keep Polyxena offstage, with her mother, to participate in their letter duet. The death of the girl, and the madness of Hecuba, is one of the most painful things in the *Metamorphoses*.

Calchas pleads for the exchange of Cressida and Antenor, that a traitor has successfully ensured that a treacherous girl will come to the Greeks, while Troy receives back the man who will betray his native city.[1]

One should not, however, suppose that the characters of the play take no action against Time. Faced with Time under his two aspects, they react according to their temperaments. Troilus, as one might expect, tries to achieve stability in love by asserting that Time has no power over the substance of love and lovers, but only over their accidents. Winning Cressida, he contemplates the possibility that here before him is a woman who (being essentially constant) will never in reality grow old.

> O that I thought it could be in a woman—
> As, if it can, I will presume in you—
> To feed for aye her lamp and flames of love;
> To keep her constancy in plight and youth,
> Outliving beauty's outward, with a mind
> That doth renew swifter than blood decays!
>
> (III.ii. 156–61)

For Troilus, as for the Shakespeare of Sonnet 116,

> Love's not Time's fool, though rosy lips and cheeks
> Within his bending sickle's compass come.

If you prize Cressida like that, then the decay of accidents is irrelevant: you have avoided Time, by fastening upon that which cannot be subject to him. Troilus is wholly prepared for the effects of Time upon love, because he has demonstrated, at least to his own satisfaction, that such effects do not matter. What he cannot be prepared for, and what, indeed, he does not even foresee as an hypothesis, is the possibility of real infidelity. There is nothing absurd (although critics sometimes call it so)[2] in his plea to Cressida (IV.iv. 57) before their parting:

> Hear me, my love: be thou but true of heart—

---

1. Earlier versions of the Troy story vary somewhat over the question of who really betrayed the city. For Chaucer (as for Shakespeare when he wrote *Lucrece*), Sinon was the arch-villain, with Antenor a good second to him. But the usual medieval tale has *Æneas* as the traitor, with Antenor to help him: Caxton and Lydgate agree in that story, as did the author of *Sir Gawayn and the Green Knight;* cf. Caxton, p. 667, '[The Greeks within Troy were led] by the conduyte of Eneas and of Antenor that were open traytours unto theyre Cyte and also to theyr Kynge and lord.'

2. E.g. Patricia Thompson, 'Rant and Cant in *Troilus and Cressida*', *E&St.* (1969), pp. 33–56.

for he can only raise the possibility of betrayal in order to reject it: the words are essentially an encouragement.

On the other side, the side of public life and action, stability can only be achieved by constant effort:

> Perseverance, dear my lord,
> Keeps honour bright. (III. iii. 150–1)

Personal reputation can never remain what it was, since Time either disregards what has been, or else destroys it; for Time in this has willing allies, and is embodied in mankind, in its volatility of liking and respect. Hence Honour, as Sidney maintained in the *Arcadia*, must be constantly renewed. This is a way to oppose Time, and to frustrate him; but it does so knowing that the very condition of continuing is to leave behind the 'husks and formless ruin of oblivion'. Essentially this way is hinted at in Agamemnon's opening words to the Greek council: it is in some degree a way of settling for second-best, since no action proceeds as you expected, and you must bear your time of trial in patience, while at the same time persevering.

(d) IDENTITY AND ATTRIBUTES

Because *Troilus and Cressida* attempts to deal with the actions of Time, and with the betrayals inseparable from man's normal experience; and because one cannot be betrayed without first having trusted (one must 'prove [one's] troth', as Nestor would think of it) the play also examines those grounds on which men base a belief, whether it be that two and two make four, or that Helen is worth fighting over. Almost everything about the play— its curious tone; its familiar material; its dual action; its Pandarus and Thersites; its learned debates; its frustrations of desire and design—is selected with that purpose in mind. Effectually, of course, Time and Experience are overlapping concepts: experience is one man's knowledge of past time; but the play does not always treat them together. Many passages in *Troilus*, therefore, are devoted to the processes of verification, and to the means by which one achieves a right judgement, whether of identity or value.

I should like to begin with the simplest cases. It is an unusual play that fails to identify speakers promptly, and dramatists have unobtrusive ways of naming those who need to be named. One becomes familiar with

As I remember, Adam

or perhaps

> And now, my cousin Hamlet, and my son.

One recognizes the skill which can make use of the necessity:

> I am glad to see you well.
> Horatio—or I do forget myself.

or even

> Who's there?
> Nay, answer me. Stand, and unfold yourself.

There can be, sometimes, a little clumsiness: in the first scene of *Troilus*, there would be something awkward in the following exchange, even if it were a first meeting:

Troil.	By whom, Æneas?
Æneas.	Troilus, by Menelaus.

But it is not a first meeting, for each speaker has been identified within the preceding five lines; and Troilus has already identified himself (by referring to himself in the third person) in the first short speech of the play. The second scene opens with Cressida's question

> Who were those went by?
>
> *Alex.*   Queen Hecuba and Helen.

and, thirty lines later, she is asking again

> Who comes here?

in order, apparently, to prove that she cannot recognize her uncle.[1] But, verbal play apart, what the scene leads to is the procession across the stage of the returning Trojan warriors; and it is there that the process of identification becomes more complex. Pandarus has been maintaining with vigour that Troilus is equal—even superior—to Hector; yet, faced with the formal sequence of armed men, he confuses Troilus with Deiphobus. In retrospect, there is more salt than one might suppose in the earlier exchange with his niece—

Pand.	Do you know a man if you see him?
Cress.	Ay, if I ever saw him before and knew him.

(I.ii.64–6)

---

1. In a sense, Pandarus has his revenge, when he intrudes into her bedchamber (IV.ii.20) and pretends that Cressida, for the sake of the play on the word 'maid', is her own maidservant.

Throughout the play Shakespeare seems to be concerned to use all the ways in which a character can be identified, or mistaken. During the Trojan debate, Troilus is interrupted by Cassandra, crying aloud offstage, before her entry; and in answer to Priam's question, replies that it is 'our mad sister, I do know her voice'—a line glossed by Hector's 'It is Cassandra'. Another figure offstage is recognized by his walk, when Diomedes brings Cressida to the Greek camp (IV.v.14–16). Later in the same scene (IV.v.75–7), the herald Æneas sharply takes up Achilles for an ungenerous remark, and his little logical game makes its dramatic point. A straightforward request for identification will sometimes produce an unexpected result, as when Agamemnon asks who Troilus may be, and gets in reply a character sketch (something like what is offered in more comic form when Alexander describes Ajax at I.ii.19–31). Thersites, challenged by Hector, does not name himself, although he identifies himself to his own condemnation, by writing himself down as disgustingly base (v.iv.27–31); but he likewise turns the pattern he has used to comic effect, when he is subsequently challenged by the bastard Margarelon, and offers in reply a brilliant sequence of variations on illegitimacy (v.vii.16–22). It is first-rate clown's technique, but Thersites tells the truth as well. Likewise, when Cressida has been kissed by the Greeks, and is departing, Ulysses offers an 'identification' of her which is a lesson in how to recognize a whore by her movements and conversation; and during that same round of kissing, Patroclus identifies himself as three different men in two separate embraces.[1]

More complicated games can be played with what remains as essentially the same situation. In the Greek debate, which he interrupts, Æneas refuses to recognize Agamemnon, because (he implies) authority is not evident in his looks. Agamemnon, in effect, has lost his identity in so far as he has not properly fulfilled his function. Just so, when the Greek generals insult Achilles by ignoring him, they leave him to deduce that he too has failed in his function: he is no longer the greatest warrior among the Greeks, and hence is 'nobody'. But 'function' is not the most obvious of characteristics: other logical categories may be used to isolate the accidents which distinguish one substance from another. Pandarus finds himself wholly at cross purposes with Paris' servant, who (like Hamlet's grave-digger) is an 'absolute knave'. Pandarus' 'honour' ceases to become a title for him; and,

---

1. As Paris (acting the part which should belong to Menelaus); hence, as Menelaus, deprived of his proper function; and finally, as himself (IV.v.28–33).

in disclaiming the right to a dukedom, he finds himself all but damned (III.i.11–16). The servant pursues his advantage in providing a periphrasis for 'Helen'—

the mortal Venus, the heart-blood of beauty, love's visible soul

—and, when Pandarus mistakes this for 'Cressida', the servant triumphs logically:

No, sir, Helen: could not you find out that by her attributes?[1]

For satirical purposes, Thersites invites Achilles and Patroclus to determine their relationships to himself and to Agamemnon, and proceeds then to prove Patroclus a fool absolute, and the other three but fools relative: the point being that the three are foolish only in respect of the roles that they have chosen to play:

> *Thers.* Agamemnon is a fool to offer to command Achilles, Achilles is a fool to be commanded of Agamemnon, Thersites is a fool to serve such a fool, and this Patroclus is a fool positive.
> *Patro.* Why am I a fool?
> *Thers.* Make that demand of the Creator, it suffices me thou art.   (II.iii.64–70)

Equally satirical, but this time part of Ulysses' plot to prepare Ajax as champion, is a passage later in the same scene (ll. 179–257). Here the technique is no longer part of a logical round-game, and the folly of Ajax is not demonstrated to Ajax himself: indeed, the business of keeping Ajax from suspecting how far he is being manipulated requires a good many asides, together with two long, fulsome speeches from Ulysses. But logically considered, the situation is comparable to those others examined above; for Ajax is teased and flattered into assuming that he himself is modest and worthy, while Achilles is proud and worthless—a confusion which is effectually an error in *self*-identification, derived from self-ignorance. (The same vices in Achilles are treated more directly, in III.iii; for there, Ulysses is able to use pride as a 'glass' for pride, and Achilles grows a little in self-knowledge by learning from reflection.)[2]

---

1. The word is discussed on p. 76.

2. A more obvious application of the moral 'glass' is found in *Ham.* III.iv. 19–20: 'You go not till I set you up a glass / Where you may see the inmost part of you.' There, however, Queen Gertrude's moral imbecility is not incurable: by ll. 89–91, she can see clearly: 'Thou turn'st my eyes into my very soul / And there I see such black and grained spots / As will not leave their tinct.' By contrast, Achilles, while aware of the damage done to his reputation, is still confused in mind and conscience: 'My mind is troubled like a fountain stirr'd,/ And I myself see not the bottom of it' (ll. 306–7).

But the ramifications of the teasing of Ajax are more than this would imply. Ajax does not merely make a false identification, he welcomes false attributes:

Nest. What a vice were it in Ajax now—
Ulyss. If he were proud—
Diom. Or covetous of praise—
Ulyss. Ay, or surly borne—
Diom. Or strange, or self-affected. (II.iii.235–9)

Further, he disclaims any knowledge of pride, and is encouraged in this by Agamemnon, in words which not only look forward to the language of Ulysses, when he applies medicine to Achilles (IV.v.), but to that of Thersites on the self-consumption of lechery (V.iv.35), and back to Æneas, disclaiming self-praise when he visits the Greek camp (I.iii.240–3):

Your mind is the clearer, Ajax, and your virtues the fairer. He that is proud eats up himself: pride is his own glass, his own trumpet, his own chronicle; and whatever praises itself, but in the deed, devours the deed in the praise.
(II.iii.155–9)

It is indeed evident from this scene that the matter of right identification is also a matter of right valuation: that a man's self-knowledge is linked with his knowledge of other men.[1] He recognizes himself, as he recognizes them, by rightly knowing the attribute of each one; and his own judgement will play him false if he fails to see those attributes rightly:

Ajax. What is he more than another?
Agam. No more than what he thinks he is. (II.iii.144–5)

That is, Achilles, great warrior though he be, diminishes himself in such measure as he tries (through pride) to augment himself. And the act by which he is diminished is twofold. It operates partly in the minds of men, so that reputation declines: pride and self-love '[devour] the deed in the praise'. But it operates also in Achilles himself: there is civil war within him between 'his mental and his active parts' (l. 175); and hence neither understanding nor action (*gnosis* or *praxis*, as Aristotle called it)[2] can function properly. The process is self-perpetuating: the more Achilles chooses to withdraw from the battle, the more he is unable to act at all; and the longer he remains inactive (as Ulysses tells him

1. This seems to be implied (though perhaps with a more specific application) in Sonnet 114.
2. *Ethics*, I.3.

later), the less will any man desire his activity, for his worth is already diminished.

The word 'attribute' is a dangerous term, which brings us to the heart of the play's arguments; and it is dangerous because ambiguous. On the one hand, it refers simply to those qualities, in any being or object, which can be seen and judged by the senses and the understanding; those qualities, in effect, by which we identify and evaluate it. We know a man by his walk and bearing, his height, his speech, his physique: as Hector observed,

> for Achilles, my own searching eyes
> Shall find him by his large and portly size.   (IV.v.160–1)

Knowing these, and his actions and opinions, we can judge his intelligence, his moral nature, his essential worth: as a consequence, we ascribe to him a reputation. And, on the other hand, the word refers primarily to that reputation itself (so that 'attribute' behaves like 'honour'). As Agamemnon remarks,

> Much attribute he hath, and much the reason
> Why we ascribe it to him.   (II.iii.118–19)

(That is to say, 'attribute' is fame—or reputation—and the cause of it is that body of 'attributes'—or qualities—because of which we ascribe his fame to Achilles.) But 'honour' is similar (setting aside for the moment its sense of 'honesty'). Achilles recognizes its nature:

> And not a man, for being simply man,
> Hath any honour, [i.e. is respected] but honour for those honours
> That are without him—as place, riches, and favour:
> Prizes of accident as oft as merit.   (III.iii.80–3)

Hence, it is easy to move from the objective position—of recognizing attributes, and judging what they are—to the subjective—of dealing at large with a reputation unanalysed, and allowing all (objective) attributes to be judged in terms of that reputation. And to say that is to have moved from questions of identity to those of value and opinion:[1] to have moved, in fact, to the Trojan debate, where (as Hector noted)

1. See especially the discussion in W. M. T. Nowottny, ' "Opinion" and "Value" in *Troilus and Cressida*', *EC*, 4 (1954), and the rejoinder by Frank Kermode.

> the will dotes that is attributive
> To what infectiously itself affects,
> Without some image of th'affected merit.
> (II. ii. 59–61)

Paradoxically, in this play, the processes both of identification and attribution seem to have the power to take from a man something of his identity and his attributes. Even recognition by others does something to push the individual back in the direction of the type: false recognition or attribution by oneself, and especially of oneself, completes the process. Part—not all—of what goes on in moral allegory takes place also in *Troilus:* the man subject to a vice moves halfway to becoming the vice;[1] so that, for brief periods, *Troilus* is indeed a morality play, and bodies forth some of the same traditional sins.

(e) PRIDE AND ENVY

Of the seven deadly sins, *Troilus* concerns itself seriously with no more than three. There are no gluttons in the play; and avarice is not a fault of which anyone is accused. Wrath appears in a context where it is at once corrected by patience, when Troilus is checked by Ulysses:

> let us depart, I pray,
> Lest your displeasure should enlarge itself
> To wrathful terms. (v. ii. 36–8)

Otherwise it belongs appropriately to an heroic action, as when Hector is wrathful at his defeat by Ajax, or, in full force of arms in the field, is generous to his inferiors, or (briefly) is angry with Achilles. That is, after all, Homeric; and, in Homer at least, it is more nearly an outward sign of courage aroused.[2] Accidie is surely there in Helen's apartment, when Venus has again disarmed Mars ('I would fain have armed today, but my Nell would not have it so'), and to some degree it touches Troilus in the first scene of the play, but it leaves him almost at once. Perhaps the chief sinner here is Achilles (or so Ulysses says: I. iii. 142–51).

Lechery is another matter. From one point of view it is the cause of the Trojan War (although Shakespeare constantly sees the war as arising from corrective justice—Helen for Hesione—

---

1. Cf. the deadly sins in *Piers Plowman*, Passus v, particularly Glutton, who also inhabits this no-man's-land of the imagination.

2. Or so Aristotle takes it: cf. his citations in *Ethics*, III. viii (p. 99): 'Hence such expressions in Homer as "into their spirit he put strength" and "Wrath he aroused and spirit" and "bitter the rage his nostrils filled".'

and not from the judgement of Paris).[1] Certainly it is apparent in Paris and Helen, in Diomedes, in Achilles, in Cressida and Troilus, though in differing degrees: the two main actions of the play are linked by their sexual patternings. Thersites is in no doubt about the motivation of the warriors; they are wenching rogues, cuckold and cuckold-maker; and his formula 'wars and lechery' has, perhaps, been too easily taken by critics as Shakespeare's judgement on the whole action. The place of lechery in the economy of the play has, at any rate, not been overlooked. What remains is pride, and envy.

Envy, if one is to believe O. J. Campbell, is a necessary but ambiguous factor in the operation of satire: Asper/Macilente (*Every Man out of his Humour*) seems to see envy as 'the emotion most likely to stimulate effective criticism of vice and folly'.[2] Certainly, such a formula will fit Thersites. He is a 'core of envy' according to Achilles (v. i. 4), and a 'damnable box of envy' for Patroclus (l. 24); and he himself, in his curse upon the Greeks, invokes the devil Envy to say 'Amen', like a clerk responding to a priest.[3] But that is all. Although Thersites accuses Ajax of being envious of Achilles (II. i. 34), envy is otherwise impersonal, a kind of ill-fortune or general ill-humour: that which may try to denigrate the truth of Troilus (III. ii. 95), or provoke the gods to divide lovers (IV. iv. 27), as Cressida supposes, or persuade Time to injure all virtue and excellence (III. iii. 174). Much more significant is the relationship between envy/envious and emulation/emulous, and the degree to which the terms overlap. On the whole, envy is plain ill-will, or (more specifically) that mortification provoked by seeing the superior advantages of others; and although it may imply ambitious rivalry, that relatively innocuous sense is found only with a qualifying adjective, and does not occur in *Troilus*. Emulation (and emulous), by contrast, refers primarily to desire or endeavour to surpass others—in fact, to ambitious rivalry— and it is only in secondary senses that it means jealousy, or grudge against superiority (= envy). Hence, in *Troilus*, emulation covers a wide range of activity, not all of which is culpable. Diomedes' 'emulous honour' (IV. i. 29) is heroic, like the 'emulous missions' of the gods themselves (III. iii. 189), or the 'gory emulation' between cousins from which Hector and Ajax withdraw. Even in

1. Again, the subdivision of justice comes from *Ethics*, v. 4 (p. 148).

2. *Comicall Satyre*, p. 57.

3. Envy, here, may be the figure who appears in the (revised) coda to *Mucedorus* (?1609/1610?), but this is only surmise, and the date of the revision is wholly uncertain.

the mouth of Ulysses, emulation's 'thousand sons' are not *primarily* malicious: the fallen horse is 'o'er-run and trampled on' by those who, being driven by ambition, have eyes elsewhere. The malice occurs in the curses of Thersites ('emulous factions' is his phrase for the war (II.iii.75)—or perhaps for the Greek dissensions), or in Hector's dismissal of the Greek sickness ('emulation in the army', II.ii.212), or in Ulysses' diagnosis of the same plague:

> an envious fever
> Of pale and bloodless emulation. (I.iii.133–4)

Little of this, it seems to me, points towards satire. It is rather a part of the play's constant preoccupation with moral analysis; and it tends to make of Thersites yet another victim of disease, rather than a 'wounded surgeon'.

Pride occupies a more central position than envy (as befits that sin which is the root of all the others), but it is mostly the preserve of Achilles and Ajax. Ulysses in the Greek debate is discussing pride, in effect, since pride (or rebellion against one's proper place in hierarchy) is what promotes the 'hollow factions', the disdain of each man for his superior (ll. 129–34); and it is pride (as well as accidie) that he demonstrates in Achilles, when he develops the exemplum of his argument (ll. 142 ff.). Pride will move both Ajax and Achilles, like dogs with a bone, if Ulysses' plot is successful. By the time of the embassy to Achilles (II.iii), pride is the word in everyone's mouth. Thersites has already demonstrated the pattern of degree inverted—

> Agamemnon is a fool to offer to command Achilles, Achilles is a fool to be commanded of Agamemnon, . . . (II.iii.64–5)

—and then (it is characteristic of Thersites to abuse both sides) decried the behaviour of Achilles in refusing obedience to Agamemnon:

> *Achill.* Patroclus, I'll speak with nobody . . . .
> *Thers.* Here is such patchery, such juggling, and such knavery!
> (ll. 71–4)

What ensues is a careful analysis of Achilles' pride[1] (by Ulysses), a proud rejection of pride (by Ajax), and a splendid ironic praise of Ajax's freedom from pride (by the whole Greek staff). The

---

1. Achilles' pride is found all too plainly in Homer: cf. *Iliad*, IX.654–5, where Diomedes is indignant at Agamemnon's embassy to Achilles—'He's proud enough beside,—/But this ambassage thou hast sent will make him burst with pride.'

process is completed by the medicinal scorn of III.iii, when Achilles sees his own pride as in a glass.

Now, the Greeks at large, because they are proud, fail to preserve degree; and once degree is observed again, then proper order is the virtue that is exercised. It is a political virtue. But, for the individual, the virtue to be aimed at has no name,[1] and the quality can only be exemplified in action. Hence, in *Troilus* it is Hector who represents the proper balance, and the mean to be aimed at; he seeks honours, but is modest. As Æneas explains, he represents that Trojan virtue, whereby courtesy preserves one from pride, although it may be mistaken for pride by those who know no better:

> In the extremity of great and little,
> Valour and pride excel themselves in Hector;
> The one almost as infinite as all,
> The other blank as nothing. Weigh him well,
> And that which looks like pride is courtesy.[2]
>
> (IV.v.78–82)

Ajax is vain and a boaster, who nevertheless claims less than his due when he pretends to be both modest and ignorant.[3] He therefore becomes a surrogate for Achilles twice over: once, when he is selected to fight with Hector, and again, when he acts out all the extremity of pride. In the end the audience sees little of that—after the mock praise of him (II.iii), there is really nothing of Ajax until the (possibly burlesque) instruction to the trumpeter (IV.v.6–11); but it does see the charade played by Thersites and Patroclus, and it hears Thersites' brilliant prosopopoeia:

> Why, a stalks up and down like a peacock, a stride and a stand; ruminates like an hostess that hath no arithmetic but her brain to set down her reckoning; bites his lip with a politic regard, as who should say 'There were wit in this head

---

1. See *Ethics*, IV.3, where pride-in-action is boastfulness (the error of excess), but the mean is nameless.

2. Æneas himself is quite capable of exercising the same virtue of courtesy. His behaviour as herald towards Agamemnon is not simply corrective, nor is it merely manœuvring for advantage. He means what he says; he is courteous, in wanting to give Agamemnon his due; and ceremony ('the men of Troy are ceremonious courtiers') is the means by which he can do so justly, without offence or arrogance. When his manner is mistaken, he explains himself—as he explains Hector's behaviour, in IV.v—but checks himself for fear the explanation itself may look like pride. The man who, in such circumstances, acts justly, will not praise himself.

3. In Aristotelian terms, he pretends to be *ironic*—claiming too little—in order to *boast*—claiming too much: see *Ethics*, IV.7 (p. 133).

and 'twould out'—and so there is; but it lies as coldly in him
as fire in a flint, which will not show without knocking. The
man's undone for ever, for if Hector break not his neck i' th'
combat, he'll break't himself in vainglory. He knows not me:
I said 'Good morrow, Ajax', and he replies 'Thanks,
Agamemnon.'—What think you of this man, that takes me for
the general?   (III.iii.250–2)

The pride of Achilles keeps him from knowing himself. The pride
of Ajax keeps him from knowing both himself and Thersites. The
sin of pride corrupts the judgement. (The proud man commits
errors of identification.) But Ajax is redeemable, all the same.
Surrogate for Achilles, he is also meant to resemble Hector; and
indeed (in heroic terms) he does so, as Homer had been the first to
recognize. When he is matched with Hector as a warrior, and
faced by Hector's courtesy and generosity, Ajax himself becomes
generous and courteous, free from pride, firm with Achilles, and
gentle towards his cousin. He lapses once more only when, like
Achilles, he seeks revenge, and 'foams at mouth' (v.v.36).

I said that the sin of pride corrupts the judgement. I might as
properly have said that it is a false judgement of oneself and of
others that leads to pride. What the self is—what those others'
selves are—is not merely part of a moral analysis, but belongs also
with proper identification and distinction. The reflexive pattern
of the language in which Ulysses describes Achilles is significant:
the 'will peculiar', the 'self-admission' of Achilles lead to 'a pride
that quarrels at self-breath'. Nothing enters his mind 'save such as
doth revolve/And ruminate himself'. The speech itself acts out the
self-regard (and the figure of the glass) which it defines. The man
who (like Ajax) is self-willed, will also love himself, but the value
which he sets upon himself will be a false one.[1] It is 'imagin'd
worth' that destroys Achilles' power to judge himself; his will
'dotes' because it is

> attributive
> To what infectiously itself affects
> Without some image of th'affected merit.

Logically, his fault is very close to that of Troilus: Hector's words
(just quoted) apply as well to him as to Troilus or Paris; but
Troilus will err more generously, in overvaluing another person.
Achilles overvalues himself only, and in doing so he sets 'his mental
and his active parts' at war. What is happening in the Greek
camp, where 'the still and mental parts' are disdained by the acts

1. Cf. II.iii.171–4.

of hand, is happening within Achilles. The consequence for the Greek army, when lost degree releases 'raging appetites',[1] is that appetite will consume itself (I.iii.124). For Achilles, the consequence of rampant will is that he 'batters down himself'.

The case of Achilles is extreme, to be compared only with that of Ajax, because they alone are distinguished for pride. But since pride, within the terms of the play, is less an intellectual error than an assertion of the passional self, one may notice in passing that in their effects the faults of Achilles or Ajax are like those of Troilus. For Troilus also finds difficulty in sustaining his own 'self'—or so Pandarus asserts, in argument with his niece:

> *Cress.*   'Tis just to each of them; he is himself.
> *Pand.*   Himself? Alas poor Troilus, I would he were—
> *Cress.*   So he is.
> *Pand.*   —Condition I had gone barefoot to India.
> *Cress.*   He is not Hector.
> *Pand.*   Himself? No, he's not himself, would a were himself.
> (I.ii.71–7)

Popular idiom here reveals a significant truth: namely, that the melancholy and love-sick young warrior is, quite radically, not what he was.[2] Hector, of course, accuses his youngest brother of failing to recognize true 'selves' when he sees them: the valued object must be 'precious in itself' and not merely precious in the eye of the observer. By this objective argument, Troilus stands condemned for the time being—that is, until Hector shifts his ground—and he appears to maintain his position until he sees Cressida unequivocally faithless. At that point he is driven to confess that both his 'self' and her 'self' are either divided or removed: the pain he feels, showing itself in outward action, forces him to promise silence and patience by saying

> I will not be myself, nor have cognition
> Of what I feel: I am all patience.   (v.ii.63–4)

One might argue that the disorder which, in its simplest and most absurd form, makes Ajax confuse Agamemnon and Thersites, now makes Troilus call what he sees 'Diomed's Cressida'. But having said that, one should at once distinguish. The disorder of Ajax comes from self-love and self-delusion on a titanic scale: he devises an heroic part for himself to play, and insists upon

---

1. The phrase is Hector's, as applied to his younger brothers.

2. The *remedium amoris* produces a similar effect, *teste* A. E. Housman: 'And now the fancy passes by, / And nothing will remain, / And all around they'll say that I / Am quite myself again.'

playing it; so that the longer he persists with it, the more he becomes his own prisoner. Troilus may appear to be 'that same young Trojan ass that loves the whore there', but then he has been denied the opportunity of seeing what Pandarus, and the Greeks, and the audience, already know. His disorder derives from loving another, and devising a part for that other to play:

> O that I thought it could be in a woman—
> As, if it can, I will presume in you—
> To feed for aye her lamp and flames of love;
> To keep her constancy in plight and youth,
> Outliving beauty's outward, with a mind
> That doth renew swifter than blood decays!
>
> (III. ii. 149–54)

It is only when Cressida appears to abandon her script, and to speak more than is set down for her, that he finds himself forced to see her as not what she was, or as not what he had thought her. Cressida herself had tried to shun herself, during the wooing in Pandarus' orchard: had spoken of 'an unkind self, that itself would leave'; and now Troilus sees the consequence of that division, as Cressida for the second time becomes 'another's fool'.

(f) STYLES AND METHODS

What appears from the methods which *Troilus* employs is not merely the relativity of Value, nor the folly of Troilus, nor the objective wisdom of Ulysses, but the fact that the play has also explored the various techniques which are open to the dramatist, and that therefore we have seen the different notions of value, the different methods and standards of judgement which may be employed on this or any other subject. *Troilus* is essentially a schematic play, an exercise in dramatic paradigms; it takes any man, or any situation, and looks at either in a variety of ways, *each one valid for a specific kind of play*. It is this which accounts for much of the difficulty which we find in characterizing the play: comedy, tragedy, satire, tragic farce and the rest have been propounded and justified; *and all are right*. Make the assumption that the play is satire, and the play reflects the assumption. Heroes appear unheroic, lovers are absurd, policy grows into an ill opinion, a sick Pandarus speaks the Epilogue; and such a pattern is bound to make any serious, heroic utterance or action appear as if in burlesque. The merely neutral details of action (if a good play may be said to embody any neutral matter) will take their colouring from context, and the battle scenes will therefore appear (as they do to at least one editor)[1] purely farcical. Yet, assume that the play is to be seen seriously, and heroes will redeem their unheroic lapses: Hector will still be a Worthy; Thersites will save his skin only by speaking the damning truth of himself; Ajax will be courteous and generous, like his cousin; and Troilus' disillusionment will be potentially tragic. But the shape of the play allows no such assumptions: the betrayal of Troilus is presented with three commentaries at once, and all different. I have already drawn the analogy (in discussing one scene) with mock-heroic form, in which double-vision is an essential ingredient; and the complications of *Troilus* seem akin to those of *The Rape of the Lock*.[2] But *Troilus* assumes no such structure except in v.ii, and we are left to cast about again for other comparisons.

Part of the difficulty of coming to terms with *Troilus* derives from a simple fact: that the structure, the language, the tone of the play—even the possible methods of acting any given scene—are all likely to be, in themselves or in relationship, ambivalent. It seems an odd thing to say, since Shakespeare's dramatic technique relies heavily in most of the plays upon the juxtaposition of similar or opposed attitudes or actions, so that the audience may make a comparative judgement.[3] But in *Troilus* it is more than usually difficult to determine one's response either to the single phenomenon or to the resultant of the things compared. The whole play seems designed at once to invite and to frustrate judgement: to insist upon the relative at the expense of the absolute. Examples may make this clear.

It is a commonplace of dramatic structure to prepare in some way for the entry of a character not yet seen. In this play Priam, the ruler of the one party, and the very image of tragic misfortune, is not prepared for at all, and has little part to play. Achilles, who first enters is II.i, in a scene of prose and near-comedy, has already been referred to as better than Troilus (by Cressida), 'a drayman, a porter, a very camel' (by Pandarus), and sardonically, as 'the great Achilles', 'the large Achilles', 'Sir Valour' (by Ulysses, who also concedes that he is 'the sinew and

1. See the Introduction to the NCS edition.

2. 'And China's earth receives the smoking tide' is heroic in diction, and mock-heroic in matter (coffee poured into porcelain cups), yet the line would be applicable to an inundation of the Hoang-ho.

3. This is only a variant of the familiar doctrine of *similis materiei dissimilis tractatio*, or else *dissimilis materiei similis tractatio*, which Ascham discusses under *Imitatio*, the fifth section of *The Scholemaster*: see *Elizabethan Critical Essays*, ed. G. Gregory Smith, 1904 (repr. 1950), Vol. I, p. 8.

the forehand' of the Greeks, but who points out also that this is 'opinion'). Thersites, who opens Act II, and who is so often taken as the voice of sanity in the play,[1] is introduced in the Greek debate (I.iii) in his Homeric form, as 'a slave whose gall coins slanders like a mint'; Ajax is referred to as oxymoronic in I.ii—a condition justified by his appearances later in the play; Helen is ironically dismissed by Troilus in I.i, just fails to appear (but is the subject of anecdote) in I.ii, is discussed as a war-aim in II.ii, praised hyperbolically at the opening of III.i, and then appears as a vapid and empty-headed woman immediately afterwards. To Troilus, in I.i, Cressida is the inaccessible *Princesse lointaine*; in the next scene she is a pert, witty girl. And, finally, Hector, said to be angry from hurt pride in I.ii, and a challenger in I.iii and II.i, is a prudent statesman in II.ii, advising the return of Helen; and only at the end of that same scene (the Trojan debate) does he reveal the fact of his challenge to the rest of the Trojan council. One may set against that the further fact that while the Trojan War is treated seriously by the Prologue, yet the first two scenes look on it as of secondary importance, and the third scene, while presenting a serious meeting of warriors, nevertheless contrives to present those very warriors with a mockery of themselves (in the report of Patroclus' acting) and with the highly mannered, almost playful, embassy of Æneas.

Choice of prose or verse can act as a rough guide to the way in which one is meant to receive any utterance, on the grounds that tragedy, serious matter, and noble speakers tend towards verse, and that comedy, and characters of the middle sort or below it, towards prose. These are of course approximations, but even so they break down with *Troilus* (as with other plays of about 1600 and after). Certain speakers use one form or the other as a general rule, and may even dominate the usage of others: Pandarus 'imposes' prose upon Troilus in I.i, just as Cressida does upon the servant Alexander in the next scene: on the other hand, Achilles uses verse whenever he wishes, even in a scene predominantly controlled by the prose of Thersites; and Thersites himself, otherwise a prose speaker, produces one ribald couplet with devastating effect, to cap the rhymed speech with which Cressida leaves the play. (Since his function in that scene is even more obviously choric than usual, the rhyme may be the less surprising.) Pandarus, usually a prose speaker, speaks rhymed verse for the Epilogue (where the formal requirement overrides the

1. A view which I do not share.

characteristics of the speaker), but is also given to song and to verse quotation. (It is not quite clear at IV.iv.15ff. whether he recites or breaks into song, but the effect is much the same.) Helen speaks prose—a silly, affected, courtly slang, carefully adjusted for the purpose of teasing Pandarus; but, like Paris in the scene which they share (III.i), she breaks into a rather mannered, not quite heroic verse (with internal rhyme) to end the scene. That scene, however, concludes with a prose line, and without rhyme: other scenes, in verse, are rich in rhyme used as dramatic pointing. For an example, one may turn to the Greek debate (I.iii); Ulysses concludes his speech on degree with a rhymed couplet (ll. 136–7): Æneas produces two rhymed couplets for his moral *sententiae* (ll. 240–3): Agamemnon answers the challenge with a speech ending with two more couplets (ll. 286–9): Nestor follows, ending with one couplet (ll. 209–300): Agamemnon leads off his guest with two couplets (ll. 305–8): Ulysses ends the exposition of his plot with a couplet (ll. 385–6); and Nestor concludes scene and act with yet another (ll. 391–2). So much rhyme, and so placed, corresponds roughly with what one finds in the *Henry IV* plays and in *Henry V* (although there the question is complicated by the presence of the Chorus): this suggests that similar effects were intended, and that rhyme in a scene apparently serious is not of itself meant to sound mockingly in the ear.[1]

At the same time, one may feel that the effect of the rhyming in *Troilus* (and one must include here the two longer speeches by Cressida which are in rhyming couplets)[2] goes beyond the norms to be expected in pointing up the structure of a scene. Agamemnon's exit with Æneas (I.iii.305–8) is virtually the end of a scene—in a play of neo-classical structure it would be so, and eighteenth-century editors did so treat it—but the rhyming remains slightly obtrusive, a hint of artifice which may detach the audience a little from what it is observing. Tail-rhyme, in such a case, needs to be considered not with head-rhyme (alliteration) but with schemes such as anaphora, in which a kind of *syntactical* rhyming occurs, and where the effect of such distancing can be very marked: the obvious case is to be found in the wooing scene (III.ii), where Troilus and Cressida predict their own fates (ll. 171–93), and where the strong sense of detachment and distance is reinforced by Troilus' preceding speech (ll. 156–68), in which he concerns

1. Other plays of the late 1590s of course include the maturer comedies: but the natures of their actions are distinct from those of the Histories or of *Troilus*.

2. I.ii.287–300 and V.ii.106–11.

himself less with the flesh-and-blood Cressida in front of him than with the model of Cressida that she might become.[1]

If, as I suggested, comparison and juxtaposition are frequently the means by which judgement is passed on the actions and language of the play, then the presence of two commentators and observers like Pandarus and Thersites ought to ensure that heroic language, for example, never remains uncriticized. What Patricia Thompson calls 'rant and cant' certainly exists in the play: the rhetoric of Troilus after he has seen Cressida unfaithful, or when he announces the death of Hector, is properly suspect, and Troilus is not alone guilty; but the problem of identifying for certain the effect of a given style is still unsolved. If we believe that Pandarus by his utterances debases the love story (and the love story is by no means unscathed), then we need to be able to judge the tone of Pandarus' speech in order to judge that of Troilus. I am not sure that we can. Pandarus, watching the lovers who are about to be parted, says, 'Ah, sweet ducks!' Plainly, he reduces the intensity of emotion in the meeting—Cressida is already hectic—but how far anyone can read his intention, and divine the nature of his sympathy, I do not know. Patricia Thompson suggests that change, not only of language but also of argument, may be significant: Hector's volte-face 'undermines' his earlier, sounder speech. It may be so. But one may equally argue, with Hunter,[2] that the 'regular collapse of the grand gesture into incompetency and frustration does not mean, however, that the gesture was never grand anyway'. This is a safer position than that which sees 'undermining' as the effect of comparison and sudden change. Best of all is to recognize that

1. Effects of distancing can be (and are) achieved by still other means. At the end of iv.ii, when Pandarus tells Cressida that she is to be sent to the Greeks, she makes her protestation of constancy (ll. 99–108), and then predicts the outward forms that her grief will take (ll. 108–11): 'I'll go in and weep / ... Tear my bright hair, and scratch my praised cheeks, / Crack my clear voice with sobs'. The effect of this is a little stilted, quite apart from the dramatic irony: there is a hint of an older rhetoric (though nothing so extreme as, say, the lamentations of Constance, in *John* iii.iv). What has happened is that Shakespeare has made use of the difference between narrative and drama. In Chaucer's *Troylus*, Criseyde tears her hair while weeping: in Henryson's *Testament*, she is cursed by Cynthia, so that her 'voice sa cleir' shall be 'unples-and, hoir and hace' (l. 338). In her 'Complaint', Cresseid herself refers to her 'cleir voice' as being 'raw as Ruik'. What was descriptive detail in the two poems, has in the play become Cressida's stage direction to herself: her words tend to objectify, and the audience perceives the effect as 'distance'—emphasized by the obtrusive 'Do, do' of Pandarus (l. 109).

2. '*Troilus and Cressida*: a tragic satire', p. 16.

rhetoric is fundamentally neutral, and that there is no constant equivalence of effect for any trope or scheme, by itself or in frequent occurrence. It is certainly clear that, in this play especially, no rhetorical norm obtains. The affected language of Helen and Pandarus (III.i), with its ludicrous iteration of 'sweet', is one form of courtly utterance; and one might be tempted to classify with it the courtly prose of Troilus in III.ii—

> What too curious dreg espies my sweet lady in the fountain of our love?   (ll. 64-5)

But one could well be wrong. The Troilus who dwells on 'Cupid's pageant'[1] is the man who wittily diminishes all the conventional hyperboles of a lover, and then propounds (with a wry twist to the Platonic view of love) a vision of that love which approaches the tragic.

Guidance may perhaps be found in the English Histories, and especially in *1* and *2 Henry IV*. Here are plays, like *Troilus*, with multiple plots; here are contrasted views of war, and battles which come to nothing (*2H4* IV.i,ii); here are multiple kings (dead Richard, Percy, Mortimer, Henry), multiple heirs (Percy, Hal), correspondent topics (purses, Percies), mock-kings (Blunt, Hal, Falstaff), mimes (the Eastcheap charades), choice of fathers (Henry, Falstaff, the Lord Chief Justice), and sardonic commentators who are out of place on a battlefield. The rejection of Falstaff is both structurally essential, and emotionally painful. Besides, the two *Henry IV* plays invite a mixed response throughout, and both exploit the inevitable conditions imposed upon Histories—namely, that the action of the play must be a compromise. No history play can escape wholly from its context in Time: we *know* what came before and after, and we can see how far the dramatist's choice of matter was indeed a compromise, no matter what rigorous selection and distortion he may exercise to achieve a formal satisfaction. Equally, each history play, considered *per se*, restricts Time by its own limitations of form, and its formal assumptions are, while the action lasts, absolute. For the audience and the critic, the action (or, more probably, actions) of these later histories will imply a structure nearer to comedy than to tragedy. Even *Richard II*, with a single action, achieves such symmetry that the audience contemplates a situation half-comic, as each King in turn explores the gap between the King's two

---

1. If by this he refers to Cupid's masque in *Faerie Queene*, III.xii, then he is in error: the masque is full of monstrous figures from allegory, including Feare (stanza 12); but Troilus' own view of love is of course distinct from that.

bodies, and tries with limited success to resolve the problems of rule. Yet each history play is liable to be tragic for many of its actors: Richard, Bushy and Green die violently, although for Bolingbroke (v.iii. 77–8).

> Our scene is alt'red from a serious thing,
> And now chang'd to 'The Beggar and the King'.

Take that opposition one stage further, and we have *1 Henry IV* with its multiple plots and commentaries, plays extempore, mimes and parodies, together with the grinning honour of Sir Walter Blunt. Move on to *2 Henry IV*, and the plots, though substantially related, are, causally, held far apart; action comes to nothing, or little, whether it be the Archbishop's rising or Falstaff's scheming. Outward appearance and reputation, at Gaultree, does more to conquer a rebel than activity might do. Inflated rhetoric collapses, and Northumberland moves from hectic threats of violence into prudent retreat. Yet reputation, in the form of the dead Hotspur, has no more military power than King Richard's name. Men are slaves of Rumour, and begin to speak of themselves as Time's subjects. Move on one step further, and one arrives at *Troilus*. But since to use such formulae might suggest that *Troilus* is so uncertain in form as to be amorphous, it may help one's understanding of the play to sketch its outlines a little more firmly, and to indicate how far a true dramatic unity has been achieved.

First, the play is manifestly not a mere chronicle history of the Trojan War.[1] It consists of two linked actions, of which the love-plot is concluded with the play's conclusion, and the war-plot, though not fully played out, is by implication at an end; for with the death of Hector, the fate of Troy is sealed.[2] Moreover, the pattern of the action was foretold in the Prologue:

> our play
> Leaps o'er the vaunt and firstlings of those broils,
> Beginning in the middle, starting thence away
> To what may be digested in a play.   (Prol. 26–9)

1. Such a chronicle is to be found in Heywood's *Iron Age*. The play represented by the Admiral's Company 'plot' may have been another.
2. This pattern is common to the *Iliad*, and to the medieval recensions of the Troy story. In Chapman's translation (*Iliad*, xxii. 337–8) Achilles is quite explicit: 'we have slaine Hector, the period / Of all Troy's glorie'. In Caxton's *Recuyell* (p. 614) the Trojans 'sayd all that from thens forth they had loste alle her hope and truste of deffence'.

That is to say, Shakespeare has designed an Aristotelian 'action', seizing upon a period of crisis in the war, and admitting no more material than will suffice to embody that action. In the public world, the Greeks have drawn together; Achilles has once more joined battle; and Hector is slain. In the private world, Troilus has found, won, and lost Cressida.

The two actions are related by form and substance. The war (and it is only to that action that the Prologue refers) is a 'cruel war', but it derives from a 'love cause'.[1] Troilus, the second Hector, is the protagonist of the love-plot. Paris, Menelaus, Troilus, Diomedes and Achilles are all directly involved with love and war, although the relationships (and the behaviour) may differ.[2] Even Hector's challenge is made in defence of a mistress. Achilles as a warrior is unreliable and unchivalrous, in marked contrast to the generous and chivalrous Hector: indeed, the opposition of the two in battle, with

> *Hect.*   Pause, if thou wilt.
> *Achill.*   I do disdain thy courtesy, proud Trojan.
>
> > (v. vi. 14–15)

set over against

> I am unarm'd: forego this vantage, Greek.
>
> > (v. viii. 9)

is already foreshadowed in the affair of the challenge, where the dancing provocation of Æneas' speech meets the sullen contempt of Achilles' recapitulation:

> Marry, this, sir, is proclaim'd through all our host,
> That Hector, by the fifth hour of the sun,
> Will with a trumpet, 'twixt our tents and Troy,
> Tomorrow morning, call some knights to arms
> That hath a stomach, and such a one that dare
> Maintain—I know not what: 'tis trash— . . .
>
> > (ii. i. 123–8)

---

1. The Trojan War is not the only campaign that sprang from such a source: Ovid's *Elegies*, ii. 12 would have reminded Shakespeare of the battle of the Lapiths and the Centaurs (which Ovid narrates in detail in *Metamorphoses* xii, as an episode in his own account of the Trojan War), of the war between Turnus and Æneas over Lavinia, and of the fight that threatened between the Romans and the Sabine fathers.

2. Paris fights to keep Helen—when he can bring himself to do so; Menelaus leads an armed force to recover her; Troilus fights both to keep Helen and to avenge himself on Diomedes; Diomedes fights to win back Helen, and to prove himself Cressida's 'knight'; while Achilles, love-sick for Polyxena, will fight nobody, until he is driven to avenge Patroclus.

But Achilles as a lover is contrasted with Troilus: Achilles becomes inert, slothful and treacherous, for he betrays the Greek cause by withdrawal from the fighting,[1] whereas Troilus remains faithful to his father's cause, and suffers (but does not commit) treason, by the infidelity of Cressida.

Both actions of the play embody common or related themes—Time; identity; valuation; Man' propensity to

> see and approve of the better,
> [And] go for the worse[2]

—and the play is so devised that the audience is constantly compelled to hold what it contemplates at a distance, and to pass judgement upon it. Indeed, it is Shakespeare's triumph in *Troilus* to have kept his audience from too close a sympathy with the characters of the play, but at the same time to have involved it closely in those abstractions of morality and metaphysics which (according to his usual practice) the characters would have embodied. We are in a world in which the incontinent action, and not the incontinent man, has moved us: in which Time is more immediately present to us than is Nestor. The art of the greater Sonnets is the same art that wrought *Troilus*.

Consequently, the play emphasizes its patterns and parallels, its comparisons and distinctions, drawing together Greek and Trojan as they become infected with false pride and dignity, both personal and national; so that failure to observe degree leads to Greek faction and inanition, whereas failure to distinguish true and false honour hurries the Trojans forward to their utter destruction. Hector, a realist in politics, becomes an idealist when he fights, and concedes, out of his 'vice of mercy' a breathing-space to the man who will cause his death.[3] Troilus, by contrast, is an idealist in love, but a realist in war, urging Hector to show no mercy and arguing that one should be (as Ulysses reports of him) 'more vindicative than jealous love'. He embodies the doctrine that Caxton claimed to find in Virgil: '*Non est*

1. In some versions of the story, he even bargained for peace with the Trojans, provided that he might have Polyxena.

2. This is Ovid's formula—'video meliora proboque, / deteriora sequor', but St Paul makes the same complaint—'For the good that I would, I do not; but the evil that I would not, that I do.' (Romans vii. 19).

3. The medieval sources saw Hector's error at the moment when he acceded to the request of his cousin Ajax, and withdrew the victorious Trojans from the pursuit of the Greeks and destruction of their fleet; whereby the Trojans 'missed to have the victorie' (Caxton, p. 590). Shakespeare creates his own context for the mistaken generosity, but the result is the same.

misericordia in bello. . . . A man ought not to be too mercifull, but take the victory when he may get it'. But the true realists are on the Greek side. Diomedes, who cherishes no illusions about Helen or Cressida, is pragmatic in his dealings with another man's mistress.[1] Achilles, enervated by the 'weak wanton Cupid', will nevertheless organise a gang-murder out of pure vindictiveness. And, finally, Ulysses, apparently free of human weakness (so far as intelligence can ensure it), diagnoses exactly the sickness of the Greeks, the vices of Achilles, and the hyperbolic extrapolations of Troilus.[2]

Intelligence and moral sense set Hector and Ulysses aside from their fellows on each party (although Nestor shows more insight than the rest), and each man lapses from his own best understanding of right conduct. Intelligence, however, is not the most obvious characteristic of Thersites and Pandarus, the two commentators and voyeurs of the play: indeed, Pandarus seems to have no great critical capacity at all, but only the ability to involve himself in a situation sufficiently to debase it. Thersites debases whatever he meets and contemplates, but does so by vituperation and dissociation. Pandarus is a romantic gone rotten. Thersites is a romantic gone sour. Both are included in the play to amuse those with a taste for scepticism and scurrility, like 'my witty young masters o' the Inns o' Court';[3] but despite the skill with which they are deployed (and especially despite the brilliant invention of Thersites' language) their true function in the play is structural. In a play which was never meant to turn the accomplishment of many years into an hour-glass, it is their business (like that of the realists against the idealists) to present to us other possible views and evaluations. Fortune may not always have time, within a given dramatic action, to beggar the estimation which we prized; but in that case a Thersites or a Pandarus, a Diomedes, a Hector, or an Achilles, will act as Fortune's surrogate. Calchas may be able to strip himself of his

1. Ironically, he employs, against her, Cressida's own technique of pretended indifference. Women also 'prize the thing ungain'd more than it is'.

2. If he has a limitation, it is the inability to be a perfect prophet. He can see the secret love of Achilles for Polyxena, and judge its likely consequences. He cannot foresee that a letter from Hecuba and her daughter will keep Achilles in his tent; or that Hector's killing of Patroclus will return Achilles to the field.

3. *Bartholomew Fair*, Induction 34–5; the Stagekeeper proposes a comic 'conceit': 'Would not a fine pump upon the stage ha' done well, for a property now? And a punk set under upon her head, with her stern upward, and ha' been sous'd by my witty young masters o' the Inns o' Court?' (which may remind us that the theatrical taste of the Inns was not at all points sophisticated.)

attributes; Achilles may find that his attributes slowly vanish of themselves; but Thersites will strip the attributes from any man, and provide a fresh set from his own imaginings. It is no wonder, in the age of the sceptic and the 'send-up', that *Troilus and Cressida* has grown in popularity, for it hits the taste of the time. Many suppose that its assertions are wholly destructive: the Emperor never had any clothes. But it may be, in effect, a little more like Strauss's *Ariadne*: a work which asserts its staginess with bravado: which emphasizes that assertion by confining its first Act to the green room and its quarrels: which puts together two plots at the *fiat* of M. Jourdain, who wishes them to be played *gleich-zeitig*: which sets the abandoned Ariadne and her retinue upstage, and leaves the forestage to the parodic mockers from the *commedia dell' arte* (and especially to Zerbinetta, for whom each new lover comes 'like a god'); and which finds in the end that the *deus ex machina* is a god indeed.

TROILUS AND CRESSIDA

A neuer writer, to an euer
reader. Newes.

Eternall reader, you haue heere a new play, neuer stal'd with the
Stage, neuer clapper-clawd with the palmes of the vulger, and yet
passing full of the palme comicall; for it is a birth of your braine,
that neuer vnder-tooke any thing commicall, vainely: And were
but the vaine names of commedies changde for the titles of
Commodities, or of Playes for Pleas; you should see all those
grand censors, that now stile them such vanities, flock to them for
the maine grace of their grauities: especially this authors Commedies, that are so fram'd to the life, that they serue for the most
common Commentaries, of all the actions of our liues, shewing
such a dexteritie, and power of witte, that the most displeased
with Playes, are pleasd with his Commedies. And all such dull
and heauy-witted worldlings, as were neuer capable of the witte
of a Commedie, comming by report of them to his representations,
haue found that witte there, that they neuer found in them-
selues, and haue parted better wittied then they came: feeling an
edge of witte set vpon them, more then euer they dreamd they
had braine to grinde it on. So much and such sauored salt of
witte is in his Commedies, that they seeme (for their height of
pleasure) to be borne in that sea that brought forth *Venus.*
Amongst all there is none more witty then this: And had I time I
would comment vpon it, though I know it needs not, (for so much
as will make you thinke your testerne well bestowd) but for so
much worth, as euen poore I know to be stuft in it. It deserues
such a labour, as well as the best Commedy in *Terence* or *Plautus.*
And beleeue this, that when hee is gone, and his Commedies
out of sale, you will scramble for them, and set vp a new English
Inquisition. Take this for a warning, and at the perrill of your
pleasures losse, and Iudgements, refuse not, nor like this the
lesse, for not being sullied, with the smoaky breath of the multitude; but thanke fortune for the scape it hath made amongst you.
Since by the grand possessors wills I beleeue you should haue
prayd for them rather then beene prayd. And so I leaue all such
to bee prayd for (for the states of their wits healths) that will not
praise it. *Vale.*[1]

1. This Epistle, found in copies of Q in the second state, occupies the leaf
signed ¶2, following the cancel title-page.

DRAMATIS PERSONÆ

THE PROLOGUE

PRIAM, *King of Troy.* *Queen Hecuba - Priam's wife.*
HECTOR
TROILUS
PARIS } *his sons.*
DEIPHOBUS
HELENUS
MARGARELON, *a bastard son of Priam.*
ÆNEAS
ANTENOR } *Trojan commanders.*
CALCHAS, *a Trojan priest, taking part with the Greeks.*
PANDARUS, *uncle to Cressida.*

AGAMEMNON, *the Greek General.*
MENELAUS, *his brother.*
ACHILLES
AJAX
ULYSSES
NESTOR } *Greek commanders.*
DIOMEDES
PATROCLUS
THERSITES, *a deformed and scurrilous Greek.*
ALEXANDER, *servant to Cressida.*
Servant to Troilus.
Servant to Paris.
Servant to Diomedes.

HELEN, *wife to Menelaus.*
ANDROMACHE, *wife to Hector.*
CASSANDRA, *daughter to Priam; a prophetess.*
CRESSIDA, *daughter to Calchas.*

Trojan and Greek soldiers.
Attendants.

Note. This list derives essentially from Malone. The Prologue first appeared as an actor in NCS.

96

TROILUS AND CRESSIDA

THE PROLOGUE

[*Enter the* Prologue, *in armour.*]

Prol. In Troy, there lies the scene. From Isles of Greece
The princes orgulous, their high blood chaf'd,
Have to the port of Athens sent their ships
Fraught with the ministers and instruments
Of cruel war: sixty and nine that wore   5
Their crownets regal, from th'Athenian bay
Put forth toward Phrygia, and their vow is made
To ransack Troy, within whose strong immures
The ravish'd Helen, Menelaus' queen,
With wanton Paris sleeps—and that's the quarrel.   10
To Tenedos they come,
And the deep-drawing barks do there disgorge

Prologue

1–31. THE PROLOGUE . . . war.] F; not in Q.   S.D.] NCS; The Prologue
(in armour). Collier[2]; not in F.   12. barks] F2 (Barkes); Barke F.

Prologue

2. *orgulous*] haughty. The word is fairly common in Middle English, especially in Romances, and frequent in Caxton's *Recuyell* (perhaps cf. also Spenser's Orgoglio).

chaf'd] heated, irritated: cf. also IV.v.259.

3. *port of Athens*] So in Caxton: 'the Kings . . . assemblid them to gyder at the port of athens'.

5. *sixty and nine*] Again Caxton is the source: 'The some of Kynges and dukes . . . were sixty and nyne'.

6. *crownets*] A by-form of *coronets*, becoming uncommon during the seventeenth century, but cf. *Ant.* IV.xii.27.

8. *immures*] walls (*quasi* enwallments).

11.] A short line of three feet (cf. l. 19): Shakespeare may have intended it to be so, in imitation of the occasional short lines of the *Aeneid* (e.g. VI.94, 'Externique iterum thalami'): that is (despite the apparent mild irony of tone in parts of the Prologue), he meant the passage to sound heroic, according to the most obvious model.

12. *barks*] It is usual to follow F2, though it seems odd that the apparent error of F, set in such large type, should have escaped notice. Perhaps *barke* is an uninflected plural.

97

Their warlike fraughtage. Now on Dardan plains
The fresh and yet unbruised Greeks do pitch
Their brave pavilions: Priam's six-gated city,　　　　15
Dardan and Timbria, Helias, Chetas, Troien,
And Antenorides, with massy staples
And co-responsive and fulfilling bolts,
Stir up the sons of Troy.
Now expectation, tickling skittish spirits　　　　20
On one and other side, Trojan and Greek,
Sets all on hazard. And hither am I come,
A Prologue arm'd, but not in confidence
Of author's pen or actor's voice, but suited
In like conditions as our argument,　　　　25
To tell you, fair beholders, that our play
Leaps o'er the vaunt and firstlings of those broils,
Beginning in the middle, starting thence away

17. Antenorides] *Theobald;* Antenonidus *F.*　　19. Stir] *F* (Stirre); Sperre *Pope*², conj. *Theobald;* Sperrs *Capell;* Sparr *Singer*², conj. *Coleridge.*

15–19. *Priam's . . . Troy*] That is, the sons of Troy stir up to warlike readiness the city of Priam, with its six gates, heavily stapled and bolted.

15. *pavilions*] Cf. *LLL* v.ii.645 for a similar association of Greek heroes and medieval chivalry.

six-gated] The names of the gates are from Caxton and Lydgate, being in the same order as in those two writers, but with spellings nearer to Caxton's. No medieval author uses a form exactly like Shakespeare's *Antenonidus,* although Lydgate is credited with *Anthonydes* (*Troy Book,* ii.600ff.). Most probably F's compositor misread his copy.

19. *Stir up*] I retain the F reading, taking *sons of Troy* as the subject. As they presume (with Theobald) that, since the city cannot arouse the Trojans, the Trojans must lock up the city, most editors emend; but emendation is needed only if we assume that *with massy . . . bolts* is an adverbial phrase qualifying the verb, rather than an adjectival phrase which belongs (like the names of the

gates to which it applies) to a parenthesis. The F reading leaves us with an awkward sentence, unusual for Shakespeare, with its subject and verb reversed; but editors who emend suppose the same syntax.

20. *skittish*] lively, spirited.

23. *Prologue arm'd*] Perhaps an allusion to the Prologue of Jonson's *Poetaster* (1601), who was also armed and apologetic (see also Introduction, p. 19).

25. *conditions*] Walker (NCS) emends to the singular, on the grounds that 'the character of the subject is martial'; but several senses of *condition* in OED require the plural form for a meaning indifferently plural or singular (e.g. 11b).

27. *vaunt*] beginning (the prefix vaunt- / vant- used as a noun; cf. *van*).

28. *Beginning in the middle*] A critical commonplace, drawn from Horace's *De Arte Poetica,* and especially proper to a play on the Trojan War (cf. especially l. 147: 'Nec gemino bellum Troianum orditur ab ovo'). There

To what may be digested in a play.
Like, or find fault: do as your pleasures are: 30
Now good, or bad, 'tis but the chance of war.   [*Exit.*]

31 S.D.] *NCS (goes); not in F.*

seems to be no point in emending
here for the sake of the metre:
Shakespeare may be allowed his
Alexandrines, as well as his trimeters
(cf. ll. 11 and 19, above).

29. *digested*] disposed, distributed;

cf. *Ham.* ii.ii.436–7, 'well digested in
the scenes'. *Not* part of the food
imagery of the play.

30–1. *are . . . war*] A perfect rhyme;
and cf. Tilley C 223.

ACT I

SCENE I

Enter PANDARUS *and* TROILUS.

Troil. Call here my varlet, I'll unarm again.
    Why should I war without the walls of Troy,
    That find such cruel battle here within?
    Each Trojan that is master of his heart
    Let him to field; Troilus, alas, hath none.   5
Pand. Will this gear ne'er be mended?
Troil. The Greeks are strong, and skilful to their strength,
    Fierce to their skill, and to their fierceness valiant;
    But I am weaker than a woman's tear,
    Tamer than sleep, fonder than ignorance,   10
    Less valiant than the virgin in the night,
    And skilless as unpractis'd infancy.
Pand. Well, I have told you enough of this: for my part
    I'll not meddle nor make no farther. He that will

ACT I

Scene 1

ACT I SCENE 1] *F* (*Actus Primus. Scoena Prima.*); *not in Q.*   3. within?] *F;* within, *Q.*

1. *varlet*] servant, page (presumably, the 'Boy' of 1. ii. 276).

2–3. *Why should . . . within?*] The war in the members (Romans vii. 23: cf. Prudentius' *Psychomachia*) was familiar throughout Christendom. Thus, the allusion to Anacreon, suggested by Theobald, need not be supposed, though it remains possible: Baldwin (*Variorum*) believes that a Latin version was consulted.

6. *gear*] affair, matter, way of behaving (an elastic term, usually having a depreciatory sense, such as 'nonsense' 'carrying-on'). Cf. *Mer. V.* 1. i. 110, and Roper's *Life of More*, ed. E. V. Hitchcock (E.E.T.S., 197, 1935, p. 83]: ' "Bone deus, bone deus, [man,] will this geare neuer be lefte?" quoth shee.'

7–8 *to . . . to . . . to . . .*] Editors usually follow Franz and gloss as 'in addition to', but Abbott's interpretation (§187), 'up to', 'in proportion to', is attractive.

14. *meddle nor make*] Cf. Tilley M 852.

have a cake out of the wheat must tarry the   15
grinding.

Troil. Have I not tarried?

Pand. Ay, the grinding; but you must tarry the <u>bolting</u>.

Troil. Have I not tarried?

Pand. Ay, the bolting; but you must tarry the leavening.   20

Troil. Still have I tarried.

Pand. Ay, to the leavening; but here's yet in the word
'hereafter' the kneading, the making of the cake,
the heating of the oven, and the baking: nay, you
must stay the cooling too, or you may chance burn   25
your lips.

Troil. Patience herself, what goddess e'er she be,
Doth lesser blench at suff'rance than I do.
At Priam's royal table do I sit,
And when fair Cressid comes into my thoughts—   30
So, traitor! 'When she comes'! When is she thence?

Pand. Well, she looked yesternight fairer than ever I
saw her look, or any woman else.

Troil. I was about to tell thee: when my heart,
As wedged with a sigh, would rive in twain,   35
Lest Hector or my father should perceive me,

---

18. must] *Q;* must needs *F.*   22. here's] *Q,F;* there's *NCS.*   23. 'hereafter']
As Dyce; hereafter *Q,F.*   24. heating of] *F (2nd setting);* heating *Q,F (1st
setting).*   25. you may] *F;* yea may *Q.*   28. suff'rance] *Q;* sufferance *F.*
31. So, traitor!] *Rowe (subst.);* So (Traitor) *F;* So traitor *Q.*   When . . .
thence?] *Camb. (subst.);* When she comes? When is she thence? *Rowe³;* then she
comes when she is thence. *Q, F (subst.).*   32–3.] *As Q;* Well, | . . . looke, |
. . . else. *F.*   34. thee:] *Camb. (subst.);* thee,—*Capell;* thee *Q.*

---

18. *bolting*] sifting (esp. flour from
bran).

24. *heating of*] F's reading (in the
second setting) might easily be an
unconscious correction, by the compositor, of Q's *heating*; but Q's
omission of a word is quite as likely.

27–8. *Patience . . . blench*] For 'lesser
blench' we should understand 'not
blench so little'. Troilus contradicts
himself: Patience ought to blench
more than he does. But Shakespeare
sometimes confuses himself when

correlating comparatives or negatives: cf. *Mac.* III. vi. 8–9, 'Who cannot
want the thought, how monstrous | It
was . . .' (where 'can' is needed).

31.] The emendation and the QF
reading imply the same sense—that
Troilus errs in even momentary
forgetfulness—but the first works by
hyperbole and the other by heavy
irony. Inversion by accident would
have been easy, and it is therefore
tempting to emend: I follow the
majority of editors.

     I have, as when the sun doth light a storm,
     Buried this sigh in wrinkle of a smile;
     But sorrow that is couch'd in seeming gladness
     Is like that mirth fate turns to sudden sadness.   40

Pand. And her hair were not somewhat darker than
     Helen's—well, go to, there were no more com-
     parison between the women. But for my part, she
     is my kinswoman; I would not, as they term it,
     praise her, but I would somebody had heard her   45
     talk yesterday as I did. I will not dispraise your
     sister Cassandra's wit, but—

Troil. O Pandarus—I tell thee Pandarus—
     When I do tell thee there my hopes lie drown'd,
     Reply not in how many fathoms deep   50
     They lie indrench'd. I tell thee I am mad
     In Cressid's love: thou answer'st, 'She is fair';
     Pour'st in the open ulcer of my heart
     Her eyes, her hair, her cheek, her gait, her voice;
     Handlest in thy discourse—O—that her hand,   55
     In whose comparison all whites are ink,

---

37. a storm] *Rowe;* a scorne *Q;* a-scorne *F.*   42. Helen's . . . to,] *Pope;*
Hellens, well go to, *Q; Helens,* well go too, *F.*   45. her, but] *Q;* it, but *F.*
52. 'She is fair'] *As Hanmer;* she is faire, *Q,F (subst.).*   53. Pour'st] *F* (Powr'st);
Powrest *Q.*   55. discourse . . . hand,] *Malone (subst.);* discourse: O that her
hand *Q;* discourse. O that her Hand *F;* discourse—O that! her Hand! *Rowe.*

37. *a storm*] Rowe's emendation has much to support it: (a) Troilus, sighing and looking profoundly depressed, lightens his expression with a smile—a trite enough figure, perhaps suiting his rhetoric here; (b) the implied misreading (*c* for *t*, and *-rne* for *-rme*) is easy in a Secretary hand; (c) Keats's defence of QF (Caroline Spurgeon, *Keats's Shakespeare*, 1928, p. 149; cited in *Variorum*) is ingenious, but does not bear analysis: 'Apollo in the act of drawing back his head, and forcing a smile upon the world' may perhaps suit one's view of Troilus, but does not correspond to l. 39.

53. *ulcer*] A curious image: one rather expects the 'gash' of l. 62, for Troilus hardly sees his love as a disease. Mrs E. Duncan-Jones (privately) suggests that Shakespeare is recalling Ronsard's *Amours* CIX, a sonnet to Cassandre which mentions Achilles' spear; and she argues that, Ronsard being fashionable about 1600 (cf. *Parnassus Plays*, ed. J. B. Leishman, 1949, I.i.1125, II.i.1268), an Inn of Court audience would recognize at least the style of the poet, though not perhaps the exact allusion. An ulcer can be the consequence of an unhealed wound: Troilus may therefore be implying that his heart, being continually wounded, cannot heal. (But see further l. 98 n.)

55. *that her hand*] that hand of hers.

Writing their own reproach, to whose soft seizure

The cygnet's down is harsh, and spirit of sense

Hard as the palm of ploughman. This thou tell'st me.

As true thou tell'st me, when I say I love her.   60

But saying thus, instead of oil and balm,

Thou lay'st in every gash that love hath given me

The knife that made it.

Pand. I speak no more than truth.

Troil. Thou dost not speak so much.   65

Pand. Faith, I'll not meddle in it—let her be as she is:

if she be fair, 'tis the better for her; and she be not,

she has the mends in her own hands.

Troil. Good Pandarus—how now, Pandarus?

Pand. I have had my labour for my travail, ill thought   70

on of her, and ill thought on of you; gone between

and between, but small thanks for my labour.

Troil. What, art thou angry, Pandarus? What, with me?

Pand. Because she's kin to me, therefore she's not

so fair as Helen. And she were not kin to me,   75

she would be as fair o' Friday as Helen is o'

Sunday. But what care I? I care not and she were

a blackamoor, 'tis all one to me.

Troil. Say I she is not fair?

Pand. I do not care whether you do or no. She's a fool   80

to stay behind her father; let her to the Greeks,

---

66. in it]*Q;* in't *F.*   71. on of you] *F;* of you *Q.*   75. were not] *F (2nd setting);* were *Q,F (1st setting).*   76. o' Friday] *Q (a Friday);* on Friday *F.*
77. what care] *F;* what *Q.*   80. *Pand.*] *Q,F (1st setting (Pan.)); Troy. F (2nd setting).*

---

57. *seizure*] clasping.

58. *spirit of sense*] one of those most refined and delicate bodily substances, which transmitted sense-impressions to the 'common' sense in the mind, and hence served to connect corporeal and incorporeal.

61. *oil and balm*] ointments, salves. Oil and *wine* was the dressing used by the Samaritan in the parable (Luke x.34), but Shakespeare may also have in mind the balm of Gilead (Jeremiah viii.22) which is associated with physicians, and with the fall of a

doomed city as well. (Ezekiel xxvii.17 mentions 'honey, and oil, and balm', and that passage is also concerned with the fall of a great city.)

66. *not meddle in it*] Perhaps cf. Tilley M 853.

68. *mends . . . hands*] Cf. Tilley M 872: Pandarus probably implies that Cressida can always have recourse to cosmetics.

76–7. *as fair . . . Sunday*] as handsome fasting (and dressed to suit) as Helen in her finery.

81. *her father*] Calchas. In *Iliad* I,

and so I'll tell her the next time I see her. For my
part I'll meddle nor make no more i'th'matter.
Troil. Pandarus—
Pand. Not I.   85
Troil. Sweet Pandarus—
Pand. Pray you speak no more to me; I will leave all
     as I found it, and there an end.   *Exit. Sound alarum.*
Troil. Peace, you ungracious clamours! Peace, rude sounds!
     Fools on both sides, Helen must needs be fair   90
     When with your blood you daily paint her thus.
     I cannot fight upon this argument;
     It is too starv'd a subject for my sword.
     But Pandarus—O gods, how do you plague me!
     I cannot come to Cressid but by Pandar,   95
     And he's as tetchy to be woo'd to woo
     As she is stubborn-chaste against all suit.
     Tell me, Apollo, for thy Daphne's love,
     What Cressid is, what Pandar, and what we.
     Her bed is India; there she lies, a pearl.   100
     Between our Ilium and where she resides,

King's Palace.

88 S.D. *Exit.*] *Q; Exit Pandar. | F.*   97. stubborn-chaste] *Theobald;* stub-
borne, chast *Q,F.*

Calchas is a Greek, son of Thestor,
who has the gift of augury from
Apollo. In Chaucer (*Troilus and
Criseyde,* 1.66ff.), who in this matter
drew on Benoît or Guido, he is a
Trojan 'devyn', who is told by
'Apollo Delphicus' that Troy will fall
to the Greeks; he himself then goes
over to the Greeks, and is well
received, on the assumption that his
foresight will be of tactical use.
(Caxton, *Recuyell,* p. 663, credits him
with devising the great horse—of
brass, not of wood—by which the
Greeks finally entered Troy.) Shakespeare has thus introduced the idea
of Cressida's defection in his first
scene, with strong irony, although
Pandarus, of course, has no notion of
it as a serious possibility.
     83. *meddle nor make*] See n. to l. 14

above.
     92. *argument*] theme (as in Prologue
l. 25).
     93. *starv'd*] trivial, lacking matter.
     96. *tetchy*] irritable, touchy.
     98. *Tell . . . love*] The allusion is
appropriate on several counts: (a)
Daphne, like Cressida, fled her lover
(as the lover saw it), and was almost
offensively coy; (b) Apollo's plea to
her is remarkably like that of Troilus
here—that is, Shakespeare is taking
his style, as well as his allusion, from
Ovid (*Metamorphoses* 1); (c) Apollo
was not only a musician but a healer,
and lamented to Daphne the wound
in his heart which even his skill could
not cure.
     101. *Ilium*] Priam's palace, always
thought of (since Benoît) as standing
apart from the city of Troy.

Cress. Then you say as I say, for I am sure he is not
    Hector.
Pand. No, nor Hector is not Troilus in some degrees.   70
Cress. 'Tis just to each of them; he is himself.
Pand. Himself? Alas poor Troilus, I would he were—
Cress. So he is.
Pand. —Condition I had gone barefoot to India.
Cress. He is not Hector.   75
Pand. Himself? No, he's not himself, would a were
    himself. Well, the gods are above, time must
    friend or end. Well, Troilus, well, I would my
    heart were in her body. No, Hector is not a better
    man than Troilus.   80
Cress. Excuse me.
Pand. He is elder.
Cress. Pardon me, pardon me.
Pand. Th'other's not come to't, you shall tell me
    another tale when th'other's come to't. Hector   85
    shall not have his wit this year.

68–9.] *As Q;* Then ... say, / ... *Hector. F.*   70. nor] *Q;* not *F.*   71. just
to ... them; he] *Rowe (subst.);* iust, to each of them he *Q,F.*   72. were—]
Capell (subst.); were. *Q,F.*   74. —Condition] *Capell* (—condition)*;* Condition
Q,F.   76. Himself? No,] *Rowe* (Himself? no,)*;* Himselfe? no? *Q,F.*   86. wit]
Rowe; will *Q,F.*

71.] That is, Hector is Hector, and
the better man, by comparison with
Troilus.

74. *Condition . . . gone*] even if, to
prove it true, I had been compelled
to go. For the hyperbole, cf. *Oth.*
IV. iii. 38–9 ('I know a lady in Venice
would have walk'd barefoot to
Palestine for a touch of his nether
lip').

76. *not himself*] unwell, out of sorts,
below his usual standard of excellence.
This superficial play with notions of
identity is nevertheless part of a
pattern: Cressida herself employs
similar ideas more seriously at
III. ii. 145–6, and effectually enacts
them in her betrayal of Troilus in
v. ii. 145 ('This is, and is not, Cressid').

77. *the . . . above*] Cf. Tilley G 201,
G 202, G 250, H 348.

77–8. *time . . . end*] Perhaps cf.
Tilley T 30 or M 874 (but Tilley has
no exact parallel). It is hard to be
sure whether Pandarus' proverbs are
meant to be merely ludicrous, like
Dogberry's, or whether they are, in
their half-facetious way, another comment on the action of Time within the
play—something to stand with the
observations of Ulysses, Agamemnon,
Troilus and Achilles. Chaucer's Pandarus is also much given to proverbs:
cf. *Troilus*, 1.624–721, and Troilus'
reply at 1.752–60.

81. *Excuse me*] A remark indicating
dissent (as now): OED gives this as
the earliest instance.

84. *not come to't*] not fully mature:
cf. IV.v.97, and v.iii.33 ('Let grow
thy sinews till their knots be strong').

86. *wit*] intelligence, understanding.

Cress. He shall not need it if he have his own.

Pand. Nor his qualities.

Cress. No matter.

Pand. Nor his beauty.   90

Cress. 'Twould not become him, his own's better.

Pand. You have no judgement, niece. Helen herself
swore th'other day that Troilus, for a brown
favour—for so 'tis, I must confess—not brown
neither—   95

Cress. No, but brown.

Pand. Faith, to say truth, brown and not brown.

Cress. To say truth, true and not true.

Pand. She praised his complexion above Paris.

Cress. Why, Paris hath colour enough.   100

Pand. So he has.

Cress. Then Troilus should have too much. If she
praised him above, his complexion is higher than
his: he having colour enough, and the other
higher, is too flaming a praise for a good com-   105
plexion. I had as lief Helen's golden tongue had
commended Troilus for a copper nose.

Pand. I swear to you I think Helen loves him better
than Paris.

Cress. Then she's a merry Greek indeed.   110

---

97. say] *Q,F;* say the *NCS.*   98. say] *This edn;* say the *Q,F.*   102. much.]
This edn; much; *Rowe;* much, *Q,F.*   104. his:] *Theobald (subst.);* his, *Q,F.*

The QF reading *will* is awkward: to
have one's will = to get one's way,
and neither Hector nor Troilus is in
any way frustrated; while the sense
'sexual desire' appears to be irrelevant. Besides, would Cressida let it
pass without comment?

    94. *favour*] appearance, look, face.

    96. *but*] merely, simply.

    97–8.] There is little to choose
between Pandarus' 'say truth' and
Cressida's 'say the truth', but plainly
the two remarks should be congruent,
or Cressida's playfulness loses some of
its point.

    103. *above*] sc. Paris. The name may

have dropped out of the text in Q:
the prose of this speech is most
irregularly and widely spaced, which
might easily have been caused by
press-correction without reference to
copy. (The point was made by the
late Philip Williams, in his Ph.D.
dissertation on the printing of the
texts of *Troilus and Cressida*.)

    107. *copper nose*] A sign of inebriety.

    110. *merry Greek*] merry fellow, per-
son of loose behaviour, wanton; cf.
Tilley M 901 (and cf. also iv.iv.55,
'A woeful Cressid 'mongst the merry
Greeks').

Pand. Nay, I am sure she does: she came to him
th'other day into the compassed window—and
you know he has not past three or four hairs on
his chin—

Cress. Indeed a tapster's arithmetic may soon bring his   115
particulars therein to a total.

Pand. Why, he is very young, and yet will he within
three pound lift as much as his brother Hector.

Cress. Is he so young a man, and so old a lifter? ⟨_not_⟩

Pand. But to prove to you that Helen loves him, she   120
came and puts me her white hand to his cloven
chin—

Cress. Juno have mercy, how came it cloven?

Pand. Why, you know 'tis dimpled: I think his smiling
becomes him better than any man in all Phrygia.   125

Cress. O, he smiles valiantly.

Pand. Does he not?

Cress. O yes, and 'twere a cloud in autumn.

Pand. Why, go to then. But to prove to you that Helen
loves Troilus—   130

Cress. Troilus will stand to the proof if you'll prove
it so.

Pand. Troilus? Why, he esteems her no more than I
esteem an addle egg.

Cress. If you love an addle egg as well as you love an   135
idle head you would eat chickens i'th'shell.

Pand. I cannot choose but laugh to think how she
tickled his chin: indeed she has a marvell's white
hand, I must needs confess—

Cress. Without the rack.   140

Pand. And she takes upon her to spy a white hair on

---

112. *compassed window*] window with
a semi-circular bay.

115. *tapster's arithmetic*] reckoning of
the most simple kind: cf. III.iii.251–3.
A tapster's intelligence was proverbially low (cf. Francis, in *1H4*
II.iv).

119. *young*] inexperienced (as opposed to *old* = practised).

lifter] thief: a term current until

the nineteenth century, and still used
in compounds (e.g. shop-lifter).

128.] I do not understand this
riposte.

131. *stand to*] Literally, 'maintain',
but Cressida quibbles obscenely.

138. *marvell's*] Perhaps an old-
fashioned pronunciation (of marvellous): cf. Polonius (*Ham.* II.i.3, 'You
shall do marvell's wisely').

his chin.

Cress. Alas poor chin, many a wart is richer.

Pand. But there was such laughing: Queen Hecuba
laughed that her eyes ran o'er—   145

Cress. With millstones.

Pand. And Cassandra laughed.

Cress. But there was a more temperate fire under the
pot of her eyes. Did her eyes run o'er too?

Pand. And Hector laughed.   150

Cress. At what was all this laughing?

Cand. Marry, at the white hair that Helen spied on
Troilus' chin.

Cress. And't had been a green hair I should have
laughed too.   155

Pand. They laughed not so much at the hair as at his
pretty answer.

Cress. What was his answer?

Pand. Quoth she, 'Here's but two and fifty hairs on
your chin, and one of them is white.'   160

Cress. This is her question.

Pand. That's true, make no question of that. 'Two and
fifty hairs,' quoth he, 'and one white: that white
hair is my father, and all the rest are his sons.'
'Jupiter,' quoth she, 'which of these hairs is Paris   165
my husband?' 'The forked one,' quoth he, 'pluck't

148. was a] *Q;* was *F.*   159. two] *Q,F;* one *Theobald.*

146. *With millstones*] i.e. there were
no tears; cf. *R3* I.iii.353.

148. *a more temperate fire*] Cassandra,
doomed to foreknow the fall of the
city and yet not be believed, was
unlikely to join with any enthusiasm
in this facetious game.

154. *green*] A colour normally
associated (as now) with inexperience:
cf. perhaps 'green geese' in *LLL*
I.i.97.

159. *two and fifty*] Editors have
struggled to save both Shakespeare's
arithmetic and the tradition which
gave Priam fifty sons: copyist's errors
and an extra-traditional bastard are
the usual alternative explanations.

However, Troilus' mild joke requires
only that the forked hair should at
first have been counted as two; and
the apparently erroneous total, and
the colloquial inversion of the numeral
(*two* and fifty), both draw attention to
the fact. The spelling of the Q at this
point shifts from *heare* to *heire*, but it is
hard to be sure that the words were
phonetically distinct. If certainty
were possible, then it might be argued
that this was evidence for the nature
of Q's copy-text—namely, that it was
meant for private reading and not for
theatrical use; but a compositor
might have noticed the pun for himself and set it down in his text. One

out and give it him.' But there was such laughing,
and Helen so blushed, and Paris so chafed, and
all the rest so laughed that it passed.

Cress. So let it now, for it has been a great while going   170
by.

Pand. Well cousin, I told you a thing yesterday; think
on't.

Cress. So I do.

Pand. I'll be sworn 'tis true; he will weep you and   175
'twere a man born in April.

Cress. And I'll spring up in his tears and 'twere a
nettle against May.   *Sound a retreat.*

Pand. Hark! they are coming from the field. Shall we
stand up here and see them as they pass toward   180
Ilium? Good niece, do, sweet niece Cressida.

Cress. At your pleasure.

Pand. Here, here, here's an excellent place, here we
may see most bravely. I'll tell you them all by
their names as they pass by, but mark Troilus   185
above the rest.

Enter ÆNEAS [and passes over].

Cress. Speak not so loud.

Pand. That's Æneas, is not that a brave man? He's
one of the flowers of Troy, I can tell you. But
mark Troilus; you shall see anon.   190

Enter ANTENOR [and passes over].

186 S.D. *and . . . over*] *Rowe (subst.)* ; *not in Q,F.*   189. can tell] *Q ;* can *F.*
190 S.D. *and . . . over*] *Rowe (subst.)* ; *not in Q,F.*

ought not to erect textual theory upon
phonological doubt.

169. *passed*] exceeded description:
cf. *Wiv.* I.i.273.

172. *told you a thing*] told you something of consequence: cf. *LLL*
v.i.139, where the speaker is the
precise Armado.

179–81.] Criseyde watches Troilus
returning from the field, in Chaucer
(II.610–51), but after Pandarus has
left her; no other Trojan hero is
present. On the other hand (as Pro-

fessor Brooks reminds me) Chaucer's
Pandarus arranged (II.1009–22) that
Troilus should ride past on a second
occasion (II.1247–88), so that Pandarus might urge his excellence to
Criseyde; and there are details which
suggest that Shakespeare recalled
that incident, and conflated it with
this (cf. especially II.1260, 'bekked on
Pandare': l. 198 (below) 'give you
the nod'; and see Introduction, p.
24).

Cress. Who's that?

Pand. That's Antenor: he has a shrewd wit, I can tell
you, and he's a man good enough; he's one
o'th'soundest judgements in Troy whosoever, and
a proper man of person. When comes Troilus?   195
I'll show you Troilus anon: if he see me, you shall
see him nod at me.

Cress. Will he give you the nod?

Pand. You shall see.

Cress. If he do, the rich shall have more.   200

Enter HECTOR [*and passes over*].

Pand. That's Hector, that, that, look you, that; there's
a fellow! Go thy way, Hector—there's a brave
man, niece—O brave Hector! Look how he
looks, there's a countenance: is't not a brave man?

Cress. O, a brave man.   205

Pand. Is a not? It does a man's heart good. Look you
what hacks are on his helmet—look you yonder,
do you see? Look you there: there's no jesting,
there's laying on, take't off who will, as they say:
there be hacks.   210

Cress. Be those with swords?

Pand. Swords, anything, he cares not: and the devil
come to him, it's all one. By God's lid it does one's
heart good.

193. a man] *F;* man *Q.*   194. judgements] *Q;* judgment *F.*   197. him]
Q; him him *F.*   200 S.D.] *Rowe (subst.); Enter Hector | Q,F; (and so at 214,
220, 229, 243)*   201. you, that; there's] *Q;* you, that there's *F;* you, that:
there's *Pope.*   205. a brave] *Q;* brave *F.*   206. man's] *F;* man *Q.*
209. there's laying] *Q;* laying *F.*   off who will] *F3;* off, who will *Q,F2;* off,
who ill *F.*

198. *give . . . nod*] (a) nod to you in
recognition; (b) call you a fool
(= noddy). OED also cites a rare
occurrence of nod = figure of scorn.

200. *the . . . more*] you will be a still
greater fool; alluding to the parable
of the talents, Matthew xxv. 29 ('For
unto every one that hath shall be
given, and he shall have abundance').

209. *there's laying . . . will*] those

were good blows and no mistake.
(The phrase is usually applied to
laying out large sums of money.)

210. *there be*] Apparently a deliberately colloquial form, characteristic of
Pandarus, but the indicative usage is
surprising. Abbott (§299) comments
on the interrogative use (as in
Cressida's question in l. 211).

213. *lid*] eyelid. The oath is trivial.

Enter PARIS [*and passes over*].

Yonder comes Paris, yonder comes Paris: look ye　215
yonder, niece, is't not a gallant man too, is't not?
Why, this is brave now: who said he came hurt
home today? He's not hurt. Why, this will do
Helen's heart good now, ha? Would I could see
Troilus now: you shall see Troilus anon.　　　220

Enter HELENUS [*and passes over*].

Cress. Who's that?
Pand. That's Helenus—I marvel where Troilus is—
　　that's Helenus—I think he went not forth today—
　　that's Helenus.
Cress. Can Helenus fight, uncle?　　　　　　225
Pand. Helenus? No—yes, he'll fight indifferent well—
　　I marvel where Troilus is. Hark, do you not hear
　　the people cry 'Troilus'?—Helenus is a priest.
Cress. What sneaking fellow comes yonder?

Enter TROILUS [*and passes over*].

Pand. Where? Yonder? That's Deiphobus.—'Tis　230
　　Troilus! There's a man, niece! Hem! Brave
　　Troilus, the prince of chivalry!
Cress. Peace, for shame, peace.
Pand. Mark him, note him. O brave Troilus! Look
　　well upon him, niece, look you how his sword is　235
　　bloodied, and his helm more hacked than
　　Hector's, and how he looks, and how he goes! O
　　admirable youth; he never saw three and twenty.
　　Go thy way, Troilus, go thy way. Had I a sister

220. shall see] *Q*; shall *F*·　226. Helenus? No—] *Hanmer* (*subst.*); *Helenus* no:
Q,F. indifferent well] *F2*; indifferent, well *Q,F.*　234. note] *Q*; not *F.*
238. never] *Q*; ne're *F.*

217. *brave*] splendid, fine.
217–18. *who said . . . today?*] Æneas,
at I.i.109.
226. *indifferent well*] This use of the
short adverbial form is noted as 'very
common *c.* 1600–1730' by the OED
(and cf. *Ham.* III.i.122 'I am myself

indifferent honest').
237. *goes*] walks: the primary sense
of the verb.
239–40.] Pandarus' hyperbole is
comically complimentary to himself:
the Graces were usually called
daughters of Zeus; and for his own

were a grace, or a daughter a goddess, he should   240
take his choice. O admirable man! Paris? Paris
is dirt to him, and I warrant Helen, to change,
would give an eye to boot.

Enter Common Soldiers [*and pass over*].

Cress. Here comes more.

Pand. Asses, fools, dolts, chaff and bran, chaff and   245
bran; porridge after meat. I could live and die in
the eyes of Troilus. Ne'er look, ne'er look, the
eagles are gone: crows and daws, crows and daws.
I had rather be such a man as Troilus, than
Agamemnon and all Greece.   250

Cress. There is amongst the Greeks Achilles, a better
man than Troilus.

Pand. Achilles? A drayman, a porter, a very camel.

Cress. Well, well.

Pand. Well, well? Why, have you any discretion?   255
Have you any eyes? Do you know what a man is?
Is not birth, beauty, good shape, discourse, manhood, learning, gentleness, virtue, youth, liberality and such like, the spice and salt that season
a man?   260

Cress. Ay, a minced man; and then to be baked with

240. or] *Q,F;* and *Hanmer.*   243. an eye] *Q;* money *F;* one eye *Pope.*
244. comes] *Q;* come *F.*   246-7. in the eyes] *Q;* i'th'eyes *F.*   251. amongst]
Q; among *F.*   259. such like] *Q;* so forth *F.*   season] *Q;* seasons *F.*

daughter to be even half a goddess,
Pandarus would need to be wedded
to a divinity.

243. *an eye*] F's *money* is not only
vulgar, but also diminishes the force
of the figure (which is not Pandarus'
intention).

245-8.] Deighton pointed out the
likeness of this iteration to the idiom
of Falstaff before Shrewsbury (*1H4*
IV.ii.63 ff.).

246. *porridge*] soup or broth, usually
made with vegetables and cereal in a
meat stock (as in Scotch broth). It
was taken before the meat course, as
now, so that Pandarus' inversion

becomes all the more forceful.

248. *crows*] Apparently associated
in Shakespeare's mind with blackness, ugliness, and carrion.

daws] Like the crow, the (jack)daw
is a member of the Corvidae. Shakespeare contrasts it with the nightin-
gale (*Tw.N.* III.iv.35). It was often a
type of foolishness (cf. Sir John Daw,
in *Epicoene*).

261. *minced*] Literally, chopped fine
(in reference to the many divisions of
Troilus' excellence, as they have just
been given); but Cressida is playing
also on the allusion to cookery in
spice, salt, season. She may hint further

no date in the pie, for then the man's date is out.

Pand. You are such a woman, a man knows not at
 what ward you lie. ~~position of defence she stands~~

Cress. Upon my back, to defend my belly; upon my   265
 wit, to defend my wiles; upon my secrecy, to
 defend mine honesty; my mask, to defend my
 beauty; and you, to defend all these; and at all
 these wards I lie, at a thousand watches.

Pand. Say one of your watches.   270

262. date is] *Q;* dates *F.*   263. such a] *Q;* such another *F.*   a man] *Q;*
one *F.*   266. wiles] *Q,F;* will *conj. Johnson.*   269. lie, at] *Q;* lie at, at *F.*

at the sense *diminished, mutilated* (see
next note).

262. *no date in the pie*] Dates were
much used for flavouring and sweeten-
ing pies and other dishes (and hence
for puns by dramatists). Here, *no date*
may imply something wanting in *the
man*, as well as leading on to *date is out*
(= is out of fashion, is past his best).
The implication (if we may judge
from Pandarus' reply) is strongly
sexual.

263. *such a woman*] There seems to
be no point in following F here:
another at l. 276 loses its sense of climax
if it be a repetition.

264. *ward*] posture of defence, in
fencing (nowadays usually distinguished by French ordinal numerals).
Cf. *1H4* II.iv.190–1 ('Thou knowest
my old ward—here I lay, and thus I
bore my point'), and Nashe, *Choice of
Valentines*, l. 152 ('Poore pacient
Grisill lyeth at her warde').

265. *back*] Apart from the obvious
anatomical sense, this may also imply
armour for the back, or a rearguard:
the OED gives no example earlier
than 1648 for the former, but the
several senses (some figurative) for the
latter suggest that the metaphor may
have had a literal precedent (see
OED sv III.8, 8b, 11, 12). There may
also be a hint of the sense 'sexual
vigour'; for although the *logic* of
Cressida's remark leaves no room for

it, the word-order of this sentence, in
an exchange full of sexual innuendo,
allows the word to suggest its improper meaning before cancelling it.
Cf. also Tilley F 594.

266. *wiles*] Johnson's conjecture
'will' is very tempting: again, there
would be a logical pattern (*wit* versus
will), together with a sexual innuendo.

266–7. *my secrecy . . . mine honesty*]
Primarily, 'my power to keep a
secret, to maintain my reputation for
chastity'; but *secrecy* might also
imply genitals (cf. OED sv 3b), as
with the plural *secrets* (cf. Deuteronomy xxv.11).

267. *mask*] Sunburned faces were
reckoned ugly: cf. *Gent.* IV.iv.150–1
('she . . . threw her sun-expelling
mask away').

268. *you . . . these*] Pandarus was in
some respect guardian to his niece;
but this remark appears to make him
almost the bawd that Cressida calls
him, at l. 286.

269. *wards*] (a) places to be guarded
(as in a castle); (b) defended entrances; (c) fencing postures (as at
l. 264).

watches] (a) times or places of guard
or look out; (b) divisions of the night
(as in Latin *vigilia*; and cf. *Oth.*
I.i.123); (c) wakefulness; (d) wakes
or revels. It is hard to tell which of
these senses Pandarus implies.

Cress. Nay, I'll watch you for that, and that's one of
the chiefest of them too. If I cannot ward what I
would not have hit, I can watch you for telling
how I took the blow, unless it swell past hiding,
and then it's past watching.   275

Pand. You are such another. (sarcastic - your a fine one.)

Enter Boy.

Boy. Sir, my lord would instantly speak with you.
Pand. Where?
Boy. At your own house, there he unarms him.
Pand. Good boy, tell him I come. [*Exit Boy.*] I doubt he   280
be hurt. Fare ye well, good niece.
Cress. Adieu, uncle.
Pand. I will be with you, niece, by and by.
Cress. To bring, uncle?
Pand. Ay, a token from Troilus.   *Exit Pandarus.*   285
Cress. By the same token, you are a bawd.
　　　Words, vows, gifts, tears, and love's full sacrifice
　　　He offers in another's enterprise;
　　　But more in Troilus thousand-fold I see
　　　Than in the glass of Pandar's praise may be;   290

272. too] *F;* two *Q.*   276 S.D.] *As Q; after 275, F.*   279. there . . . him]
Q; not in F.   280 S.D.] *Capell; not in Q,F.*   283. I will be] *Q;* Ile be *F.*
284. bring, uncle?] *Hudson;* bring, Uncle. *F4;* bring vncle: *Q;* bring Vnkle. *F.*
285 S.D.] *F (after 286); not in Q.*

272-3. *ward . . . hit*] protect my
virginity (continuing the metaphor
from fencing). Quibbles of this kind
usually turn on *hit | mark*, i.e. on terms
of archery (cf. Donne, *Poems*, ed.
H. J. C. Grierson, 1912, I. 461), but
perhaps the better analogy is found
in *LLL* IV.i.119, 125 ff. See also the
quibbles in 'Silver White' (*Secular
Lyrics of the XIVth and XVth Centuries*,
ed. R. H. Robbins, 1955).

276. *You . . . another*] = you're a fine
one! (sarcastically; perhaps contemptuously): cf. Tilley A 250.

279. *there*] Presumably = *where*, but
the usage would be uncommon *c.* 1600.
Perhaps Shakespeare was affected by
the language of his sources.

283. *I will be with you*] (a) I will
visit you; (b) I will be even with you.

284. *To bring*] An intensive: OED
knows nothing of it, and examples are
more surely found than explanations.
Be with you to bring is evidently a
threat, probably jocular (though
serious in *Spanish Tragedy*, III.xii.22).
Schmidt suggests that it bore an
obscene sense when addressed to
women. Pandarus chooses to take it
literally.

290. *glass of Pandar's praise*] Not an
uncommon figure (cf. *LLL* IV.i.18),
but it takes its place with the comments on reflection by Ulysses and
Achilles (III.iii).

Yet hold I off. Women are angels, wooing:
Things won are done; joy's soul lies in the doing.
That she belov'd knows naught that knows not this:
Men prize the thing ungain'd more than it is.
That she was never yet that ever knew   295
Love got so sweet as when desire did sue.
Therefore this maxim out of love I teach:
'Achievement is command; ungain'd, beseech.'
Then though my heart's content firm love doth bear,
Nothing of that shall from mine eyes appear. *Exit.*   300

[SCENE III]

Sennet. Enter Agamemnon, Nestor, Ulysses, Diomedes,
        Menelaus, *with* Others.   (reflects Act. II ii)

Agam. Princes:
        What grief hath set these jaundies on your cheeks?

299. Then] *Q; That F.*   content] *Q; Contents F.*

Scene III

S.D. *Sennet.] F; not in Q.*   1–2. Princes . . . cheeks?] *F; one line, Q.*
2. these] *Q; the F.*   on] *F; ore Q.*

291. *wooing*] while being wooed.

292. *Things . . . doing*] there is
neither interest nor value in the prize
gained: the struggle to achieve is
what gives value (an argument found
also in the Trojan debate, in II.ii). In
Q, this line is marked, like l. 294, as
a *sententia*, by the use of inverted
commas: Q and F agree in distinguishing l. 298 by both commas
and the use of italic type. (Italic type
is used for I.iii.117, and commas for
V.ii.113.)

294. *prize*] Q's *price* is the older
form of the same verb; but the situation is complex (see OED sv *prize*).

297. *out of love*] as from love's book.

298.] Won, the woman is commanded: wooed, she is besought. Cressida
apparently agrees with Mrs Peachum
(*Beggar's Opera*, Air IX): 'O Polly,
you might have toy'd and kist. / By
keeping men off, you keep them on.'

299. *Then . . . content*] F's *contents* is
really an indifferent variant, the
plural form being often construed as
singular in the seventeenth century;
but *that* (= so that) deserves more
respect, being the ground of a slightly
different argument. In Q, Cressida's
final couplet is a separate statement:
in F, it is a consequence of l. 297.

Scene III

S.D.] Diomedes remains mute, but
is necessarily present at a full council.

1–30.] According to Coriolanus,
his mother habitually used arguments
similar to those used here by Agamemnon (*Cor.* IV.i.3–9).

2. *these jaundies*] Jaundice is 'a
morbid condition caused by obstruc-
tion of the bile' (OED), of which the
symptoms are yellowness (*jaunesse*) of
skin, fluids and tissues, together with
physical weakness, loss of appetite,

The ample proposition that hope makes
In all designs begun on earth below
Fails in the promis'd largeness: checks and disasters   5
Grow in the veins of actions highest rear'd,
As knots, by the conflux of meeting sap,
Infects the sound pine and diverts his grain
Tortive and errant from his course of growth.
Nor, princes, is it matter new to us   10
That we come short of our suppose so far
That after seven years' siege yet Troy walls stand,

8. Infects] Q; Infect F.

and constipation. The word is, strictly, singular (cf. the forms *iaunes*, *iaunyce*) and the *d* is a phonetic accretion: in 1600 it was indifferently singular or plural (cf. the true plural forms of other complaints—mumps, measles, etc). The F reading gives no indication of number: Q *may* be wrong in reading *ore* (= o'er) instead of F *on*; but it is hard to know what ways of thinking about disease are implied in lay usage. Symptoms, considered figuratively, could be seen *in* the face (cf. *Rom.* v.iii.94–5: 'Beauty's ensign yet / Is crimson in thy lips and in thy cheeks'); and Shakespeare's only other use of the word *jaundice* does not help (*Mer. V.* 1.i.85: 'creep into the jaundice').

3. *proposition*] OED explains as 'putting forward for acceptance; an offer' (citing this line), although sense 6 ('something put forward as a scheme or plan of action') is equally plausible.

5–6. *checks . . . rear'd*] The general drift is obvious, but particular terms are hard to gloss. *Disasters* is only in part figurative (= misfortune): otherwise, it holds some of its literal meaning of adverse planetary influence. *Checks* = restraints upon action (perhaps by a supernatural power), but Shakespeare uses the *verb*, at least, to imply the slowing of growth in plants (cf. Sonnets 5, 1.7, and 15, 1.6); so that in the present passage, the con-

nection, by way of *Grow*, with *sap* and *pine*, is clear. *Veins* = apparently the general metaphorical sense of 'inward parts', perhaps 'vessels': *rear'd* = raised; but *veins* again looks forward to the vegetable metaphor (cf. Chaucer, *Canterbury Tales*, General Prologue, l. 3: 'bathed every veyne in swich licour').

8. *Infects*] spoils, affects injuriously. I follow Q, although *Infect* (F) is grammatically correct, and Q was obviously influenced by the singular *sap* (as if that were the subject); yet such solecisms are common in Shakespeare.

9. *Tortive*] twisted, contorted. Apparently a Shakespearean coinage: eighteenth-century editors complained of the vocabulary of this play as 'bombastical' (e.g. Tyrwhitt, *Var.* '78), and indeed some of its less usual words seem a little affected, as Marston's do.

11. *suppose*] expectation (OED, citing this line: the other example of the sense is Munday's (1602)—about the date of this play, so that credit for the usage, if it be distinct, can hardly be given). A better interpretation might be sense 4 (purpose, intention), for Agamemnon speaks of *designs*, *aim*, and *surmised shape*, as well as of *hope*.

12. *seven years*] This fits Caxton's chronology, in that Hector died in the seventh year of the siege; but it is

Sith every action that hath gone before
Whereof we have record, trial did draw
Bias and thwart, not answering the aim   15
And that unbodied figure of the thought
That gave't surmised shape. Why then, you princes,
Do you with cheeks abash'd behold our works,
And call them shames which are indeed naught else
But the protractive trials of great Jove   20
To find persistive constancy in men,
The fineness of which metal is not found
In fortune's love? For then the bold and coward,
The wise and fool, the artist and unread,
The hard and soft, seem all affin'd and kin;   25
But in the wind and tempest of her frown,
Distinction, with a broad and powerful fan
Puffing at all, winnows the light away,
And what hath mass or matter by itself
Lies rich in virtue and unmingled.   30
Nest. With due observance of thy godlike seat,
Great Agamemnon, Nestor shall apply
Thy latest words. In the reproof of chance
Lies the true proof of men. The sea being smooth,

---

13. every] *F;* euer *Q.*   19. call] *Q;* thinke *F.*   shames] *Q;* shame *F.*
27. broad] *Q;* lowd *F.*   31. thy godlike] *Theobald;* the godlike *Q;* thy godly
F; thy goodly *Pope.*

---

too late for the death of Patroclus, and
too early for Achilles' love for
Polixena.

15. *Bias and thwart*] crookedly and
sideways (both terms are adverbial).

20. *protractive*] lengthening out,
delaying (apparently no recorded
example before this).

21. *persistive*] Apparently another
coinage: curiously enough, *persistent*,
the modern term, has not been found
earlier than the nineteenth century.

22. *metal*] Cf. the Biblical images of
refining and purgation, in Job
xxiii.10, and Zechariah xiii.9 (and
perhaps Hebrews xii.6).

24. *artist*] learned man, scholar.

25. *affin'd*] connected, related.

27. *fan*] implement for winnowing

(cf. Matthew iii.12).

30. *virtue*] excellence, ability, distinction.

31. *observance of*] respect for.

seat] dignity of office (implied by a
chair or throne belonging to it).

32. *apply*] gloss, expound (as with a
learned text). Nestor intends to draw
from Agamemnon's general principles
the particular lesson appropriate to
the Greeks.

33–4.] Cf. Tilley C 715: 'Great
courage is in greatest dangers tried'.

34–6. *The sea . . . breast*] Cf. Tilley
S 174 ('In a calm sea every man may
be a pilot') and Erasmus, *Adagia*
104E ('Tranquillo quilibet guber-
nator est').

How many shallow bauble boats dare sail   35
Upon her patient breast, making their way
With those of nobler bulk;
But let the ruffian Boreas once enrage *(North. North East Win)*

(sea God) The gentle Thetis, and anon behold
The strong-ribb'd bark through liquid mountains cut,
Bounding between the two moist elements
Like Perseus' horse. Where's then the saucy boat   41
Whose weak untimber'd sides but even now
Co-rivall'd greatness? Either to harbour fled,
Or made a toast for Neptune. Even so   45
Doth valour's show and valour's worth divide
In storms of fortune; for in her ray and brightness

36. patient] *F;* ancient *Q.*

35. *bauble*] trivial, toy-like: an attributive use, again possibly a coinage by Shakespeare, who elsewhere uses the noun for boat-shaped objects—*Shr.* IV.iii.82: 'a paltry cap, / A custard-coffin, a bauble, a silken pie'—and even for a fleet—*Cym.* III.i.27-8: 'his shipping / (Poor ignorant baubles!)'.

36. *patient*] F seems plainly right here: the problem is merely how Q produced *ancient*. It has been suggested that its copy read *pacient*, and that damage deleted the *p*, thus leaving what was read as *ācient*. Evidence is wanting, but some such theory is needed to explain the Q reading.

38. *Boreas*] the N.N.E. wind: frequently the N. wind.

39. *Thetis*] a sea-goddess, and mother of Achilles: by metonymy, the sea, at least since Virgil's fourth Eclogue. Deighton cited Marlowe, *2 Tamburlaine,* I.vi.41-2: 'The sun . . . / Shall hide his head in Thetis' watery lap.'

40.] There seems to be a close parallel (especially in view of *ruffian Boreas* at l. 38) with *Oth.* II.i.7-9: 'If it ha' ruffian'd so upon the sea, / What ribs of oak, when the huge mountains melt, / Can hold the mortise?'

41. *two moist elements*] air and water. Each of the four elements had two qualities: fire, hot and dry; air, hot and wet; water, cold and wet; earth, cold and dry.

42. *Perseus' horse*] Pegasus, the winged horse, ridden by both Perseus and Bellerophon. He was born of the blood of the dead Medusa, upon whom he was begotten by Poseidon (which may explain why Shakespeare associates him with both moist elements: he was derived from the sea-god, and he could fly).

saucy] impudent.

43. *untimber'd*] without a frame of strong timbers; perhaps, undecked, without cross-members (not otherwise noted by OED until 1814—in a passage based on this speech—but not therefore a coinage by Shakespeare). *Timbered* usually had the sense of well-made, strong; and *untimbered* may be merely a simple antonym.

44. *Co-rivall'd*] vied with. Q uses the obsolete, F the modern spelling (considering the verb as being formed from the noun); but OED gives the verb only as *corrival*, citing Marston.

45. *toast*] fragment of toasted bread, taken in wine.

The herd hath more annoyance by the breese
Than by the tiger; but when the splitting wind
Makes flexible the knees of knotted oaks,   50
And flies flee under shade, why then the thing of courage,
As rous'd with rage, with rage doth sympathize,
And, with an accent tun'd in self-same key,
Retires to chiding fortune.

Ulyss.   Agamemnon,
Thou great commander, nerves and bone of Greece,   55
Heart of our numbers, soul and only sprite,
In whom the tempers and the minds of all
Should be shut up, hear what Ulysses speaks.
Besides th'applause and approbation
[*To Agamemnon.*] The which, most mighty for thy
    place and sway,   60
[*To Nestor.*]   And thou, most reverend for thy
    stretch'd-out life,

51. flee] *Capell;* fled *Q,F.*   54. Retires] *Q,F(subst.)*; Returns *Pope;* Replies
Hanmer; Retorts *Hudson, conj. Dyce.*   55. nerves] *Q;* nerve *F.*   56. sprite]
Q (spright); spirit *F.*   59. th'applause] *Q;* the applause *F.*   60 S.D.] *Rowe*
(subst.); not in Q,F.   61 S.D.] *Rowe (subst.); not in Q,F.*   61. thy] *F;* the *Q.*

48. *breese*] gadfly: it is usual to distinguish the word, by this spelling, from breeze (= light wind), although the form is archaic.

50. *knees*] Craig noticed but rejected as irrelevant the fact that timber naturally grown bent is used for ship-building and is called knee-timber. The term is most often applied to oak and makes better sense of the metaphor. Knee-timber is the toughest and least flexible of wood, and was by nature the shape required: cf. Bacon, *Essays,* 'Of Goodness, and Goodness of Nature' ('knee-timber, that is good for ships that are ordained to be tossed').

51.] An Alexandrine: F has used it to make space (with ten lines to go to the foot of a page): cf. the white space round the S.D. at I.ii.254, and at I.ii.290 (both in the first column of this same page).

flee] Capell's emendation preserves grammar and the proper sequence of tenses, and rests upon the assumption that Q misread *e* as *d*—the most likely of all mistakes if Q's copy were in Secretary hand.

52. *sympathize*] correspond to, match.

54. *Retires to*] rages against. Hulme relates the root *-tire* to tear (= rant, bluster, 'go on') (pp. 261–2).

55. *nerves*] sinews; the usual sense in Shakespeare. The plural form (= strength of the body) is almost invariably employed; whereas *bone* (= firmness of frame) is as frequently found in the singular. I therefore follow Q: F has merely tried to be consistent.

56. *sprite*] Shakespeare normally uses the form *spirit* for those senses relevant here (animating principle, vital power) as well as for energy or mettle: *sprite* probably indicates the pronunciation for both forms.

57. *tempers*] dispositions.

58. *shut up*] enclosed: embodied; perhaps subsumed.

61. *stretch'd-out life*] Nestor's exact

I give to both your speeches, which were such
As Agamemnon and the hand of Greece
Should hold up high in brass; and such again
As venerable Nestor, hatch'd in silver,   65
Should with a bond of air, strong as the axletree
On which heaven rides, knit all the Greekish ears
To his experienc'd tongue—yet let it please both,
Thou great, and wise, to hear Ulysses speak.

67. On . . . rides] *Q;* In which the Heavens ride *F.*   the Greekish] *Q;* all
Greekes *F.*

age is doubtful; but he was by this
time ruling over a third generation
(cf. iv.v.195-6, 'I knew thy grandsire, / And once fought with him').
The point is clear from Lydgate
(1.4147-97), who describes the fight,
and from Homer (*Iliad*, 1.273), who
counts the generations.

62-7. *which were . . . rides*] This
passage presents difficulty largely
because of Shakespeare's fluid syntax
and ambiguous imagery. Ulysses
begins by praising both Agamemnon
and Nestor, while deferentially implying that he himself has something
of value to say: he therefore offers
variations on two traditional images.
First, Agamemnon's speech was such
that the speaker (and the hand of
Greece) should hold it up in brass;
and, secondly, Nestor's was such that
all the Greeks (and not merely the
generals then present) should have
been bound to his eloquence by a
bond paradoxically strong—mere air
as mighty as the axis of the universe.
The drift is clear; but it may seem odd
(a) that Agamemnon should hold up
his own inscribed speech; (b) that the
exact nature of 'the hand of Greece'
should be uncertain; and (c) that
while the 'brass' applies to the monumental status of the speech, the
'silver' applies (strictly) to Nestor
himself. Symmetry and logic have
deferred to the power of association.
(The alternative to this reading is
drastic: to take Agamemnon (l. 63)
and Nestor (l. 65) as vocatives, to

emend *and the hand* to *all the hands,* and
(necessarily) to read *thy experienc'd* for
his experienc'd.)

66-7. *axletree . . . rides*] In the
Ptolemaic astronomy, the heavens
and all the heavenly bodies revolved
about the earth.

67-8.] For an illustration of this
figure, see George Puttenham, *The
Arte of English Poesie,* iii.ii: 'At least
waies, I find this opinion confirmed
by a pretie deuise or embleme that
Lucianus alleageth he saw in the
pourtrait of *Hercules* . . . where they
had figured a lustie old man with a
long chayne tyed by one end at his
tong, by the other end at the peoples
eares, who stood afar of and seemed
to be drawen to him by the force of
that chayne fastned to his tong, as
who would say, by force of his
perswasions' (*Elizabethan Critical
Essays,* ed. G. Gregory Smith, 1904,
Vol. ii, p. 147). The remainder of the
paragraph is an interesting defence of
the wisdom and eloquence of old men.

67. *Greekish*] The older adjectival
form, supplanted by *Greek* during the
seventeenth century. Shakespeare uses
the older form, together with *Greek*
and *Grecian,* with no apparent preference, except that *Greekish* occurs
only in this play. F's version of this
line strikes me as especially awkward
for an actor to speak. Walker (NCS)
dismisses it as 'a typical Compositor B
perversion'; but it might equally well
be authorial.

69. *great, and wise*] The punctuation

Agam. Speak, Prince of Ithaca, and be't of less expect   70
    That matter needless, of importless burden,
    Divide thy lips, than we are confident
    When rank Thersites opes his mastic jaws
    We shall hear music, wit, and oracle.
Ulyss. Troy yet upon his basis had been down   75

70–5. *Agam.* . . . . *Ulyss.*] *F; not in Q.*   73. mastic] *F; mastiff Rowe; mastive*
Var. '21; nasty conj. Orger.   75. basis] *F; bases Q.*

of F may suggest that Ulysses is politely distinguishing Nestor from Agamemnon.

70–4.] Plainly Ulysses expects, and should receive, a reply: he has been elaborately diffident, and he has made a request. The lines omitted by Q are ponderous, and that may be why they are wanting, but they are in Agamemnon's usual style.

70. *expect*] expectation: noted as rare by OED, which, however, cites an example from 1597. (For the form, cf. *suppose* at l. 11 above.)

71. *importless*] without significance: trivial.

73. *rank*] Usually glossed as 'foul', 'gross', 'disgusting'; but other senses may be relevant: e.g. rancid, strong-smelling, licentious, festering.

mastic] A difficult term (but cf. masticate). Commentators have suggested that it is the name of a substance used for filling teeth, (though OED gives no such sense). Emendations proposed include *mastiff* (Thersites is always biting—cf. *indistinguishable cur* at v.i.27), *mastix* (scourge or satirist; but the word is usually found in combination—*Histriomastix* etc.—although the emendation *might* imply an allusion to the War of the Theatres), and even *nasty* (which is right in sense, but is unlikely to have given rise to the more difficult reading *mastic*). There is nothing else in the play which can be offered as certain reference to the War of the Theatres, and one ought not therefore to emend in order to support such a theory. Mastic was known to

have medicinal properties, and the OED's citation from Gerard is of interest: Shakespeare almost certainly knew the *Herball* (cf. J. W. Lever's note on *LLL* v.ii.887–8: *RES*, n.s. 3, 1952, p. 117), and Gerard's spelling is that of the F ('The Rosen is called . . . in Latine *Lentiscina Resina*, and likewise Mastiche: in Shops Mastix: . . . in English Masticke'). Shakespeare *may* have known that mastic was used in the East as a chewing gum: he may even have known that the Greek μαστίχη was perhaps connected with the verbs 'to chew' or 'to gnash the teeth': he could see the analogy with *masticate* for himself. On the other hand, he may have looked no further than Sidney's *Arcadia* II (1593), the second Eclogue: '. . . an old acquaintance of his called Mastix (one of the repiningest fellows in the world, and that beheld nobody but with a mind of mislike).'

75–137.] Ulysses' speech is discussed in Appendix IV, pp. 321–2. Editors have demonstrated that it is an argument familiar during the sixteenth century, depending as it does on the notion of order as a harmony of parts, under the rule of a single head, and finding analogies in the natural world. The force of the speech, by itself, is considerable; but in context it has little effect; and it is not a text to which the play is a sermon.

75. *basis*] Q's *bases* is possible—Shakespeare uses the plural elsewhere—but ll. 75–6 seem to argue from singulars.

And the great Hector's sword had lack'd a master
But for these instances.
The specialty of rule hath been neglected,
And look how many Grecian tents do stand
Hollow upon this plain, so many hollow factions.   80
When that the general is not like the hive
To whom the foragers shall all repair,
What honey is expected? Degree being vizarded,
Th'unworthiest shows as fairly in the mask.
The heavens themselves, the planets, and this centre   85

77. *instances*] 'case[s] adduced in objection to or disproof of a universal assertion' (OED). The term belongs to scholastic logic: Ulysses, although appealing in the end to the passions, begins as a strict disputant.

78. *specialty*] Either as in OED 5 ('a thing specially belonging or attached to one person; a special possession, distinction, favour, or charge'), or as in OED 7 ('*Law*. A special contract, obligation, or bond, expressed in an instrument under seal'). Shakespeare elsewhere uses the second sense only in the plural.

79. *look how many*] just as many (corresponding to its correlative *so many* in l. 80: cf. the Latin *toties . . . quoties*). The formula *look how / look what* usually introduces a comparison, and needs no intrusive comma after *look*: cf. *Venus and Adonis*, ll. 299, 815; Sonnet 37, l. 13. The point was clarified by Mark Eccles, *JEGP*, XLII (1943), p. 386.

80. *Hollow*] Hanmer omitted the word—plausibly, for the sake of the metre: Steevens, on the other hand, omitted *hollow* for the same reason. But emendation is not necessary: the hollowness of the factions (empty, unproductive, 'not answering inwardly to outward appearance' (OED), insincere, false) matches that of the tents (the least substantial of all shelters).

82. *foragers*] Shakespeare's only use of the noun. His normal use of *forage*

(both noun and verb) concerns preying or ravaging, a sense hardly proper here; but other writers use *foragers* in its military sense (= those who go out to collect food for the army), which answers well to the function of those worker bees (now always known as foragers) which gather the nectar. The term embodies the metaphor implied throughout ll. 81–3.

83. *Degree*] rank, especially high rank, but perhaps also order of precedence, and hierarchy (cf. l. 86). To *vizard* one is to vizard the other.

84. *mask*] Corresponding to the 'vizard' implied in the verb (*vizard*) of l. 83, and not the 'masque' supposed by Deighton; i.e. if the ruler be hidden by a mask, as the subject is, then both are indistinguishable: similarly, if the principle of order be hidden (= lost), then value ('the unworthiest') is lost also. Ulysses, like Troilus in II.ii, is erecting a theory of value upon an assertion, but whereas Troilus' assertion is personal, that of Ulysses is general and analogical. (It is not, however, a point likely to be noticed by an audience that agreed with Ulysses.) Ulysses begins, in these lines, with the relationship of worth and identity: Troilus ends in v.ii with an enactment of the same notion.

85. *centre*] the earth, which was the point about which, in the Ptolemaic system, all other heavenly bodies moved.

Observe degree, priority, and place,
Insisture, course, proportion, season, form,
Office, and custom, in all line of order.
And therefore is the glorious planet Sol
In noble eminence enthron'd and spher'd   90
Amidst the other; whose med'cinable eye
Corrects the influence of evil planets,
And posts like the commandment of a king,
Sans check, to good and bad. But when the planets
In evil mixture to disorder wander,   95

92. influence . . . planets] *Q;* ill Aspects of Planets evill *F.*   94. check] *Q;*
check, *F.*

86. *degree*] order of precedence.

87. *Insisture*] a nonce-word, and dictionaries and commentators can only guess. Relevant senses of the Latin *insisto* are 'stop', 'stand still': 'persist', 'hold on'; and *insistere vestigia* = follow / tread in the steps (cf. the order *insisture, course* . . .). Two senses are therefore plausible: (a) steady continuance of motion; (b) the moment of (apparent) stasis, when a planet, as viewed from the earth, seems to pause before reversing its former motion. Walker (NCS) objects to the latter interpretation (from Baldwin, *Variorum*) as too technical; but Shakespearean characters are familiar with such a complex notion of astronomy as the retrograde motion of Mars (e.g. Helena in *All's W.* I.i.194; Claudius in *Ham.* I.ii.114), and the two senses of stasis and motion suggested here are the primary senses for the verb *insist* in 1600.

88. *line*] rule, principle (Schmidt): a metaphorical sense derived from the cord or string used, in building or surveying, to determine directions or planes (cf. *Tp.* IV.i.239, 'we steal by line and level').

89. *planet*] any heavenly body having apparent motion against the fixed stars, and therefore (in the Ptolemaic system) including the sun (which was still called a planet as late as 1727).

90. *spher'd*] set in a sphere, i.e. placed in the transparent sphere in which each planet was thought to move.

91. *other*] uninflected plural form, common from the tenth to the eighteenth century.

med'cinable] healing, curative.

92.] Q's reading is to be preferred: F's *aspects* (= way in which planets looked on each other) was commonly used for the way in which they looked upon the earth, and hence *might* have been confused with the influence which they exerted; but even so, such an interpretation confuses cause and effect (*aspect* produces *influence*). Besides, ill and evil are almost tautologous, and the inversion of noun and adjective (*planets evil*) is very awkward (although not unknown elsewhere in Shakespeare).

93. *posts*] travels as fast as may be. The postal service was primarily for the transmission of royal and governmental documents: post-masters were to provide relays of fast horses. The subject of *posts* is *eye*: the sun itself kept due order (as, by implication, Agamemnon also should do).

94. *check*] I follow Q, Cambridge, and Deighton: the word refers forward to the next phrase, and not (as with F's comma) back to *posts*.

95. *mixture*] (effectually), relationship (cf. OED sv, especially 1 e =

What plagues and what portents, what mutiny,
What raging of the sea, shaking of earth,
Commotion in the winds, frights, changes, horrors,
Divert and crack, rend and deracinate
The unity and married calm of states   100
Quite from their fixure! O, when degree is shak'd,
Which is the ladder of all high designs,
The enterprise is sick. How could communities,
Degrees in schools, and brotherhoods in cities,
Peaceful commerce from dividable shores,   105
The primogenity and due of birth,

96. mutiny,] *Q;* mutiny? *F.*   97. sea,] *Q;* Sea? *F.*   earth,] *Q;* Earth? *F.*
98. winds,] *Q;* Windes? *F.*   101. fixure!] *F;* fixure: *Q.*   102. of] *Q;* to *F.*
106. primogenity] *Q* (primogenitie); primogenitiue *F.*

sexual intercourse, a sense often implied punningly in respect of planetary conjunction—e.g. *2H4* II.iv.261–2: 'Saturn and Venus this year in conjunction! What says th' almanac to that?').

to disorder] so that disorder will ensue.

99. *Divert*] turn awry, against the course of nature.

deracinate] uproot, extirpate (Schmidt): apparently not found before Shakespeare either for the literal sense (*H5* v.ii.47) or for the figurative (here only, in the plays).

101. *fixure*] fixedness, stability. OED cites its first example from Drayton (1603), but presumably the present occurrence is the earlier (1602/3, and not 1609). For the form, cf. II.iii.110, *flexure*, dating from 1592, but see also OED under the article *-ure.*

102.] Cf. Tilley S 848.

of] I follow Q with hesitation. *Degree* and *ladder* are semantically connected, and one need not suppose that the ladder is merely the symbol of degree: that, degree being necessary, but *not* as a means of ascent, the ladder belongs to the designs, and hence *of* is correct. Yet that which is the condition of an action might be considered a means to that action; and the connection of *ladder* with *high*

(which entails the reading *to*) could be Shakespeare's, just as much as a compositor's or scribe's. To read *of* is to require strict logic: to read *to* is to admit associations of sense and image.

103. *sick*] Health, as much as order, is the theme of the speech; and health depended upon proper regulation and balance within the body. The sun (= Agamemnon) has (quite apart from his astrological function) a *med'cinable eye* (l. 91), and rulers were not only holy but healing: cf. the practice of touching for the 'Evil', which was emphasized in Edward the Confessor (*Mac.* IV.iii.141 ff.), and which persisted as late as the infancy of Samuel Johnson (Boswell's *Life,* ed. R. W. Chapman, 1953, p. 32).

104. *Degrees*] academic ranks.

brotherhoods] guilds, societies: perhaps 'corporations', 'companies' (Johnson).

105. *commerce*] Stressed on the second syllable.

dividable] Stressed on the first syllable. Almost certainly, the suffix has the active sense, and the term means 'dividing', 'separating'; but it has not elsewhere been found with this meaning.

106. *primogenity*] right of succession or inheritance of the first-born. The

Prerogative of age, crowns, sceptres, laurels,
But by degree stand in authentic place?
Take but degree away, untune that string,
And hark what discord follows. Each thing melts   110
In mere oppugnancy; the bounded waters
Should lift their bosoms higher than the shores,
And make a sop of all this solid globe;
Strength should be lord of imbecility,

110. melts] *Q;* meetes *F.*

usual term was *primogeniture*: it occurs (meaning 'the fact of being first-born') as early as the thirteenth century, but the two senses concerning legal inheritance date respectively from 1602 and 1631. To assume that Shakespeare wrote *primogeniture* is to assume also that Q and F have both misread (or that F was affected by *prerogative*, immediately below). To assume that F is right means that Q omitted one letter (which is easy enough), but it means also that F has produced a nonce-word. Since F is quite as likely to have been affected by *prerogative*, it seems better to trust Q. There is, after all, the noun *primogenit* (twelfth to seventeenth century), normally used in legal and theological contexts, and which could lead to another nonce-word by the addition of -*y* (cf. OED under the article -*y suffix*[3], '. . . a living formative for abstract nouns of quality or condition'). Of the possibility that *primogenitiue* should have stood in Q, we may note that Q's form *primogenitie* occurs on B4, a page apparently set by Eld's Compositor B; and this man preferred -*ie* for abstract nouns in -*y* (cf. *specialtie, prioritie, mutinie, unitie,* all on the same page). Had the reading occurred on a page set by Eld A (who preferred -*y*) one might have argued with more confidence that the letter -*u*- had been dropped; but since B, if faced with *primogenity* in his copy, was likely to spell it with -*ie,* one cannot therefore deduce that he omitted a letter, merely because -*ie* stands as what he

set. Whatever form one chooses implies that *due of birth* is not a separate entity but a synonym or gloss.

108. *authentic*] 'as possessing original or inherent authority . . .; entitled to obedience or respect' (OED).

110. *melts*] I follow Q, while admitting the propriety of F's reading. *Meets* carries with it the sense of violent contrast and opposition, and seems to imply that the process of collision is endless: on the other hand, *melts,* although apparently less forceful, looks forward to the universal self-destruction of ll. 119–24, and embodies the disfiguring, the unshaping, of creation and all creatures which leads to it. (*Melt* and its synonyms are Shakespeare's recurrent metaphor for dissolution of identity, as Professor Brooks notes: cf. *Ant.* IV.xiv.10, 'The rack dislimns'; IV.xv.63, 'The crown o' the earth doth melt'.) Notice also the association (referred to in the note to l. 40, above) of stormy seas and *melting* (*Oth.* II.i.7–9).

111. *oppugnancy*] antagonism, conflict, opposition.

112. *bosoms*] Used (though normally in the singular) by Shakespeare for the surface of the earth or sea, or for that part of the air which supports a flying object.

113. *sop*] fragment of food dipped or soaked in liquid, as in John xiii.26. (Cf. the *toast* of l. 45; but Ulysses is more extravagant and apocalyptic than Nestor.)

114.] The strong would rule the

And the rude son should strike his father dead;   115
Force should be right—or rather, right and wrong,
Between whose endless jar justice resides,
Should lose their names, and so should justice too.
Then everything includes itself in power,
Power into will, will into appetite,   120
And appetite, an universal wolf,

117. resides] (recides) _Q, F;_ presides _Hanmer._   118. lose] _F3;_ loose _Q,F._
their] _Q;_ her _F._   119. includes] _F;_ include _Q, Johnson._

weak (_imbecility_ = feebleness, impo-
tence), with the consequence that
youth would overmaster age—which
ought, in terms of the thesis of the
speech, to be dominant by reason of
experience and wisdom. Of this, l. 115
gives a particular instance, complicated by breaking a natural tie;
but age of itself should be enough to
awaken reverence: cf. _Oth._ 1.ii.60–1
('Good signior, you shall more command with years / Than with your
weapons'). There is no difficulty in
the lines, read thus; and the ingenuity
of early editors was pointless.

116.] Cf. Tilley M 922.

117. _resides_] keeps its place _or_
inheres in. Shakespeare's grammar
causes some difficulty: nothing can
remain between a fight, but only
between the warring parties. _Justice_
is not equated with _right_: it lies somewhere between the _claims_ of two
parties to a quarrel, one of whom is
predominantly right, but whose case
is not identical with strict and impartial judgement. Justice, therefore,
inheres in their state of opposition: it
derives from their contest (cf. Aristotle, _Ethics,_ v. 4).

119–20.] Everything (because only
power has authority) grows merely
powerful: powerful things grow merely
self-willed (depending upon their
own judgements): self-will grows into
self-gratification. _Will,_ of course, is an
ambiguous term, and embodies already the sliding from egotism to lust.

119. _includes_] Johnson followed Q,
thus apparently reading _everything_ as

plural, and it is tempting to follow
him; but there seems to be no certain
evidence that _everything_ was thought of
as plural (despite its sense of _all_), and
plenty that writers have used it
specifically as a singular (= each
thing). The omission of _-s_ in Q would
have been easy: I therefore follow F.
The sense is more difficult. OED suggests 'to enclose within [non-material]
limits': Schmidt, 'to terminate', 'to
come to in the end'. Capell put the
latter sense in the words 'converts
itself into'. Walker (NCS) prefers the
idea of 'embodiment', and compares
this with 'shut up' (l. 58), though
giving no argument except from context. The only Shakespearean parallel
supports Schmidt (_Gent._ v.iv.158).
The problem is complicated because,
while the present line reads _includes . . .
in,_ the next line twice reads _into._
Either Shakespeare intended OED's
sense for this line, and Schmidt's for
l. 120, or he had in mind _both_ senses
for both lines, but the notions of pro-
gressive constriction and of development towards an end affected his
choice of preposition.

121–4. _wolf . . . eat up himself_] This
celebrated image, of cannibalism as
the last consequence of disorder, is
found also in _Lr_ iv.ii.49–50
('Humanity must perforce prey on
itself, / Like monsters of the deep')
and in the Shakespearean addition to
Sir Thomas More, ll. 86–7 ('men like
ravenous fishes / Would feed on one
another'). The importance of the
image in the canon is discussed by

So doubly seconded with will and power,
Must make perforce an universal prey,
And last eat up himself. Great Agamemnon,
This chaos, when degree is suffocate,　　125
Follows the choking;
And this neglection of degree it is
That by a pace goes backward, with a purpose
It hath to climb. The general's disdain'd
By him one step below, he by the next,　　130
The next by him beneath: so every step,
Exampled by the first pace that is sick
Of his superior, grows to an envious fever
Of pale and bloodless emulation.

127. it is] *Q;* is it *F.*　　128. with] *Q;* in *F.*

R. W. Chambers (*Shakespeare's Hand in the Play of Sir Thomas More*); the history of the image before Shakespeare used it, in the note to the *Lear* passage by Muir (New Arden edn). Baldwin (in *Variorum*) sees the appetite as the *envious fever* (l. 133) and cites St Augustine: *Inuidus vir . . . ut lupus rapax insanit inaniter . . . ad nihilum redigitur.* There seems no reason to suppose that any *one* appetite is meant, since other passions, or rather, deadly sins, are described in this way in the play (e.g. II.iii.156, 'He that is proud eats up himself'; v.iv.32–5, 'What's become of the wenching rogues? I think they have swallowed one another. I would laugh at that miracle; yet in a sort lechery eats itself').

125. *suffocate*] smothered, stifled. Shakespeare uses only this uninflected form of the participle: the inflected form appears to have superseded it in the mid-seventeenth century.

127. *neglection*] disregard. Shakespeare uses this form, and *neglect*, and *negligence*, indifferently.

128–9.] 'That goes backward step by step . . . with a design in each man to aggrandise himself, by slighting his immediate superiour' (Johnson). Inversion of proper order produces retrogression, not progress.

132. *Exampled*] justified by precedent.

132–3. *sick . . . superior*] i.e. the superior is the disease. (For the conceit of person as disease cf. *Ado* I.i.81, 'If he have caught the Benedick'.)

133–4. *envious . . . emulation*] Shakespeare's normal use of *bloodless* implies pallor and lifelessness: Johnson glossed bloodless emulation as 'An emulation not vigorous and active, but malignant and sluggish', thus emphasizing not only the torpor of envy (blood = vigour, life) but also the infection which it carried. OED does not recognize (save for one example in the Douai Bible) a fully pejorative sense for *emulation*, but gives as the worst sense 'grudge against the superiority of others'. Schmidt, on the other hand, includes *envy* in the sense of the whole group of words *emulation / emulator / emulous*, with the single exception of the last at IV.i.29. *Envious fever* at any rate, intensifies this implication. Envy had been represented as pale, at least since Ovid, (*Metamorphoses*, II.775, 'Pallor in ore sedet'), and in Alciati's *Emblems* LXXI (see note in *Variorum*), but there was a strong medieval tradition as well: cf. Langland, *Piers Plowman* (B-text), Passus

And 'tis this fever that keeps Troy on foot,   135
Not her own sinews. To end a tale of length,
Troy in our weakness stands, not in her strength.

Nest. Most wisely hath Ulysses here discover'd
The fever whereof all our power is sick.

Agam. The nature of the sickness found, Ulysses,   140
What is the remedy?

Ulyss. The great Achilles, whom opinion crowns
The sinew and the forehand of our host,   *seat of strength*
Having his ear full of his airy fame,   *fragile, vulnerable*
Grows dainty of his worth, and in his tent   145   *too nice*
Lies mocking our designs: with him Patroclus
Upon a lazy bed the livelong day
Breaks scurril jests,   *(vulgarly abusive.)*

137. stands] *Q;* liues *F.*

v. 78, 'He was as pale as a pelet · in
the palsye he semed'.

137. *stands*] I prefer Q's reading to
F's *lives*: the drift of the argument has
been that the Greeks are sick (although
not mortally so) and the Trojans
therefore strong; hence Troy *stands*,
and does not lie prone.

139. *power*] armed force.

142.] Ulysses pointedly makes no
direct reply to Agamemnon's question: his speech is apparently intended
to stir the Greek leaders to action by
moving their passions, and any more
specific answer would have come later;
but the entry of Æneas relieves him of
the necessity.

opinion] repute, public estimation.

143. *sinew . . . forehand*] *sinew* =
tendon, but also = seat of strength,
and hence strength itself: *forehand* is
usually explained as advantage; the
advantageous position (tactically considered—that is, forward, or ahead);
that which holds such a position. The
adjective (in archery) appears to
carry with it implications of great
strength. But the phrase here may
perhaps be meant to stand for
forehand sinew, i.e. the strongest member.

144. *airy*] Walker (NCS) suggests

'lofty' and 'in everyone's mouth' (cf.
aura popularis), which is attractive:
Latin *aereus* meant high, and that
sense was also to be found in Marlowe
(*Dr Faustus*, 1.126, 'Shadowing more
beauty in their airy brows'). Yet I
cannot avoid feeling that something
pejorative may also have been implied: the *bond of air* (1.iii.66) which
knitted Nestor's tongue to his auditors
was meant to be paradoxically slight;
Shakespeare's commonest sense for
airy seems to have been *insubstantial*;
and the association here with *fame*
(which might also mean mere rumour,
as well as reputation) appears to
emphasize the fragility, the vulner-
ability of the excellence which is
attributed to Achilles.

145. *dainty*] too nice, too solicitous.
Oddly enough (in view of the ensuing
phrase) the word derives, through Old
French, from Latin *dignitatem* (worthiness): *dainty of his worth*, therefore,
opposes the good and ill senses of
what is essentially the same word.

147. *livelong*] OED glosses as 'an
emotional intensive of long'. Shakespeare uses it only twice. Apparently,
exasperation is beginning to show
through the formal speech of Ulysses.

148. *scurril*] scurrilous.

And with ridiculous and awkward action,
Which, slanderer, he imitation calls,   150
He pageants us. Sometime, great Agamemnon,
Thy topless deputation he puts on,
And like a strutting player, <u>whose conceit</u> ⎤   *whose wit lies*
Lies in his hamstring and doth think it rich ⎦   *in his thighs*
To hear the wooden dialogue and sound   155
'Twixt his stretch'd footing and the scaffoldage,
Such to-be-pitied and o'er-wrested seeming
He acts thy greatness in; and when he speaks,

---

149. awkward] *F*; sillie *Q*.   156. scaffoldage] *F4* (*subst.*); scoaffollage *Q*;
scaffolage *F*.   157. o'er-wrested] *Pope*; ore-rested *Q,F*.

---

149. *awkward*] Q's *silly* is poor and
tautologous, but not easy to account
for. There can be no doubt, in view
of the strongly mimetic quality of the
following lines, that *awkward* must
have been intended.

151. *pageants*] mimics, imitates as in
a pageant. A nonce-word (although
the stricter sense of the verb is retained
by Milton, cf. OED sv 2).

152. *topless*] supreme, having no
superior. OED gives this as a nonce-
word, in this sense, but I see no real
distinction between the figurative
meaning here and that cited from
Marston (*Antonio's Revenge*, I.i.85,
'My topless villainy'), in which case
Marston and Shakespeare vie for the
credit of the figurative sense, as
applied to an abstraction. But Marlowe's 'topless towers of Ilium' is also
likely (granted a Trojan context) to
have been in Shakespeare's mind.

deputation] Editors gloss as 'deputed
office', with the emphasis on *office*, and
certainly *depute* (vb) = ordain, assign,
appoint. On the other hand, Shakespeare uses the words *deputy, depute,
deputation* with some implication of
substitution; and there is something
to be said for Schmidt's gloss, at this
place, of 'vicegerency' ('thy dignity as
Jove's substitute').

153. *strutting player*] Whether the
term means 'flaunting, swaggering'

(OED 5) or 'affecting an air of
dignity or importance' (OED 7)
hardly matters: Shakespeare twice
uses *strut* elsewhere of pretentious
actors (*Ham.* III.ii.33, *Mac.* v.v.25).
The word dates a style of acting:
cf. W. A. Armstrong, in *Sh.S.*, 7
(1954), pp. 82–9, and A. J. Gurr,
ibid., 16 (1963), pp. 95–101.

153–4. *whose . . . hamstring*] whose
wits are in his thighs.

154. *rich*] Probably 'splendid, fine';
although Schmidt suggests 'delight-
ful'.

155. *wooden . . . sound*] Primarily, of
course, the sound of the actor's step
on the stage, but by implication the
empty, brainless exchanges of Achilles
and Patroclus.

156. *scaffoldage*] I follow the usual
practice of editors, and emend: the
word is in any case unusual, and may
be taken to be related to scaffold,
which is otherwise a normal term for
stage. (For the form of the stage see
C. Walter Hodges, *The Globe Restored*,
1953.)

157. *o'er-wrested*] strained (nonce-
word, ignored by OED). To wrest is
to tighten or twist—often, a stringed
instrument—but also to pervert, to
distort, or even to sprain. (It is
especially frequent as applied to
violent distortion of the sense of
Scripture.)

'Tis like a chime a-mending, with terms unsquar'd,
Which, from the tongue of roaring Typhon dropp'd,
Would seem hyperboles. At this fusty stuff   161
The large Achilles, on his press'd bed lolling,
From his deep chest laughs out a loud applause:
Cries 'Excellent! 'Tis Agamemnon right!
Now play me Nestor: hem and stroke thy beard,   165
As he being dress'd to some oration.'
That's done, as near as the extremest ends
Of parallels, as like as Vulcan and his wife;
Yet god Achilles still cries 'Excellent!

159. unsquar'd] *F;* unsquare *Q.*   164. right] *Q;* iust *F.*   165. hem] *Q;*
hum *F.*   169. god] *Q,F;* good *F2.*

159. *like . . . a-mending*] Steevens
claims to have heard the process, but
does not explain it. Bells properly cast
of the right metal should be in tune in
all three of their notes: the 'hum-note'
(an octave below the fundamental
note sounded by the bell) can be
flattened slightly by thinning the
metal near the crown of the bell. The
sound of filing a whole chime of bells
may be imagined. (See article *Bell* in
Enc.Brit., 11th edn.) Cf. also Hotspur's
image for harsh noise (*1H4* III.i.125:
'I had rather hear a brazen canstick
turn'd').

unsquar'd] Q's *unsquare* is not found
in OED: Schmidt glosses it, with F's
unsquared, as 'not suitable, not shaped
and adapted to the purpose'. The
verb *square* = to make timber etc.
square or rectangular in cross-section,
but OED also notes two figurative
senses, both meaning to adjust, adapt,
harmonize, or render appropriate,
and both Q and F readings could be
derived from such verbs, although the
participial form is the more obvious.
The possible error of *-d* / *-e* is simple
enough.

160. *Typhon*] Otherwise *Typhoeus*: a
monster, one of the Titans, representing the earthquake and the volcano,
and hence capable of deafening
sounds. According to Ovid (*Meta-*

morphoses, v.321) he is buried under
Sicily, and spits fire and rock through
Etna. His earlier ragings had terrified
even the Olympian gods into dis-
guising themselves in order to escape
him.

161. *fusty*] not fresh; mouldy, stale.
Deighton suggested a connection with
fustian, but the metaphor in the text
suits the rest of the food imagery in
the play.

164. *right*] precisely, exactly. F's
just means the same, although Achilles
may perhaps be allowed some consistency: cf. l. 170. Shakespeare seems
to use the words indifferently.

165. *play me*] Cf. l. 170 *play him me,*
and see Abbott, §220.

hem] F's *hum* is truly an indifferent
variant: both represent a nervous
cough or interjection: both are used
in phrases suggesting hesitancy (*hum /
hem* and *haw*); but *hum* perhaps carries
more sense of disapprobation. I follow
Q merely as copy-text.

166. *dress'd to*] prepared, made
ready for.

168. *Vulcan*] In Greek, Hephaestos:
a lame god, son of Zeus and Hera
(*Iliad,* 1.572), and by trade a smith:
hence, deformed and dirty. He was
wedded to Aphrodite.

169. *god*] F2's reading *good* has
attracted many editors, and must be

'Tis Nestor right: now play him me, Patroclus,   170
Arming to answer in a night alarm.'
And then, forsooth, the faint defects of age
Must be the scene of mirth, to cough and spit,
And with a palsy fumbling on his gorget_ *armor for throat*
Shake in and out the rivet: and at this sport   175
Achilles Sir Valour dies, cries 'O, enough, Patroclus,
Or give me ribs of steel: I shall split all
In pleasure of my spleen.' And in this fashion
All our abilities, gifts, natures, shapes,
Severals and generals of grace exact,   180
rhetorical Achievements, plots, orders, preventions,
Excitements to the field, or speech for truce,

---

174. palsy fumbling] *Q,F;* palsy-fumbling *Tyrwhitt;* palsied fumbling *Capell.*

---

taken as a heavy sarcasm. Yet *god* is also a sarcasm, and hyperbole (Achilles was the son of Thetis), and suits the irony of the situation: Achilles is too great to be concerned with the mere mortals who would command him. Ulysses hints at a similar irony later (III.iii.94).

171. *answer*] respond (to an hostile action or threat): sometimes formally, as to a challenge (cf. II.i.129: 'who shall answer him?').

172. *faint . . . age*] i.e. defects of age and feebleness.

173. *scene*] spectacle, dramatic show.

174. *palsy fumbling*] The phrase need not have troubled editors: *palsy* was an adjective until the early eighteenth century.

gorget] armour for the throat.

175. *and at*] Pope omitted *and* (which indeed occurs already in the line); but I suspect that scansion was his argument; and perhaps one ought not to correct too often for that reason.

176. *Sir Valour*] i.e. Achilles. 'Sir' is not infrequently used derogatorily, with a variety of grammatical forms: e.g. 'Sir Oracle' (*Mer. V.* I.i.93), 'Sir Prudence' (*Tp.* II.i.281), 'Sir Smile' (*Wint.* I.ii.196), 'Sir you of Troy' (this scene, l. 244).

177. *all*] Editors do not gloss, and perhaps one can be too precise: the word may merely refer back to *ribs* (and by implication the trunk or torso); but I suspect that *all* here is adverbial (= altogether): cf. *Tim.* III.i.142 ('dispossess her all').

178. *spleen*] a ductless abdominal gland, considered to be the seat of several emotions (melancholy, laughter, malice, etc.), and hence used for the emotions themselves, and sometimes of the occasions of them; here, probably, the fit of laughter itself, but perhaps 'fantasy' or 'caprice'. The ambiguity is to be expected: *Sir Valour dies*, for example, is perfect mock-heroic.

180. *severals and generals*] (excellence of) individuals and the whole group. Strictly, these are adjectives used as nouns: the plural form is invariably used for *severals*, which in this instance has determined the number of the second term.

of grace exact] Probably, 'precise and graceful': i.e. the Greek generals are professionally excellent, and their excellence is itself a grace.

181. *preventions*] defensive measures, precautions.

182. *Excitements*] exhortations.

Success or loss, what is or is not, serves
As stuff for these two to make paradoxes.
Nest. And in the imitation of these twain,   185
    Who, as Ulysses says, opinion crowns — *designates*
    With an imperial voice, many are infect. *as absolute commander*
    Ajax is grown self-will'd, and bears his head
    In such a rein, in full as proud a place
    As broad Achilles; keeps his tent like him;   190
    Makes factious feasts; rails on our state of war
    Bold as an oracle; and sets Thersites,
    A slave whose gall coins slanders like a mint,
    To match us in comparisons with dirt
    To weaken and discredit our exposure,   195
    How rank soever rounded in with danger.
Ulyss. They tax our policy and call it cowardice,

189. place] *Q,F;* pace *Pope.*   190. keeps] *Q;* and keepes *F.*   195. and] *F;*
our *Q.*

184. *stuff*] Not quite as in l. 161:
here, rather, = raw material, something to be worked up.

paradoxes] statements contrary to
received opinion or belief (OED, the
primary sense); otherwise, absurdities
(cf. *Oth.* II.i.138-9: 'These are old
paradoxes, to make fools laugh i'the
alehouse').

186-7. *crowns . . . voice*] designates
absolute commander. As Deighton
pointed out, however, nobody thought
of *Patroclus* as a leader.

187. *infect*] This uninflected form of
the past participle became obsolete
soon after Shakespeare's death.

188-9. *bears . . . rein*] bridles (as
Johnson noted of his own time, the
metaphor survived): carries his head
haughtily.

189. *place*] high rank, dignity.
Pope's *pace* is nevertheless attractive,
since it carries on the figure of Ajax
as a horse (and cf. III.iii.126: 'A very
horse, that has he knows not what!';
also Thersites' jibe at II.i.17-20).

190. *broad*] Probably alluding to
Achilles' size, although editors have
suggested 'puffed up'. (Chapman

attributes 'broad language' to Achilles: *Iliad*, I.224.)

191. *war*] Perhaps = preparedness
for war; but here, and at l. 198,
Shakespeare seems to be using the
word in senses not recognized by the
OED until the time of Milton and
Dryden (instruments of war: soldiers
etc. in fighting array).

193. *slave*] abject wretch: man of no
moral sensibility or feeling.

gall] bile, or secretion of the liver:
also, gall-bladder, and its bitter contents: hence, bitterness, asperity,
rancour.

195. *and*] Q's *our* would represent a
simple misreading in Secretary hand.
The suggestion *or* (reported in the
Cambridge edition) gives a feeble
sense for the climax of a speech.

exposure] vulnerable situation.

196. *rank*] thickly.

197-210.] Walker (NCS) compares
this speech with Ovid, *Metamorphoses*,
XIII.360-9: 'Quippe manu fortes nec
sunt tibi Marte secundi, / consiliis
cessere meis, tibi dextera bello / utilis:
ingenium est, quod eget moderamine
nostro; / tu vires sine mente geris,

Count wisdom as no member of the war,
hinder foresight Forestall prescience, and esteem no act
But that of hand. The still and mental parts,   200
That do contrive how many hands shall strike
When fitness calls them on and know by measure
Of their observant toil the enemy's weight—
Why, this hath not a finger's dignity.
They call this bed-work, mapp'ry, closet-war;   205
So that the ram that batters down the wall,
For the great swinge and rudeness of his poise,
They place before his hand that made the engine,
Or those that with the fineness of their souls
By reason guide his execution.   210

refers to military staff work & intell. operation

202. calls] *Q ;* call *F.*   203. enemy's] *NCS, conj. Delius;* enemies *Q,F (subst.).*
205. mapp'ry] *Q,F (subst.) ;* mappery *Capell.*   207. swinge] *Q ;* swing *F.*

mihi cura futuri; / tu pugnare potes, / pugnandi tempora mecum / eligit Atrides; tu tantum corpore prodes, / nos animo; quantoque ratem qui temperat, anteit / remigis officium, quanto dux milite maior, / tantum ego te supero, nec non in corpore nostro / pectora sunt potiora manu: vigor omnis in illis.'

197. *tax*] censure, denigrate.

policy] sagacity, prudence; stratagems. The term (together with *politic* and *politician*) acquired strong pejorative associations through its supposed connection with the doctrines of Niccolo Machiavelli, but only Thersites uses it so in this play, and then in opposition to its other sense of *government* (cf. v.iv.9, 12; v.iv.17).

198. *member*] part of the body (cf. the continuing image in l. 200 of *hand . . . mental parts*).

war] see note to l. 191 above.

199. *Forestall*] (perhaps) hinder, prevent: the sense 'beset' 'obstruct' (OED 3) read figuratively, would also suit the context, but no other figurative use is noted.

prescience] foresight.

200–3. *The still . . . weight*] A neat summary of military staff-work and·

intelligence operations.

203. *enemy's*] Delius conjectured that the noun was singular, as indeed it should be, if Ulysses be considering the particular and not the general case (cf. *H5* iv.i.76).

205.] Work to be done reclining: mere map-reading and sketching: planning of war in the study (all that is implicit in the phrase 'armchair general'). This practical soldier's contempt is shared by Iago (*Oth.* i.i.19–31) and by Antony (*Ant.* iii.xi.38–40). Ulysses speaks with some feeling on the point: he and Diomedes had made a reconnaissance by night for the Greeks (*Iliad* x).

207. *For*] because of.

swinge] impetus, forcible motion. Editors generally have followed F, but *swinge* has more sense of violence and great momentum than has any meaning of *swing* (and cf. the senses for the verb). Note also Chapman, *Iliad*, vii.173: 'At least for plaine fierce swinge of strength'.

rudeness] roughness, violence.

poise] heavy blow, forcible impact (but the primary sense 'weight' may be intended).

209. *souls*] intellectual powers.

Nest. Let this be granted, and Achilles' horse
    Makes many Thetis' sons.   *Tucket.*
Agam.   What trumpet? Look, Menelaus.
Menel. From Troy.

Enter ÆNEAS.

Agam. What would you 'fore our tent?
Æneas. Is this great Agamemnon's tent, I pray you?   215
Agam. Even this.
Æneas. May one that is a herald and a prince
    Do a fair message to his kingly eyes?
Agam. With surety stronger than Achilles' arm
    'Fore all the Greekish lords, which with one voice   220
    Call Agamemnon head and general.
Æneas. Fair leave and large security. How may

212 S.D.] *F; not in Q.*   218. eyes] *Q; eares F.*   220. lords] *This edn;* heads
Q,F; host *conj. Kinnear.*

212 S.D. *Tucket*] Strictly, the signal for advancing, given to cavalry by a trumpet (despite F's *trumpets* at l. 258): cf. Æneas' remark at l. 262, which refers to a single trumpeter. The word is connected with *toccata* (touch) and with *tuck* (OED sb²) = brief sounding of a trumpet, or tap upon a drum.

212. *Menelaus*] Editors sometimes omit, because the name is extra-metrical: one might argue as justly that it is indecorous for Menelaus to run errands for Agamemnon; but since he answers the question put to him, he must be presumed to have run the errand also. (He is, in any case, treated most unceremoniously in the kissing of Cressida in iv.v.)

218. *fair*] benign, peaceable, gentle.
message] the business entrusted to a messenger or ambassador. *To do a message* was a common formula: hence, Q's *eyes* is to be preferred to F's *ears* (although, of course, speech was necessary).

219. *Achilles' arm*] Walker (NCS) explains by reference to Erasmus' *Adagia*—arma Achillea being prover-bially the best protection. She reads

arms, to agree with the adage. Editors have sometimes objected that Aga-memnon would hardly swear by Achilles, after what has passed: Johnson, indeed, proposed Alcides; but nothing need prevent Agamem-non (without appealing to Erasmus) from making capital out of the reputa-tion of his greatest warrior. After all, he goes on at once to claim the absolute authority (ll. 220–1) which has just been denied him (ll. 186–7).

220. *lords*] Q and F agree in reading *heads*, but if Q were wrong, F might well follow suit. Kinnear proposed *host*, which makes good sense. *Lords* (this edn) is perhaps graphically nearer to *heads*, and represents a formula found elsewhere (cf. iii.iii.138: 'these Grecian lords'). Error of anticipation is quite easy (*head* occurs in the next line), although the error might as readily be there (*head* for *lord*); but, as Walker points out, there is something absurd in all the Greek heads with one voice calling Agamemnon head (or indeed any-thing else at all).

A stranger to those most imperial looks
Know them from eyes of other mortals?

Agam.   How?

Æneas. Ay: 225
I ask, that I might waken reverence,
And bid the cheek be ready with a blush
Modest as morning when she coldly eyes
The youthful Phoebus.
    Which is that god in office, guiding men?   230
Which is the high and mighty Agamemnon?

Agam. This Trojan scorns us, or the men of Troy
Are ceremonious courtiers.

Æneas. Courtiers as free, as debonair, unarm'd,
As bending angels: that's their fame in peace;   235
But when they would seem soldiers, they have galls,
Good arms, strong joints, true swords, and—Jove's
    accord—

---

225. Ay] *Q,F* (I); *separate line, Steevens.*   227. bid] *Q;* on *F.*   228–9.] *As
F; one line, Q.*   230. god in office,] *Rowe;* god, in office *Q;* God in office *F.*
235. fame] *F;* same *Q.*   237. swords, and—Jove's accord—] *Theobald (subst.);*
swords, & great *Ioues* accord *Q;* swords, & *Ioues* accord, *F;* swords; and Loves'
a lord *conj. Steevens;* swords, great Jove's own bird *conj. Kinnear;* swords, and
great Jove's accent; *Sisson.*

---

223. *A stranger . . . looks*] Both sides
were supposed to have fought in
armour, with the face entirely covered:
hence Nestor's remark to Hector at
IV.v.194–5) 'But this thy countenance
still lock'd in steel, / I never saw till
now'). Major warriors need introductions to each other in that scene: the
exception is Ulysses, who, with
Diomedes, had been on an embassy
to Ilium (IV.v.215). Yet Diomedes
and Æneas need introductions also,
in IV.i: presumably they knew each
other in the field—as Nestor knew
Hector—by armorial bearings: the
situation, while suited to Shakespeare's own age, suits also his
medieval sources—cf. also *pavilions*
(Prologue) and *Sir Diomed* (IV.v.88).
Nevertheless, Æneas is making some
capital out of the conventional situation: if he hesitates in seeking *most*

imperial looks and *a god in office*, he
insults Agamemnon; and Agamem-
non's rejoinder (l. 244) shows that the
point was taken. (His next remark
gives Æneas a way of retreat.)
    227. *bid*] A verb seems to be called
for, as a parallel to *waken:* F's *on,*
while syntactically possible, is highly
unidiomatic.
    234. *debonair*] mild, gracious, cour-
teous. Significantly, this is its only use
by Shakespeare: Deighton noted that
it was common in Chaucer (citing
Troilus and Criseyde, I.181), but it is
found also in Malory, and in Caxton's
Recuyell.
    235. *bending*] courteous (Schmidt):
i.e. bowing.
    236. *galls*] 'spirit to resent injury or
insult' (OED).
    237. *strong joints*] The general sense
is clear, but the phrase may be more

Nothing so full of heart. But peace, Æneas,
Peace, Trojan, lay thy finger on thy lips.
The worthiness of praise distains his worth   240
If that the prais'd himself bring the praise forth;
But what the repining enemy commends,
That breath fame blows; that praise, sole pure,
    transcends.
Agam. Sir you of Troy, call you yourself Æneas?
Æneas. Ay, Greek, that is my name.   245

241. that the] *Q;* that he *F.*

suggestive than appears. The usual meaning of *joint* is 'limb' or 'member' (cf. *LLL* v.i.124: 'his great limb or joint'); but perhaps these joints have firm ligaments controlling them (= articulation)—cf. i.iii.55 ('nerves and bone'); v.viii.12 ('thy sinews, and thy bone'); as well as Hector's remark to Troilus at v.iii.33 ('Let grow thy sinews till their knots be strong'). In that case the phrase means that the Trojans are men of physical maturity.

Jove's accord] Many suggestions have been made, both to explain and to emend this passage: Theobald's slight alteration of the F punctuation (which I have interpreted by dashes) is as elegant as any. Walker (NCS) cites Erasmus as authority for reading the phrase as 'an asseveration, often used, as here, in ironic apology for boasting speech' (cf. *H5* i.ii.307: 'God before'). Those editors who dislike such syntax emend the Q (which has no comma after *accord*), thus making *and . . . heart* one continuous syntactical unit: hence, Steevens' suggestion *Love's a lord* and Kinnear's *great Jove's own bird.* Not all editors approve of Q's metre: hence, some follow F (in omitting *great*) and some, Kinnear (in omitting *and*). Those who accept *Jove's accord* as an absolute construction are not always content with the result. Sisson placed a semi-colon at the end of the line, and emended Q to *great Jove's accent*—a reading which has the merit of syn-

tactical ingenuity, and of graphic plausibility. (I suspect, however, that such pointing leaves Æneas with a halting climax to his boast.) Theobald's reading is the most economical.

238. *full of heart*] courageous.

239.] Cf. Tilley F 239.

240-1.] A commonplace: cf. the behaviour of Achilles and of Ajax in ii.iii, and especially the comment of Agamemnon at ii.iii.158-9 ('whatever praises itself, but in the deed, devours the deed in the praise'): Proverbs xxvii.2 ('Let another man praise thee, and not thine own mouth; a stranger, and not thine own lips'); Tilley P 547, C 554, M 476: Howell's comments on Ben Jonson at dinner (*Epistolae Ho-Elianae*, ii.xiii: 'One thing interven'd, which almost spoil'd the relish of the rest, that *B.* began to engross all the discourse, to vapour extremely of himself, and, by vilifying others, to magnify his own *Muse.* T. Ca[rew] buzz'd me in the ear, that tho' *Ben.* had barrell'd up a great deal of knowledge, yet it seems he had not read the *Ethiques*, which, among other precepts of Morality, forbid self-commendation').

244. *Sir you of Troy*] Sir Trojan (after Walker, NCS). Agamemnon is vulgarly direct and disrespectful, in contrast with the self-conscious and elaborate rhetoric with which Æneas addresses himself.

245. *Ay, Greek*] Whether Æneas means 'cheat', 'card-sharper', or 'roysterer' hardly matters: he has met

Agam. What's your affairs, I pray you?

Æneas. Sir, pardon, 'tis for Agamemnon's ears.

Agam. He hears naught privately that comes from Troy.

Æneas. Nor I from Troy come not to whisper with him.

    I bring a trumpet to awake his ear,   250

    To set his sense on the attentive bent,

    And then to speak.

Agam.   Speak frankly as the wind.

    It is not Agamemnon's sleeping hour:

    That thou shalt know, Trojan, he is awake,

    He tells thee so himself.

Æneas.   Trumpet, blow loud: 255

    Send thy brass voice through all these lazy tents,

    And every Greek of mettle, let him know

    What Troy means fairly shall be spoke aloud.

                              Sound trumpet.

    We have, great Agamemnon, here in Troy

    A prince call'd Hector—Priam is his father—   260

    Who in this dull and long-continu'd truce

246. affairs] *Q*; affayre *F*.   249. whisper with] *Q*; whisper *F*.   251. sense] *F*; seat *Q*.   the] *F*; that *Q*.   255. loud] *F*; alowd *Q*.   258 S.D.] *As Q; The Trumpets sound. | F*.   261. this] *F*; his *Q*.

Agamemnon on his own level. Both at once mend their manners (ll. 246–7), while maintaining the assumption that the Greek leader is not yet recognized.

249. *whisper with*] Both transitive and intransitive form were common. Shakespeare seems to use the intransitive elsewhere only in *All's W.* IV.iii.286 (a prose scene; and there is therefore no check from metre): here, F is more regularly metrical, although one cannot argue only from that. I follow Q, simply as copy-text.

250. *trumpet*] trumpeter (necessary to identify—and hence to protect—a herald in the performance of his office).

251.] A difficult line: Q's *that* is almost certainly affected by the ensuing *att-*, and *seat* is not obviously appropriate; yet F's *sense*, although most editors accept it, is a little flat

(especially for Æneas) and it jingles with *attentive bent*. I find it hard to decide, in point of meaning, between *seat* (= chair of office, and by implication him who sits in it) and *sense* (= hearing, primarily); and I think that *sense* (written as *sence*) could have been read as *seate* (especially in view of the iteration of *-at-* and *att-*). It is fair to admit that the same degree of liberty, and a similar argument, could produce the reading *To set his seat upon th'attentive bent*.

252. *frankly*] freely, without restraint.

255. *loud*] Æneas completes Agamemnon's pentameter, and one ought perhaps to preserve metre as far as possible. Besides, *aloud* occurs at the end of l. 258, and anticipation would be easy.

257. *mettle*] ardour, courage, high spirit.

Is resty grown. He bade me take a trumpet
And to this purpose speak: kings, princes, lords,
If there be one among the fair'st of Greece
That holds his honour higher than his ease,   265
That feeds his praise more than he fears his peril,
That knows his valour and knows not his fear,
That loves his mistress more than in confession
With truant vows to her own lips he loves,
And dare avow her beauty and her worth   270
In other arms than hers—to him this challenge:
Hector, in view of Trojans and of Greeks,
Shall make it good, or do his best to do it,
He hath a lady wiser, fairer, truer,
Than ever Greek did couple in his arms;   275

262. resty] *Q; rusty F.*   266. That feeds] *This edn; And feeds Q; That seekes F.*   275. couple] *Q; compasse F.*

262. *resty*] inactive, indolent (OED 2). F's *rusty* is plausible, and may be connected with *mettle*, although whether in the mind of author or of compositor, who can say? The primary sense of resty (= restive) would also suit, although *that* sense is perhaps more usually applied to horses. Under sense 2, OED significantly cites Jonson, *Silent Woman*, I.i ('He would grow resty else in his ease. His virtue would rust without action').

268-9.] Who shows his love for his mistress in valiant deeds, and not in idle promises made to her in safety. *Truant vows* may be those of an idler, a worthless fellow, or of one who neglects his proper business (cf. *1H4* v.i.94: 'I have a truant been to chivalry').

269. *to her own lips he loves*] = when lip to lip with her: the elliptical expression, and the slightly playful language, is of a piece with the puns in *arms* (l. 271) and in *couple* (l. 275).

274. *wiser, fairer, truer,*] Hector's challenge is traditional in form, in that it opposes the challenger's mistress against the whole world; but the qualities are those to which Shakespeare normally appeals: cf. *Mer. V.* II.vi.56 ('like herself, wise, fair, and true'); and *Ado* II.iii.222-4 ('They may say the lady is fair . . . and virtuous . . . and wise'). John Speed, *History of Great Britain* (1611), p. 1190, notes that, outside Lisbon, in May 1589, the Earl of Essex challenged the Spaniards to break a lance in disputing the honour of Queen Elizabeth and of their own mistresses.

275. *couple*] F's *compass* implies merely an embrace: *couple* seems to have (as editors have noted) heraldic associations, since *coupled* = conjoined (= the linking of sub-ordinaries on a field). But this will not quite do: to make good sense (if there were an heraldic allusion), we should need the term *impale* (= to join the arms of man and woman in one achievement); yet such a word is not supported by the text, when Æneas is referring primarily to the *woman*, and not to any arms to which she may be entitled. Various senses suggesting mating or marrying might be adduced, without elucidating the phrase. Walker (NCS) sees a reference to bearing a token of

And will tomorrow with his trumpet call
Midway between your tents and walls of Troy
To rouse a Grecian that is true in love.
If any come, Hector shall honour him:
If none, he'll say in Troy, when he retires,   280
The Grecian dames are sunburnt and not worth
The splinter of a lance. Even so much.

Agam. This shall be told our lovers, Lord Æneas.
If none of them have soul in such a kind,
We left them all at home; but we are soldiers,   285
And may that soldier a mere recreant prove
That means not, hath not, or is not in love.
If then one is, or hath, or means to be,
That one meets Hector: if none else, I am he.

Nest. Tell him of Nestor, one that was a man   290
When Hector's grandsire suck'd. He is old now;
But if there be not in our Grecian host
A noble man that hath no spark of fire

288. hath, or] *F;* hath a *Q.*   292. host] *Q;* mould *F.*   293. A noble] *Q;*
One Noble *F.*   no spark] *Q;* one spark *F.*

the mistress about the armour (cf.
v.ii.168: 'That sleeve is mine that
he'll bear on his helm'); but the syntax will hardly permit that, any more
than the purely heraldic interpretation. I follow Q with hesitation.

276. *trumpet*] See note to l. 250,
above.

281. *sunburnt*] Ladies wore masks to
protect their complexions, for sunburn
was accounted a blemish (cf. note to
i.ii.267, above, and *Ado* ii.i.299–300:
'Thus goes everyone to the world but
I, and I am sunburnt'). I see no
reason for Partridge's interpretation
(= man-burnt, i.e. infected with
venereal disease).

282. *splinter . . . lance*] Shakespeare's
only other use of the noun *splinter*
(*Cor.* iv.v.110) refers to the breaking
of lances, and this seems to have been
the primary use until his time (together with the splitting of a ship
upon a rock). Æneas is maintaining a
properly chivalric style. It is just
possible that *splinter* is a verbal noun

(= splintering), and hence, by extension, the act of tilting.

Even so much] Apparently some such
formula was usual at the end of an
herald's speech (cf. Montjoy, in *H5*
iii.vi.141: 'So far my king and master,
so much my office').

284–5.] Agamemnon's meaning is
clear, although his logic is not
impeccable.

284. *soul*] emotions: capacity for
feeling.

287. *means not, hath not*] i.e. means
not to be, hath not been (and likewise
with the ellipsis in l. 288).

288. *hath, or*] Q's obvious error (*a*
for *or*) is an easy misreading.

292. *host*] F's *mould* may have been
caused by *old* in the preceding line
(immediately above *hoste*) and perhaps by *gould* at l. 295: we know that
compositors were as liable to errors of
anticipation as scribes, and that they
read their copy through, not one line
at a time, but a page at a time.

293. *A . . . no*] F's *One . . . one* is tidy

To answer for his love, tell him from me
I'll hide my silver beard in a gold beaver,   295
And in my vambrace put my wither'd brawns,
And, meeting him, will tell him that my lady
Was fairer than his grandam, and as chaste
As may be in the world. His youth in flood,
I'll prove this troth with my three drops of blood.   300
Æneas. Now heavens forfend such scarcity of youth.
Ulyss. Amen.
Agam. Fair Lord Æneas, let me touch your hand:

296. my wither'd brawns] *Q* (*subst.*); this wither'd brawne *F*.   297. will tell]
F; tell *Q*.   300. prove this troth] *Q*; pawne this truth *F*.   301. forfend] *Q*;
forbid *F*.   youth] *F*; men *Q*.   302–3. *Ulyss.* Amen. / *Agam.* Fair] *F* (*subst.*);
Vlis. Amen: faire *Q*.

and logical; but there are too many
solecisms in Shakespeare's logic, and
that where the reading is unquestion-
able, for emendation by F to be
required: one has here, after all, only
the habitual double negative. F's
reading seems more awkward, and
less intensive, than it was perhaps
meant to be.

295. *beaver*] Strictly, 'the lower part
of the face-guard of a helmet, when
worn with a visor' (OED), but
apparently, in the sixteenth century,
confounded with the visor itself (as in
Ham. I.ii.229). Nestor's heraldry is
defective: he puts metal upon metal.

296. *vambrace*] (variant of F's *vant-
brace*): defensive armour for the arm.
To judge from the examples cited by
OED, the plural form may have been
uninflected: at least, there are some
ambiguous instances; and in view of
the uncertainty over number in other
words (cf. *jaundies*: I.iii.2) I prefer to
read as plural, assuming that such a
plural may be possible, and declining
to suppress the evidence for it. (See
next note.)

brawns] muscular part, esp. of arm,
leg, or thumb (here, = arms). For
Nestor to point too clearly (as with
F's *this withered brawn*) to his en-
feebled arm, would be less hyperbolic

than ludicrous.

299. *His . . . flood*] in the prime of
his vigour (an absolute construction).
Baldwin (*Variorum*) was tempted to
suppose *blood* as the original reading
(cf. *LLL* IV.ii.3); but images of flux
are fairly frequent in this play (e.g.
II.iii.132–4: 'ebbs and flows . . . / Rode
on his tide'; II.iii.165: 'stream of his
dispose'; III.iii.159: 'Like to an
enter'd tide').

300. *prove . . . troth*] If, with F, we
read *pawn*, then presumably Nestor
says that he will set the truth at
hazard at the cost of his life—which
is to set an odd sense on *truth*; *prove* is
therefore likely to be correct, and if
prove, then *troth* (= truth, as frequently in Shakespeare).

301. *forfend*] *forbid* is the more common word in Shakespeare: if F
paraphrased in l. 300, it may have
done so here.

youth] Q is probably wrong here,
being affected by the ensuing *Amen*;
but its error is not of the same kind as
I suppose in F.

303. *Agam.*] Q made a second error
here: *Amen* was also responsible for
the omission of the speech-heading
Agamemnon. (Yet Q's speech-headings
are not always reliable: cf. II.i.39ff.,
II.iii.221 ff.).

To our pavilion shall I lead you, sir.
Achilles shall have word of this intent;   305
So shall each lord of Greece, from tent to tent.
Yourself shall feast with us before you go,
And find the welcome of a noble foe.

Exeunt all but Ulysses and Nestor.

Ulyss. Nestor.
Nest. What says Ulysses?   310
Ulyss. I have a young conception in my brain:
    Be you my time to bring it to some shape.
Nest. What is't?
Ulyss. This 'tis:
    Blunt wedges rive hard knots; the seeded pride   315
    That hath to this maturity blown up

---

304. you, sir] *Q;* you first *F.*   308 S.D.] *Capell (subst.); Exeunt. | Manet*
Vlysses, and Nestor. F; not in *Q.*   314. This 'tis] *F;* not in *Q.*

304. *sir*] Walker (NCS) argues for
F's *first* saying that Agamemnon has
already addressed Æneas. Further,
the graphic confusion (*sir | first*) is
easy. But Agamemnon's speech does
not run very naturally—it is, with its
two couplets, a piece of dramatic
punctuation, the end of a movement
(almost, the end of a scene)—and I
assume that after l. 303 there should
be a pause: Agamemnon leaves his
seat, does Æneas the courtesy of
moving to *him* (instead of insisting
that Æneas approach), and then, at
l. 304, turns and prepares to conduct
him to his pavilion. The momentary
silence implied by the touching of
hands is enough to justify a new mode
of address.

312. *my time*] Nestor is often enough
associated with Time; here, he becomes the period of gestation.

314.] Q's omission of a short speech
has sometimes pleased editors, who
explain that the reading avoids an
ugly sibilance; and so it does, but the
sound was intended. Admittedly,
although Ulysses begins a little
abruptly in Q, in reply to Nestor's
enquiry, his elliptical manner is not
new (cf. l. 142, where he appears

almost to ignore Agamemnon's question); but at this moment there is a
dramatic point to be made. Nestor
does not remain because the two had
agreed it already: he does so because
Ulysses calls to him, quietly. Both
should have formed up and moved
out ceremonially, and neither, for five
lines, wishes to draw attention to his
absence. For that space of time, both
speak in low tones, half-whispering,
and the sibilants in ll. 309–14 allow
this to be emphasized. From l. 315
onward, conversational tones will suit.

315. *Blunt . . . knots*] Erasmus,
Adagia, 'Malo nodo malus quaerendus
cuneus': cf. Tilley D 357. A favourite
proverb with Shakespeare.

316. *blown up*] swollen, puffed up.
No one word will serve as gloss. *Blow*
refers back to *seed*, because seed is set
just as eggs are laid (cf. fly-blown),
but also because the seed-head of a
plant expands at the point at which
the seeds will disperse; the dispersal
is windborne, and the wind therefore
blows them (cf. further, Keats's comment on the passage, in *Variorum*).
Again, it is *pride* of which the seed is
ripe, and pride is often enough
associated with being blown (up) (cf.

In rank Achilles must or now be cropp'd,
Or, shedding, breed a nursery of like evil
To overbulk us all.
Nest. Well, and how?   320
Ulyss. This challenge that the gallant Hector sends,
However it is spread in general name,
Relates in purpose only to Achilles.
Nest. True: the purpose is perspicuous as substance
Whose grossness little characters sum up;   325
And in the publication make no strain
But that Achilles, were his brain as barren
As banks of Libya—though, Apollo knows,
'Tis dry enough—will with great speed of judgement,
Ay, with celerity, find Hector's purpose   330
Pointing on him.
Ulyss. And wake him to the answer, think you?
Nest. Why, 'tis most meet: who may you else oppose

324. True] *Q; not in F.*   as] *Q; even as F.*   327. were] *F; weare Q.*
333. Why] *Q; Yes F.*

OED's citation sv 23: 'Croesus . . . he
perceived to be blowen and puft up
with pride'): so also *Tw.N.* II.v.43.
   317. *rank*] full (and coarse) in
growth.
   318. *nursery*] plot of ground kept for
raising young plants.
   319. *overbulk*] outgrow (a nonce-
word).
   324. *perspicuous*] obvious, apparent.
   324–5. *substance . . . up*] Hector's
intention is as clear as if it had been
explicitly calculated and set out.
Nestor puns on *substance* = (a) matter,
(b) wealth or riches, (c) contents or
purport, and on *grossness* = (a) mass,
bulk, (b) exaggerated obviousness
(with perhaps a hint of the sense of
the adverb *grossly* (OED 6c) =
roughly, sketchily, inexactly).
   326. *publication*] promulgation, an-
nouncement.
   make no strain] do not doubt. *Strain*
is usually glossed as 'strong (muscular)
effort', but it is at least possible that it
means 'strained construction or inter-

pretation' (OED 6).
   328. *banks of Libya*] Libya was
generally construed as the whole of
north Africa (cf. map in the Elzevir
Virgilii Opera of 1636), and hence a
place of sandy deserts; whether
banks = ridges, slopes, or whether
it = shores (sea-banks) hardly matters: Libya, from Atlas to the tide-
mark, was proverbially barren.
   Apollo] As the god associated with
light, medicine, the Muses, and
oracles, Apollo may be fairly taken as
the polar opposite to the stupidity of
Achilles.
   329. *dry*] barren, sterile. Dryness
implied infertility, as moisture did
increase, in all the body (cf. *Oth.*
III.iv.32–40); and an idiot's brain
was thought to be hard and desiccated
(cf. *AYL* II.vii.39).
   333. *Why*] More emphatic than F's
Yes.
   oppose] set as antagonist or opponent
(not often intransitive, but cf. IV.v.75,
IV.v.94, V.iii.57).

That can from Hector bring his honour off
If not Achilles? Though't be a sportful combat,   335
Yet in the trial much opinion dwells;
For here the Trojans taste our dear'st repute
With their fin'st palate; and trust to me, Ulysses,
Our imputation shall be oddly pois'd
In this vile action; for the success,   340
Although particular, shall give a scantling
Of good or bad unto the general,
And in such indexes, although small pricks
To their subsequent volumes, there is seen
The baby figure of the giant mass   345
Of things to come at large. It is suppos'd
He that meets Hector issues from our choice;
And choice, being mutual act of all our souls,
Makes merit her election, and doth boil,

334. his honour] F (subst.); those honours Q.   336. the] Q; this F.   340. vile]
Q (vilde); wilde F.

334. *his honour*] Shakespeare normally uses the singular form, and
there is no antecedent for Q's *those*.

336. *opinion*] credit, repute.

339. *imputation*] reputation (seldom
used in the pejorative sense which is
now usual). Nestor, like Ulysses in
III. iii, sees men's repute as subject to
change, and only maintained by
continual effort.

pois'd] weighed in the mind, evalu-
ated. (Nestor thinks of men judging
weight by lifting and holding an
object in the hand.)

340. *vile*] trivial, of little worth. F's
wild (= rash) also makes good sense;
and misreading, either way, would be
easy.

341. *particular*] specific, limited (sc.
to Achilles).

scantling] OED explains as 'sample
. . . specimen' (sense 6), but 2c
(= 'the measure or degree of [a
person's] capacity or ability') seems
equally appropriate. Either sense will
fit the ensuing figure of *indexes* | *volumes*
and *baby* | *giant*: the notion of *pars pro
toto* is there already in *taste . . . repute*

and *particular* | *general*.

343-4. *indexes . . . volumes*] Editors
explain *index* as (a) a summary prefixed, and (b) a pointer (usually, the
hand with index finger extended, set
marginally to draw attention to
matter of importance). Shakespeare's
usage allows the former, though hardly
the latter (cf. *Oth.* II. i. 254: 'index and
prologue'). The syntax here suggests
that *index* may be a synonym for
prick; but *prick* may stand to *volume*
as point to bulk or quantity—or
rather, might do so, if that sense of
volume occurred as early as the play.
Apparently, it does not; but OED
cites one usage (6a, and perhaps 6b)
which combines the notions of *book*
and *size*. Hence, *index* = (a) summary,
and (b) index finger: *prick* = (a) mark
or tick, and (b) small particle:
volume = (a) book, and (b) size or
mass of book.

344. *subsequent*] Pronounced subsé-
quent.

346. *at large*] full-size.

348. *souls*] powers of intelligence.

349. *election*] Usually glossed as 'act

As 'twere from forth us all, a man distill'd   350
Out of our virtues: who miscarrying,
What heart receives from hence a conquering part
To steel a strong opinion to themselves?—
Which entertain'd, limbs are his instruments,
In no less working than are swords and bows   355
Directive by the limbs.

Ulyss. Give pardon to my speech: therefore 'tis meet
Achilles meet not Hector. Let us like merchants
First show foul wares, and think perchance they'll sell:
If not,   360
The lustre of the better shall exceed
By showing the worse first. Do not consent

352. receives . . . a] *Q;* from hence receyues the *F.*   354–6.] *F; not in Q.*
354. are] *F2;* are in *F.*   355. In] *F;* E'en *NCS.*   357–62.] *As Capell;* Give
. . . meete, / . . . Marchants / . . . sell; / . . . exceed, / . . . consent, *Q;* Give
. . . speech: / . . . *Hector:* / . . . Wares, / . . . not, / . . . shew, / . . . consent, *F.*
359. First . . . wares,] *Q;* shew our fowlest Wares, *F.*   361–2.] shall exceed
/ . . . first *Q;* yet to shew, / shall shew the better. *F.*

of choice', which is hardly possible here: the context requires 'object of choice', for which OED, at any rate, gives no warrant. Professor Brooks suggests that 'makes merit her election' = makes merit her criterion of choice.

351. *virtues*] courage, valour (? perhaps, physical energy).

352–3.] The inversion (*receives from hence* / *from hence receives*) is indifferent, although a copyist might be more likely to reverse an inversion than to create one: I follow Q, as copy-text. Much more important is the variant *a* / *the*, since, even if we accept Capell's excellent suggestion of reading the lines as a question, the sense of *part* varies according to the article prefixed to it. F in effect says, '(If our champion miscarry), how will the Trojans (= party of the conqueror) rate themselves as our superiors!'— and needs no mark of interrogation. Q says, 'How can we expect each Greek to derive his share of confidence (from our champion's failure)?'—and must be read as a question.

354–6.] These involved lines obviously gave some difficulty, and Nestor's argument can be taken without them: he *says* what would happen if the Greek champion were to fail, but his rhetorical question makes clear the consequence which would follow from the victory which the Greeks would naturally desire. In ll. 354–6, he is explicit: the 'strong opinion' which derives to the successful champion's side will operate in the limbs of all, in just the same way that the limbs in turn manage the weapons. Clearly, *his* (l. 354) refers to *opinion* (= its): *entertained* = received. Few editors retain *in* at l. 354. At l. 355, *In* is ingeniously emended by Walker to *E'en*, but I believe the emendation to be unnecessary: *working* is a verbal substantive, not a participle, and means 'influence, effectiveness' (OED).

357–65.] The collation shows how far there was confusion here; but I think that the text is worse than the variants suggest. (See discussion in Introduction, pp. 8–10.)

That ever Hector and Achilles meet,
For both our honour and our shame in this
Are dogg'd with two strange followers.   365
Nest. I see them not with my old eyes: what are they?
Ulyss. What glory our Achilles shares from Hector,
     Were he not proud, we all should share with him;
     But he already is too insolent,
     And it were better parch in Afric sun   370
     Than in the pride and salt scorn of his eyes,
     Should he 'scape Hector fair. If he were foil'd,
     Why then we did our main opinion crush
     In taint of our best man. No, make a lott'ry,
     And by device let blockish Ajax draw   375
     The sort to fight with Hector. Among ourselves
     Give him allowance for the better man;
     For that will physic the great Myrmidon,
     Who broils in loud applause, and make him fall
     His crest that prouder than blue Iris bends.   380
     If the dull brainless Ajax come safe off,

364-5.] *As F; as prose, Q.*   368. share] *Q*; weare *F.*   370. it] *Q;* we *F.*
373. did] *F;* do *Q.*   377. for the better] *Q;* as the worthier *F.*

367-8. *shares . . . share*] Ulysses puns on 'cleaves' and 'divide with others'. F's *wear* implies that Hector would lose tokens of honour to Achilles, but the sense is perhaps a little strained.

370. *it were better*] it would be preferable *for us.*

Afric] Shakespeare's usual form of the word: for the adjectival use, uninflected, of a proper noun, cf. *Britain court (Cym.* II.iv.37); *Lethe wharf (Ham.* I.v.33); etc. (see Schmidt).

371. *salt*] bitter.

372. *fair*] fortunately, successfully.

373. *main opinion*] general reputation.

crush] destroy, overcome.

374. *taint*] disgrace, discredit.

376. *sort*] lot: an infrequent use of the word, (but cf. *sors* (Latin) as in *sortes virgilianae*). The term *lot* became the norm for all senses.

377. *allowance*] praise: (perhaps) acknowledgement.

379. *broils*] glows, is excited. The word is, of course, commonly used of the cooking of food; but metaphorical senses are not unusual (cf. OED 3, 4a, 4b, 4c), and suggestions of cookery in this line are perhaps not wholly appropriate, however contemptuous Ulysses may be.

fall] let fall. (An idiom from Scandinavian usage, current recently on Tyneside, as Professor Brooks assures me.)

380. *crest*] comb, feathers, mane (i.e. any sign of pride). Ulysses sees Achilles as a horse in a state of excitement: cf. *Caes.* IV.ii.23-6 ('But hollow men, like horses . . . / . . . fall their crests'). On the other hand, further senses of crest are possible: e.g. 'erect plume or tuft of feathers . . . on the top of a helmet' (OED 2); apex

We'll dress him up in voices: if he fail,
Yet go we under our opinion still
That we have better men. But, hit or miss,
Our project's life this shape of sense assumes: 385
Ajax employ'd plucks down Achilles' plumes.
Nest. Ulysses,
Now I begin to relish thy advice,
And I will give a taste thereof forthwith
To Agamemnon: go we to him straight.   390
Two curs shall tame each other: pride alone
Must tar the mastiffs on, as 'twere their bone.   *Exeunt.*

387–8. Ulysses . . . relish] *Var. '73; Ulysses,* now I relish *Pope;* Now *Vlysses* I begin to relish *Q,F (subst.).*   389. thereof] *Q; of it F.*   392. tar] *F (tarre); arre Q.*   their] *F; a Q.*

of helmet (hence, the helmet itself) (OED 6); and I think that they were intended. The purely heraldic senses are irrelevant.

blue Iris] messenger of the gods, and goddess of the rainbow. Admittedly the rainbow is not *only* blue: Ovid invariably stresses the many colours of Iris, and Virgil (*Aeneid,* IV.610) refers to *mille coloribus;* but there is not therefore sufficient reason to argue (as *Variorum* does) that the flower is intended. Shakespeare refers to the flower always as the *flower-de-luce.*

bends] curves in a bow: cf. OED sv 8, citing Gascoigne (1577) ('The Rainbow bending in the skie').

382. *dress him up*] OED notes of the verb that it may imply attire appropriate 'to a part which one aspires to play'.

383. *go . . . opinion*] Not usually glossed: apparently 'we continue to

maintain our belief', or perhaps 'we [shall] continue according to our belief'.

384. *hit or miss*] Cf. Tilley H 475.

387–8.] Either one follows Pope and Johnson, and omits *begin to,* or one transfers a word to a new line; and to set *Now* in isolation is to gain nothing, for the scansion will still be faulty (*Ulysses* is stressed on the second syllable).

391. *Two . . . other*] Cf. Tilley C 918.

392. *tar*] incite. I follow F, as editors usually do; but there may be good sense in the Q reading, despite the ease with which one can explain the loss of a letter (Mus*t* tarr / Mus*t* arr). *Arr(e)* is simply the snarl or growl of a dog (see citations in OED), and can also mean 'vex', 'worry': there is, however, no known example of the phrase 'to arr on' (which would be required here).

[ACT II]

[SCENE I]

Enter AJAX *and* THERSITES.

Ajax. Thersites—

Thers. Agamemnon—how if he had boils, full, all over, generally?

Ajax. Thersites—

Thers. And those boils did run—say so—did not the   5
general run then? Were not that a botchy core?

Ajax. Dog!

Thers. Then would come some matter from him: I see none now.

Ajax. Thou bitch-wolf's son, canst thou not hear?   10
Feel then.   *Strikes him.*

Thers. The plague of Greece upon thee, thou mongrel beef-witted lord!

ACT II

Scene I

2–3. boils . . . generally?] *Q; Biles (full) all over generally, F.*   6. run then?]
8. Then] *Q;* Then there *F.*   *Capell;* run then, *Q;* run, *F.*   10. thou not]
Q; ᵁ̥ not *F.*   11 S.D.] *F; not in Q.*

Scene I

6. *botchy core*] Punning on (a) car-buncular, (b) bungled, or lumpy; and (a) boil, (b) heart.

8. *matter*] (a) pus, (b) good sense, reasoned argument.

12. *plague of Greece*] Perhaps the plague mentioned by Homer, *Iliad* I (so Steevens) or by Lydgate, III.4876–83—just before the dream of Andromache (Malone); but Thersites seems

to see the Greeks as perpetually plagued.

mongrel] Ajax was half-Greek, half-Trojan, his mother Hesione being Priam's sister: cf. 'This blended knight' (IV.v.86).

13. *beef-witted*] Perhaps 'ox-brained' (cf. I.ii.20–1), but it was conventionally supposed that a diet of beef dulled the wits: cf. *H5* III.vii.149–52, and *Tw.N.* I.iii.84–5.

Ajax. Speak then, thou vinewed'st leaven, speak! I
    will beat thee into handsomeness!   15
Thers. I shall sooner rail thee into wit and holiness,
    but I think thy horse will sooner con an oration
    than thou learn a prayer without book. Thou
    canst strike, canst thou?—A red murrain o' thy
    jade's tricks.   20
Ajax. Toadstool! Learn me the proclamation.
Thers. Dost thou think I have no sense, thou strikest
    me thus?
Ajax. The proclamation.
Thers. Thou art proclaimed fool, I think.   25
Ajax. Do not, porpentine, do not, my fingers itch—
Thers. I would thou didst itch from head to foot: and
    I had the scratching of thee, I would make thee
    the loathsomest scab in Greece. When thou art
    forth in the incursions thou strikest as slow as   30
    another.

14. vinewed'st] *Knight;* whinid'st *F;* vinew'd *Johnson;* vnsalted *Q.*   17. ora-
tion] *F;* oration without booke *Q.*   18. thou] *Q;* y̆ *F.*   learn a] *F;*
learne *Q.*   22. strikest] *Q;* strik'st *F.*   25. fool] *Q;* a foole *F.*   27–8. foot:
... thee] *This edn, conj. apud Camb.;* foot, ... thee, *Q,F (subst.).*   29. loath-
somest] *Q;* loathsom'st *F.*   29–31.] *Q; not in F.*

14. *vinewed'st*] mouldiest. I adopt
the usual form of the F reading: cf. the
name for the Dorset cheese—Blue
Vinny. (Q's *unsalted* is difficult: salt is
no part of leaven, and to take *leaven*
as = doctrine (Matthew xvi. 12)
would give two mixed and awkward
metaphors: unsalted leaven = tasteless doctrine.) Ajax wants the truth
from Thersites, and not malicious
abuse: hence, he probably alludes to
1 Corinthians v. 8 ('not with the old
leaven, neither with the leaven of
malice and wickedness').

17.] Contemptuous comparison of
man and horse occurs also at
I. iii. 211–12, III. iii. 126, 304–5.

con] learn by rote.

19. *red murrain*] a plague! (*red* being,
apparently a simple intensive).

21. *Toadstool*] Resembling Thersites in being (in many cases)
poisonous.

Learn me] tell me. Deighton glossed
as 'ascertain for me', but the sense
'tell', 'teach' is very common in
Shakespeare. It may be significant
that Caliban's use of it (*Tp.* I. ii. 366–7)
is also associated with the 'red plague'
(cf. l. 19, above).

22. *sense*] (a) intelligence, (b) capacity for physical sensation.

26. *porpentine*] porcupine. Professor
Brooks reminds me of J. Hall,
Virgidemiarum (1598), Lib. V, Sat.
III, ll. 1–2, where the porcupine is
made the emblem of Satire ('The
Satire should be like the Porcupine, /
That shoots sharp quills out in each
angry line').

my fingers itch] Cf. Capulet in rage to
Juliet (*Rom.* III. v. 164).

Ajax. I say the proclamation.

Thers. Thou grumblest and railest every hour on
Achilles, and thou art as full of envy at his greatness as Cerberus is at Proserpina's beauty—ay,   35
that thou bark'st at him.

Ajax. Mistress Thersites!

Thers. Thou shouldst strike him.

Ajax. Cobloaf!

Thers. He would pun thee into shivers with his fist,   40
as a sailor breaks a biscuit.

Ajax. You whoreson cur!   [*Beats him.*]

Thers. Do! do!

Ajax. Thou stool for a witch!

Thers. Ay, do! do! thou sodden-witted lord, thou hast   45
no more brain than I have in mine elbows: an
asinico may tutor thee. Thou scurvy-valiant ass,
thou art here but to thrash Trojans, and thou art
bought and sold among those of any wit, like a
barbarian slave. If thou use to beat me, I will   50
begin at thy heel, and tell what thou art by inches,
thou thing of no bowels thou!

38–43.] *As F; as one speech by Thersites, Q.*   42 S.D.] *Pope: not in Q,F.*
46. brain] *Q,F;* brain in thy head *Capell (conj.).*   47. Thou] *F;* you *Q.*
scurvy-valiant] *Dyce;* scuruy valiant *Q,F.*   48. thrash] *Q;* thresh *F.*

35. *Cerberus*] Three-headed dog,
guardian of Hades: supposed to fight
with, and mutilate, suitors for the
hand of Proserpina; hence, effectually,
envious of her beauty (*Variorum* note).

37.] A jeering reference to Thersites' scolding tongue. (Ajax is trying
very hard to hurt.)

39 ff.] See Introduction, pp. 11–12.

40. *pun*] pound (of which it is an
early variant).

44. *stool for a witch*] i.e. small, low,
contemptible object: Ajax is abusing
Thersites' appearance (cf. l. 21
Toadstool) but perhaps (very doubtfully) with an allusion to the ducking-
stool for scolds (cf. l. 37). Walker
(NCS) ingeniously argues that the
confusion of speeches has wrongly
given this to Ajax: that Thersites is
punning; and that *stool* = privy (the

usual pun on *Ajax / a jakes*: cf. *LLL*
v. ii. 571–2). But Shakespeare is normally more obvious than this on the
subject, and none of the present
exchange is subtle: it seems better to
follow QF.

45–6.] Capell's conjecture gives a
rhetorical balance to the insult, which
persists in the modern version (X has
more brain in his little finger than Y
has in his whole body), but is not
therefore right: cf. Tilley W 548.

47. *asinico*] little ass (from Spanish
asnico, dim. of *asno*).

49. *bought and sold*] handled like
something inanimate; there is almost
certainly some suggestion of the proverbial sense 'tricked, betrayed': cf.
Tilley B 787, and *R3* v. iii. 305–6.

51. *by inches*] methodically, bit by bit.

52. *bowels*] feelings.

Ajax. You dog!

Thers. You scurvy lord!

Ajax. You cur!   [*Beats him.*]   55

Thers. Mars his idiot! do, rudeness: do, camel: do, do!

Enter ACHILLES *and* PATROCLUS.

Achill. Why, how now, Ajax, wherefore do ye thus?
How now, Thersites, what's the matter man?

Thers. You see him there, do you?

Achill. Ay: what's the matter?   60

Thers. Nay look upon him.

Achill. So I do: what's the matter?

Thers. Nay but regard him well.

Achill. Well?—why, so I do.

Thers. But yet you look not well upon him, for who-   65
somever you take him to be, he is Ajax.

Achill. I know that, fool.

Thers. Ay, but that fool knows not himself.

Ajax. Therefore I beat thee.

Thers. Lo, lo, lo, lo, what modicums of wit he utters—   70
his evasions have ears thus long. I have bobbed
his brain more than he has beat my bones. I will
buy nine sparrows for a penny, and his pia mater

55 S.D.] *Rowe; not* in *Q,F.*   56 S.D.] *F; not* in *Q.*   57. ye thus] *Q;* you
this *F.*   58. man?] *F;* man. *Q.*   59. there,] *F;* there? *Q.*   60. matter?]
F3; matter. *Q,F.*   64. Well?] *Kittredge;* well, *Q,F.*   so I do] *Q;* I do so *F.*
72. I] *F;* It *Q.*

59–65. *see him . . . look upon him . . .
regard him well . . . look not well upon
him*] Typical clown's routine.

65–6. *whosomever*] Variant form of
whosoever, perhaps more old-fashioned.
Professor Jenkins points out to me
that, in *Hamlet, -somever* forms tend to
occur in Q2, and *-soever* forms in F.

66. *Ajax*] If the pun on this name
occurs at all in the play, it is here.

71. *evasions*] defensive arguments,
self-excuses.

have ears thus long] are asinine.
(Thersites mimes, with fingers to his
head.)

bobbed] beaten, struck.

73. *nine sparrows for a penny*] The
average price between that of
Matthew x.29 (two for a farthing)
and Luke xii.6 (five for two farthings),
as *Variorum* noted.

pia mater] one of the membranes
covering the brain: hence sometimes
used for the brain itself. Holofernes
shows how ambiguously it could
appear ('these are begot in the
ventricle of memory, nourished in the
womb of *pia mater*, and delivered upon
the mellowing of occasion': *LLL*
iv.ii.66–9). Cf. also *Tw.N.* i.v.115–
16: 'one of thy kin has a most weak
pia mater.'

is not worth the ninth part of a sparrow. This lord,
Achilles—Ajax, who wears his wit in his belly and   75
his guts in his head—I'll tell you what I say of him.
Achill. What?
Thers. I say, this Ajax—   [*Ajax offers to strike him.*]
Achill. Nay, good Ajax.
Thers. Has not so much wit—   80
Achill. Nay, I must hold you.
Thers. As will stop the eye of Helen's needle, for whom
he comes to fight.
Achill. Peace, fool!
Thers. I would have peace and quietness, but the fool   85
will not: he there, that he: look you there.
Ajax. O thou damned cur, I shall—
Achill. Will you set your wit to a fool's?
Thers. No I warrant you, the fool's will shame it.
Patro. Good words, Thersites.   90
Achill. What's the quarrel?
Ajax. I bade the vile owl go learn me the tenor of the
proclamation, and he rails upon me.
Thers. I serve thee not.
Ajax. Well, go to, go to.   95
Thers. I serve here voluntary.
Achill. Your last service was suff'rance—'twas not
voluntary, no man is beaten voluntary: Ajax was
here the voluntary, and you as under an impress.

76. I'll] *F;* I *Q.*   78 S.D.] *After Rowe (following 77); not in Q,F.*   80. wit—]
F3; wit. *Q,F.*   84. fool!] *Q* (foole?); foole. *F.*   89. the] *Q;* for a *F.*
92. the vile owl] *Q;* thee vile Owle, *F;* thee, vile Owl, *F4.*   97. suff'rance]
Q; sufferance *F.*

75–6. *his wit in his belly and his guts
in his head*] Cf. Burton, *Anatomy of
Melancholy*, Democritus Junior to the
Reader (Everyman edn, p. 67),
which also cites Cornelius Agrippa,
Ep. 28, Lib. 7.
82. *eye . . . needle*] An obscene
quibble: cf. *H5* II.i.32–5: 'we cannot
lodge and board a dozen or fourteen
gentlewomen that live honestly by the
prick of their needles, but it will be
thought we keep a bawdy-house

straight.'
88.] Cf. Proverbs xxvi.4: 'Answer
not a fool according to his folly, lest
thou also be like unto him' (also cf.
Tilley F 510); but v.5 reverses the
proverb.
90.] *Bona verba quaeso* (a familiar
tag from Terence, *Andria*, l. 204, pleading for restraint); cf. *Wiv.* I.i.112–13,
and Kyd, *Spanish Tragedy*, IV.i.184.
99. *as . . . impress*] (a) conscripted;
(b) marked as by a seal or stamp.

Thers. E'en so—a great deal of your wit too lies in   100
your sinews, or else there be liars. Hector shall
have a great catch and a knock out either of your
brains: a were as good crack a fusty nut with no
kernel.

Achill. What, with me too, Thersites?   105

Thers. There's Ulysses, and old Nestor, whose wit was
mouldy ere your grandsires had nails on their toes,
yoke you like draught-oxen and make you plough
up the wars.

Achill. What? what?   110

Thers. Yes, good sooth: to, Achilles: to, Ajax: to—

Ajax. I shall cut out your tongue.

Thers. 'Tis no matter, I shall speak as much wit as
thou afterwards.

Patro. No more words, Thersites; peace.   115

Thers. I will hold my peace when Achilles' brach bids
me, shall I?

Achill. There's for you, Patroclus.

Thers. I will see you hanged like clotpolls ere I come
any more to your tents: I will keep where there is   120
wit stirring, and leave the faction of fools.   *Exit.*

Patro. A good riddance.

Achill. Marry, this, sir, is proclaim'd through all our host,
That Hector, by the fifth hour of the sun,

102. and . . . out] *Kittredge (subst.); and knocke at Q; if he knocke out F.*
103. a were] *Q; he were F.*   107. your] *Theobald; their Q,F.*   on their
toes] *F; not in Q.*   109. wars] *Q; warre F.*   111. sooth . . . to—] *As
Theobald; sooth, to Achilles, to Aiax, to—Q,F.*   113. wit] *Capell, NCS; not in
Q,F.*   115. Thersites; peace.] *Q (Thersites peace.); Thersites. | F.*   116. brach]
Rowe; brooch, Q,F (Brooch).   119. clotpolls] *Kittredge; Clotpoles F;
Clatpoles Q.*   124. fifth] *F (fift); first Q.*

105. *with me*] trying to be even with
me: 'getting at' me.

107. *your*] Probably written *y^r* in
Q's copy, as Malone saw.

111. *to . . . to*] Thersites is crying on
his team.

113. *wit*] If Q and F are right, then
Thersites' retort must be elliptical
(*speak* = speak good sense). It seems
more likely that something was
omitted: I follow Capell.

116. *brach*] Rowe's emendation is
generally accepted, and wholly plausible (supposing *brach* were read as
broch). In view of Achilles' comment,
it seems unlikely that Thersites meant
(or was taken to mean) that Patroclus
was a catamite: *brach* = bitch (hence,
effeminate but favoured creature).

119. *clotpolls*] dunderheads.

124. *fifth*] Much more likely than
Q's *first*: this is a public tournament,

Will with a trumpet 'twixt our tents and Troy,   125
Tomorrow morning, call some knights to arms
That hath a stomach, and such a one that dare
Maintain—I know not what—'tis trash—Farewell.

Ajax. Farewell: who shall answer him?

Achill. I know not, 'tis put to lott'ry: otherwise   130
He knew his man.

Ajax. Oh, meaning you? I will go learn more of it.   *Exeunt.*

[SCENE II] (Reflects lii)

Enter PRIAM, HECTOR, TROILUS, PARIS, *and* HELENUS.

Priam. After so many hours, lives, speeches spent,
Thus once again says Nestor from the Greeks:
'Deliver Helen, and all damage else—
As honour, loss of time, travail, expense,
Wounds, friends, and what else dear that is consum'd   5
In hot digestion of this cormorant war—
Shall be struck off.' Hector, what say you to't?

Hect. Though no man lesser fears the Greeks than I,
As far as toucheth my particular,
Yet, dread Priam,   10
There is no lady of more softer bowels,
More spongy to suck in the sense of fear,

---

128. Maintain—I] *Hanmer;* Maintaine I *Q,F.*   132 S.D.] *Pope: Exit | F; no in Q; Exeunt* Ach. *and* Pat. *Capell (after 131).*

Scene II

9–10.] *As Collier; one line, Q,F.*   9. toucheth] *Q;* touches *F.*

not a private duel. Thersites (III.iii.293) expects a decision by 11 a.m.

127. *stomach*] inclination (i.e. metaphorical 'appetite'); cf. IV.v.263, III.iii.219. There may also be a hint of the sense 'courage'.

Scene II

1–7.] Priam's formal language belongs to his function as president of debate, reporting a diplomatic ex-change: hence the lists at l. 1, and ll. 4–5. He is more to the point, and briefer, than Agamemnon.

2. *once . . . Nestor*] There was no major embassy by Nestor in Shake-speare's sources: Ulysses and Dio-medes were the chief ambassadors.

6. *cormorant*] sea-bird of supposedly gluttonous appetite: cf. *LLL* I.i.4 ('cormorant devouring Time').

11. *softer bowels*] more merciful nature.

More ready to cry out 'Who knows what follows?'
Than Hector is. The wound of peace is surety,
Surety secure; but modest doubt is call'd   15
The beacon of the wise, the tent that searches
To th'bottom of the worst. Let Helen go.
Since the first sword was drawn about this question
Every tithe soul 'mongst many thousand dismes
Hath been as dear as Helen—I mean, of ours.   20
If we have lost so many tenths of ours
To guard a thing not ours nor worth to us
(Had it our name) the value of one ten,
What merit's in that reason which denies
The yielding of her up?

Troil.   Fie, fie, my brother: 25
Weigh you the worth and honour of a king
So great as our dread father's in a scale
Of common ounces? Will you with counters sum
The past-proportion of his infinite,
And buckle in a waist most fathomless   30
With spans and inches so diminutive
As fears and reasons? Fie for godly shame!
Helenus. No marvel though you bite so sharp of reasons,
You are so empty of them. Should not our father

13. 'Who . . . follows?'] *As Pope;* who knowes what followes *Q,F.*
14–15. surety, / Surety] *F;* surely / Surely *Q.*   17. worst. Let] *F;* worst let
Q; wound. Let *Hanmer.*   go.] *F2;* go, *Q,F.*   25. up?] *Q;* vp. *F.*
27. father's] *Q;* Father *F.*   29. past-proportion] *Johnson;* past proportion *Q,F.*
33. sharp of] *Q;* sharp at *F.*   34. them.] *Rowe;* them, *F;* them *Q.*   father]
F; father; *Q.*

14–15. *The . . . secure*] 'peace is most
endangered by overconfidence'; and
cf. *Mac.* III.v.32–3 ('And you all
know, security / Is mortals' chiefest
enemy').

16. *tent*] roll of gauze or other
(medicated) material, used for prob-
ing a wound.

19–20. *Every . . . Helen*] 'Every soul
that has been taken as a tithe by war
is as dear as Helen, and of such tithes
there have been many thousands'
(Deighton): i.e. of the Trojan forces,
war has taken one man in ten.

19. *dismes*] tenths: i.e. 'tithe souls',

all the tithe men who have been taken
from all the tens.

27. *father's*] Since it is *the worth and
honour* that is being weighed, the
grammar of Q says so. F's *father* is
affected by the proximity of *king.*

29. *past-proportion*] immeasurable
quantity.

infinite] infinity: cf. *Ado* II.iii.102.

33. *bite . . . reasons*] Q's *bite of* is an
older form than F's *bite at:* OED gives
no evidence for this late use. But if Q
be wrong, why is its error historically
possible?

Bear the great sway of his affairs with reason   35
Because your speech hath none that tell him so?
Troil. You are for dreams and slumbers, brother priest,
   You fur your gloves with reason; here are your reasons:
   You know an enemy intends you harm,
   You know a sword employ'd is perilous,   40
   And reason flies the object of all harm.
   Who marvels then when Helenus beholds
   A Grecian and his sword, if he do set
   The very wings of reason to his heels,
   And fly like chidden Mercury from Jove,   45
   Or like a star disorb'd? Nay, if we talk of reason,
   Let's shut our gates and sleep: manhood and honour
   Should have hare hearts, would they but fat their
      thoughts
   With this cramm'd reason: reason and respect

35. reason] *Q; reasons F.*   36. tell him so?] *Q; tells him so. F.*   45–6.] *As*
Q; Or . . . Reason, / And . . . Ioue, F.   46. disorb'd?] *Q; disorb'd. F.*
47. Let's] *F; Set's Q.*   48. hare] *Q; hard F.*

35. *reason*] faculty which orders
thought. F's *reasons* is unnecessary:
singular and plural play off against
each other in these speeches, and one
need not emend for rhetorical con-
gruence. Rowe's *with reasons* (l. 38) is
thus too careful to avoid the alternative sense of 'with (good) reason':
Troilus is bludgeoning his brother
with both words.

37 ff.] Troilus' attack on Helenus
may derive either from Caxton
(p. 524) or from Lydgate (II. 3001–69).

38. *You . . . reason*] 'you comfort
yourself with arguments of prudence'.
Obviously contemptuous, although
commentators differ on the precise
implication: it is perhaps unlikely
that there is any connection of *fur*
with academic dress, although Whiter
thought so (*Specimen of a Commentary*,
pp. 130–5: see *Variorum* note).

41. *object*] 'presentation of something to the eye' (OED, citing this
passage); cf. *objection* (4).

45. *chidden Mercury*] When an infant,
Mercury [= Hermes] stole Apollo's

cattle: Apollo arraigned him before
Jove [= Zeus], who commanded that
Mercury should take Apollo at once
to Pylos, to restore the cattle, which
was promptly done (*Hymn to Hermes*).
The theft only is told in *Metamorphoses* II; the whole theft and rebuke
(as in the *Hymn*) is briefly alluded to
in Horace, *Odes*, trans. P. Francis, I. x
('When from the god who gilds the
pole, / Even yet a boy, his herds you
stole, / With angry voice the
threat'ning power / Bade thee the
fraudful prey restore'), and it is perhaps from Ovid and Horace, rather
than from the Greek *Hymn*, that
Shakespeare drew—especially as the
next lines of the Ode refer to Priam
and Agamemnon.

46. *star disorb'd*] 'shooting star'
(Baldwin, *Variorum*).

48. *hare*] Noted for timidity: cf.
III. ii. 87–8 ('the voice of lions and the
act of hares').

49. *cramm'd*] fattened (perhaps,
forcibly fed).

respect] consideration, caution.

    Make livers pale, and lustihood deject.   50
Hect. Brother,
    She is not worth what she doth cost the keeping.
Troil. What's aught but as 'tis valued?
Hect. But value dwells not in particular will:
    It holds his estimate and dignity   55
    As well wherein 'tis precious of itself
    As in the prizer. 'Tis mad idolatry
    To make the service greater than the god;
    And the will dotes that is attributive
    To what infectiously itself affects,
    Without some image of th'affected merit.   60
Troil. I take today a wife, and my election
    Is led on in the conduct of my will:
    My will enkindled by mine eyes and ears,

50. Make] *Q;* Makes *F.*   51–2.] *This edn;* Brother, . . . keeping. *Q;* Brother . . . worth / What . . . holding. *F;* Brother, . . . cost / The holding. *Theobald.* 57. mad] *Q;* made *F.*   59. attributive] *Q;* inclineable *F.*

50. *livers*] seat of courage and passion.

52. *keeping*] Cf. ll. 82, 150.

53.] Cf. Tilley W 923.

54. *particular*] of one man.

55. *his*] Cf. Abbott §228 (*his* = its).

57–8. *'Tis . . . god*] Noble cites Matthew xxiii. 19 ('whether is greater, the gift, or the altar that sanctifieth the gift?'); but the whole passage attacking the scribes and Pharisees in that chapter seems to be relevant, and Shakespeare alludes to it several times in the play (especially v. 27, cf. v.viii. 1, and v. 33, cf. iii.i. 129). The rejection of Cassandra's warnings (l. 122 and also v.iii) is analogous to vv. 34–8.

59. *attributive*] bestowing or ascribing (the qualities which are admired): i.e. the doting lover sees nothing intrinsically of value in the beloved, but merely imputes value, without (as Hector explains) any evidence for its presence. F's *inclineable* is a weak substitute for *attributive*, and makes *affects* tautologous.

60. *infectiously*] morbidly.

affects] loves, is delighted with.

61. *affected merit*] excellence in the object admired.

62. *I . . . wife*] A mere postulate; 'suppose I were to marry'. Troilus' hypothesis, not unnaturally, hints at his real concerns.

62–6. *I . . . judgement*] Troilus' vocabulary is orthodox, and even learned—*election* = act of deliberate choice (cf. *Ethics*, iii.2)—but his psychology may be suspect. *Eyes* and *ears* ought to offer evidence, and *will and judgement* would then decide the matter between them; whereas Troilus' choice is effected by enflamed *will*. One might save the appearances by saying that this is not his own behaviour, but that of any young man whose passions dominate him (i.e. the whole passage is mere postulate): whatever the truth of it, Troilus can see clearly that, in any matter involving will and judgement, those faculties are truly *dangerous shores* in respect of the eyes and ears

Two traded pilots 'twixt the dangerous shores   65
Of will and judgement—how may I avoid,
Although my will distaste what it elected,
The wife I choose? There can be no evasion
To blench from this and to stand firm by honour.
We turn not back the silks upon the merchant   70
When we have soil'd them, nor the remainder viands
We do not throw in unrespective sieve
Because we now are full. It was thought meet
Paris should do some vengeance on the Greeks;
Your breath with full consent bellied his sails;   75
The seas and winds, old wranglers, took a truce

65. shores] F; shore Q.   68. choose] Q; chose F.   71. soil'd] Q; spoyl'd F.
72. sieve] Q (siue); same F; place F2; sink Delius; safe conj. Delius (1846).
75. with] Q; of F.

which ply between them (traded pilots = skilled navigators). Once a man is committed, he may, says Troilus, be obliged to stand firm by his decision: to appeal, in that condition, to will or to reason alone is to risk shipwreck. Cf. Aquinas, Summa Theologiae, 1 a–2 ae. xiii. 1, c & ad. 2: 'Choice is materially an act of the will, formally an act of the reason. The decision or judgement, drawn by the reason as a conclusion, is followed by choice in the will.'

66. avoid] get rid of, expel, banish (OED 5).

67. distaste] disrelish, dislike, regard with aversion. Apparently a new word (literal sense 1586, this sense 1592: OED), and possibly a translation of Italian (di)sgustare or of French desgouster. Shakespeare uses it on six occasions, of which four occur in this play.

68–9. There . . . honour] One cannot evade one's responsibility and yet remain honourable.

68. evasion] subterfuge, fallacious argument.

69. blench] flinch, shrink from.

this] i.e. the election of l. 62 (or rather, in this case, the moral consequences of that choice).

71. soil'd] F's spoyl'd is less specific

and forceful. The food image which follows is very potent, and invites the more exact and active word.

72. unrespective] confused, without distinction or order.

sieve] basket (for fragments), 'a common voider' (Johnson); cf. the baskets at Matthew xv. 37 and Mark vi. 43, for the fragments of the loaves and fishes. It is, however, odd to have consecutive words ending in -ive / -ieve: unrespective is plainly right, being like tortive, persistive, protractive, in I.iii; and sieve may be wrong. J. H. Walter suggests (privately) that one should read sure (= sewer): cf. v.i. 76.

74. do . . . on] cf. R3 I.ii. 87: 'For doing worthy vengeance on thyself'.

75. with . . . consent] Q's reading makes it clear that the full consent is the immediate cause of the swelling sails: breath = both speech and expiration. F's of simplifies the phrase, perhaps to its loss.

bellied] swelled. Apparently the earliest use of the verb in this sense; but Shakespeare had already played with the idea in MND II.i. 128–9: 'When we have laugh'd to see the sails conceive / And grow big-bellied with the wanton wind'.

76. wranglers] quarrellers: (perhaps) disputants, debaters.

And did him service: he touch'd the ports desir'd,
And for an old aunt whom the Greeks held captive,
He brought a Grecian queen, whose youth and freshness
Wrinkles Apollo's, and makes stale the morning.   80
Why keep we her?—The Grecians keep our aunt.
Is she worth keeping?—Why, she is a pearl
Whose price hath launch'd above a thousand ships,
And turn'd crown'd kings to merchants.
If you'll avouch 'twas wisdom Paris went—   85
As you must needs, for you all cried 'Go, go':
If you'll confess he brought home worthy prize—
As you must needs, for you all clapp'd your hands
And cried 'Inestimable!': why do you now
The issue of your proper wisdoms rate,   90
And do a deed that never Fortune did—

80. stale] *F;* pale *Q.*   87. he] *F;* be *Q.*   91. never Fortune] *Q;* Fortune neuer *F.*

78. *old aunt*] Hesione, daughter of Laomedon, and sister of Priam. She was to have been sacrificed to a sea-monster: Herakles, by compact, slew the monster, was cheated of his bargain, sacked Troy, killed Laomedon, and gave Hesione to Telamon, by whom she became mother of Teucer. Shakespeare follows his sources (e.g. Lydgate, III.2046–8) in making her the mother of Ajax also.

80. *stale*] F's reading continues the contrast with both *youth* and *freshness* (cf. OED 4: 'past the prime of life'; and OED 2: 'having lost its freshness [sc. of food and drink]'). Cf. also *Wint.* IV.i.12–14: 'so shall I do / To th'freshest things now reigning, and make stale / The glistering of this present'.

82. *pearl*] Here = object of supreme worth (as in Matthew xiii.45–6). Troilus makes Cressida a pearl (at I.i.100), and himself a merchant.

83.] Ovid (*Metamorphoses*, XII.7), Virgil (*Aeneid*, II.198), Caxton (II, p. 546, 'twelfe honderd and foûr

and twenty shippis') all warrant this total: the immediate source is Marlowe, *Dr Faustus* (v.i.107), and not *2 Tamburlaine*, II.iv.87–8 (as the rhythm of the line makes plain).

price] value, worth: pre-eminence. The collocation of *pearl* and *price* makes quite clear the allusion to Matthew xiii.46 (one pearl of great price).

87. *worthy*] The Q reading is closer to l. 82 and to the whole context: it is not easy to see F's *noble* as a misreading.

90. *proper*] own.

rate] chide, reprove. Deighton supposed a sense 'condemn' (which the context would bear, but which OED does not support). Perhaps *issue* should be understood as 'offspring', rather than 'consequence, upshot', which is the more usual sense in Shakespeare.

91.] i.e. value something above price, and then arbitrarily account it valueless. Fortune herself was never so inconsistent.

Beggar the estimation which you priz'd
Richer than sea and land? O theft most base,
That we have stol'n what we do fear to keep;
But thieves unworthy of a thing so stol'n,　　　　95
That in their country did them that disgrace
We fear to warrant in our native place.
Cass. [*Within.*] Cry, Trojans, cry!
Priam.　　　　　　　　What noise, what shriek is this?
Troil. 'Tis our mad sister, I do know her voice.
Cass. [*Within.*] Cry, Trojans!　　　　　　　　100
Hect. It is Cassandra.

Enter CASSANDRA *raving.*

Cass. Cry, Trojans, cry! Lend me ten thousand eyes,
And I will fill them with prophetic tears.
Hect. Peace, sister, peace.
Cass. Virgins and boys, mid-age and wrinkled eld,　　105
Soft infancy, that nothing canst but cry,
Add to my clamours! Let us pay betimes
A moiety of that mass of moan to come.

101 S.D.] *Q* (*after* 97); *Enter Cassandra with her haire about her eares* | *F* (*after* 97).
105. eld] *Collier, conj. Theobald;* elders *Q;* old *F.*　　106. canst] *Q;* can *F.*
107. clamours] *Q;* clamour *F.*

92. *Beggar*] deprive of value (lit. 'impoverish').

estimation] object of value (lit. 'value').

95-7.] 'But we are even more unworthy of the prize we gained in the rape of Helen, when in our very city we are afraid to justify the disgrace we did the Greeks [by that rape] in their homeland.'

95. *But*] Capell objected that the word was unnecessary; but the argument proceeds *a fortiori*—to fear to keep an object stolen is not the same as to fear to justify the theft (especially when the theft was abroad, in Greece, and the justification at home, in Troy).

105. *eld*] Theobald's suggestion is attractive, and I follow it: as he observed, 'all the rest' (= *mid-age, infancy, virgins* and *boys*) 'are substan-

tives'. OED notes *old* (F) as a noun (= old man, old woman) but gives no example after 1532; whereas *eld* occurs elsewhere in Shakespeare for 'people of former times' and 'old age' (e.g. *Meas.* III.i.36). F's *old* may, therefore, be only a misreading of *eld.* Yet *elders* may be right. The sense of 'parents, forefathers' occurs no later than the Geneva Bible (2 Timothy i.3: 'I thanke God, whome I serue from my elders'), although *elders* = seniors is still current. Either meaning would fit, if the contrast be with *infancy* (l. 106): if with *virgins* and *mid-age,* then 'seniors' only would answer.

107. *betimes*] before it is too late.

108. *moiety*] part (usually less than half, although OED gives 'half' as the primary sense). Shakespeare seems frequently to use the word as implying a payment which is due, or a share

Cry, Trojans, cry! Practise your eyes with tears!
Troy must not be, nor goodly Ilion stand: 110
Our firebrand brother Paris burns us all.
Cry, Trojans, cry! A Helen and a woe:
Cry, cry! Troy burns, or else let Helen go.   *Exit.*
Hect. Now, youthful Troilus, do not these high strains
Of divination in our sister work   115
Some touches of remorse? Or is your blood
So madly hot, that no discourse of reason,
Nor fear of bad success in a bad cause,
Can qualify the same?
Troil.   Why, brother Hector,
We may not think the justness of each act   120
Such and no other than event doth form it,
Nor once deject the courage of our minds

122–3. minds / . . . mad:] *Rowe (subst.)*; mindes, / Because *Cassandra's* madde,
Q; mindes; / Because *Cassandra's* mad, *F*.

legally bestowed; cf. *Lucr.*, Dedication; Sonnet 46, l. 12; *Mer. V.* iv.i.26;
Ham. i.i.93.

109. *Practise . . . tears*] learn to weep.
The formula 'practise [noun] with
[noun]' is uncommon; but perhaps
cf. *Meas.* iii.i.162–3: 'to practise his
judgement with the disposition of
natures.'

111. *firebrand brother*] The pregnant
Hecuba dreamed that she was
delivered of a firebrand, which burned
Troy: Virgil, *Aeneid*, vii.320, x.704–5.
(Falstaff's page confuses the story
with that of Meleager, *2H4* ii.ii.85–6.)

114–15. *strains . . . divination*] prophetic utterances. (For *strain* v. OED
12b, 'passage of song or poetry'; but
perhaps 12c is the more appropriate
sense, 'stream or flow of impassioned
or ungoverned language'—obviously
developed from 12b, but not noted
before 1649.)

116. *touches*] sensations, feelings
(OED 13b): (perhaps) trace, 'smack'
(OED 19, cf. 2c).

117. *discourse of reason*] process of
ratiocination. Strictly, *discourse* alone
is enough (= rationality, reasoning),
but the intensive phrase was used

from the fifteenth until the nineteenth
century.

119. *qualify*] moderate. (The object
of *this* verb, in Shakespeare's usage, is
frequently passion, humour, heat, or
fire.)

120–6. *We . . . gracious*] It has been
objected (by Walker, in NCS) that
this makes the goodness of the quarrel
depend merely upon the fact that
their honours are engaged in it. But
that is not what Troilus says: he
argues (a little elliptically) that,
although Cassandra is mad, the rest
of the Trojans decided to commit
themselves in honour to defend Helen.
They may, he implies, be proved im-
prudent by the consequences; but
justice cannot be made merely pragmatic. Their honours have *ratified* the
goodness of the quarrel: they have not
created it. The real difficulty lies in the
phrase *make it gracious*, which may
mean either 'create the appearance of
desirable qualities in it' or 'make it
evidently as gracious as it really is'.
Troilus implies the latter sense, Hector the former. The two senses torment
Troilus throughout v.ii.

121. *event*] outcome.

Because Cassandra's mad: her brain-sick raptures
Cannot distaste the goodness of a quarrel
Which hath our several honours all engag'd   125
To make it gracious. For my private part,
I am no more touch'd than all Priam's sons;
And Jove forbid there should be done amongst us
Such things as might offend the weakest spleen
To fight for and maintain.   130
Paris.   Else might the world convince of levity
As well my undertakings as your counsels.
But I attest the gods, your full consent
Gave wings to my propension, and cut off
All fears attending on so dire a project.   135
For what, alas, can these my single arms?
What propugnation is in one man's valour
To stand the push and enmity of those
This quarrel would excite? Yet I protest,
Were I alone to pass the difficulties,   140
And had as ample power as I have will,
Paris should ne'er retract what he hath done,
Nor faint in the pursuit.
Priam.   Paris, you speak
Like one besotted on your sweet delights.
You have the honey still, but these the gall: 145

---

124. *distaste*] make distasteful (= call in question).

129. *spleen*] courage, spirit. (A dangerous word, in this context: it can also mean 'caprice, passion, impetuosity'.)

131. *convince*] convict, prove guilty.

133. *attest*] call to witness.

134. *propension*] inclination: here, almost = 'desire', for it has *wings*. Paris's mind is moving rapidly from the propensity to the passion then generated, and thence to the course of action (*project*) which ensued.

135. *dire*] frightening. *Dirus* (Lat.) = cursed, cruel, deadly, damnable; the *dirae sorores* were the Furies.

136. *single*] of one man.

137. *propugnation*] defence, protection.

138. *push*] attack, enmity. But note that *stand the push* apparently means 'be exposed to, put up with (perforce)'; cf. *1H4* III.ii.66, *2H4* II.ii.36, where in both places the tone is contemptuous. Paris seems to be speaking simultaneously of the war and of a personal feud.

140. *pass*] experience, suffer (cf. *Oth.* I.iii.167: 'the dangers I had pass'd').

145.] Cf. Tilley H 556.

gall] Shakespeare's constant antonym for sweetness: cf. *Rom.* I.i.192.

So to be valiant is no praise at all.

Paris. Sir, I propose not merely to myself
     The pleasures such a beauty brings with it,
     But I would have the soil of her fair rape
     Wip'd off in honourable keeping her.   150
     What treason were it to the ransack'd queen,
     Disgrace to your great worths, and shame to me,
     Now to deliver her possession up
     On terms of base compulsion! Can it be,
     That so degenerate a strain as this   155
     Should once set footing in your generous bosoms?
     There's not the meanest spirit on our party
     Without a heart to dare or sword to draw
     When Helen is defended: nor none so noble
     Whose life were ill bestow'd, or death unfam'd,   160
     Where Helen is the subject. Then, I say,
     Well may we fight for her whom we know well
     The world's large spaces cannot parallel.

Hect. Paris and Troilus, you have both said well,
     And on the cause and question now in hand   165
     Have gloz'd, but superficially—not much
     Unlike young men, whom Aristotle thought

146. So] *Q,F;* So, *Theobald.*   166. gloz'd,] *Q,F;* gloz'd *Theobald.*

146. *So*] in that way.
praise] merit, virtue.
149. *soil*] moral stain or tarnish.
150. *honourable*] Probably an adjective used adverbially (so Schmidt, and Abbott §1); although it might be possible to see it as an adjective, and *keeping* as a noun. (*Keeping of* would be the expected form.)
151. *ransack'd*] carried off as plunder.
153. *her possession*] i.e. possession of her.
154. *On . . . compulsion*] Cf. *1H4* II.iv.231–6: 'What, upon compulsion? . . . Give you a reason on compulsion? . . . I would give no man a reason upon compulsion, I.'
155. *strain*] 'admixture in a character of some quality somewhat contrasting with the rest' (OED 8b).

156. *generous*] noble; i.e. *generosus* (Lat.): playing on the word *degenerate.*
157. *on our party*] i.e. on the Trojan side.
161. *subject*] cause, occasion (of arms); cf. I.i.93: 'It is too starv'd a subject for my sword'.
166. *gloz'd*] glossed, commented. The reference to scholastic method is certainly the primary sense here, but Hector may hint at the uncomplimentary 'talked smoothly and speciously' (OED 3).
167. *Aristotle*] An obvious (and trivial) anachronism. (For the significance of Aristotle's writings in the rest of the speech, see Appendix III.) Rowe, offended by such a solecism, chose to read 'graver sages'.

Unfit to hear moral philosophy.
The reasons you allege do more conduce
To the hot passion of distemper'd blood   170
Than to make up a free determination
'Twixt right and wrong: for pleasure and revenge
Have ears more deaf than adders to the voice
Of any true decision. Nature craves
All dues be render'd to their owners: now   175
What nearer debt in all humanity
Than wife is to the husband? If this law
Of nature be corrupted through affection,
And that great minds, of partial indulgence
To their benumbed wills, resist the same,   180
There is a law in each well-order'd nation
To curb those raging appetites that are

173. adders] *Q,F;* adders' *conj. apud Camb.*   179–80. minds, . . . indulgence /
To . . . wills,] *Rowe (subst.);* mindes . . . indulgence, / To . . . wills *Q,F.*

168. *moral philosophy*] The sixteenth-century term for political philosophy, although early commentators supposed it to be an error (cf. *Variorum* note, which suggests moreover how common the phrase was). Aristotle's opinion may be found in the *Ethics,* 1.3 (i.e. very early in the work, where any casual reader might find it), and was well known: otherwise, Erasmus' *Colloquies* ('De colloquiorum utilitate'), which quotes Aristotle, may be the source.

170. *distemper'd*] diseased, disordered (of the body): deranged (of the mind): disturbed, disproportioned (of the bodily humours). Effectually, all three senses are present.

171. *determination*] judicial decision.

172. *'Twixt . . . wrong*] Hector takes much the same (Aristotelian) view of Justice as Ulysses does (cf. note to I.iii.117).

173. *ears . . . adders*] Proverbial: cf. Tilley A 32, and Psalm lviii ('Even like the deaf adder that stoppeth her ears; which refuseth to hear the voice of the charmer, charm he never so wisely'). (I cite the Book of Common

Prayer as likely to be the version most familiar to Shakespeare.)

175. *All . . . owners*] Cf. Tilley D 634, and Romans xiii.7.

176–7. *What . . . husband?*] Cf. Aristotle, *Ethics,* v.6: 'Hence justice between husband and wife comes nearer true justice than does that between master and slaves, or that between the father and his family. It is in fact justice between husband and wife that is the true form of domestic justice.'

176. *humanity*] human nature.

178. *affection*] (a) passion, lust (as opposed to reason); (b) bias, partiality (OED 8).

179. *that*] Cf. Abbott §285.

of] = through.

partial indulgence] sympathetic or lenient gratification of a desire. (The phrase also has a technical significance in Roman Catholic usage.)

180. *benumbed*] insentient: 'That is, inflexible, immoveable, no longer obedient to superior direction' (Johnson).

182. *curb*] restrain. Almost always used figuratively by Shakespeare: cf.

Most disobedient and refractory.
If Helen then be wife to Sparta's king,
As it is known she is, these moral laws   185
Of nature and of nations speak aloud
To have her back return'd: thus to persist
In doing wrong extenuates not wrong,
But makes it much more heavy. Hector's opinion
Is this in way of truth: yet ne'ertheless,   190
My spritely brethren, I propend to you
In resolution to keep Helen still
For 'tis a cause that hath no mean dependence
Upon our joint and several dignities.
Troil. Why, there you touch'd the life of our design: 195
Were it not glory that we more affected
Than the performance of our heaving spleens, *(passion of..)*
I would not wish a drop of Trojan blood *anger*
Spent more in her defence. But, worthy Hector,
She is a theme of honour and renown,   200
A spur to valiant and magnanimous deeds,

186. nations] *Q;* Nation *F.*   195. Why,] *Theobald;* Why *Q;* Why? *F.*

Lucr., l. 706, 'curb his heat'; *Mer. V.* I.ii.23-4, 'the will of a living daughter curb'd'; *Shr.* IV.i.196, 'curb her mad and headstrong humour'; *Cor.* III.i.38, 'curb the will of the nobility'.

183. *refractory*] stubborn, perverse, rebellious.

185-6. *moral . . . nations*] A common distinction, although the law of nations is really a derivative from natural law (and that from divine law): cf. Hooker, *Of the Laws of Ecclesiastical Polity,* I.iii-x; Aristotle, *Ethics,* v.7.

189-90. *Hector's . . . truth*] Hector admits both an absolute and a relative standard: absolutely, it is wrong to keep Helen and to continue the war; but on the other hand, honour is also properly concerned, and their honours would be impugned if they did *not* keep Helen.

191. *spritely*] animated, gay.

propend] incline, am disposed (not used elsewhere in Shakespeare).

193. *For*] because, in so far as; cf. *Meas.* II.i.27-8 ('You may not so extenuate his offence / For I have had such faults').

dependence] consequence: i.e. the propriety of keeping Helen will appear, in so far as our honours are known to be engaged in the quarrel. (There is a further sense of *dependence* —'affair of honour, awaiting settlement': OED 6b—which, while not fitting the logic of the sentence, may explain Shakespeare's choice of the word in arguing from the motives of an honourable dispute.)

194. *several*] particular, individual.

196. *glory*] fame, renown.

affected] aimed at, aspired to.

197. *performance . . . spleens*] operation of proud tempers: 'execution of spite and resentment' (Johnson).

200. *theme*] cause, motive for action.

201. *magnanimous*] fitting the noble nature, the 'great in mind' (cf. *Ethics,* IV.3; the desire of men like

Whose present courage may beat down our foes,
And fame in time to come canonize us;
For I presume brave Hector would not lose
So rich advantage of a promis'd glory   205
As smiles upon the forehead of this action
For the wide world's revenue.

Hect.   I am yours,
You valiant offspring of great Priamus.
I have a roisting challenge sent amongst
The dull and factious nobles of the Greeks   210
Will strike amazement to their drowsy spirits.
I was advertis'd their great general slept
Whilst emulation in the army crept:
This, I presume, will wake him.   *Exeunt.*

[SCENE III]

Enter THERSITES *solus.*

Thers. How now, Thersites! What, lost in the labyrinth
of thy fury? Shall the elephant Ajax carry it thus?
He beats me, and I rail at him. O worthy satisfaction! Would it were otherwise—that I could
beat him, whilst he railed at me. 'Sfoot, I'll learn   5

211. strike] *F;* shrike *Q.*

Scene III

Troilus to perform glorious deeds is discussed at IV. 4).

202. *courage*] spirit, boldness (OED 3, 3d). The courage is that of the Trojans (derived from the very doing of the deeds).

203. *canonize*] Accented on the second syllable (cf. *Ham.* I.iv.47).

204. *presume*] take it for granted that.

206. *forehead*] forefront, beginning.

207. *revenue*] Accented on the second syllable.

209. *roisting*] wild, boisterous.

211. *strike*] Q's *shrike* (= shriek) is implausible: the tone of Hector's challenge is rather contemptuous than melodramatic; and the form *shrike* could only arise as a misreading

of *strike* if the copy were in an Italian hand, rather than in Shakespeare's normal Secretary hand.

212. *advertis'd*] notified, informed (stress on second syllable).

213. *emulation*] 'envious contention' (Schmidt).

Scene III

2. *elephant Ajax*] Cf. I.ii.21, 'slow as the elephant'.

carry it] have the better of it.

5–6. *I'll . . . devils*] Perhaps an allusion to the association of the comic clown with devils: cf. Marlowe, *Dr Faustus*, I.iv, III.iii, and Greene, *Friar Bacon and Friar Bungay*, ll. 2011–73.

to conjure and raise devils but I'll see some issue of
my spiteful execrations. Then there's Achilles:
a rare enginer. If Troy be not taken till these two
undermine it, the walls will stand till they fall of
themselves. O thou great thunder-darter of   10
Olympus, forget that thou art Jove the king of
gods: and Mercury, lose all the serpentine craft of
thy caduceus, if ye take not that little little less
than little wit from them that they have; which
short-armed ignorance itself knows is so abundant   15
scarce, it will not in circumvention deliver a fly
from a spider without drawing their massy irons
and cutting the web. After this, the vengeance on
the whole camp—or rather, the Neapolitan bone-
ache; for that methinks is the curse depending on   20
those that war for a placket. I have said my
prayers, and devil Envy say 'Amen'. What ho!
my Lord Achilles!

13. ye] *Q;* thou *F.*   17. their] *Q;* the *F.*   19. Neapolitan] *Q; not in F.*
20. depending] *Q;* dependant *F.*

6. *but I'll*] unless I may: Walker
conjectures *but I.*
8. *enginer*] (a) maker of military
works or machines; (b) contriver,
plotter.
12–13. *serpentine . . . caduceus*] Serpents entwined themselves about the
rod of Mercury, who, besides being
Jove's messenger, typified prudence,
skill, cunning, and even theft and
perjury, if gracefully performed (cf.
Metamorphoses II, and *Wint.* IV.iii.24–6,
'. . . Autolycus; who, being as I am,
littered under Mercury, was likewise
a snapper-up of unconsidered trifles').
13. *caduceus*] the staff of Mercury,
which he received from Apollo:
originally adorned with white ribbons,
it later appears entwined about with
two serpents. Mercury carried it as
herald or messenger of the gods, and
as conductor of souls to the Underworld (= psychopomp); it had
magical powers, bestowed prosperity,
and could turn objects to gold; and it

was the symbol of the settlement of
quarrels.
15. *short-armed*] Ignorance is necessarily lacking in reach (= understanding, penetration, policy).
16. *circumvention*] craft, artifice.
17. *irons*] swords: cf. *Tw.N.* IV.i.38
(also jestingly).
19–20. *Neapolitan bone-ache*] venereal
disease (probably syphilis) usually
supposed to have originated in Naples:
cf. Buttons of Naples = 'syphilitic
buboes' (Nares, cited OED: *button* 11).
21. *placket*] apron, petticoat, or
skirt: hence (derisively) a woman.
Also, a slit in the skirt, and, by
analogy, the pudendum.
22. *Envy*] Traditionally, one of the
seven deadly sins. R. Simpson
(*Academy*, IX, 1876, p. 402) first
noticed that, in the revised epilogue
to *Mucedorus* (1610 edn), Envy *is* made
to say Amen; but the date of the
revision is unknown.

Patro. [*Within.*] Who's there?—Thersites? Good Ther-
      sites, come in and rail.   25
Thers. If I could a' remembered a gilt counterfeit, thou
      couldst not have slipped out of my contemplation:
      but it is no matter—thyself upon thyself! The
      common curse of mankind, folly and ignorance,
      be thine in great revenue: Heaven bless thee from   30
      a tutor, and discipline come not near thee! Let
      thy blood be thy direction till thy death: then if
      she that lays thee out says thou art a fair corse, I'll
      be sworn and sworn upon't, she never shrouded
      any but lazars. Amen.   35

Enter PATROCLUS.

      Where's Achilles?
Patro. What, art thou devout? Wast thou in prayer?
Thers. Ay, the heavens hear me!
Patro. Amen.
Achill. [*Within.*] Who's there?   40
Patro. Thersites, my lord.
Achill. [*Within.*] Where? where?—O where?—Art
      thou come?

Enter ACHILLES.

      Why, my cheese, my digestion, why hast thou not
      served thyself in to my table so many meals?   45

24 S.D.] *NCS, anon. conj. apud Camb.; Enter Patroclus | F (after 23); not in Q.*
Thersites? Good] *Q (subst.); Thersites. Good F.*   26. a'] *Q;* have *F.*   gilt]
F; guilt *Q.*   27. couldst] *Q;* would'st *F.*   33. art] *F;* art not *Q.*
35 S.D.] *NCS, anon. conj. apud Camb.; after 23, F.*   37. in] *Q;* in a *F.*
39.] *Q; not in F.*   40 S.D.] *This edn (also at 42); not in Q,F.*   42. Where?
where?—O where?] *Q (subst.);* Where, where, *F.*   43 S.D. *Enter* ACHILLES.].
Here, this edn; before 40, Q,F.

24 *S.D.*] It is possible for Patroclus
to enter here (as in F) and to watch
Thersites without hearing him, but it
is surely better that he should remain
offstage during most of this ensuing
speech. (F's entry might be a promp-
ter's 'warning' or an entry from a
distance.)

26. *gilt counterfeit*] false coin (=slip):

hence *slipped out* (l. 27).

28. *thyself upon thyself*] 'For you to
remain yourself is your own worst
punishment.'

32. *blood*] fleshly or passional
nature.

44. *cheese*] Traditionally a digestive
after meals: cf. Tilley C 269.

45. *in to*] (QF *into*) Last words in a

Come, what's Agamemnon?

Thers. Thy commander, Achilles: then tell me
    Patroclus, what's Achilles?

Patro. Thy lord, Thersites: then tell me I pray thee,
    what's Thersites?   50

Thers. Thy knower, Patroclus: then tell me Patroclus,
    what art thou?

Patro. Thou mayst tell that knowest.

Achill. O tell, tell.

Thers. I'll decline the whole question. Agamemnon   55
    commands Achilles, Achilles is my lord, I am
    Patroclus' knower, and Patroclus is a fool.

Patro. You rascal!

Thers. Peace, fool, I have not done.

Achill. He is a privileged man: proceed, Thersites.   60

Thers. Agamemnon is a fool, Achilles is a fool, Ther-
    sites is a fool, and, as aforesaid, Patroclus is a fool.

Achill. Derive this: come.

Thers. Agamemnon is a fool to offer to command
    Achilles, Achilles is a fool to be commanded of   65
    Agamemnon, Thersites is a fool to serve such a
    fool, and this Patroclus is a fool positive.

Patro. Why am I a fool?

Thers. Make that demand of the Creator, it suffices me
    thou art. Look you, who comes here?   70

50. Thersites] *Q;* thy selfe *F.*   53. mayst] *F* (maist)*;* must *Q.*   58–62.] *F;*
not in Q.   65–6. of Agamemnon] *F; not in F.*   67. this] *Q; not in F.*
69. of the Creator] *Tatlock;* to the Creator *F;* of the Prouer *Q.*   70 S.D.] *Q;*
after 68, F. DIOMEDES *and* AJAX] *As Capell; Diomed, Aiax & Calcas | Q,F (subst.).*

crowded line in Q: F followed. The
usual phrase is *to serve in a meal* (i.e.
in = adv.).

53. *mayst*] Q's *must* is perhaps too
emphatic for the tone of this by-play;
Patroclus is merely off-hand here, and
only acknowledges being stung at l. 58.

55. *decline*] 'recite formally or in
definite order' (OED 20b: 'transferred sense of the grammatical
term').

60. *privileged man*] fool officially
recognized, and therefore at liberty

to be disrespectful with impunity (cf.
l. 94 below; *AYL* ii.vii.47–9: 'I must
have liberty / Withal, as large a
charter as the wind, / To blow on
whom I please, for so fools have';
Tw.N. i.v.93–4).

67. *fool positive*] absolute fool: the
rest are fools only in respect of the
reason given.

69. *Creator*] Q's *Prover* is nonsense—
Thersites is himself the 'prover'—but
a misreading of *Creator* is perhaps just
possible.

Enter AGAMEMNON, ULYSSES, NESTOR, DIOMEDES,
and AJAX.

Achill. Patroclus, I'll speak with nobody. Come in with
 me, Thersites.   *Exit.*
Thers. Here is such patchery, such juggling, and such
 knavery! All the argument is a whore and a
 cuckold: a good quarrel to draw emulous factions, 75
 and bleed to death upon. Now the dry serpigo on
 the subject, and war and lechery confound all! [*Exit.*]
Agam. Where is Achilles?
Patro. Within his tent, but ill dispos'd, my lord.
Agam. Let it be known to him that we are here. 80
 He sate our messengers, and we lay by
 Our appertainings, visiting of him.
 Let him be told so, lest perchance he think
 We dare not move the question of our place,
 Or know not what we are.   85
Patro. I shall say so to him.   [*Exit.*]
Ulyss. We saw him at the opening of his tent:
 He is not sick.
Ajax. Yes, lion-sick—sick of proud heart. You may call

71. Patroclus] *F;* Come *Patroclus* / *Q.* 72 S.D.] *F; not in Q.* 74–5. a
whore . . . cuckold] *Q;* a Cuckold and a Whore *F.* 75. emulous factions]
Q; emulations, factions *F.* 76–7. Now . . . all] *F; not in Q.* 77 S.D.]
Theobald; not in Q,F. 81. He sate our] *Q;* He sent our *F;* He shent our
Theobald; He sent us *Hanmer;* We sent our *Collier, conj. Theobald;* He rates our
conj. Dyce. 82. appertainings] *Q;* appertainments *F.* 83. so, lest] *Q;* of,
so *F.* 86. say so] *Q;* so say *F.* 86 S.D.] *Rowe*[3]*; not in Q,F.* 89. lion-
sick] *Rowe;* Lion sick *Q,F (subst.).* of] *Q;* of a *F.*

73. *patchery*] fool's play, clownage,
cheating (cf. *juggling*), and cf. *patch* =
domestic fool or clown (after Cardinal
Wolsey's fool). (See also *MND*
III. ii. 9, IV. i. 208, and Professor Brooks's
notes *ad loc.*)

75. *emulous*] actuated by a spirit of
rivalry: competitive.

factions] parties in rivalry.

76. *serpigo*] General term for creeping skin disease.

79. *ill dispos'd*] indisposed, unwell.

81. *sate*] ignored. Q's reading was
successfully defended by Hulme (*Ex-
plorations*, p. 260). F's apparent cor-

rection (*sent*) tempted editors to
emend further—either the subject
(We *sent*), or the verb (*He* shent).

82. *appertainings*] that which belongs
to an office: visible and apparent
signs of authority. Both Q and F
readings (*appertainings, appertainments*) each appear only once in the
canon.

84.] 'We dare not assert that we are
his commander.'

89. *lion-sick*] The lion was proverbially proud (as Ajax goes on to
explain).

89–91. *You . . . pride*] Ajax rejects

it melancholy if you will favour the man, but by   90
my head 'tis pride. But why? why? Let him show
us a cause. A word, my lord.   [*Takes Agamemnon aside.*]
Nest. What moves Ajax thus to bay at him?
Ulyss. Achilles hath inveigled his fool from him.
Nest. Who, Thersites?   95
Ulyss. He.
Nest. Then will Ajax lack matter, if he have lost his
          argument.
Ulyss. No: you see, he is his argument, that has his
          argument, Achilles.   100
Nest. All the better: their fraction is more our wish
          than their faction; but it was a strong composure a
          fool could disunite.
Ulyss. The amity that wisdom knits not, folly may
          easily untie.   105

Enter PATROCLUS.

Here comes Patroclus.
Nest.   No Achilles with him.
Ulyss. The elephant hath joints, but none for courtesy:
          His legs are legs for necessity, not for flexure.

90. if you] *Q; if F.*   92. a] *Q; the F.*   A ... lord] *F; not in Q.*   92 S.D.]
Malone; not in Q,F.   99. argument, that] *Q;* argument that *F.*   100.
argument, Achilles] *F3;* argument *Achilles* | *Q,F.*   102. composure] *Q;*
counsell that *F;* composure that *Johnson.*   104. knits not,] *Q;* knits, not *F.*
105 S.D.] *F; not in Q.*   106. him.] *Q;* him? *F.*   108. flexure] *Q;* flight *F.*

the sophisticated explanation of
humorous imbalance (*melancholy*), and
affects a plain man's bluntness. He
also accuses Achilles of a sin (*pride =*
the chief of the deadly seven), rather
than of an affectation.
     98. *argument*] (a) theme, subject;
(b) disputation.
     99–100.] Ulysses says, in effect,
'Observe that Achilles, having stolen
Thersites, is now Ajax' theme, and
Ajax has thereby acquired matter for
everlasting dispute' (i.e. an Achillean
[= endless] argument, concerning
Achilles). Grey (*Notes*, 1754) observed
the source of this quibble in Erasmus,

Adagia (Chil. 1, Cent. 7, Prov. 41).
     101–2. *their fraction . . . faction*]
Better that Ajax and Achilles should
quarrel, than that they should form
an alliance [sc. against us].
     102. *composure*] connection.
     107–8.] Despite the assertion of
Aristotle (*Historia Animalium*), ele-
phants were for long believed to have
inflexible knee-joints; but the belief
rested on a proverb usually included
in Erasmus, *Adagia* ('Homo genibus
elephantinis'), which made the comparison between the beast and the
proud man.

Patro. Achilles bids me say he is much sorry
    If any thing more than your sport and pleasure   110
    Did move your greatness and this noble state
    To call upon him; he hopes it is no other
    But for your health and your digestion sake,
    An after-dinner's breath.
Agam.   Hear you, Patroclus:
    We are too well acquainted with these answers;   115
    But his evasion, wing'd thus swift with scorn,
    Cannot outfly our apprehensions.
    Much attribute he hath, and much the reason
    Why we ascribe it to him; yet all his virtues,
    Not virtuously on his own part beheld,   120
    Do in our eyes begin to lose their gloss—
    Yea, like fair fruit in an unwholesome dish,
    Are like to rot untasted. Go and tell him
    We come to speak with him, and you shall not sin
    If you do say we think him over-proud   125
    And under-honest, in self-assumption greater
    Than in the note of judgement; and worthier than
        himself
    Here tend the savage strangeness he puts on,
    Disguise the holy strength of their command,
    And underwrite in an observing kind   130

---

114. after-dinner's] *Rowe* (*subst.*); after Dinners *Q,F.*   120. on] *Q;* of *F.*
122. Yea] *Q;* Yea, and *F.*   124. come] *Q;* came *F.*   128. tend] *Q;* tends
F.   on,] *F;* on *Q.*

111. *state*] council, group of nobles.

113. *digestion*] uninflected genitive (to avoid two sibilants together); cf. Franz §199.

114. *breath*] 'gentle exercise' (Schmidt): cf. iv.v.92.

117. *apprehensions*] (a) understandings; (b) power of arrest.

118. *attribute*] (a) quality ascribed or recognized; (b) reputation accorded. Cf. *Ham.* i.iv.20–2 ('it takes / From our achievements, though perform'd at height, / The pith and marrow of our attribute').

119–20. *all . . . beheld*] The play on *virtues / virtuously* is a little forced: it might be more effective, were we to read *beheld* as = kept, sustained (OED notes no example later than 1525). Mason's conjecture *upheld* was sensible.

127.] A rather awkward Alexandrine.

note of judgement] 'distinctive mark of good judgment' (Deighton).

128. *tend*] wait on, attend.

savage strangeness] barbarous reserve.

130. *underwrite*] submit to.

in . . . kind] with deference or respect.

His humorous predominance—yea, watch
His course and time, his ebbs and flows, as if
The passage and whole stream of this commencement
Rode on his tide. Go tell him this, and add
That if he overhold his price so much   135
We'll none of him, but let him, like an engine
Not portable, lie under this report:
'Bring action hither, this cannot go to war.'
A stirring dwarf we do allowance give

132. course and time] *Q*; course and times *Pope*; pettish lines *F*; pettish lunes *Hanmer.*   and flows] *Q*; his flowes *F*.   as] *F*; and *Q*.   133. stream . . . commencement] *This edn, conj. Malone*; streame of his commencement *Q*; carriage of this action *F*.

131. *humorous*] capricious, impulsive (from imbalance of the humours in the body).

131–4. *yea . . . tide*] I retain those readings which support the sustained image of varying tidal streams (*course, time, ebbs, flows, passage, stream, rode, tide*), and which show the relation of the speech to those others throughout the play which deal with wild waters and with merchants crossing seas (I.i.102–4; II.ii.65, 75, 83–4; and I.iii.111–13, V.ii.170–1). F's *lines* has no *obvious* meaning in the context: Hanmer's emendation (*lunes*) is attractive, the word being found elsewhere in Shakespeare (*Wint.* II.ii.30). Yet *lines* (emended to *lunes*) occurs in *Wiv.* IV.ii.17, and OED notes *on a line* = in a rage (Warwickshire dialect).

132. *course*] flow, current: direction of flow: cf. *Oth.* III.iii.460–2, '. . . the Pontic sea, / Whose icy current and compulsive course, / Ne'er feels retiring ebb, but keeps due on'.

time] rhythm; time of oscillation or revolution (as of a tide, or of the moon).

133. *passage*] channel, route.

stream] (a) current, flow (especially of tidal water); (b) motion; drift or tendency (OED cites Chapman, *Iliad*, I.272: 'Give not stream / To all thy power'; but perhaps better cf. *Tim.* IV.i.27: ''gainst the stream of

virtue'; v.iv.6; *Meas.* III.ii.138; *All's W.* IV.iii.24).

commencement] beginning (cf. I.iii.1–17): Schmidt glosses 'undertaking, enterprise'; perhaps = thing begun. Yet *commencement* is interpreted as *comitia* (e.g. by Littleton's *Latin Dictionary*, 1735), which in turn may be 'assembly, convocation, parliament'. Emendation to *commercement* (= business) is unnecessary.

135. *overhold*] overestimate, hold at too high a rate. Apparently a nonceword.

136. *engine*] military machine, usually gun, ram, or catapult; cf. I.iii.208, and *Cor.* v.iv.18–20: 'When he walks, he moves like an engine, and the ground shrinks before his treading'.

137.] The deliberate iteration of *portable . . . report* is an example of what Puttenham called Auricular Figures, '. . . those which worke alteration in th'eare by sound . . . And so long as this qualitie extendeth but to the outward tuning of the speach, reaching no higher then th'eare and forcing the mynde little or nothing, it is that vertue which the Greeks called *Enargia* and is the office of the auricular figures to performe' (*Arte of English Poesie*, III.x).

139. *stirring*] active.

allowance] praise, approbation.

Before a sleeping giant. Tell him so.   140
Patro. I shall, and bring his answer presently.   [*Exit.*]
Agam. In second voice we'll not be satisfied:
   We come to speak with him. Ulysses, enter you.
                             Exit Ulysses.
Ajax. What is he more than another?
Agam. No more than what he thinks he is.   145
Ajax. Is he so much? Do you not think he thinks him-
   self a better man than I am?
Agam. No question.
Ajax. Will you subscribe his thought, and say he is?
Agam. No, noble Ajax; you are as strong, as valiant,   150
   as wise; no less noble, much more gentle, and
   altogether more tractable.
Ajax. Why should a man be proud? How doth pride
   grow? I know not what pride is.
Agam. Your mind is the clearer, Ajax, and your virtues 155
   the fairer. He that is proud eats up himself: pride
   is his own glass, his own trumpet, his own
   chronicle; and whatever praises itself, but in the
   deed, devours the deed in the praise.

               Enter ULYSSES.

Ajax. I do hate a proud man as I do hate the engender- 160
   ing of toads.
Nest. [*Aside.*] And yet he loves himself: is't not strange?

141 S.D.] *Rowe; not in Q,F.*   143. enter you] *F*; entertaine *Q*.   143 S.D.]
F; not in Q.   146. much?] *F3*; much: *Q*; much, *F*.   154. pride] *Q*; it *F*.
155. Ajax] *F; not in Q*.   160. as I do] *Q*; as I *F*.   162 S.D.] *Johnson; not
in Q,F.*   162. And] *Q; not in F.*

142.] 'We will not tolerate a mere
messenger.'

143. *enter you*] Q's *entertain* is a
plausible error (= engage an enemy,
OED 9c: engage in a task, 16), but
the syntax seems to be against its
reading.

149. *subscribe*] admit, agree with.

156. *He . . . himself*] Pride is as much
a form of self-consumption as lechery
(v.iv.35) or civil disorder (I.iii.119–
24).

158–9. *whatever . . . praise*] Agamemnon agrees, in this, with Æneas
(I.iii.240–3), but the matter was a
commonplace: cf. Proverbs xxvii.2,
and S. Guazzo, *Civile Conversation*,
trans. George Pettie, Tudor Translations series (1925), II.iii.

158. *but*] except, save.

160–1. *the . . . toads*] An image of
profound loathing for Othello also
(*Oth.* IV.ii.62–3).

Ulyss. Achilles will not to the field tomorrow.

Agam. What's his excuse?

Ulyss.   He doth rely on none,
But carries on the stream of his dispose   165
Without observance or respect of any,
In will peculiar and in <u>self-admission</u>.
Agam. Why will he not, upon our fair request,
Untent his person, and share th'air with us?

Ulyss. Things small as nothing, for request's sake only,   170
He makes important; possess'd he is with greatness,
And speaks not to himself but with a pride
That quarrels at self-breath. Imagin'd worth
Holds in his blood such swol'n and hot discourse
That 'twixt his mental and his active parts   175
Kingdom'd Achilles in commotion rages

---

168. Why will] *Q*; Why, will *F*.   169. th'air] *Q*; the air *F*.   170. request's]
Pope; requests *Q,F*; request *Var.* '73.   173. worth] *Q*; wroth *F*.

163. *will not to*] will not go to:
omission of the verb of motion is
common (cf. Abbott §405).

165. *carries on*] maintains, keeps up
(OED's first example in this sense).
Shakespeare's usual idiom is *holds up*
(cf. *MND* III.ii.239).

167. *In will peculiar*] self-willed (cf.
Hector at II.ii.54: 'But value dwells
not in particular will').

in self-admission] trusting only his
own judgement.

170. *for . . . only*] merely because
they *were* requested.

171. *possess'd . . . greatness*] His
assurance of his own superiority
(which = *pride*, the chief deadly sin,
and that by which the devils fell) now
possesses him, as if a devil had
entered him.

172–3. *And . . . self-breath*] This is
surely hypothetical and hyperbolic:
Achilles is hardly in soliloquy.
Ulysses appears to infer, from the
contempt of Achilles' address to him,
that Achilles disdains speech of *any*
kind: cf. the burlesque of such pride
in Ajax, at III.iii.268 ff.

173–7. *Imagin'd . . . himself*] Pride

is now precisely equated with the self-
consuming civil war of I.iii.119–24;
cf. note to l. 156 above. The error of
Achilles is to dwell on imaginary
worth attributed to *himself*: that of
Troilus, on such worth attributed to
another. The personal and metaphysical disorders which follow are
much alike.

175. *mental . . . parts*] mind and
body; yet Achilles' sickness is more
profound than such an antithesis
would suggest. Perhaps cf. *Caes.*
II.i.66–7: 'The genius and the mortal
instruments / Are then in council'
(where *mortal instruments* is surely
other than the power of physical
act?). There may be (in the *Troilus*
line) a hint of Aristotle's distinction
between *gnosis* and *praxis* (*Ethics*, I.3).

176–7. *Kingdom'd . . . himself*] cf.
Tilley K 89, which derives from
Matthew xii.25: 'Every kingdom
divided against itself is brought to
desolation'. Perhaps cf. also Proverbs
xxv.29: 'He that hath no rule over
his own spirit is like a city that is
broken down, and without walls'.

176. *Kingdom'd*] fashioned like a

And batters down himself. What should I say?
He is so plaguy proud that the death-tokens of it
Cry 'No recovery'.
Agam.   Let Ajax go to him.
Dear lord, go you and greet him in his tent.   180
'Tis said he holds you well, and will be led
At your request a little from himself.
Ulyss. O Agamemnon, let it not be so!
We'll consecrate the steps that Ajax makes
When they go from Achilles. Shall the proud lord   185
That bastes his arrogance with his own seam
And never suffers matter of the world
Enter his thoughts, save such as do revolve
And ruminate himself—shall he be worshipp'd
Of that we hold an idol more than he?   190
No: this thrice worthy and right valiant lord
Shall not so stale his palm, nobly acquir'd,
Nor, by my will, assubjugate his merit—
As amply titled as Achilles is—
By going to Achilles.   195
That were to enlard his fat-already pride
And add more coals to Cancer when he burns
With entertaining great Hyperion.

177. down himself] *Q;* gainst it sclfc *F.*   188. do] *F;* doth *Q.*   192. Shall]
Q; Must *F.*   194–5.] *As Johnson; one line, Q,F.*   194. titled] *F;* liked *Q,*
196. fat-already] *Capell;* fat already, *Q,F.*

kingdom. (Rare, as a form; but the
notion is a commonplace: cf. *Caes.*
ii. i. 67–8; *Cor.* i. i. 95–6.)

178. *plaguy*] Steevens wished to
omit the word, as both vulgar and
extra-metrical; but it refers literally
to a plague (= pride) of which
Achilles already shows the sympto-
matic spots.

death-tokens] signs of mortal sickness
(usually, plague): cf. 'Lord's tokens'
(*LLL* v. ii. 423).

181. *holds*] regards.

186. *seam*] fat, grease.

187–9. *And never . . . himself*] A
difficult passage: Achilles only allows
the business of the outer world to
enter his thoughts in so far as that

leads him to reflect on himself and
his own excellence.

188. *revolve*] consider, meditate on.

192. *stale*] 'lower (oneself, one's
dignity) in estimation by excessive
familiarity' (OED v², 2 b).

palm] emblem of superiority or
victory. (Hence, *stale his palm* =
cheapen his laurels.)

193. *assubjugate*] subdue, render
inferior.

196–8.] Cf. Tilley F 785.

197. *Cancer*] Zodiacal sign (the
Crab) which the sun enters on 21 June,
at the summer solstice: hence, a symbol of intense natural heat.

198. *Hyperion*] the Titan guiding
the sun's chariot, and hence, the sun.

This lord go to him? Jupiter forbid,
And say in thunder 'Achilles, go to him!'   200
Nest. [*Aside.*] O, this is well: he rubs the vein of him.
Diom. [*Aside.*] And how his silence drinks up this applause!
Ajax. If I go to him, with my armed fist
    I'll pash him o'er the face.
Agam. O no, you shall not go.   205
Ajax. And a be proud with me, I'll feeze his pride:
    Let me go to him.
Ulyss. Not for the worth that hangs upon our quarrel.
Ajax. A paltry, insolent fellow!
Nest. [*Aside.*] How he describes himself!   210
Ajax. Can he not be sociable?
Ulyss. [*Aside.*] The raven chides blackness.
Ajax. I'll let his humours blood.
Agam. [*Aside.*] He will be the physician that should be
    the patient.   215
Ajax. And all men were o' my mind—
Ulyss. [*Aside.*] Wit would be out of fashion.
Ajax. —a should not bear it so, a should eat swords
    first. Shall pride carry it?
Nest. [*Aside.*] And 'twould, you'd carry half.   220

201–2 S.D.] *As Johnson; not in Q.,F.*   202. this] *F; his Q.*   203–4.] *As Rowe³;
as prose, Q.,F.*   204. pash] *F; push Q.*   206–7.] *As Q; as prose, F.*   206. a]
F; he Q.   210 S.D.] *As Capell (also 212, 214, 217, 220, 221, 223); not in
Q.,F.*   213. let] *F; tell Q.*   humours] *F; humorous Q; humour's Hudson;
humours' Staunton.*   216. o'] *Rowe³; a F; of Q.*

(Properly, the Titan is Helios, and borrows the name Hyperion from his father.)

201. *rubs . . . him*] encourages his humour.

202.] Cf. Sonnet 114, ll. 9–10: 'O 'tis the first: 'tis flatt'ry in my seeing, / And my great mind most kingly drinks it up'.

204. *pash*] strike or bruise violently; Q's *push* is probably simple mis-reading. Despite the tone of Ajax' remarks here, the word could quite properly be used seriously in heroic contexts (see OED citations).

206. *feeze*] do for, settle. A vulgar usage: cf. Sly's quarrel, *Shr.* Ind. i.1·

212.] Cf. Tilley R 34; yet Tilley cites only this passage and Webster, *White Devil*, v.iii. 88.

213.] Ajax sees Achilles as altogether dominated by excess of humours, to be cured only by blood-letting: *humours* = indirect object. (Cf. S. Rowlands, *The Letting of Humours Blood in the Head-Vaine*, 1611 [1600].) Q's reading is careless.

218. *eat swords*] be wounded, stabbed; *eat's words* (conj. Grey) is too mild for the threatening tone Ajax has adopted.

Ulyss. [*Aside.*] A would have ten shares.

Ajax. I will knead him, I'll make him supple.

Nest. [*Aside.*] He's not yet through warm. Force him
 with praises—pour in, pour in, his ambition is dry.

Ulyss. [*To Agamemnon.*] My lord, you feed too much on this
  dislike.   225

Nest. Our noble general, do not do so.

Diom. You must prepare to fight without Achilles.

Ulyss. Why, 'tis this naming of him does him harm.
 Here is a man—but 'tis before his face,
 I will be silent.

Nest.   Wherefore should you so? 230
 He is not emulous, as Achilles is.

Ulyss. Know the whole world, he is as valiant—

Ajax. A whoreson dog, that shall palter with us thus.
 Would he were a Trojan!

Nest. What a vice were it in Ajax now— 235

Ulyss. If he were proud—

Diom. Or covetous of praise—

Ulyss. Ay, or surly borne—

Diom. Or strange, or self-affected.

Ulyss. Thank the heavens, lord, thou art of sweet composure,
 Praise him that gat thee, she that gave thee suck; 241
 Fam'd be thy tutor, and thy parts of nature

221. *Ulyss.*] *F; Aiax. | Q.* 221–2. shares. | *Ajax.* I will] *F;* shares. I will *Q.*
222–3. supple. | *Nest.* [*Aside.*] He's] *As Theobald;* supple, he's *Q,F* (*subst.*).
224. praises] *F;* praiers *Q.* pour in, his] *F;* poure, his *Q.* 225 S.D.] *As
Capell; not in Q,F.* 228. does] *Q;* doth *F.* 229–30.] *As prose, Q.*
229. man—] *Rowe;* man *Q;* man, *F.* 232. valiant—] *Q;* valiant. *F.*
233. with us thus] *Q;* thus with vs *F.* 239. self-affected] *F3;* selfe affected
Q,F. 241. gat] *Q;* got *F.* 242. Fam'd] *Q;* Fame *F.*

221–2.] See Introductipn, p. 12.

221. *ten shares*] = the whole;
Ulysses emends Nestor's sarcasm.

223. *Force*] (= farce) stuff: cf.
forcemeat.

233.] *that shall*] who thinks he can;
who sets up to.

241–8.] Cf. Ovid, *Metamorphoses,*
IV.322–6 (noted by Warburton in
Theobald), and *Shr.* IV.v.38–40 (based
upon Golding's translation of the
same lines: noted by Steevens).

Steevens suggested, here, an allusion
to Luke xi.27: 'Blessed is the womb
that bare thee, and the paps which
thou has sucked' ('the pappes which
gaue thee sucke': Book of Common
Prayer, 1549).

241. *she*] Treated as if uninflected:
cf. Abbott §211; Franz §287a–h;
O. Jespersen, *Progress in Language*
(1909), p. 154.

242–3.] F's hyperbole and paradox
—Ajax' *nature* is better than the

Thrice fam'd beyond, beyond all erudition;
But he that disciplin'd thine arms to fight,
Let Mars divide eternity in twain   245
And give him half; and, for thy vigour,
Bull-bearing Milo his addition yield
To sinewy Ajax. I will not praise thy wisdom,
Which like a bourn, a pale, a shore, confines
Thy spacious and dilated parts. Here's Nestor,   250
Instructed by the antiquary times—
He must, he is, he cannot but be wise;
But pardon, father Nestor, were your days
As green as Ajax', and your brain so temper'd,
You should not have the eminence of him,   255
But be as Ajax.
Ajax. [*To Nestor.*]   Shall I call you father?
Nest. Ay, my good son.
Diom.   Be rul'd by him, Lord Ajax.
Ulyss. There is no tarrying here: the hart Achilles

---

243. beyond, beyond all] *F;* beyond all thy *Q.*   244. thine] *Q;* thy *F.*
249. bourn] *F;* boord *Q.*   250. Thy] *F;* This *Q.*   254. Ajax'] *Hanmer;*
Aiax | Q,F.   256 S.D.] *This edn; not in Q,F.*   257. *Nest.*] *Q; Vlis. | F.*

---

erudition of others—is preferable to
Q's *beyond all thy erudition.* Walker
(NCS) explains *thy* as caught from
l. 242: the words (in Q) are in perfect
register vertically.

247. *Bull-bearing*] There may be a sly
allusion to the proverb 'He may bear
a bull that hath borne a calf': cf.
Erasmus, *Adagia* 90 D ('Taurum tollet,
qui vitulum sustulerit') and Tilley
B 711 (= small sins in youth lead to
great sins in age: cf. Jonson, *Epigrams,*
'On Mill, my Lady's Woman'). *Bull-bearing Milo,* in this sense, must have
gone from bad to worse, and Ajax has
outdone him.

Milo] athlete of Crotona, of
immense strength: said to have carried some yards, slain with his fist,
and eaten, a young bull, all in one
day.

addition] title granted in honour of
some excellence (cf. *Cor.* i.ix.65).

249. *bourn*] boundary.
pale] fence, barrier.

251. *antiquary*] ancient, of antiquity;
OED gives this as the primary sense,
and cites (besides this) an example
from 1877: otherwise, used elliptically as substantive. Stressed on the
first syllable.

252.] The three verbs are not quite
congruous (cf. i.iii.288).

254. *green*] inexperienced, raw:
sometimes used pejoratively; cf. *H5*
ii.iv.136, *Ant.* i.v.74.

temper'd] composed, disposed.

255. *have . . . him*] be (counted)
superior to him.

257. *Nest.*] There is no point in
giving this speech to Ulysses. *All* the
Greeks have flattered Ajax; and it is
to Nestor (to whom he has just been
so flatteringly compared) that Ajax
naturally turns for direction.

Keeps thicket. Please it our great general
To call together all his state of war:　　260
Fresh kings are come to Troy. Tomorrow
We must with all our main of power stand fast;
And here's a lord—come knights from east to west
And cull their flower—Ajax shall cope the best.

Agam.　Go we to council: let Achilles sleep.　　265
Light boats sail swift, though greater hulks draw deep.

Exeunt.

259. great] *Q; not in F.*　　264. cull] *F; call Q.*　　266. sail] *Q; may saile*
F.　　hulks] *Q; bulkes F.*

259. *Keeps thicket*] Ulysses thinks in terms of hunting; cf. I.i.115, V.vi.30–1.

260. *state of war*] military staff.

261.] Metrically defective.

262. *main*] full might.

264. *cope*] prove a match for: cf. I.ii.34.

265. *council*] Q's *counsel* is no error, but an alternative spelling.

266. *hulks*] large cargo vessels. F's *greater bulks* may in some way be connected with IV.iv.126 (*great bulk Achilles*).

[ACT III]

[SCENE I]

Enter PANDARUS *and a* Servant.

Music sounds within.

Pand. Friend, you, pray you, a word: do you not follow
    the young Lord Paris?
Serv. Ay sir, when he goes before me.
Pand. You depend upon him, I mean.
Serv. Sir, I do depend upon the Lord. 5
Pand. You depend upon a notable gentleman, I must
    needs praise him.
Serv. The Lord be praised!
Pand. You know me, do you not?
Serv. Faith, sir, superficially. 10
Pand. Friend, know me better: I am the Lord Pandarus.
Serv. I hope I shall know your honour better.
Pand. I do desire it.
Serv. You are in the state of grace?
Pand. Grace? Not so, friend: honour and lordship are 15

ACT III

Scene 1

S.D. *Enter . . .* Servant.] *F; Enter Pandarus* | *Q.*   *Music sounds within.*] *F*
(after II.iii.266); not in Q.   1. you not] *Q;* not you *F.*   4. mean.] *Q;*
meane? *F.*   6. notable] *Q;* noble *F.*   15. Grace?] *Q;* Grace, *F.*

5. *Lord*] quibbling on Lord (Paris)
and Lord (God). Until l. 15, the
servant plays with ideas of devotion
and theology, Pandarus with rank.
    10. *superficially*] (a) outwardly;
(b) a little, slightly.
    12.] 'I hope that I shall find you
grow a better man' (taken by
Pandarus to mean 'I hope to be

better acquainted with your lordship').
    14.] 'You are in charity, and free
from mortal sin' (taken by Pandarus
to mean 'You are a Duke').
    15. *honour and lordship*] Cf. *Ethics*
(trans. J. Wilkinson, 1547): 'honors
and lordships maketh a man knowen'.

184

my titles. What music is this?

Serv. I do but partly know, sir: it is music in parts.

Pand. Know you the musicians?

Serv. Wholly, sir.

Pand. Who play they to?   20

Serv. To the hearers, sir.

Pand. At whose pleasure, friend?

Serv. At mine, sir, and theirs that love music.

Pand. Command, I mean, friend.

Serv. Who shall I command, sir?   25

Pand. Friend, we understand not one another: I am
too courtly, and thou art too cunning. At whose
request do these men play?

Serv. That's to't indeed, sir: marry, sir, at the request
of Paris my lord, who is there in person; with him,   30
the mortal Venus, the heart-blood of beauty, love's
visible soul—

Pand. Who, my cousin Cressida?

Serv. No, sir, Helen: could not you find out that by her
attributes?   35

Pand. It should seem, fellow, that thou hast not seen the
Lady Cressida. I come to speak with Paris from
the Prince Troilus: I will make a complimental
assault upon him, for my business seethes.

Serv. [*Aside.*] Sodden business: there's a stewed phrase   40
indeed!

16. titles] *Q;* title *F.*   18. musicians?] *Q;* Musitians. *F.*   24. friend] *F;*
not in Q.   27. art] *F; not in Q.*   30. who is] *Q;* who's *F.*   32. visible]
Hanmer; invisible *Q,F;* invincible *conj. Becket;* indivisible *NCS, conj. Daniel.*
soul—] *This edn;* soule: *Q;* soule. *F.*   34. not you] *Q;* you not *F.*   36.
fellow, that] *F;* fellow *Q.*   37. Cressida] *F; Cressid | Q.*

32. *visible soul*] A paradox, like
mortal Venus; *invisible soul* is tauto-
logical (in that a soul is necessarily
unseen); *invincible soul* (conj. Becket)
is perhaps a transferred epithet (since
it is *Love* which is unconquerable);
and *indivisible* (NCS, after Daniel) as
applied to a soul, is as much a
tautology as *invisible*. Of the servant's
three affected phrases, the first is an
oxymoron, the second an hyperbolic
metaphor, and this, the last, a kind of
ellipsis—Helen is that soul (= quint-
essence) of the concept of Love,
which (until she manifested it in her
person) was never seen.

38–9. *complimental assault*] constant
attack of complimentary speeches
(which follows).

39. *seethes*] is about to boil over (= I
am in a hurry).

40. *Sodden*] (= p. part. of *seethe*)
(a) boiled, saturated; (b) stewed:
hence, of the stews or brothels.

Enter PARIS *and* HELEN [*with* Attendants].

Pand. Fair be to you, my lord, and to all this fair company; fair desires in all fair measure fairly guide
them—especially to you, fair queen: fair thoughts
be your fair pillow.   45

Helen. Dear lord, you are full of fair words.

Pand. You speak your fair pleasure, sweet queen. Fair
prince, here is good broken music.

Paris. You have broke it, cousin, and by my life you
shall make it whole again: you shall piece it out   50
with a piece of your performance.

Helen. He is full of harmony.

Pand. Truly, lady, no.

Helen. O sir—

Pand. Rude, in sooth: in good sooth, very rude.   55

Paris. Well said, my lord; well, you say so in fits.

Pand. I have business to my lord, dear queen. My lord,

41. S.D. *with* Attendants] *Theobald* (*attended*); not in *Q*,*F*.   51–2. perform-
ance. | *Helen.* He] *Alexander, anon. conj. apud Camb.;* performance. *Nel,* he] *Q*,*F*,
(*subst.*).

42–6.] It is just possible to distinguish senses of *fair* proper to each
usage here, but the difficulty would
hardly have been so apparent to the
speakers (despite the way in which
Helen caps Pandarus' compliment,
l. 46). Courts, like all restricted
societies, generate their own idiom,
and devise many nice distinctions in
the use of every common word or
phrase (as do schools, and units of the
armed services).

48. *broken music*] Possibly, music in
parts (polyphonic music), but more
probably music played by instruments
of different families (e.g. woodwind
and strings). Broken consorts were
characteristic of court music: see
F. W. Sternfeld, '*Troilus and Cressida*:
Music for the Play', *English Institute
Essays* (1952).

49. *broke*] interrupted.

52.] I give this speech to Helen
(despite Paris' tendency to address or
refer to her as 'Nell') because (a)

Helen, throughout the scene, is gently
teasing Pandarus with mocking compliments; (b) Pandarus is more likely
to reply to a remark *by* Helen, than
to a polite observation *to* Helen;
(c) in Q, the latter part of E(i) is a
little crowded—the speech occurs
low on E4—and there are several
times, as here, two short speeches to a
line, so that it would be easy to misread a speech-heading as a mode of
address (*Nel.* mis-set for *Hel.*, which
is the speech-heading elsewhere on
this page).

55. *Rude*] [I am] lacking in
accomplishments.

56. *fits*] (a) short strains of music
(or a dance); (b) recurrent spasms or
paroxysms: cf. Pandarus' last speech
(l. 55), which repeats itself, with slight
variation.

57.] From this point onward,
Pandarus tries to distract Helen's
attention with trivialities, while speaking his message aside to Paris. Helen

will you vouchsafe me a word?

Helen. Nay, this shall not hedge us out: we'll hear you
    sing, certainly.   60

Pand. Well, sweet queen, you are pleasant with me.—
    But marry, thus, my lord: my dear lord and most
    esteemed friend, your brother Troilus—

Helen. My Lord Pandarus, honey-sweet lord—

Pand. Go to, sweet queen, go to—commends himself   65
    most affectionately to you—

Helen. You shall not bob us out of our melody; if you
    do, our melancholy upon your head.

Pand. Sweet queen, sweet queen, that's a sweet queen,
    i'faith.   70

Helen. And to make a sweet lady sad is a sour offence.

Pand. Nay, that shall not serve your turn; that shall it
    not, in truth, la. Nay, I care not for such words:
    no, no.—And my lord, he desires you that if the
    King call for him at supper, you will make his   75
    excuse.

Helen. My Lord Pandarus.

Pand. What says my sweet queen, my very very sweet
    queen?

Paris. What exploit's in hand? Where sups he tonight?   80

Helen. Nay, but my lord—

Pand. What says my sweet queen?—My cousin will fall
    out with you: you must not know where he sups.

---

58. word?] *F2;* word. *Q.,F.*   67–8.] *As Hanmer; as verse, Q.,F.*   75. supper,]
F; super. *Q.*   83. you: / you . . . sups] *As Capell;* you. / *Hel.* You . . . sups
Q.,F.

constantly attempts to persuade Pandarus to sing; Pandarus just as constantly fends her off, and does his embassy. Helen, despite the erroneous agreement of Q and F at l. 83, never finds out what they discuss.

59. *hedge us out*] keep us away (from your private talk); but cf. Schmidt 'elude us', and NCS 'fob us off'.

61. *pleasant*] playful, mocking.

67. *bob us out of*] cheat us of, deprive us of.

69–70; 72–4; 78–9.] Pandarus
speaks to Helen more and more as one might to a small child (cf. iv.ii, iv.iv).

83–4.] I allocate the speeches substantially as Capell—an arrangement which helps explain *My cousin will fall out with you*: i.e. Pandarus won't betray his secret explicitly, but feels that he can drop a hint to Paris— Cressida (= *my cousin*) will be annoyed if Paris persists in such questions.

Paris. I'll lay my life, with my disposer Cressida.

Pand. No, no, no such matter, you are wide: come,   85
your disposer is sick.

Paris. Well, I'll make's excuse.

Pand. Ay, good my lord: why should you say Cressida?
No, your poor disposer's sick.

Paris. I spy.   90

Pand. You spy? What do you spy?—Come, give me an
instrument. Now, sweet queen.

Helen. Why, this is kindly done.

Pand. My niece is horribly in love with a thing you
have, sweet queen.   95

Helen. She shall have it, my lord, if it be not my Lord
Paris.

Pand. He? No, she'll none of him: they two are twain.

Helen. Falling in after falling out may make them three.

Pand. Come, come, I'll hear no more of this: I'll sing   100
you a song now.

Helen. Ay, ay, prithee, now. By my troth, sweet lord,
thou hast a fine forehead.

84. I'll lay my life] *Q; not in F.*   87. make's] *Kittredge, conj. Capell;* makes *Q;*
make *F.*   89. your poor] *F;* your *Q.*   94. horribly] *Q;* horrible *F.*   102.
lord] *F;* lad *Q.*

84. *my disposer*] she who can do what
she will with me (OED *dispose* v 8).
That this is the sense of the word is
suggested by ll. 94–9: Helen half-
suspects an affair between Paris and
Cressida.

90. *I spy*] Alluding to the children's
game: Paris facetiously hints that he
has understood Pandarus' implications.

91–3.] Pandarus at length consents
to sing, in order to turn the conversation and evade the teasing of Paris.
Helen still does not see what is going
on.

94–5.] Pandarus includes Helen
once more in the conversation; perhaps his remark implies merely that
Helen has a lover and Cressida has
not.

98. *they . . . twain*] they are on ill
terms; cf. Tilley T 640.

99.] Helen's wit is bawdy—copula-
tion may well lead to conception—but
she is merely elaborating a proverb.
Cf. *Paradise of Dainty Devices* (refrain
of a poem by R. Edwardes): 'The
falling out of faithful friends renewing
is of love'. The ultimate source is
Terence, *Andria,* 555 ('Amantium
irae amoris integratio est') by way of
Erasmus, *Adagia* 740B; see Tilley
F 40, and F. P. Wilson, *Oxford
Dictionary of English Proverbs,* p. 242.

103. *thou . . . forehead*] Possibly a
hint of cuckoldry (cf. Tilley F 589)
but Pandarus appears to be single,
and the proverb is not dated before
1678. The forehead was supposed to
reveal the mind (cf. Tilley F 590, and
Erasmus, *Adagia* 524B, 'Ex fronte
perspicere'), and may have been a
general pointer to one's moral
nature: cf. Ezekiel iii.9: 'As an

Pand. Ay, you may, you may.

Helen. Let thy song be love: this love will undo us all.   105
          O Cupid, Cupid, Cupid!

Pand. Love? Ay, that it shall, i'faith.

Paris. Ay, good now, love, love, nothing but love.

Pand. In good troth it begins so.   [*Sings.*]

> *Love, love, nothing but love, still love, still more!*   110
>   *For O love's bow*
>   *Shoots buck and doe;*
>   *The shaft confounds*
>   *Not that it wounds,*
> *But tickles still the sore.*   115
> *These lovers cry O ho, they die!*
>   *Yet that which seems the wound to kill*
> *Doth turn O ho, to Ha, ha, he!*
>   *So dying love lives still.*
> *O ho, a while, but Ha, ha, ha!*   120
> *O ho, groans out for Ha, ha, ha!—Heigh ho!*

---

108. love, love, . . . love] *Q,F* (*subst.*)*; as song title* (*italics*) *conj. Delius.*   109–
10. *Pand.* In . . . so. | *Love*] F (*subst.*)*;* Pand: *Love | Q.*   109 S.D.] *Dyce; not in Q,F.*   111–14.] *As Pope; For . . . Doe | The . . . wounds | Q ; For . . . Bow | Shootes . . . Doe | The . . . wounds | F.*   113. *shaft confounds*] F; *shafts confound Q.*
116.] *Q,F; These . . . cry | O . . . die | Johnson.*   121. *Heigh ho!*] *Q,F; as speech. Var. '85, conj. Ritson.*

adamant harder than flint have I made thy forehead'.

104. *you may*] 'Go along with you!'

105. *this . . . all*] The *Variorum* note suggests that this is a quotation from a song, citing Field, *A Woman is a Weathercock* ('What, musing and writing? O, this love will undo us all'): it is possible, yet I find it odd that both Helen and Paris should quote songs, and that Pandarus should take his cue only from Paris. (Professor Brooks suggests that Helen and Paris quote the *same* song, and that, if so, Helen's line is the name of the tune.)

108. *good now*] please; 'an interjectional expression denoting acquiescence, entreaty, expostulation, or surprise' (OED): cf. *Ham.* I.i.73: 'Good now, sit down, and tell me'.

109.] Despite Q's omission of the line, Pandarus' reply is clearly needed.

113–14.] 'The shaft doesn't hurt that which it pierces.'

115. *sore*] wound; (perhaps) buck of the fourth year (cf. *LLL* IV.ii.56 ff.).

117. *wound to kill*] fatal wound.

121. *Heigh ho*] Taken by editors to be an interjection by Pandarus. There is, however, no good reason for excluding it from the song, because (a) both Q and F set the phrase in italic type, as with the song (although agreement of Q and F is not conclusive); (b) musically, two long notes for *Heigh ho!* would make the last line of the verse as long as the first (six beats); (c) the second part of the song plays, very largely, with sounds suggestive of sexual enjoyment (of which this might well be another);

Helen. In love, i'faith, to the very tip of the nose.

Paris. He eats nothing but doves, love, and that breeds
hot blood, and hot blood begets hot thoughts, and
hot thoughts beget hot deeds, and hot deeds is   125
love.

Pand. Is this the generation of love? Hot blood, hot
thoughts, and hot deeds? Why, they are vipers.
Is love a generation of vipers? Sweet lord, who's
afield today?   130

Paris. Hector, Deiphobus, Helenus, Antenor, and all
the gallantry of Troy. I would fain have armed
today, but my Nell would not have it so. How
chance my brother Troilus went not?

Helen. He hangs the lip at something: you know all,   135
Lord Pandarus.

Pand. Not I, honey-sweet queen; I long to hear how
they sped today.— You'll remember your brother's
excuse?

Paris. To a hair.   140

Pand. Farewell, sweet queen.

Helen. Commend me to your niece.

136. Pandarus.] *Q; Pandarus? | F.*

(d) it is not unprecedented for a song
to end with broken utterance and an
imperfect cadence: cf. the end of
John Dowland's 'In darkness let me
dwell'; (e) Helen's remark (l. 122)
may be, quite plausibly, a comment
upon the style of Pandarus' singing,
and not (as Ritson supposed: *Remarks*,
1783) upon his involuntary sigh.

123. *doves*] Like pigeons (the two
kinds were frequently confused),
associated with love—first, from their
behaviour (cf. billing and cooing),
and secondly, from association with
the doves that drew Venus' chariot.
Not *necessarily* an aphrodisiac—Paris
is facetious—but certainly a meat that
heated the blood.

124–6. *hot . . . love*] A typical piece
of wit, suppressing the false analogies
(one hot thing is like another: like
begets like) beneath the ambiguous

common term *hot* = (a) impassioned,
angry; (b) sexually excited.

128. *vipers*] Sometimes referred to
St Paul's shipwreck in Malta (Acts
xxviii.3: 'There came a viper out of
the heat, and fastened on his hand');
but I suspect that Proverbs xxiii is the
source, with its association of strange
women with whores (v. 27), the excit-
ing effects of wine (v. 31), and the
consequences of indulgence (v. 32:
'At last it biteth like a serpent, and
stingeth like an adder'). *Adder* became
viper for the sake of the joke in the
next line.

129. *generation of vipers*] Cf. Matthew
iii.7, xii.34, xxiii.33; and Luke iii.7.

132. *gallantry*] nobility; 'gallants'
collectively. (Earliest example in
OED, both for this sense and for the
form of the word.)

140.] Cf. Tilley H 26.

Pand. I will, sweet queen.   [*Exit.*] *Sound a retreat.*
Paris. They're come from the field: let us to Priam's hall
    To greet the warriors. Sweet Helen, I must woo you 145
    To help unarm our Hector. His stubborn buckles,
    With these your white enchanting fingers touch'd,
    Shall more obey than to the edge of steel
    Or force of Greekish sinews: you shall do more
    Than all the island kings—disarm great Hector.   150
Helen. 'Twill make us proud to be his servant, Paris.
    Yea, what he shall receive of us in duty
    Gives us more palm in beauty than we have,
    Yea, overshines ourself.
Paris. Sweet, above thought I love thee.   *Exeunt.* 155

[SCENE II]

Enter PANDARUS *and* Troilus' Man [*, meeting*].

Pand. How now, where's thy master? At my cousin
    Cressida's?
Man. No sir, he stays for you to conduct him thither.

Enter TROILUS.

Pand. O here he comes! How now, how now?
Troil. Sirrah, walk off.   [*Exit Man.*]   5
Pand. Have you seen my cousin?
Troil. No, Pandarus. I stalk about her door
    Like a strange soul upon the Stygian banks

---

143 S.D. *Exit.*] *Rowe; not in* Q,F.   144. the field] Q; field F.   147. these]
F; this Q.   154–5. ourself. / *Paris.* Sweet,] *Pope;* our selfe. / *Par:* Sweet Q;
our selfe. / *Sweete* F.   155. thee] F; her Q, *Johnson.*

Scene II

S.D.] *Enter Pandarus and Troylus Man* / F; *Enter. Pandarus Troylus, man* / Q; Enter
a *Servant,* and *Pandarus,* meeting / *Capell.*   3. he stays] F; stayes Q.   5 S.D.]
Kittredge; Exit *Servant* / *Capell; not in* Q, F.   8. Like] F; Like to Q.

150. *island kings*] Greeks: cf.
Prologue, ll. 1–2.

Scene II
7. *stalk*] move in stately fashion, like
a ghost; cf. *Ham.* 1.i.53, 69.

Staying for waftage. O be thou my Charon,
And give me swift transportance to those fields   10
Where I may wallow in the lily beds
Propos'd for the deserver! O gentle Pandar,
From Cupid's shoulder pluck his painted wings
And fly with me to Cressid!
Pand. Walk here i'th'orchard, I'll bring her straight.   *Exit.*
Troil. I am giddy: expectation whirls me round.   16
    Th'imaginary relish is so sweet
    That it enchants my sense: what will it be
    When that the wat'ry palate tastes indeed
    Love's thrice-repured nectar? Death, I fear me,   20

---

12. Pandar] *Q; Pandarus | F.*   15 S.D.] *As Dyce; Exit Pandarus | F; not in Q.*
19. palate tastes] *Hanmer;* pallats taste *Q,F, Rowe, Pope.*   20. thrice-repured]
This edn; thrice repured *Q;* thrice reputed *F.*

---

9. *waftage*] passage by water; cf.
Err. IV.i.96: 'A ship you sent me to,
to hire waftage.'

Charon] infernal ferryman, who
bore the souls of the dead over Styx to
Elysium.

10. *transportance*] conveyance.

11. *wallow*] roll or turn, as upon a
bed. The word has acquired as its
primary sense (for modern ears) 'take
delight in gross pleasures or a de-
moralizing way of life' (OED 6), and
editors usually so gloss it; but there
are many senses without this strong
moral disapproval: e.g. OED 2 'roll
about . . . while lying down'; OED 3
'roll about or lie prostrate in or upon
some . . . yielding substance'. Shakespeare may have remembered Chaucer, *Troilus and Criseyde*, V.211: 'To
bedde he goth, and walweth ther and
torneth'.

lily beds] Probably less classical
(*Aeneid*, VI.883) than Biblical (the
Song of Solomon ii.16, iv.5, vi.1–2,
vii.2): in any case, Virgil's lilies are
merely part of the Elysian flora,
whereas those of Solomon have an
obvious sexual symbolism.

13.] Cf. *Faerie Queene*, III.xii.23, 'And
clapt on hie his coulourd winges
twaine'.

15.] Pandarus' business-like literal-
ism is in strong contrast to Troilus'
slightly strained hyperbole.

16–23.] For similar fear of excessive
delight, cf. Lyly, *Endymion*, III.iv.96–
102: '. . . lest imbracing sweetnesse
beyond measure, I take a surfeit
without recure'. Portia (*Mer. V.*
III.ii.111–14) also fears love's abundance, but does not go on (as Troilus
does) to apprehend loss of 'distinction' in her senses: the perceptual
confusion in that play is of a different
order, and belongs to Bassanio (see
note to ll. 35–8 below).

19. *wat'ry*] moistened by saliva;
salivating.

20. *repured*] F's *reputed* is the more
common word and hence the more
likely to be a mis-reading (this
example of *repured* (as pp. adj.) being
the only one given by OED); there-
fore, *praestat difficilior lectio*. In any case
the contrast of fine / crude throughout
the speech requires the Q reading
here.

Sounding destruction, or some joy too fine,
Too subtle-potent, tun'd too sharp in sweetness
For the capacity of my ruder powers.
I fear it much; and I do fear besides
That I shall lose distinction in my joys,   25
As doth a battle, when they charge on heaps
The enemy flying.

Enter PANDARUS.

Pand. She's making her ready, she'll come straight.
You must be witty, now: she does so blush, and
fetches her wind so short, as if she were frayed   30
with a spirit! I'll fetch her: it is the prettiest
villain; she fetches her breath as short as a new-
ta'en sparrow.   *Exit.*

21. Sounding] *Q,F;* Swounding *Camb.;* Swooning *Pope.*   22. subtle-potent]
Theobald; subtill, potent] *Q,F (subst.).*   tun'd] *Q;* and *F.*   27 S.D.] *F;*
not in Q.   30. frayed] *Capell (subst.);* fraid *Q,F;* 'fraid *Hanmer.*   31. spirit]
Q; sprite *F.*   32. as short] *Q;* so short *F.*   33 S.D.] *Dyce; Exit Pand. | F;*
not in Q.

21. *Sounding destruction*] dissolution
of consciousness by swooning (of
which *sounding* is an alternative form).
The phrase is less likely to be paren-
thetic (a gloss upon Death), than the
second term in a series of *three*
possible consequences: (1) death (at
worst), or (2) sounding destruction,
or (at least) (3) some joy too fine.
Orger's conjecture (*distraction*) is
plausible—Shakespeare elsewhere uses
the senses of 'violent perturbation of
mind' (*Ant.* IV.i.9) and 'mental de-
rangement' (Sonnet 119)—but one
would in that case have to read the
present phrase as 'perturbation great
enough to cause unconsciousness',
which seems a little forced.

22. *tun'd . . . sweetness*] F's *and* produces an oxymoron (excess in one
kind produces its contrary: cf. *Paradise Lost,* III.380: 'Dark with excessive
bright'). Q's *tun'd* uses a figure from
music to explain a paradox of taste:
to raise sweetness to an extreme pitch

would be to lose the sense of sweetness
altogether.

26. *battle*] armed force, army.
26-7.] Cf. the image used by
Ulysses, III.iii.161-3.

29. *witty*] alert; in full command of
the five wits.

30. *frayed*] frightened.

31. *spirit*] ghost, supernatural
apparition. Shakespeare seems to use
sprite and *spirit* indifferen'ly: I follow
Q.

32. *villain*] Like *rogue*, a term used
affectionately or facetiously, especially
of children and women; also, an
inferior kind of hawk (which may be
intended here: cf. ll. 42-3 and 52
below).

32-3. *new-ta'en sparrow*] In normal
conditions, birds have a higher
metabolic rate (and hence, pulse-rate
and rate of breathing) than men: a
terrified bird, *a fortiori*, breathes very
fast indeed (as observation shows).

Troil. Even such a passion doth embrace my bosom.
My heart beats thicker than a feverous pulse,   35
And all my powers do their bestowing lose,
Like vassalage at unawares encount'ring
The eye of majesty.

Enter PANDARUS *and* CRESSIDA.

Pand. Come, come, what need you blush? Shame's a
baby. Here she is now; swear the oaths now to her   40
that you have sworn to me.—What, are you gone
again?—You must be watched ere you be made
tame, must you? Come your ways, come your
ways: and you draw backward we'll put you
i'th'fills. Why do you not speak to her? Come,   45
draw this curtain, and let's see your picture—
alas the day, how loath you are to offend daylight!
And 'twere dark, you'd close sooner. So, so; rub
on and kiss the mistress. How now, a kiss in fee-
farm! Build there, carpenter, the air is sweet.—   50
Nay, you shall fight your hearts out ere I part you:

36. lose] *F3;* loose *Q,F.*   37. unawares] *F;* unwares *Q.*   39. Come . . .
blush] *As separate line, Q,F.*   46. picture—] *Q,F;* picture. [*Snatching her mask*] /
Johnson.   47. day,] *F;* day? *Q.*

35–8.] Boyle (*ES*, xxx. 36) first
noted a similarity to *Mer. V.*
iii.ii.175–82 (cf. note to ll. 16–23
above).

35. *thicker*] Here, perhaps, 'faster';
but *thick* really implies many things
close together, or in rapid succession,
and hence (in a temporal sense) in
irregular and uncontrolled haste (cf.
2H4 ii.iii.24: 'speaking thick, which
nature made his blemish'; *Mac.*
i.iii.97–8: 'As thick as hail, / Came
post with post').

36. *bestowing*] employment, use.

39–40. *Shame's a baby*] Typical of
Pandarus' nurse-like speech. The
phrase sounds proverbial.

42–3. *You . . . you?*] As indeed a
hawk may be, for three days and
nights together (cf. *villain*, l. 32; *the
falcon as the tercel*, l. 52).

45. *fills*] shafts of a cart (variant of
thills; but *fills* / *phills* seems to be usual
with Shakespeare: cf. *Mer. V.* ii.ii.91).

46. *draw . . . picture*] Cressida is
veiled, as Olivia is (*Tw.N.* i.v.236–7).

48. *close*] (a) join, combine; (b)
agree, come to terms; (c) grapple,
come to grips.

48–9. *rub . . . mistress*] A series of
puns from bowling: *rub* = move, but
slowly, and perhaps curve inwards
(spoken to a wood that the player
would retard); *kiss* = touch gently;
mistress = jack.

49–50. *in fee-farm*] held in per-
petuity.

50.] For building where the air is
sweet, cf. *Mac.* i.vi.1–9 and *2H4*
v.iii.5–8.

51. *fight . . . out*] Cf. *close* (=grapple)
above, l. 48.

the falcon as the tercel, for all the ducks i'th'river
—go to, go to.
Troil. You have bereft me of all words, lady.
Pand. Words pay no debts, give her deeds; but she'll   55
    bereave you o'th'deeds too, if she call your
    activity in question.—What, billing again? Here's
    'In witness whereof the parties interchangeably—'
    Come in, come in: I'll go get a fire.   [*Exit Pandarus.*]
Cress. Will you walk in, my lord?   60
Troil. O Cressid, how often have I wished me thus.
Cress. Wished, my lord? The gods grant—O my lord—
Troil. What should they grant? What makes this
    pretty abruption? What too curious dreg espies my

---

52. falcon as] *Theobald;* faulcon, as *Q,F.* (*subst.*).   59. fire.] *F2;* fire? *Q,F.*
59 S.D.] *F2* (*subst.*); *not in Q,F.*   61. Cressid] *Q* (*Cressid*); *Cressida | F.*
62. grant—O my lord—] *This edn;* graunt? O my Lord? *Q;* grant? O my
Lord, *F;* grant; O my Lord! *Rowe.*

---

52. *the falcon . . . river*] It is not clear
whether this means (a) falcon and
tercel are equally matched for flying
against duck, and both will kill well;
or (b) falcon and tercel are equal,
wagering whatever sum you care to
name. The phrase may be a memory
of Chaucer's Pandarus (*Troilus and
Criseyde,* IV.413: 'Both heroner and
faucoun for ryvere').
    54. *You . . . words*] Bassanio uses the
same words to Portia, in a moment of
excitement and confusion (*Mer. V.*
III.ii.175).
    55. *Words . . . deeds*] Cf. Tilley W820.
    pay no debts] probably with allusion
to 1 Corinthians vii.3: 'Uxori vir deb-
itum reddat' (Vulgate), as the Wife
of Bath well knew (Wife of Bath's
Prologue, ll. 129–30: 'Why sholde
men elles in hir bookes sette / That
man shal yelde to his wyf hire dette?').
    deeds] copulation (as also at
V.iii.112): cf. *do* (OED 16b).
    56. *bereave*] deprive (Pandarus
plays with Troilus' *bereft,* l. 54).
    57. *billing*] kissing: cf. *AYL* III.iii.
72–3: 'and as pigeons bill, so wedlock
would be nibbling'. There may be an

allusion to another sense of *bill* (= set
down in a list, book, or reckoning:
indict: petition): Pandarus goes on to
quote a common legal formula.
    58.   *interchangeably*]   reciprocally:
Pandarus uses a formula especially
to be found in indentures (= legal
documents in duplicate, divided from
the same sheet by a sinuous line: each
party signed one half, and delivered
it to the other). Since the point of an
indenture was that the two halves had
to fit perfectly together, Pandarus may
be playing with a sexual implication.
    60.] An invitation repeated verba-
tim at l. 98: see Appendix I, p. 304.
    64. *abruption*] interruption of speech
(earliest example in OED). The
dialogue from this point until the
re-entry of Pandarus is both riddling
and affected, and may be a parody of
court speech.
    curious] Usually = fine, delicate;
but Troilus' formula *too curious* may
require 'minute (in enquiry); unduly
refined; recondite' (cf. *Ham.* V.i.198:
''Twere to consider too curiously to
consider so').
    dreg] Unexpectedly singular, which

sweet lady in the fountain of our love?   65
Cress. More dregs than water, if my fears have eyes.
Troil. Fears make devils of cherubins; they never see
    truly.
Cress. Blind fear, that seeing reason leads, finds safer
    footing than blind reason stumbling without fear.   70
    To fear the worst oft cures the worse.
Troil. O let my lady apprehend no fear: in all Cupid's
    pageant there is presented no monster.
Cress. Nor nothing monstrous neither?
Troil. Nothing but our undertakings, when we vow to   75
    weep seas, live in fire, eat rocks, tame tigers;
    thinking it harder for our mistress to devise
    imposition enough than for us to undergo any

---

66. fears] *Pope;* teares *Q,F.*   71. worse] *Q,F;* worst *Hanmer.*   72–3.] *As*
Pope; O let . . . fear, / In . . . monster. *Q,F.*   74. Nor] *Q;* Not *F.*   neither?]
F; neither. *Q.*

---

supports the condemnation implicit in *too curious*: Cressida is making mountains out of molehills.

65. *fountain*] Possibly an allusion to the Song of Solomon iv. 12–15: 'A garden inclosed is my sister, my spouse; a spring shut up, a fountain sealed . . . A fountain of gardens, a well of living waters, and streams from Lebanon.' (But cf. also note to III. iii. 305.)

66. *fears*] Pope's reading is usually adopted. Cressida's hesitation (l. 62) is no indication of weeping; and even if she were to weep, the figure of tears full of eyes is likely to complicate the allegory of ll. 68–9.

67. *Fears . . . cherubins*] Almost a proverb; cf. *MND* v. i. 21–2, and Tilley B 738. (The reverse is more common: cf. Tilley D 231.)

cherubins] The normal plural from the thirteenth until the seventeenth century (based on ecclesiastical Latin and medieval French). *Cherubims* was used in translations of the Bible, from

Wyclif onward, and *cherubim* in the seventeenth century as a regular Hebrew plural; but the word has 'no root or certain etymology in Hebrew' (OED).

69. *seeing*] An adjective: *seeing reason* = reason which has its sight.

71. *To . . . worse*] Cf. Tilley W 912.

72–3.] Troilus may be wrong, in Spenser's view: Cupid's pageant (*Faerie Queene*, III. xii. 25) is wholly monstrous; but one can hardly be sure how easily such a point would be taken by an audience.

75–6.] Troilus is deliberately extravagant, but his examples are not therefore his own invention. For *weep seas*, cf. Donne, 'A Valediction: of Weeping', ll. 14–22; for *live in fire*, see the miniature by Nicholas Hilliard, in which a lover (in a penitential white shirt) is seen against a background of flame. Dante's lovers (*Purgatorio*, xxv. 112–xxvi. 148) also live in fire during their purgation.

difficulty imposed. <u>This is the monstruosity in
love, lady: that the will is infinite, and the exe-</u> 80
<u>cution confined: that the desire is boundless, and
the act a slave to limit.</u>

Cress. They say all lovers swear more performance than
they are able, and yet reserve an ability that they
never perform: vowing more than the perfection 85
of ten, and discharging less than the tenth part of
one. They that have the voice of lions and the act
of hares, are they not monsters?

Troil. <u>Are there such? Such are not we. Praise us as we
are tasted, allow us as we prove.</u> Our head shall 90
go bare till merit cover it: <u>no perfection in reversion shall have a praise in present. We will not
name desert before his birth, and, being born, his
addition shall be humble. Few words to fair faith:</u>

[Marginalia: Tr. argument parallels again (I.iii. 1-30) & a close analogue to the Trojan Debate. (II.ii. 120-1)]

---

79. This is] *F;* This *Q.* monstruosity] *Q,F;* monstrosity *F3.* 91. cover...
perfection] *This edn (conj. Delius);* louer part no affection *Q;* crowne it: no perfection *F.* 94. humble. Few . . . faith:] *As Capell;* humble: few wordes to
faire faith. *Q,F (subst.).*

---

79. *monstruosity*] (= monstrosity):
the earlier form, persisting until about
1800; 'monstrosity' appeared in the
mid-sixteenth century. Troilus may
be using the sense 'monster' (OED 2),
and continuing his allusion to Cupid's
pageant—(*this* is, after all, the only
'monster' in it).

79–82.] Troilus is more metaphysical than Cressida. *Her* comment
(ll. 83–7) is unmistakably sexual,
although it derives (as his does) from
his mockery of lovers' hyperboles. But
Troilus' lines express a profound
regret: not merely that lovers should
be less than they claim to be, but that
no love can ever find its proper and
sufficient mode of utterance—all
speech and all action comes short. His
argument is an exact parallel to that
of Agamemnon (I.iii. 1–30), and a
close analogue to that of the Trojan
debate (II.ii. 120–1).

83–4.] Cf. Tilley L 570.

87–8. *voice . . . hares*] Proverbial in

German (Löwenmaul, Hasenherz)
and perhaps in English too: cf. *Cor.*
I.i. 170: 'Where he should find you
lions, finds you hares'. Walker (NCS)
cites Erasmus, *Adagia*, 'Inconstantia:
Leo prius, nunc leporem agit'.

89–92.] I am not sure why Troilus
continues to use the plural pronoun
here: he is speaking of himself, not of
lovers in general.

89–90. *Praise . . . prove*] Cf. Tilley
P 83.

91–2. *merit . . . reversion*] Delius's
conjecture is attractive: *cover* (couer)
might as easily yield the misreading
crown (? Croune) as *lover* (louer). With
cover (= put on [one's hat]) cf. *go
bare.*

in reversion] to be enjoyed in future.

92–3.] Like Ulysses and Nestor,
Troilus uses images of gestation and
childbirth; cf. I.iii. 311–12, 344–6.

94. *addition*] title.

Few . . . faith] Cf. Tilley W 828.

Troilus shall be such to Cressid as what envy can   95
say worst shall be a mock for his truth, and what
truth can speak truest, not truer than Troilus.

Cress. Will you walk in, my lord?

Enter PANDARUS.

Pand. What, blushing still? Have you not done talking
yet?   100

Cress. Well, uncle, what folly I commit, I dedicate to
you.

Pand. I thank you for that: if my lord get a boy of you,
you'll give him me. Be true to my lord: if he flinch,
chide me for it.   105

Troil. You know now your hostages: your uncle's
word, and my firm faith.

Pand. Nay, I'll give my word for her too: our kindred,
though they be long ere they be wooed, they are
constant being won. They are burs, I can tell you: 110
they'll stick where they are thrown.

Cress. Boldness comes to me now, and brings me heart:
Prince Troilus, I have lov'd you night and day
For many weary months.

Troil. Why was my Cressid then so hard to win?   115

Cress. Hard to seem won; but I was won, my lord,
With the first glance that ever—Pardon me:

98 S.D.] *F; not in Q.*   109. be wooed] *Q;* are wooed *F.*   117. glance . . .
Pardon] *As Rowe;* glance; that euer pardon *Q,F;* glance that ever: pardon
F2.   me:] *This edn;* me *Q;* me, *F;* me—*Rowe.*

95–6. *what . . . truth*] 'The worst
insult that envy can offer will be
merely a sarcasm at the expense of
Troilus' constancy.'

101. *folly*] lechery: a common sense
in Shakespeare: cf. v.ii.18, and *Oth.*
v.ii.133: 'She turn'd to folly, and she
was a whore'. Frequent also in the
Old Testament (e.g. Deuteronomy
xxii.21: 'She hath wrought folly in
Israel, to play the whore in her
father's house'). Since, despite editors,
the present scene apparently takes
place in and about the house of
Calchas (cf. IV.i.38, and *Variorum*

note to III.ii), it may have been this
text which was in Shakespeare's mind.

110. *burs*] (probably) seed-vessels of
goose-grass (also called 'cleavers'),
rather than burdock, as Schmidt suggests, but the seed of burdock *will*
stick, if thrown. Cf. *AYL* I.iii.13–14:
'They are but burs, cousin, thrown
upon thee in holiday foolery'. Cf.
Tilley B 724.

111. *thrown*] A sexual innuendo: cf.
III.iii.206–7: 'And better would it fit
Achilles much / To throw down
Hector than Polyxena'.

If I confess much you will play the tyrant.
I love you now, but till now not so much
But I might master it. In faith I lie—   120
My thoughts were like unbridled children, grown
Too headstrong for their mother.—See, we fools!
Why have I blabb'd? Who shall be true to us
When we are so unsecret to ourselves?—
But though I lov'd you well, I woo'd you not;   125
And yet, good faith, I wish'd myself a man,
Or that we women had men's privilege
Of speaking first. Sweet, bid me hold my tongue,
For in this rapture I shall surely speak
The thing I shall repent. See, see, your silence,   130
Cunning in dumbness, from my weakness draws
My very soul of counsel. Stop my mouth.

Troil.   And shall, albeit sweet music issues thence. [*Kisses her.*]
Pand.   Pretty, i'faith.
Cress.   My lord, I do beseech you pardon me: 135
'Twas not my purpose thus to beg a kiss.
I am asham'd. O heavens, what have I done?
For this time I will take my leave, my lord.
Pand.   Leave?—And you take leave till tomorrow
morning—   140
Cress.   Pray you, content you.
Troil.   What offends you, lady?
Cress.   Sir, mine own company.

119. till now not] *Q;* not till now *F.*   121. children, grown] *F2;* children
grone *Q;* children grow *F.*   122. See, we fools!] *Theobald (subst.);* See we
fooles *Q,F.*   123. blabb'd?] *F2;* blab'd: *Q,F.*   124. ourselves?] *F;* our
selves. *Q.*   131. Cunning] *Pope;* Comming *Q,F.*   132. My . . . counsel]
Q; My soule of counsell from me *F.*   133 S.D.] *Rowe; not in Q,F.*   139.
Leave?] *Kittredge;* Leaue: *Q,F.*

121-2. *My . . . mother*] A figure
which Shakespeare uses for fundamental disorder; cf. *Meas.* i.iii.30–1:
'The baby beats the nurse, and quite
athwart / Goes all decorum'. (The
more serious version occurs in the
present play, i.iii.115: 'And the rude
son should strike his father dead'.)
   131. *Cunning*] Baldwin (*Variorum*)
defends *coming*, arguing that Silence

is allegorical, and would therefore
naturally come in dumbness. But this
is mere tautology: the paradox of
cunning in dumbness is essential as a
gloss upon the paradox of silence
coaxing Cressida's very judgement
from her.
   132. *Stop my mouth*] A common
expression in Shakespeare (cf. *Ado*
ii.i.292).

Troil. You cannot shun yourself.

Cress. Let me go and try.   145
    I have a kind of self resides with you,
    But an unkind self, that itself will leave
    To be another's fool. I would be gone:
    Where is my wit? I know not what I speak.

Troil. Well know they what they speak that speak so wisely.

Cress. Perchance, my lord, I show more craft than love,   151
    And fell so roundly to a large confession
    To angle for your thoughts. But you are wise,
    Or else you love not; for to be wise and love
    Exceeds man's might: that dwells with gods above.   155

Troil. O that I thought it could be in a woman—
    As, if it can, I will presume in you—
    To feed for aye her lamp and flames of love;

148–9. I . . . speak] *As Q*; Where is my wit? / I would be gone: I speake I know not what *F*.   150. that speak] *Q*; that speakes *F*.   155. might: that] *Capell (subst.);* might that *Q*; might, that *F*.   157. presume] *Q,F*; presume't *Deighton, conj. W. J. Craig.*   158. aye] *F*; age *Q*.

146–8.] Cressida is already divided within herself (although not so absolutely as Troilus sees her in v.ii). Hers is a moral and intellectual confusion: she desires Troilus, and yet she wishes still to keep the tactical advantage of uncertainty (as at iv.ii.17–18).

148. *fool*] perhaps = idiot, gull, although the word could also imply affection or pity.

148–9.] Metrically the verses are transposable; but it seems better to retain Q's order (in which *Where is my wit?* can refer to *both* remaining hemistiches, i.e. *I would be gone* and *I know not what I speak*) than to adopt F's (in which Cressida questions her good sense, for being uncertain, and makes incoherent speech her reason for going).

152–5.] Verity's explanation (see *Variorum* note) seems satisfactory. Cressida says, in effect, 'I tried to entrap you into confession, and you wouldn't be caught, being either too ~~wd~~ or not in love', and then,

remembering the proverb (Tilley L 558), adds 'but you can't be both wise and in love'.

152. *roundly*] frankly.

154. *Or else*] or rather.

154–5. *for . . . might*] Tyrwhitt pointed out the parallel in *Shepherd's Calendar* (March) although (as Malone saw) the ultimate source is Publilius Syrus. The sentiment is too common for further source-hunting to be of use.

157. *presume*] Elliptically, for 'presume that it may indeed be'.

158. *aye*] Q's *age* would be a simple misreading in most hands. The implicit contrast with *youth* (l. 159) may have encouraged the error.

flames] Walker (NCS, after Tannenbaum) reads *flame*, which is attractive. But while *lamp and flame* would be a typical Shakespearean figure (= flame of [her] lamp), we are not therefore required, as an alternative, to see the QF reading as providing two objects for *feed* (of which *flames* would be taken as Petrarchan symbolism).

To keep her constancy in plight and youth,
Outliving beauty's outward, with a mind   160
That doth renew swifter than blood decays!
Or that persuasion could but thus convince me
That my integrity and truth to you
Might be affronted with the match and weight
Of such a winnow'd purity in love—   165
How were I then uplifted! But alas,
I am as true as truth's simplicity,
And simpler than the infancy of truth.

Cress. In that I'll war with you.

Troil.   O virtuous fight,
When right with right wars who shall be most right! 170
True swains in love shall, in the world to come,
Approve their truth by Troilus; when their rhymes,
Full of protest, of oath, and big compare,
Wants similes, truth tir'd with iteration
(As true as steel, as plantage to the moon,   175

160. beauty's] *Capell;* beauties *Q,F.*   172. truth] *Q;* truths *F.*   174. Wants]
Q,F; Want *F2.*   similes, truth] *F;* simile's truth *Q.*   175. plantage] *Q,F;*
planets *Pope;* tidage *conj. Hudson.*

Rather, one image has suggested another, and the *flame* of the lamp has changed into the flames (*flammae*) of love.

159. *plight*] 'good or proper condition, health' (OED 5b): I follow Lee's interpretation.

160. *outward*] outward appearance (cf. *Cym.* I.i.23: 'So fair an outward, and such stuff within'). As the collation shows, *beauty's outward* has caused difficulty, but there need be none: the perfect woman would keep her fidelity young, despite the ageing of her youthful beauty; her body might in time destroy itself, but her mind would maintain its constancy. (See also note to l. 165.)

164. *affronted*] confronted, balanced.

165. *winnow'd purity*] unmixed with imperfections (i.e. bran, husk). Shakespeare uses a similar figure for his own affection, in Sonnet 125, l. 11 ('Which is not mix'd with seconds').

It may be significant that the poem contains not only a profession of simple faith, like that of Troilus, but also an analogy with the use of *outward* (above) in l. 2 ('With my extern the outward honouring'). For the image of winnowing (but applied to snow), cf. also *MND* III.ii.141–2 and *Wint.* IV.iv.365–6.

167.] Cf. Tilley T 565.

172. *Approve*] confirm, attest.

173. *compare*] comparison (*comparison* sometimes = sarcasm).

174. *Wants*] Singular form affected by singular nouns immediately before; see also Abbott §333. But *wants similes* might be awkward to speak distinctly. (For the collocation of *similes* and *iteration*, cf. *1H4* I.ii.77, 88, where Falstaff complains of *unsavoury similes* and *damnable iteration.*)

175. *As . . . steel*] Cf. Tilley S 840.

plantage . . . moon] Perhaps *plantage* is (as OED supposes) a Shakespearean

As sun to day, as turtle to her mate,
As iron to adamant, as earth to th'centre)
Yet, after all comparisons of truth,
As truth's authentic author to be cited,
'As true as Troilus' shall crown up the verse   180
And sanctify the numbers.

Cress.   Prophet may you be!
If I be false, or swerve a hair from truth,
When time is old and hath forgot itself,
When water-drops have worn the stones of Troy,
And blind oblivion swallow'd cities up,   185
And mighty states characterless are grated
To dusty nothing—yet let memory,
From false to false, among false maids in love,

---

178. Yet, after] *F* (*subst.*); After *Q*.   183. and] *F;* or *Q*.

---

coinage, meaning 'growing (cultivated) plants', by analogy with herbage. No commentator (and no gardener, either) doubts the relationship between the waxing moon and the growth of new plants or seed; but many doubt the form *plantage*. It may, but probably does not, derive from *plantago* (= plantain), for why should Shakespeare use here a Latinate form for that which he knew by its vernacular name (cf. *LLL* III.i.70)? Yet *plantage* = 'act of planting or cultivation' will not do: the context requires a natural and inevitable connection between the things named, and gardeners plant seeds at will, not by divine thrusting on.

176. *as . . . mate*] Cf. Tilley T 624.

177. *adamant*] magnet. Properly, a very hard crystalline substance: by confused etymology in early medieval Latin writers, *adamant* was supposed to derive from adamare (= be attracted to).

centre] i.e. of the globe itself.

178. *Yet*] Q's line halts, and F's *Yet* is plausible. The asseverations of Troilus and Cressida are meant to be balanced, and although Cressida says

Yea at l. 193, it is merely for emphasis. Her declaration is poised, structurally, on l. 187, and there she says 'yet'.

comparisons] 'illustration by similitudes' (Johnson).

179.] Troilus is the very soul of truth, and hence any reference to the truth of Troilus is like the appeal to an authoritative work.

180. *crown up*] (probably) put the finishing touch to (OED 9): cf. 'Finis coronat opus' (proverbial in Latin); *2H6* v.ii.28, '*La fin couronne les œuvres*'; *All's W.* IV.iv.35, 'still the fine's the crown'; Tilley E 116, 'The end crowns (tries) all'. Verbs+*up* normally imply completion (cf. eat up, burn up); however, the sense here may be 'bless, endow with honour' (OED 11); cf. Psalm lxv.11 ('Thou crownest the year with thy goodness'), and consider the implication of *sanctify the numbers*.

184.] Cf. Tilley D 618 (Job xiv.19, and Erasmus, *Adagia* 782E).

185. *blind*] regardless.

186. *characterless*] i.e. without any written or inscribed mark: hence, unrecorded.

grated] ground, pulverized.

Upbraid my falsehood. When they've said 'As false
As air, as water, wind, or sandy earth,   190
As fox to lamb, or wolf to heifer's calf,
Pard to the hind, or stepdame to her son'—
Yea, let them say, to stick the heart of falsehood,
'As false as Cressid'.

Pand. Go to, a bargain made: seal it, seal it, I'll be the   195
witness. Here I hold your hand, here my cousin's.
If ever you prove false one to another, since I have
taken such pains to bring you together, let all
pitiful goers-between be called to the world's end
after my name: call them all Pandars: let all   200
constant men be Troiluses, all false women
Cressids, and all brokers-between Pandars. Say
'Amen'.

Troil. Amen.

Cress. Amen.   205

Pand. Amen. Whereupon I will show you a chamber
with bed, which bed, because it shall not speak of
your pretty encounters, press it to death. Away.

Exeunt [Troilus and Cressida].

189. they've] *Rowe;* th'have *Q;* they 'aue *F.*   190. wind, or] *Q;* as Winde,
as *F.*   191. or wolf] *Q;* as Wolfe *F.*   196. witness. Here] *Rowe;* witnes here
Q,F (subst.).   cousin's] *Rowe;* Cozens *Q;* Cousins *F.*   198. pains] *F;* paine
Q.   200. Pandars] *Pope;* Panders *Q,F (and so at 202).*   201. constant] *Q,F;*
inconstant *Hanmer.*   202. brokers-between] *Theobald;* brokers betweene *Q,F.*
206–7. chamber with bed] *Sisson (after Hanmer);* Chamber *Q,F;* bedchamber
Theobald.   208 S.D.] *Capell;* Exeunt *Q;* after 210, *F.*

190. *water*] Cf. Tilley W 86, and
Wint. I.ii.132.

193. *stick*] pierce, stab.

198. *taken such pains*] Invariably
plural in form, though often singular
in grammar (which might account
for Q's *paine*).

199. *pitiful*] compassionate. 'Wretched, miserable' is possible; but
Pandarus is here emphasizing his
sympathy and willing help.

201. *constant*] Hanmer's emendation
is pointless: each character has insisted upon his primary quality (truth,
falsehood, pimping), and Pandarus

recognizes the pattern.

202. *brokers-between*] A mocking
parallel with goers-between. 'Broker'
already had the sense of bawd or
pimp: cf. *John* II.i.582: 'This bawd,
this broker, this all-changing word'.

206–7. *chamber with bed*] Sisson's
emendation seems inevitable; *wᵗ bedwʰ
bed* would be enough to cause error by
compositor or copyist.

207–8. *because . . . death*] Pressing to
death was the punishment for 'a
person arraigned for felony who stood
mute and would not plead' (OED
press 1 b).

And Cupid grant all tongue-tied maidens here
Bed, chamber, pander to provide this gear!   *Exit*. 210

[SCENE III]

Flourish. Enter AGAMEMNON, ULYSSES, DIOMEDES, NESTOR,
MENELAUS [, AJAX,] *and* CALCHAS.

Calch. Now, princes, for the service I have done,
Th'advantage of the time prompts me aloud
To call for recompense. Appear it to your mind
That, through the sight I bear in things to come,
I have abandon'd Troy, left my possession,   5

210. pander] *Q* (Pander)*; and* Pander *F.*   S.D.] *Q; Exeunt | F.*

Scene III

S.D.] *As Theobald (subst.) ; Enter Vlisses, Diomed., Nestor, Agamem, Chalcas. | Q ;
Enter Vlysses, Diomedes, Nestor, Agamemnon, Menelaus and Chalcas. Flourish. | F.*
1. done] *Q; done you F.*   3. your mind] *F; mind Q; your minds NCS.*
4. things to come] *F4; things to loue Q,F; things to Jove | Johnson; things of
love Deighton; things, to love conj. Steevens.*

209. *maidens*] virgins of either sex.
210. *pander*] It is strictly correct to
read *pandar*, since the *-er* ending comes
from analogy with agent-substantives,
and from verbs in -er; but since the
modern form is *pander* (both noun and
verb) it seems perhaps too nice to
retain the older form. The pander who
offers his services to the audience at
the end of a dramatic performance is
found in the Early Middle English
mime *Dame Sirith*. The Dame (probably a man in disguise) tricks the unwilling girl into accepting her lover,
and then invites further customers to
come forward: 'And wose is onwis |
And for non pris | Ne con geten his
leuemon, | I shal, for mi mede, |
Garen him to spede, | For ful wel I
con.'

Scene III

3.] An Alexandrine.
appear it] let it appear (= sub-

junctive).
4. *bear*] am endowed with.
to come] QF *to loue* can hardly be
right as it stands: Calchas was a seer,
who knew 'by calkulyinge' (*Troilus
and Criseyde*, 1.71); and to point the
passage as Steevens wished (. . . *things,
to love | I have abandon'd Troy*) is to
pervert the sense of the play—anyone
on the Greek side who saw the war as
a matter of whore and cuckold said so
in just those terms. Johnson's *to Jove*
is forced, since it was Apollo who
revealed to Calchas the crucial information about Troy's fate. Rowe's
to come has the merit of agreeing with
Caxton (see pp. 523, 526, 544, and
NCS note), and of supposing a misreading of a kind already found in Q
(initial *c* (or *C*): l—cf. III.ii.91,
cover: lover).
5. *possession*] The singular form
appears as frequently as the plural in
Shakespeare's usage.

Incurr'd a traitor's name, expos'd myself—
From certain and possess'd conveniences
To doubtful fortunes, sequest'ring from me all
That time, acquaintance, custom, and condition
Made tame and most familiar to my nature;   10
And here, to do you service, am become
As new into the world, strange, unacquainted.
I do beseech you, as in way of taste,
To give me now a little benefit
Out of those many register'd in promise   15
Which, you say, live to come in my behalf.
Agam. What would'st thou of us, Trojan? Make demand.
Calch. You have a Trojan prisoner call'd Antenor,
Yesterday took: Troy holds him very dear.
Oft have you—often have you thanks therefor—   20
Desir'd my Cressid in right great exchange,
Whom Troy hath still denied; but this Antenor,
I know, is such a wrest in their affairs
That their negotiations all must slack,
Wanting his manage; and they will almost   25
Give us a prince of blood, a son of Priam,
In change of him. Let him be sent, great princes,
And he shall buy my daughter; and her presence
Shall quite strike off all service I have done
In most accepted pain.
Agam.   Let Diomedes bear him,   30

14. benefit] benefit. *Q*; benefit: *F.*   17. demand.] *Rowe;* demand? *Q,F.*
20. you thanks therefor—] *This edn;* you thankes therefore) *Q;* you, thankes
therefore) *F.*   30. Diomedes] *Q,F;* Diomede *Hanmer;* Diomed *Steevens.*

8. *sequest'ring*] separating, divorcing.
(The word has strong legal and ecclesiastical overtones.)

10. *tame*] accustomed, accommoda-
ted to one's habits.

13. *taste*] (a) small quantity as
sample; (b) trial, proof (cf. *Lr*
I.ii.47, 'an essay, or taste of my
virtue').

15. *many*] sc. benefits.

20. *therefor*] for it, on that account.

21. *right . . . exchange*] in exchange
for a Trojan of great note.

22. *still*] continually.

23. *wrest*] (a) tuning-key; (b) peg
for tightening a (surgical) ligature;
(c) wrench. The implication of discord following the absence of Antenor
is probably to be found, but *slack*
(l. 24) does not necessarily imply a
musical metaphor.

30. *In . . . pain*] 'in hardships to
which I have most cheerfully sub-
mitted' (Deighton). It is difficult to
be wholly sure of Calchas' tone, but I
think that he is gently persuasive: I

And bring us Cressid hither: Calchas shall have
What he requests of us. Good Diomed,
Furnish you fairly for this interchange;
Withal, bring word if Hector will tomorrow
Be answer'd in his challenge: Ajax is ready.   35
Diom. This shall I undertake, and 'tis a burden
Which I am proud to bear. *Exeunt* [*Diomedes and Calchas*].

ACHILLES *and* PATROCLUS *stand in their tent.*

Ulyss. Achilles stands i'th'entrance of his tent.
Please it our general pass strangely by him
As if he were forgot; and, princes all,   40
Lay negligent and loose regard upon him.
I will come last. 'Tis like he'll question me
Why such unplausive eyes are bent, why turn'd on him.
If so, I have derision medicinable
To use between your strangeness and his pride,   45
Which his own will shall have desire to drink.

35. answer'd] *F;* answered *Q.*   36. burden] *Johnson;* burthen *Q,F.*   37. *Exeunt . . . Calchas*].] *Capell (subst.) ; Exit | Q,F.*   S.D. ACHILLES *and* PATROCLUS *stand*] *Q (subst.) ; Enter* Achilles *and* Patroclus *F.*   39. pass] *Q ;* to passe *F.*   43. bent, . . . him.] *Johnson (subst.) ;* bent? why turnd on him, *Q ;* bent? why turn'd on him? *F ;* bent on him? *Pope ;* bent on him: *Theobald*[2].

doubt if he be (almost sarcastically) pointing out, as Johnson suggested, that his efforts have been most acceptable to the Greeks.

34. *tomorrow*] Agamemnon's emphasis falls on this word. Since the decision to rig the lottery, nothing further has been said of arrangements for the combat, but arrangements have clearly been made: all that now rests is for Hector to agree to the day.

37 S.D.] Q's reading is obviously connected with the form of words used by Ulysses at l. 38: F's is just as clearly adapted to the conventions of stage practice. Either, or both, or neither, may be Shakespearean; Q may represent the authorial form (being descriptive rather than technical) and F, the stage adaptation.

39. *strangely*] as with a stranger; in a distant or reserved manner.

41. *loose*] slight, casual.

43.] An Alexandrine. It is possible that *why turn'd* represents a gloss in Q (as Walker, NCS, suggests); but if *bend . . . turn* be a tautology, it recurs in *Ant.* 1.i.4–6 ('now bend, now turn | The office and devotion of their view | Upon a tawny front'), where error can hardly be suspected. Ulysses uses the two verbs to help enact the behaviour of Achilles to the other Greeks. (Both he and Philo are a little excited, and more than a little contemptuous.)
unplausive] disapproving.

44. *derision medicinable*] Editors have sometimes suggested a change in the scheme, since Ulysses does not directly mock Achilles. *Variorum* points out, correctly, that it is the act of strangeness which is derisive; and consequently, if Achilles asks why (that is, if he recognizes that he has been

It may do good: pride hath no other glass
To show itself but pride; for supple knees
Feed arrogance, and are the proud man's fees.

Agam. We'll execute your purpose, and put on   50
A form of strangeness as we pass along.
So do each lord, and either greet him not
Or else disdainfully, which shall shake him more
Than if not look'd on. I will lead the way.

[*They cross the stage.*]

Achill. What, comes the general to speak with me?   55
You know my mind: I'll fight no more 'gainst Troy.

Agam. What says Achilles? Would he aught with us?

Nest. Would you, my lord, aught with the general?

Achill. No.

Nest. Nothing, my lord.   60

Agam. The better.   [*Exeunt Agamemnon and Nestor.*]

Achill. Good day, good day.

Menel. How do you? How do you?   [*Exit.*]

Achill. What, does the cuckold scorn me?

Ajax. How now, Patroclus.   65

Achill. Good morrow, Ajax.

Ajax. Ha?

Achill. Good morrow.

Ajax. Ay, and good next day too.   *Exit.*

54 S.D.] *This edn; they pass forward | Capell.*   55. What, comes] *F4:* What
comes *Q,F.*   57. Achilles?] *Pope; Achilles | Q ; Achilles, | F.*   61 S.D.] *Capell*
(subst.); not in Q,F.   63 S.D.] *Capell (Exit Men.); not in Q,F.*   66. Ajax.]
F4; Aiax? | Q,F.   67. Ha?] *Rowe³; Ha. Q,F (subst.).*   69 S.D.] *Dyce;*
Exeunt | Q,F; Exit Ajax Capell.

slighted), then the derision will be
available for Ulysses to use. It exists
when once put into words by Achilles:
it is medicinable in the mouth of
Ulysses. That is why the cure is used
between the strangeness and the pride.

47–8. *pride . . . pride*] only pride can
show pride an image of what pride is
like. Ulysses is arguing (as is clear
from the remainder of this sentence)
that a proud man expects his 'pride'
to be thought of as a normal state: he
sees nothing odd in it, and indeed
does not recognize it as pride at all.

Hence, the proud Achilles can only be
shown that pride is indeed his vice if
other men seem proud to him (i.e.
behave *abnormally*, according to his
expectation); their actions will discover their opinion of him, and he may
then enquire into the grounds of his
opinion of himself (the 'imagin'd
worth' of II. iii. 173).

65–7.] Ajax, characteristically, ini-
tiates *his* exchange, but, when
addressed, can think of no reply in
time (*Ha?*).

Achill. What mean these fellows? Know they not Achilles?
Patro. They pass by strangely. They were us'd to bend,   71
　　To send their smiles before them to Achilles,
　　To come as humbly as they use to creep
　　To holy altars.
Achill.　　　　　　What, am I poor of late?
　　'Tis certain, greatness once fall'n out with fortune   75
　　Must fall out with men too. What the declin'd is,
　　He shall as soon read in the eyes of others
　　As feel in his own fall; for men, like butterflies,
　　Show not their mealy wings but to the summer,
　　And not a man, for being simply man,   80
　　Hath any honour, but honour for those honours
　　That are without him—as place, riches, and favour:
　　Prizes of accident as oft as merit—
　　Which when they fall, as being slippery standers,
　　The love that lean'd on them, as slippery too,   85
　　Doth one pluck down another, and together

---

70. fellows?] *F;* fellows *Q.*　　73-4. To come . . . altars] *As Rowe*[3]*; one line; Q,F.*
73. use] *Dyce*[2]*, conj. S. Walker;* vs'd *Q,F.*　　81. but honour for] *Q ;* but honour'd
for *F;* but honor'd by *F2;* but honour by *Johnson.*　　82. riches, and] *Q,F;*
riches, *F2.*　　86-7.] *As F;* Doth . . . fall, / But . . . mee, / *Q.*

---

73. *use*] As NCS points out, the
Greeks still reverence holy altars,
though not Achilles. Further, *us'd*
occurs two lines above, and the misreading *d:e* is the easiest to commit (in
the Secretary hand): either misreading (*d:e*) or assimilation to *us'd*
(l. 71) may be the cause of the
apparent error.

79. *mealy*] Butterfly wings are
covered with minute chitinous scales,
resembling fine flour. OED cites
Browne, *Pseudodoxia Epidemica,*
III.xv.141: 'all farinaceous, or mealy-
winged animals, as Butter-flies and
Moths'.

80-2.] 'No man is venerated merely
for being what he is, but for dignities
and distinctions which are really
extrinsic to him.'

84-7. *when . . . fall*] 'All respect
founded on outward honours is as

unstable as the honours; and if the
honours be withdrawn, so is the
respect.' The syntax is difficult; *which*
finds its antecedent in *honours* (l. 81),
and ought to be the subject of *pluck
down* (l. 86); but by that point
Shakespeare is thinking of the mutual
(destructive) dependence of *love* and
honours, so that both *pluck down* in turn
(*one pluck down another*): that is, if you
lack honours, you have no love, and
if love is wanting, you will lack
honours.

84. *slippery standers*] A favourite
topos for political moralizing in the
sixteenth century (cf. *Mirror for
Magistrates,* ll. 417-18, 'The terrible
tower where honour hath his seate, /
Is hye on rockes more slypper than
the yse'). Unstable footing is in any
case implicit in the figure of the
Wheel of Fortune.

Die in the fall. But 'tis not so with me:
Fortune and I are friends; I do enjoy
At ample point all that I did possess,
Save these men's looks; who do, methinks, find out   90
Something not worth in me such rich beholding
As they have often given. Here is Ulysses:
I'll interrupt his reading.
How now, Ulysses!
Ulyss.   Now, great Thetis' son.
Achill. What are you reading?
Ulyss.   A strange fellow here   95
Writes me, that man, how dearly ever parted,
How much in having, or without or in,
Cannot make boast to have that which he hath,
Nor feels not what he owes, but by reflection,
As, when his virtues shining upon others   100
Heat them, and they retort that heat again
To the first giver.
Achill.   This is not strange, Ulysses.
The beauty that is borne here in the face
The bearer knows not, but commends itself

93–5.] *As Steevens;* Ile . . . *Vlisses?* / Now . . . Soune. / What . . . reading? /
A . . . here *Q ,F.*   96. me,] *F;* me *Q.*   100. shining] *F;* ayming *Q.*   102.
giver] *F;* giuers *Q.*

89. *At . . . point*] to the highest
degree, to the full (OED *point* 25).

91. *beholding*] regard.

94. *great . . . son*] Achilles was the
son of King Peleus of the Myrmidons,
and of the Nereid Thetis.

95. *A strange fellow*] *Variorum*
appendix, pp. 411–15, gives a full
account of the various suggestions
made by way of identification. That
Plato (*Alcibiades* 1) and Cicero
(*Tusculan Disputations*) have something like the argument of the ensuing dialogue is clear; but that they
are neither the only nor the more
immediate sources is clearer still.
Both Ulysses and Achilles derive their
theses from sixteenth-century commonplaces.

96. *Writes me*] Cf. Abbott §220.

how . . . parted] 'however excellently endowed' (Johnson).

97. *How . . . having*] however much
he has.

99. *Nor . . . not*] On the double
negative, see Abbott §406.

owes] has, owns (the usual Shakespearean sense).

100. *his . . . others*] Cf. Aquinas,
Summa Theologiae, 2 a–2 ae. clxxxviii.
6: 'Better to light up than merely to
shine'.

shining] F's reading better sustains
the notion of radiant heat and light.

101. *retort*] cast or throw back:
reflect.

104. *but commends*] subject-pronoun
omitted: cf. Abbott §404; *but* = unless
('it' understood).

To others' eyes; nor doth the eye itself,   105
That most pure spirit of sense, behold itself,
Not going from itself; but eye to eye oppos'd
Salutes each other with each other's form;
For speculation turns not to itself
Till it hath travell'd and is mirror'd there   110
Where it may see itself. This is not strange at all.
Ulyss. I do not strain at the position—
It is familiar—but at the author's drift,
Who in his circumstance expressly proves
That no man is the lord of anything,   115
Though in and of him there be much consisting,
Till he communicate his parts to others;
Nor doth he of himself know them for aught,
Till he behold them form'd in the applause

105–6.] *Q; not in F.*   110. travell'd] *Q; trauail'd F.*   mirror'd] *Hudson;*
married *Q,F.*   112. strain] *Q; straine it F.*   115. man] *Q; may F.*   116.
be] *Q; is F.*   119. form'd in the applause] *Capell; formed in the applause Q;*
formed in th'applause *F.*

105–11.] The unaided eye does not
see itself (being unable to divide itself,
and hence leave itself); but two eyes,
each looking at the other, can each
act as a mirror to the other, and show
the other itself; for the power of sight
(= the eye) cannot see itself until it
has been projected upon some reflect-
ing surface.

105–6.] F's omission is quite
natural: the compositor's eye was
doubtless misled by the three succes-
sive lines ending in *itself*.

105–7. *nor doth . . . itself*] Cf. Tilley
E 231a (= Erasmus, *Similia* 578B).

106. *spirit of sense*] See note to
I.i.58.

107–8. *but eye . . . form*] Usually
noted of lovers 'looking babies' in
each other's eyes: cf. Donne, 'The
Exstasie', ll. 11–12.

109. *speculation*] eye, act of seeing,
vision.

110. *mirror'd*] The context seems to
require the emendation (although the
verb *mirror* is not apparently used
elsewhere until Keats).

112. *position*] opinion or tenet
advanced.

113. *drift*] general line of argument.

114. *circumstance*] (discussion of)
subordinate detail.

116.] 'Though his nature and his
acts be notable.'

118. *know . . . aught*] recognize that
they have any value.

119–20. *Till . . . extended*] Recognition of the man's worth (= *applause*)
is at once an extension of his being
and his works (= *Where they're
extended*) and an act bringing them
into formal existence (= *form'd*)—
that is, the man's parts have no
identity without form: they are as
chaos, matter without shape, which
only appreciative recognition can
give them. Walker (NCS) refers to
Meas. I.i.29–40, to Erasmus, *Adagia*
(Occulta), and to Persius ('Scire
tuum nihil est, nisi te scire hoc sciat
alter'): one might add to these the
argument of Sonnets 1–17, and the
parable of the Talents, Matthew
xxv.14–30 (especially the state of the

Where th'are extended; who, like an arch, reverb'rate
The voice again; or, like a gate of steel   121
Fronting the sun, receives and renders back
His figure and his heat. I was much rapt in this,
And apprehended here immediately
Th'unknown Ajax. Heavens, what a man is there!   125
A very horse, that has he knows not what!
Nature, what things there are
Most abject in regard and dear in use!
What things again most dear in the esteem
And poor in worth! Now shall we see tomorrow—   130
An act that very chance doth throw upon him—
Ajax renown'd. O heavens, what some men do,
While some men leave to do!
How some men creep in skittish Fortune's hall,

120. th'are] Q; they are F; they're F3.   reverb'rate] Q,F, Johnson; reverb'rates F2; reverberate Tatlock; reverberates Capell.   125. Th'unknown] Q; The unknowne F.   125–7. Ajax. Heavens... are] As Q; Aiax; / Heauens... Horse / That... are F.   127. are] F2; are. Q,F.   130–1. tomorrow—... him—] NCS; tomorrow, / ... him Q; tomorrow, / ... him? F.   134. Fortune's] Rowe; fortunes Q,F.

man with one talent, who was deprived even of that one).

120. Where th'are extended] (perhaps) 'of those they reach' (NCS); but may not the sense be '(in respect of which) they have spatial magnitude'? (OED 5b)—i.e. they would exist only in a conceptual sense, were there no recognition. (Cf. Cym. i. i. 24–5: 'You speak him far. / I do extend him, ...')
who] Ellipsis has transformed the applause to those who offer it: hence, the plural verb.

121. gate of steel] Daniel proposed glass (perhaps remembering Gascoigne, The Steel Glass?), because he supposed gate to be too imprecise. The phrase occurs in Sonnet 65, l. 8, although without any suggestion of reflection. A gate of steel may as properly reflect light as an arch may reflect sound.

122. Fronting] facing, standing opposed to.

122–3. receives ... heat] What is

returned to the sun is both its form and its most evident qualities. Achilles' activity will be reflected in the behaviour of all the Greeks.

123. rapt] transported.

124. apprehended] saw the implication of: understood the significance of.

125. unknown Ajax] Ajax has done nothing yet which can give him reputation, nor even make him known for what he is; but the fight with Hector will 'create' an Ajax of great consequence, and it is the fame (Ajax renown'd, l. 132) which will effect it.

126. horse] Not an intelligent beast: cf. ii. i. 17, iii. iii. 303–4.

129–30. What ... worth] For example, Helen, and Cressida (as Diomedes sees them: iv. i. 69–75, and iv. iv. 114–18, 127–32).

134. creep] advance surreptitiously; cf. Ado iv. i. 224, Tw.N. i. v. 302. The word suggests nothing reprehensible at this date, although editors have

> *Do nothing to court Fortunes favors.*

While others play the idiots in her eyes!   135
↓ How one man eats into another's pride,
While pride is fasting in his wantonness!
To see these Grecian lords!—why, even already
They clap the lubber Ajax on the shoulder,
    clumsy & stupid
As if his foot were on brave Hector's breast,   140
And great Troy shrieking.
Achill. I do believe it, for they pass'd by me
    As misers do by beggars, neither gave to me
    Good word nor look. What, are my deeds forgot?
Ulyss. Time hath, my lord, a wallet at his back   145
    Wherein he puts alms for oblivion,   — *Time corrodes*

Also see il. 142. u.

---

137. fasting] *Q;* feasting *F.*   wantonness!] *Rowe;* wantonesse. *Q;* wanton-
nesse *F.*   140. on] *F;* one *Q.*   141. shrieking] *Q* (shriking); shrinking *F.*

---

sometimes assumed that it did, and
that those playing the fool were
therefore the favourites of Fortune
(cf. Tilley F 600: 'Fortune favours
fools'). But notice that, in the three
dual comparisons (ll. 130–7), Ulysses
in each case approves the first term
(*some men do | some men creep | one man
eats*) and despises the second (*some
men leave to do | others play the idiots |
pride is fasting*).

    skittish] volatile, fickle.

    135.] 'While others do nothing to
↓ court Fortune's favours.'

    136–7.] 'One man takes advantage
of the (idle) pride of another, while
the proud man perversely destroys his
reputation, as a man fasting may
starve himself.'

    139. *lubber*] big-grown, clumsy, and
stupid. (It is not quite clear whether
the word is adjective or noun: OED
notes it as '*attrib.* and *appositive* passing
into *adj.*' from *c.*1530 onwards.)

    141. *shrieking*] F's *shrinking* may
seem to be more decorous for *great
Troy*; but a shriek was any high-
pitched cry, at the presence of some
horror (here, the death of Hector).
Q's spelling *shriking* has its analogue
at II.ii.98 (*shrike*): both passages were
apparently set by compositor A
(D2ᵛ, G2). One might defend F by

supposing the form *shriking* in the
copy (misread by Q); but F might
easily have misread *shriking* as *shriking*,
in its turn.

    145–50.] Ulysses is master of the
elliptical reply: cf. his answer to
Agamemnon at I.iii.142.
↓ **145.** The wallet hung behind the
shoulder was a common figure (as
Variorum note makes clear). What
mattered was that the bag hung
behind: traditionally, a bag carried
before you bore your neighbour's
vices, and one behind you, your own,
which (emblematically) you therefore
forgot. Time's wallet is thus an
emblem of forgetfulness: Shakespeare,
alone, it seems, associated Time with
the figure. It may be worth noting
that a barrister's robe still includes a
small bag which hangs behind the
shoulder from a long strip of doubled
fabric: it is supposed that his fees
were surreptitiously placed therein by
the client, while the barrister (necessarily) looked elsewhere. (I owe this
suggestion to Miss K. Kelleher.)

    146–7.] The monster is *oblivion*,
despite the efforts of commentators to
make it Time, or alms, or to emend.
The syntax is admittedly ambiguous,
and l. 147 might refer to one of several
antecedents. Walker (NCS) argues

A great-siz'd monster of ingratitudes.
Those scraps are good deeds past, which are devour'd
As fast as they are made, forgot as soon
As done. Perseverance, dear my lord,   150
Keeps honour bright: to have done is to hang
Quite out of fashion, like a rusty mail
In monumental mockery. Take the instant way;
For honour travels in a strait so narrow
Where one but goes abreast. Keep then the path;   155
For emulation hath a thousand sons
That one by one pursue; if you give way,

148–50.] As Var. '73; Those ... past, / Which ... made, / Forgot ... Lord Q,F.

that the monster is Time, and inter-
prets *alms for oblivion* as 'things to be
forgotten' (i.e. oblivion is simply
forgetfulness, and not part of an
allegory). But, although Time is certainly *edax rerum* (cf. *devour'd*, l. 148),
he is also thief, midwife, chronicler,
and many other things; while
oblivion is, in Shakespeare, repeatedly associated with ingratitude (cf.
Tw.N. III.iv.345–78, and *Lr passim*).
Significantly, in *AYL* II.vii.174–90,
both ingratitude and forgetfulness
have teeth or stings. One may also
cite *Lucr.*, l. 947 ('[Time's glory is ...]
To feed oblivion with decay of
things'). Almost as persuasive is
Meas. v.i.10–14 (despite the Duke's
irony): 'O, but your desert speaks
loud, and I should wrong it / To lock
it in the wards of covert bosom, /
When it deserves with characters of
brass / A forted residence 'gainst the
tooth of time / And razure of oblivion'.
This speech not only unites Time and
oblivion as destroyers (as in the
present passage) but joins them with
other concepts from *Troilus*—e.g.
desert (cf. l. 144 above), *characters of
brass* (cf. I.iii.62–4).

150–3.] It is significant that,
whereas Achilles played with two
contrasting senses of honour (ll. 80–3),
Ulysses concerns himself more largely
with that honour which is manifested

in external display. Perseverance
keeps a polish on honour (l. 151);
momentary inaction leaves one un-
fashionable, and one becomes no
better than the (rusty) armour on a
tomb—impressive, but useless. For
the practice of adorning tombs with
armour, see, for example, Canterbury
Cathedral (tomb of the Black Prince).

150. *Perseverance*] Stressed on the
second syllable. The line wants a foot.

151–3.] Cf. Tilley W 866 ('As good
be out of the world, as out of fashion').

154–5.] The phrasing is loose:
honour = those engaged in the pursuit
of honour (a normal ellipsis); but
one ... abreast = men travel in single
file. R. Noble (*Shakespeare's Biblical
Knowledge*, 1935, p. 215) suggests a
parallel with Matthew vii.14 ('Strait
is the gate and narrow is the way');
but that passage implies that the goal
is reached with difficulty through un-
popular ways: here, the point lies in
the very numbers that vie for supremacy. *Strait* = narrow passage.

156. *emulation*] ambition: usually
seen in this play as a vice of the
Greeks. The pursuit of honour
(= ambition) entails destructive
rivalry (ll. 157–60): cf. *R2* I.iii.129–31
('the eagle-winged pride / Of sky-
aspiring and ambitious thoughts, /
With rival-hating envy').

Or <u>hedge</u> aside from the direct forthright,
Like to an <u>enter'd tide</u> they all rush by   *Shakespere uses*
And leave you hindmost;   *imagery of sea as an*   160
Or, like a gallant horse fall'n in first rank,   *irrestible force.*
You Lie there for pavement for the abject rear,
O'er-run and trampled on. Then what they do in   *(I iii - iii-13)*
      present,
Though less than yours in past, must o'er-top yours;
For Time is like a <u>fashionable host</u>   165
That slightly shakes his parting guest by th'hand,
And with his arms out-stretch'd, as he would fly,
Grasps in the comer. Welcome ever smiles,
And farewell goes out sighing. O let not virtue seek
Remuneration for the thing it was;   170

Again Ulysses stresses the import. of FASHION & its disregard of immediate past.

160. hindmost] *F;* him, most *Q.*   161–3. Or . . . on] *F; not in Q.*   162.
abject rear] *Hanmer;* abiect, neere *F.*   164. past] *F;* passe *Q.*   168. Wel-
come] *Pope;* the welcome *Q,F;* For welcome *Johnson.*   169. farewell] *Q;*
farewels *F.*   O let] *F;* Let *Q.*   170–1. was . . . wit] *As Steevens;* was. For
beauty, wit *Q;* was: for beautie, wit *F.*

158. *hedge*] Something less tautologous than Q's *turn* seems to be
required, yet most senses of *hedge*
imply chicanery, shuffling, or sharp
practice, and the context here asks
only for a moment's hesitation, a
drawing of rein.

forthright] straight path, that which
lies before one (cf. *instant way*, l. 153).

159. *enter'd tide*] Shakespeare's image
for an irresistible force frequently
derives from the sea; cf. i.iii.111–13,
and *Oth.* iii.iii.460–3.

161–3. *Or . . . on*] These lines (found
only in F) look odd at first, in that
Lie there is not quite congruous with
the preceding clauses to which it is
parallel (*they all rush by* and [they]
leave you hindmost), but the sense is
simply [*You*] *lie there.*

162. *Lie . . . pavement*] Cf. Isaiah
li.23: '. . . and thou hast laid thy body
as the ground, and as the street, to
them that went over'.

abject rear] Those who say, with
Nym, 'the knocks are too hot; and
for mine own part, I have not a case

of lives' (*H5* iii.ii.3–4): *abject* = mean,
poor-spirited.

rear] Hanmer's emendation is necessary: to read *abject, near o'er-run* (as
Pope did) is to make Achilles into a
pavement, and then to have nobody
stand upon him.

165.] Again, Ulysses places the
emphasis upon *fashion* (cf. l. 152) and
its disregard of the immediate past.

165–8.] Like Thersites, Ulysses is a
master of mimetic speech (cf.
i.iii.172–6).

168. *Grasps in*] embraces (OED and
Schmidt give only this example with
in).

169. *O*] To include the exclamation
(following F) hardly mends the metre,
but the word is fitting. Ulysses seldom
uses it (being little given to apostrophe, and then perhaps only with
irony: cf. ii.iii.183); but there is one
similar example at i.iii.101, where
(as here) the exclamation introduces
a general moral position.

170. *the thing it was*] A formula often
used by Shakespeare, and especially

For beauty, wit,
High birth, vigour of bone, desert in service,
Love, friendship, charity, are subjects all
To envious and calumniating Time.
One touch of nature makes the whole world kin—   175
That all with one consent praise new-born gauds,
Though they are made and moulded of things past,
And give to dust that is a little gilt
More laud than gilt o'er-dusted.
The present eye praises the present object: 180

178. give] Theobald, conj. Thirlby; goe Q,F; shew Johnson.

from 1600 onwards (? perhaps with a half-memory of Exodus iii.14: 'I AM THAT I AM'): cf. Sonnet 121, l. 9; *Tw.N.* I.v.173–4, IV.ii.15–16; *Oth.* V.ii.1–3; *Mac.* I.iii.109, I.v.20–1, I.vii.1–2, II.ii.1; *2H4* V.v.56. The closest parallel is, of course, in Sonnet 49, l. 7 ('love, converted from the thing it was'), where the context concerns loss of reputation, disregard by another person, and the dereliction that ensues.

172. *vigour of bone*] physical energy, health and strength of body. Not quite a parallel to the use of *bone* in I.iii.55, where *nerves and bone* makes a comprehensive statement about bodily strength.

173. *Love . . . charity*] I think that Ulysses is proposing three concepts in a rising scale of value; cf. *Summa Theologiae*, 2a–2ae. xxiii.1, where Aquinas places love-with-friendship above *mere* love. Charity, of course, is the highest love of all ('the love of God, the end of all human activity and desire, and here there are no limits': 2a–2ae.xxvii.6). Love, in the usual sense, *must* be limited, since it is desire for a secondary good: charity is love of a primary good. (Aristotle similarly prizes friendship [Philia] above love, which for him was merely biological attraction: *Ethics* VIII.) Charity is subject to Time, like all

other concepts, in so far as it is an act of the will of a human creature.

174. *calumniating*] Time destroys evidence, and leaves only fragmentary traces: hence, it misrepresents what once was. It is *envious* in that envy wishes to destroy, rather than that others should have: this links the action of Time with that of the Greeks (I.iii), of Ajax (II.i) and of the Gods (IV.ii).

175–9.] Ulysses assumes the absolute truth of his argument. Not merely is honour to be kept bright only by perseverance, but such constant action is necessary because all men are alike, in loving the new, and despising the old.

175.] This line is always misrepresented when quoted out of context (as if it meant that any 'natural' human act emphasized the kinship of mankind). Significantly, Ulysses means that mankind shows its kinship in acting discreditably.

touch of nature] natural trait or characteristic.

176. *gauds*] toys, trivialities, worthless objects.

177.] 'Although there may be nothing truly new in them' (i.e. although they are old things thinly disguised).

178. *give*] Q's *goe* is a simple minim error (*u* read as *o* imperfectly closed).

Then marvel not, thou great and complete man,
That all the Greeks begin to worship Ajax,
Since things in motion sooner catch the eye
Than what stirs not. The cry went once on thee,
And still it might, and yet it may again   185
If thou wouldst not entomb thyself alive
And case thy reputation in thy tent,
Whose glorious deeds but in these fields of late
Made emulous missions 'mongst the gods themselves,
And drave great Mars to faction.

Achill.   Of this my privacy 190
I have strong reasons.

Ulyss.   But 'gainst your privacy
The reasons are more potent and heroical:
'Tis known, Achilles, that you are in love
With one of Priam's daughters.

Achill.   Ha, known?

Ulyss.   Is that a wonder?

183. sooner] *Q;* begin to *F.*   184. stirs not] *Q;* not stirs *F.*   once] *Q;* out
F.   194. Ha, known?] *This edn;* Ha? knowne. *Q;* Ha? knowne? *F;* Ha!
known? *Rowe.*

181. *complete*] Accented on the first
syllable.

182.] The word spoken so ironically
at II.iii.189–90 ('shall he be worshipp'd / Of that we hold an idol
more than he?').

183–4. *Since . . . not*] Ulysses means
(in accordance with the drift of his
whole argument) that an active Ajax
is bound to be preferred to a torpid
Achilles. (It is his own application of
Agamemnon's sarcasm at II.iii.139–
40: 'A stirring dwarf we do allowance
give / Before a sleeping giant'.)

184. *The . . . thee*] You were once in
everyone's mouth. (*The cry goes*
usually = it is rumoured; but see
v.v.35: 'Crying on Hector').

187. *case*] hide, disguise, shut up.

188–90. *Whose . . . faction*] Perhaps
referring to the incidents of *Iliad* xx.

188. *but . . . late*] only recently upon
this battlefield.

189. *missions*] Variously glossed as

'sending (of the gods) from Heaven
about mortal business' (Johnson,
substantially); 'descent of deities to
combat on either side' (Steevens);
'sending of help' (Onions). It is hard
to resist the assumption that the
sixteenth century knew a sense like
that of the twentieth century—i.e. a
military sortie or operation. The
persistence of such a sense unrecorded
would not be without parallel: cf. the
occurrence, in R.A.F. usage, of a
phrase otherwise noted only in Langland, *Piers Plowman* (B-text, x.123):
'I wolde his eye were in his ers · and
his fynger after'.

194.] Approximately an Alexandrine: Achilles' *Ha* is extra-metrical;
but in short dialogue exchanges one
cannot always expect perfect line-
length.

one . . . daughters] Polyxena, who was
afterwards sacrificed by Neoptolemus,
at the request of his dead father

The providence that's in a watchful state   195
Knows almost every grain of Pluto's gold,
Finds bottom in th'uncomprehensive deep,
Keeps place with thought, and (almost like the gods)
Do thoughts unveil in their dumb cradles.
There is a mystery, with whom relation   200
Durst never meddle, in the soul of state,
Which hath an operation more divine
Than breath or pen can give expressure to.
All the commerce that you have had with Troy
As perfectly is ours as yours, my lord;   205

196. grain . . . gold] *F;* thing *Q;* grain of Plutus' gold *Malone, conj. Steevens.*
197. th'uncomprehensive deep] *Rowe;* the vncomprehensiue depth *Q;* th'vncomprehensiue deepes *F.*   198. place] *Q,F;* pace *Hanmer.*   199. Do] *Q,F*
(Doe)*; Does F2.*   200. whom] *Q,F;* which *Pope.*

Achilles (Ovid, *Metamorphoses,* XIII. 448 ff. and cf. Seneca, *Troades*). In Caxton, Achilles bargained secretly after Hector's death for the hand of Polyxena, in return for persuading the Greeks to make peace: when they refused to do so, he withdrew, with his forces, from the fighting.

195. *providence*] prudence, foresight.
196. *almost . . . gold*] Q's *almost everything* is probably a scribe's (or compositor's) guess at difficult copy. (For a similar failure of one text, where another preserves the sense, cf. Robert Daborne, *The Poor Man's Comfort* (Malone Society Reprint), l. 44: 'you will inforce my . . .' (MS): 'You will enforce my love?' (Q).)

Pluto's] *Variorum* note shows how readily the Elizabethans confounded Plutus and Pluto: Shakespeare need not be faulted. In any case, what matters is the logic of the speech: each thing known to the *watchful state* is hyperbolically inaccessible, and the gold must therefore be hidden in the underworld.

197. *uncomprehensive*] inconceivable, unimaginable; perhaps 'unfathom-able' (Deighton).
198. *Keeps place*] agrees with, accords with.
198–9. *almost . . . cradles*] Not only

does *providence* understand what is thought (and is proverbially swift) but it knows it before it can be uttered.

199. *Do*] Probably plural by attraction (*gods* immediately precedes it).

cradles] Editors sometimes emend, to restore the metre, and (less justi-fiably) to avoid a transferred epithet (*dumb* applying more properly to *thoughts* than to *cradles*).

200–3.] Sometimes taken (e.g. by *Variorum*) to refer to the Greek (and perhaps the Elizabethan) intelligence service (*relation* = report). Walker (NCS) demurs, arguing that *mystery* bears its theological sense (OED 2); and if her objection is sound, then it may be supported by *divine* (= par-taking of the nature of deity). I believe, however, that *mystery* = mat-ter unexplained or inexplicable (OED 5) and that *divine* = of unusual excellence (but perhaps cf. *Meas.* v. i. 367–8: 'your Grace, like power divine, / Hath looked upon my passes'). The direct reference to the intelligence service follows at once, in ll. 204–5.

204. *commerce*] Stressed on the second syllable (cf. I. iii. 105).

205. *ours as yours*] known to us as to you.

And better would it fit Achilles much
To throw down Hector than Polyxena.
But it must grieve young Pyrrhus now at home,
When Fame shall in our islands sound her trump
And all the Greekish girls shall tripping sing   210
'Great Hector's sister did Achilles win,
But our great Ajax bravely beat down him.'
Farewell, my lord: I as your lover speak.
The fool slides o'er the ice that you should break. [*Exit.*]
Patro. To this effect, Achilles, have I mov'd you.   215
A woman impudent and mannish grown
Is not more loath'd than an effeminate man
In time of action. I stand condemn'd for this:
They think my little stomach to the war
And your great love to me restrains you thus.   220
Sweet, rouse yourself; and the weak wanton Cupid
Shall from your neck unloose his amorous fold,
And, like a dew-drop from the lion's mane,
Be shook to air.
Achill.   Shall Ajax fight with Hector?
Patro. Ay, and perhaps receive much honour by him.   225
Achill. I see my reputation is at stake:
My fame is shrewdly gor'd.

---

209. our islands] *Q ;* her Iland *F ;* his island *Rowe*³.   214 S.D.] *Pope; not in*
Q,F.   223. like a] *F ;* like *Q.*   224. air] *Q ;* ayrie ayre *F.*

208. *Pyrrhus*] the other name of
Neoptolemus, son of Achilles. He was
at length brought to Troy by Ulysses,
together with Philoctetes, since without those two Troy could not be taken
(Sophocles, *Philoctetes*, l. 115).

209. *our islands*] Cf. Prologue l. 1,
and III.i.150. (F is wrong: Fame has
no peculiar island.)

212. *him*] i.e. Hector.

213. *lover*] one who wishes well, cf.
Cor. v.ii.14.

213–14. *speak . . . break*] A perfect
rhyme.

214.] Perhaps too ingeniously
glossed by editors (see examples in
Variorum note). 'Break the ice' = begin
the action, start what none else is
willing to do: cf. *Shr.* I.ii.265. Hence,

Ajax will be merely play-acting, in
his meeting with Hector, by comparison with the serious fighting which
only Achilles is capable of performing.

217. *effeminate*] cowardly, inert.

219. *my . . . war*] my marked un-
willingness to fight.

221–4.] Patroclus is pleading that
Polyxena should be abandoned: he is
not referring to himself, nor to
Achilles' affection for him.

221. *wanton*] playful, trifling (rather
than 'lascivious', I think, despite the
erotic sense of 'Cupid'). Cf. *LLL*
v.ii.752–3: 'As love is full of un-
befitting strains; / All wanton as a
child, skipping and vain'.

227. *shrewdly gor'd*] severely wounded. To *gore* (literally) is always, for

Patro.   O then beware:
    Those wounds heal ill that men do give themselves.
    Omission to do what is necessary
    Seals a commission to a blank of danger,   230
    And danger, like an ague, subtly taints
    Even then when we sit idly in the sun.
Achill. Go call Thersites hither, sweet Patroclus.
    I'll send the fool to Ajax, and desire him
    T'invite the Trojan lords after the combat   235
    To see us here unarm'd. I have a woman's longing,
    An appetite that I am sick withal,
    To see great Hector in his weeds of peace,

Enter THERSITES.

    To talk with him, and to behold his visage
    Even to my full of view. A labour sav'd.   240
Thers. A wonder.
Achill. What?
Thers. Ajax goes up and down the field, asking for
    himself.
Achill. How so?   245
Thers. He must fight singly tomorrow with Hector, and
    is so prophetically proud of an heroical cudgelling

232. we] *F; they Q.*   238 S.D.] *As F; after 240, Q.*

Shakespeare, to wound with a spear
or an arrow (i.e. to stab, not to cut).

228.] Apparently a proverb: not in
Tilley. (Perhaps cf. *John* v. vii. 112–14:
'This England never did, nor never
shall, / Lie at the proud foot of a
conqueror, / But when it first did help
to wound itself'.)

229–30.] If you neglect what you
must do, then whatever threatens you
has full scope to do what hurt it will.
(There seems to be an echo—perhaps
unconscious—of the phrase 'sins of
omission and commission', which
OED first cites from a sermon of
1597.)

230. *Seals a commission*] confirms a
form of authority.

blank] warrant lacking specific
detail (cf. blank cheque, blank
charter).

231. *taints*] infects: cf. *Tw.N.*
III. iv. 133.

232. *we*] Q's *they* perhaps refers
back to *men* (l. 228).

236–40. *I have . . . view*] According
to Lydgate (III. 3772–8) Achilles had
'gret affeccioun / In his herte, boþe
day and nyȝt, / Of worþi Hector for
to han a siȝt', because 'vnarmyd he
myȝt him neuer se'. In Caxton (p.
602), 'Achylles behelde hym gladly'.

240. *Even . . . view*] 'to the fullest
satisfaction of my eyes' (Deighton).
Cf. *Tw.N.* I. i. 26–7: 'The element
itself, till seven years' heat, / Shall not
behold her face at ample view'.

243–4.] Presumably an implied pun
on Ajax/a jakes.

247. *heroical cudgelling*] Thersites
uses the language of burlesque:
cudgelling is for countrymen with

that he raves in saying nothing.

Achill. How can that be?

Thers. Why, a stalks up and down like a peacock, a   250
stride and a stand; ruminates like an hostess that
hath no arithmetic but her brain to set down her
reckoning; bites his lip with a politic regard, as
who should say 'There were wit in this head, and
'twould out'—and so there is; but it lies as coldly   255
in him as fire in a flint, which will not show without knocking. The man's undone for ever, for if
Hector break not his neck i'th'combat, he'll
break't himself in vainglory. He knows not me: I
said 'Good morrow, Ajax,' and he replies 'Thanks,   260
Agamemnon.'—What think you of this man, that
takes me for the general? He's grown a very land-
fish, languageless, a monster. A plague of opinion!
A man may wear it on both sides, like a leather
jerkin.   265

250. Why, a] *Q* (a)*;* Why he *F.*   254–5. 'There . . . out'] *As quotation, Camb.*
254. this] *Q;* his *F.*   263. monster.] *F* (monster:)*;* monster, *Q.*

quarter-staves (cf. II.i.102–3: 'and a
knock out either of your brains'). On
the other hand, *break not his neck
i'th'combat* (l. 258) refers to a form of
death normal in jousting. Perhaps
Thersites refers to fighting at barriers.

248. *he . . . nothing*] 'His carriage
and silent gestures are witness to his
frenzy.' Ajax' actions are eloquent, as
Thersites' language is mimetic (especially ll. 250–61). The words cry out
for the actor's gesture: Thersites has
already *put on his presence* (ll. 269–70),
and this very speech is *the pageant of
Ajax* (l. 271).

253. *with . . . regard*] Ajax tries hard
to appear wise: he strikes all the
proper attitudes. (Shakespeare found
such conduct matter for comedy
elsewhere: cf. Malvolio, who practised *a demure travel of regard* (*Tw.N.*
II.v.53) and *an austere regard of control*
(II.v.67); who had *the humour of state*
(l. 52), who *read politic authors* (ll.

161–2) and who was determined to be
proud (l. 161) in the process of
realizing his fantasy.)

262–3. *a very . . . monster*] Caliban is
just such a creature (cf. *Tp.* II.ii.25–6:
'A fish: he smells like a fish; a very
ancient and fish-like smell'); and he
and Ajax sometimes share a language:
cf. *Tp.* I.ii.365–6 ('You taught me
language; and my profit on't / Is, I
know how to curse') with II.i.1–50.

263. *opinion*] 'Favourable estimate
of oneself or one's own abilities; either
in bad sense (self-conceit, arrogance,
dogmatism) or in good sense (self-
confidence)' (OED 5c). Hence, Ajax
can 'wear' his own opinion of himself
as arrogance (as hitherto), or as self-
confidence (as now, when he is prepared to meet Hector). It is still the
same pride.

265. *jerkin*] reversible (i.e. unlined)
leather jacket.

Achill. Thou must be my ambassador to him, Thersites.

Thers. Who, I? Why, he'll answer nobody: he professes not answering; speaking is for beggars, he wears his tongue in's arms. I will put on his presence: let Patroclus make demands to me. You   270
shall see the pageant of Ajax.

Achill. To him, Patroclus. Tell him I humbly desire the valiant Ajax to invite the valorous Hector to come unarmed to my tent, and to procure safe-conduct for his person, of the magnanimous, and   275
most illustrious, six or seven times honoured captain-general of the Grecian army, Agamemnon, et cetera. Do this.

Patro. Jove bless great Ajax!

Thers. Hum!   280

Patro. I come from the worthy Achilles—

Thers. Ha?

266. to him] *F; not in Q.*   267. I? Why,] *Theobald;* I: why *Q;* I: why, *F;* I? why *F3.*   270. presence: . . . me. You] *This edn;* presence, let . . . demands to me. You *Q;* presence; let . . . his demands to me, you *F;* presence. Let . . . demands to me, you *NCS.*   273. valorous] *Q;* most valorous *F.*   277. captain-general] *Hanmer (subst.);* Captaine Generall *Q;* Captaine, Generall *F.* Grecian] *F; not in Q.*   278. et cetera] *F* (&c.); *not in Q.*

266.] Even Thersites becomes an ambassador or go-between.

267–8. *he . . . answering*] It is not clear whether Ajax merely does not profess to answer a question, or whether (more positively) he professes silence, and cuts everybody. In view of *speaking is for beggars,* one ought perhaps to prefer the latter, and to read *not-answering.* (The case is different with Hotspur, who loquaciously denies fluency: *1H4* v.ii.91: 'For I profess not talking'.)

268–9. *he . . . arms*] Cf. *Mac.* v.viii.7: 'My voice is in my sword'.

270. *presence*] air, port, carriage.

let . . . me] i.e. Patroclus (the *fool positive* of II.iii.67) is to play 'feed' to Thersites, the professional fool.

271. *pageant*] We are probably meant to see Ajax as part of a City pageant, rather than of a Court

masque: perhaps as a traditional figure, like Gog or Magog. (Yet to *play his pageant* is several times used by Malory when a knight begins to display his prowess at a tourney. Perhaps *pageant* hesitates between knightly and bourgeois senses. [I owe this observation to Professor Brooks.])

278. *et cetera*] I question Dyce's opinion that this was a cue for actors to gag: it seems to me to be of a piece with the ironic pretentiousness of Achilles' preceding lines (*magnanimous, and most illustrious, six or seven times honoured*). On the other hand, while Achilles should *say* 'et cetera', Patroclus is plainly being invited to extemporize.

282. *Ha?*] = eh? Contrast *Ha!* (l. 289) which may imply either contempt (= Bah!) or knowing satisfaction (= Oho!).

Patro. Who most humbly desires you to invite Hector
    to his tent—

Thers. Hum?   285

Patro. And to procure safe-conduct from Agamemnon.

Thers. Agamemnon?

Patro. Ay, my lord.

Thers. Ha!

Patro. What say you to't?   290

Thers. God buy you, with all my heart!

Patro. Your answer, sir.

Thers. If tomorrow be a fair day, by eleven of the clock
    it will go one way or other. Howsoever, he shall
    pay for me ere he has me.   295

Patro. Your answer, sir.

Thers. Fare ye well, with all my heart.

Achill. Why, but he is not in this tune, is he?

Thers. No, but out of tune thus. What music will be in
    him when Hector has knocked out his brains, I   300
    know not—but I am sure, none, unless the fiddler
    Apollo get his sinews to make catlings on.

Achill. Come, thou shalt bear a letter to him straight.

Thers. Let me bear another to his horse, for that's the
    more capable creature.   305

Achill. My mind is troubled, like a fountain stirr'd,

---

291. buy you] *Q,F;* bu'y you *NCS;* be wi' you *Rowe.*   293. eleven of the] *Q*
(a leuen of the)*; eleuen a *F;* eleven o' *Theobald.*   299. out of] *Q;* he's out
a *F.*   304. bear] *Q;* carry *F.*

---

293. *of the clock*] Shakespeare uses
both *'clock* and this phrase; but on the
whole *o'clock* serves for brief exchanges
(e.g. 'What is't o'clock?') and *of the
clock* for fuller and more continuous
prose (e.g. *Meas.* iv. ii. 119: 'by four of
the clock'). The *tone* seems to be
irrelevant: the full form can still be
used in jocular speech: cf. *2H4*
i. ii. 186–8, 'My lord, I was born about
three of the clock in the afternoon,
with a white head, and something of
a round belly'.

298. *tune*] disposition, humour.

301–2. *fiddler Apollo*] Again, bur-

lesque language: the term *fiddler* is
contemptuous: Apollo as musician
usually played the lute (Apollo
Citharoedus).

302. *catlings*] catgut for stringed
instruments: strings of the smallest
size.

305. *capable*] intelligent, competent.

306.] Perhaps cf. Proverbs xxv. 26:
'A righteous man falling down before
the wicked is as a troubled fountain,
and a corrupt spring'; also *Shr.*
v. ii. 143–4: 'A woman mov'd is like
a fountain troubled, / Muddy, ill-
seeming, thick, bereft of beauty'.

And I myself see not the bottom of it.

[Exeunt Achilles and Patroclus.]

Thers. Would the fountain of your mind were clear
again, that I might water an ass at it: I had rather
be a tick in a sheep than such a valiant ignorance.   310

[Exit.]

307 S.D.] *Capell (subst.); Exit | Rowe; not in Q,F.*   310 S.D.] *Capell; Exeunt |
Rowe; not in Q,F.*

[ACT IV]

[SCENE I]

Enter on one side ÆNEAS, [*and* Servant] *with a torch; on the other,*
PARIS, DEIPHOBUS, ANTENOR, DIOMEDES, [*and* Others]
with torches.

Paris. See, ho! who is that there?
Deiph. It is the Lord Æneas.
Æneas. Is the prince there in person?
  Had I so good occasion to lie long
  As you, Prince Paris, nothing but heavenly business 5
  Should rob my bed-mate of my company.
Diom. That's my mind, too. Good morrow, Lord Æneas.
Paris. A valiant Greek, Æneas: take his hand;
  Witness the process of your speech, wherein
  You told how Diomed a whole week by days 10
  Did haunt you in the field.
Æneas.   Health to you, valiant sir,
  During all question of the gentle truce;
  But when I meet you arm'd, as black defiance
  As heart can think or courage execute.

ACT IV

Scene 1

S.D. [*and . . . torch*] *Var. '73; with a torch | F; not in Q.* DIOMEDES, [*and*
Others*]] Malone; Diomed the Grecian | Q,F.* 5. you] *F;* your *Q.* 9. speech,
wherein] *Q* (speech: wherein)*; speech within: F.* 10. a] *Q;* in a *F.*

 3. *prince*] i.e. Paris.
 5. *heavenly business*] (presumably)
worship.
 9. *Witness . . . speech*] 'as the drift of
your [former] speech made clear'.
Æneas, that is, has already testified
that Diomedes is valiant.
 10. *a . . . days*] every day of one week.

 11. *haunt*] hang about, dog the heels
of (cf. Webster, *Duchess of Malfi*,
I.i.29: 'I do haunt you still').
 12. *During . . . truce*] during all the
negotiations in the peaceful time of
truce.
 14. *As . . . think*] Cf. Nashe (*Works*,
ed. R. B. McKerrow), III.33.14: 'as

Diom. The one and other Diomed embraces.   15
　　Our bloods are now in calm, and, so long, health!
　　But when contention and occasion meet,
　　By Jove, I'll play the hunter for thy life
　　With all my force, pursuit, and policy.
Æneas. And thou shalt hunt a lion that will fly   20
　　With his face backward. In human gentleness,
　　Welcome to Troy! Now by Anchises' life,
　　Welcome indeed! By Venus' hand I swear
　　No man alive can love in such a sort
　　The thing he means to kill, more excellently.   25
Diom. We sympathize. Jove, let Æneas live—
　　If to my sword his fate be not the glory—
　　A thousand complete courses of the sun!
　　But in mine emulous honour let him die
　　With every joint a wound, and that tomorrow!   30
Æneas. We know each other well.
Diom. We do, and long to know each other worse.
Paris. This is the most despiteful gentle greeting,
　　The noblest hateful love, that e'er I heard of.
　　What business, lord, so early?   35
Æneas. I was sent for to the King; but why, I know not.

---

16. and, so long,] *Warburton;* and so long *Q,F.*   17. But] *F;* Lul'd *Q.*
meet] *Q;* meetes *F.*   21. backward ... gentleness,] *Theobald*[2] *(subst.);* backward, in humane gentlenesse: *Q,F (subst.).*   33. despiteful gentle] *Q;*
despightful'st gentle *F;* despiteful-gentle *conj. S. Walker.*   34–5.] *As F; as
prose, Q.*   34. noblest hateful] *Q,F;* noblest-hateful *conj. S. Walker.*

---

heart can think or tongue can tell';
also *2H6* IV. vii. 119.

15.] Diomedes here accepts Æneas'
challenge. This chivalrous contest
within the play derives from real
enmity in the source (cf. Caxton,
Recuyell, p. 561) during the embassy
to Troy of Ulysses and Diomedes.

17.] 'When we may conveniently
fight.'

19. *policy*] stratagems.

20–1. *a . . . backward*] A reference,
since this is a chivalrous encounter, to
heraldry. What Æneas has in mind
is a lion *passant regardant*, i.e. walking
with his face turned back over his

shoulder.

22–3. *Anchises' . . . hand*] As Deighton noted (after Blakeway), Æneas
swears by each of his parents in turn.
But Warburton (who saw an allusion
to Venus being wounded in the hand
by Diomedes, while protecting Æneas:
Iliad v) may have been on the right
track: Æneas also alludes to the
vulnerable part or quality of each
parent.

26. *sympathize*] are of one disposition; cf. I. iii. 52.

28. *complete*] Stressed on the first
syllable.

Paris. His purpose meets you: 'twas to bring this Greek
  To Calchas' house, and there to render him,
  For the enfreed Antenor, the fair Cressid.
  Let's have your company, or, if you please,   40
  Haste there before us. [*Aside.*] I constantly believe,
  Or rather, call my thought a certain knowledge,
  My brother Troilus lodges there tonight.
  Rouse him, and give him note of our approach,
  With the whole quality wherefore: I fear   45
  We shall be much unwelcome.
Æneas. [*Aside.*]   That I assure you:
  Troilus had rather Troy were borne to Greece
  Than Cressid borne from Troy.
Paris. [*Aside.*]   There is no help:
  The bitter disposition of the time
  Will have it so. [*Aloud.*] On, lord, we'll follow you. 50
Æneas. Good morrow, all.   *Exit Æneas* [*with servant*].
Paris. And tell me, noble Diomed, faith, tell me true,
  Even in the soul of sound goodfellowship,
  Who in your thoughts deserves fair Helen best—
  Myself, or Menelaus?

---

37. 'twas] *Q;* it was *F.*   38. Calchas'] *Pope; Calcho's | Q; Calcha's | F.*
41 S.D.] *NCS; not in Q,F; (and so at 46, 48, 50).*   41. believe] *Q;* doe thinke *F.*
45. wherefore: I fear] *Capell;* wherefore: | I feare *Q;* whereof, I feare *F.*
47–8.] *As F; as prose, Q.* 49–50. time | Will . . . so] *As Pope;* time will . . .
so: *Q,F* (*subst.*). 51 S.D.] *As Dyce* (*subst.*)*; Exit Æneas | F; not in Q.*
53. the] *F; not in Q.*   goodfellowship] *Capell;* good fellowship *Q,F.*
54. deserves . . . best] *Q;* merits faire *Helen* most *F.*

---

37. *His . . . you*] Not simply 'What
he meant I shall now tell you', but
also, 'Here is Antenor (released), and
Diomedes (who is to take Cressida,
in exchange for Antenor)'.

41–50.] Walker (NCS) is most certainly right in reading this passage as
a series of asides.

41–2. *believe . . . thought*] While F's
do think maintains a formal series
(*think/thought*) it need not therefore be
counted authoritative: the sense *I
believe* (= I think) was common from
the thirteenth century onwards (cf.
OED *believe* 7).

44. *note*] intelligence, information.

45. *quality*] 'nature, with reference
to origin: hence, cause, occasion'
(OED 8b).

54. *deserves . . . best*] I follow Q, not
being persuaded that Diomedes picks
up and plays with Paris' word (cf.
NCS note). After all, if one is seeking
rhetorical play with *merits*, there is
sufficient within the bounds of
Diomedes' own speech. Besides, while
merits (F) might easily have been
picked up into l. 54 from l. 56, it is
not so simple to explain *deserves.* Loose
paraphrase is not a characteristic of Q.

Diom.   Both alike: 55
He merits well to have her that doth seek her,
Not making any scruple of her soilure,
With such a hell of pain and world of charge;
And you as well to keep her that defend her,
Not palating the taste of her dishonour,   60
With such a costly loss of wealth and friends.
He, like a puling cuckold, would drink up
The lees and dregs of a flat tamed piece;
You, like a lecher, out of whorish loins
Are pleas'd to breed out your inheritors.   65
Both merits pois'd, each weighs nor less nor more,
But he as thee, each heavier for a whore.
Paris. You are too bitter to your country-woman.
Diom. She's bitter to her country: hear me, Paris—
For every false drop in her bawdy veins   70
A Grecian's life hath sunk; for every scruple
Of her contaminated carrion weight
A Trojan hath been slain. Since she could speak,
She hath not given so many good words breath

57. soilure] *F;* soyle *Q.*   66. nor less] *Q;* no lesse *F.*   67. he . . . each]
This edn; he as he, each *Dyce, conj. Johnson;* he as he, the *Q;* he as he, which *F.*

57. *making any scruple of*] being
reluctant, sticking at.
  soilure] sullying, staining.
58. *charge*] trouble.
60. *palating*] perceiving (on your
palate).
62. *puling*] whining, plaintive (an
odd term, in view of the laconic
brevity of Menelaus).
63. *flat . . . piece*] cask of wine
spoiled by exposure to the air; but
punning on *piece* = woman (usually
derogatory).
65. *to . . . inheritors*] to beget your
heirs. The formula *out of . . . to breed
out* appears to be mere duplication
(cf. Abbott §407): for *breed out* cf.
Wint. v.i.11–12: 'the sweet'st companion that e'er man / Bred his hopes
out of'.
66. *pois'd*] weighed, set in the
balance.

67. *each*] Johnson's brilliant conjecture needs justification. F must
have varied from Q deliberately, yet
which (F) is puzzling: one might
accept Johnson's interpretation ('He
as he. Which heavier for a whore?')
if it did not contradict l. 66. Yet a
compositor might have read *each* in
his copy, and set *which*—a fairly easy
'aural' error. Neither Paris nor
Menelaus is much the heavier—
whores were proverbially light
(= wanton)—but each is heavy
(= gloomy) in that he has part share
in a whore whether he possess her or
not.
68.] Paris is polite, but ironic.
71. *scruple*] ₁ oz.: small measure
of weight used by apothecaries.
72. *carrion*] vile, rotten (as a putre-
fying carcass).

As for her Greeks and Trojans suffer'd death.   75
Paris. Fair Diomed, you do as chapmen do,
  Dispraise the thing that they desire to buy;
  But we in silence hold this virtue well,
  We'll not commend, that not intend to sell.
  Here lies our way.   *Exeunt.* 80

[SCENE II]

Enter TROILUS *and* CRESSIDA.

Troil. Dear, trouble not yourself; the morn is cold.
Cress. Then, sweet my lord, I'll call mine uncle down;
  He shall unbolt the gates.
Troil.   Trouble him not:
  To bed, to bed! Sleep kill those pretty eyes,
  And give as soft attachment to thy senses   5
  As infants empty of all thought.
Cress.   Good morrow, then.
Troil. I prithee now, to bed.
Cress.   Are you aweary of me?
Troil. O Cressida, but that the busy day,
  Wak'd by the lark, hath rous'd the ribald crows,

77. they] *Q*; you *F.*   79. that . . . to] *This edn, conj. Lettsom;* what wee intend to *Q,F* (*subst.*)*;* what we intend not *Warburton.*

79.] If the Trojans hold the virtue *in silence*, they mean two things: (a) they will not sell Helen, and (b) they decline to observe the obvious antithesis (i.e. as *chapmen*, they ought to be praising what the Greeks dispraise). Johnson's comment is best: 'I believe the meaning is only this: though you practise the buyer's art, we will not practise the seller's'. (Perhaps cf. Sonnet 21, l. 14: 'I will not praise that purpose not to sell'.)

Scene II

4. *kill*] overwhelm, suppress. An extravagant expression, but perhaps cognate with some Petrarchan imagery and hyperbole (which involved

the metaphorical death of the lover), and certainly connected with *attachment* (= arrest) in l. 5. Emendations have been ingenious, but are mostly based on the mistaken assumption that the *infants* (l. 6) require a context altogether soft and gentle.

8–11.] The contrast with the aubade in *Rom.* III.v.1–11 has often been noticed.

9. *ribald crows*] 'ribald', of course, because of their raucous crying, but the whole phrase is both deflating and ominous. Shakespeare may have had in mind Ovid's story of Apollo and Coronis (*Metamorphoses*, II.631–2) in which a raven reveals a wife's infidelity, despite a crow's warning;

And dreaming night will hide our joys no longer,   10
I would not from thee.

Cress.   Night hath been too brief.

Troil. Beshrew the witch! With venomous wights she stays
As tediously as hell, but flies the grasps of love
With wings more momentary-swift than thought.
You will catch cold, and curse me.

Cress.   Prithee, tarry.   15
You men will never tarry.
O foolish Cressid, I might have still held off,
And then you would have tarried. Hark: there's one up.

Pand. [*Within.*] What's all the doors open here?

Troil. It is your uncle.   20

Enter PANDARUS.

Cress. A pestilence on him! now will he be mocking:
I shall have such a life.

Pand. How now, how now, how go maidenheads? Here,

Scene II

10. joys] *Q;* eyes *F.*   13. tediously] *Q;* hidiously *F.*   14. momentary-swift] *Pope;* momentary swift *Q;* momentary, swift *F.*   15–17. Prithee . . . off] *As Capell;* Prithee . . . tarry, / . . . of, *Q,F (subst.).*   19 S.D.] *F; not in Q.*   20 S.D.] *F; not in Q.*   23–4.] *As Pope;* How . . . maiden-heads, / Heere . . . Cresseid? / *Q, F (subst.).*   23–4. Here, you,] *This edn;* Here, you *Capell;* Heere you *Q;* Heare you *F.*

---

but he is more likely to have remembered Chaucer's version (*Maunciple's Tale*) in which the *crow* reveals the truth—that is to say, it was crows that he associated with unfaithful women. (Apollo's wrath and remorse may also lie behind Troilus' outburst in v.ii, and his final cursing of Pandarus.) Shakespeare's crows are sometimes merely proverbial (in contrast to swans: *Rom.* I.ii.89); but they are also anti-heroic, being contrasted with eagles (I.ii.248 and *Caes.* v.i.85), and they may be omens of death and defeat (like the Duke of Dorset's owls, in Max Beerbohm, *Zuleika Dobson*).

12–14.] Clearly, a contrast is intended between the night of lovers—

whom time gallops withal—and a night of misery, which seems endless; but *venomous wights* is no exact parallel to *grasps of love*. The context implies loathed company (as opposed to one's mistress).

12. *witch*] Cf. *H5* IV. Chorus. 20–2: 'the cripple tardy-gaited night / Who, like a foul and ugly witch, doth limp / So tediously away'.

17–18.] Cressida refers back to her earlier technique of delay and teasing (I.ii.291–300).

19. *What's*] why are; cf. Abbott §253.

23. *how go*] what is the state of the market in; cf. *2H4* III.ii.37–8: 'How a good yoke of bullocks at Stamford Fair?' (For the ribald tone, cf. *1H4*

> you, maid—where's my cousin Cressid?

Cress. Go hang yourself, you naughty mocking uncle!   25
> You bring me to do—and then you flout me too!

Pand. To do what? To do what? Let her say what.
> What have I brought you to do?

Cress. Come, come, beshrew your heart: you'll ne'er be
> good, nor suffer others.   30

Pand. Ha, ha! Alas, poor wretch! Ah, poor capocchia!
> Has't not slept tonight? Would he not—ah,
> naughty man—let it sleep? A bugbear take him!

Cress. Did not I tell you? Would he were knock'd i'th'
> head!   *One knocks.* 35
> Who's that at door? Good uncle, go and see.
> My lord, come you again into my chamber.—
> You smile and mock me, as if I meant naughtily.

Troil. Ha, ha!

Cress. Come, you are deceiv'd: I think of no such thing.   40
> How earnestly they knock: pray you, come in.   *Knock.*
> I would not for half Troy have you seen here.

> >   *Exeunt [Troilus and Cressida].*

Pand. Who's there? What's the matter? Will you beat
> down the door? [*Opening it.*] How now, what's the
> matter?   45

[*Enter ÆNEAS.*]

31. Ah] *Dyce (subst.)*; a *Q,F (and so at 32).*   32. Has't] *NCS, conj. Tannenbaum;* hast *Q,F.*   35 S.D.] *After 36, Q; after 33, F.*   35–6.] *As Q; as prose F.* 42 S.D.] *Capell; Exeunt | Q,F.*   44 S.D.] *Capell; not in Q,F.*

II.iv.358–9: 'we shall buy maidenheads as they buy hob-nails, by the hundreds.')

23–4. *Here . . . Cressid*] An obvious joke: Cressida was (presumably) a maid when he last saw her, and, being no longer the same, is supposed to be unrecognizable.

26. *to do*—] Perhaps Cressida was about to add *naught* (cf. *R3* I.i.99, and l. 38 below). Pandarus may take the verb absolutely and obscenely (= copulate), but perhaps rather in its normal sense (with abundant insinuation).

31, 32. *Ah*] Pandarus' arch, facetious form of speech seems to justify reading Q's *a* as *ah*; cf. IV.iv.11 (*Ah, sweet ducks!*), where *ah* again appears as *a* in Q. The present passage occurs at the foot of H1ᵛ, set by compositor B: IV.iv.11 is on H3, probably set by B (but the page is apparently divided between A and B).

31. *capocchia*] simpleton (Ital.).

37. *chamber*] Normally an innocent word; but cf. the proverb, 'She lies backward, and lets out her forerooms' (Tilley F 594).

Æneas. Good morrow, lord, good morrow.

Pand. Who's there? My Lord Æneas? By my troth, I
knew you not. What news with you so early?

Æneas. Is not Prince Troilus here?

Pand. Here? What should he do here?   50

Æneas. Come, he is here, my lord; do not deny him.
It doth import him much to speak with me.

Pand. Is he here, say you? It's more than I know, I'll be
sworn. For my own part, I came in late. What
should he do here?   55

Æneas. Ho, nay then! Come, come, you'll do him
wrong ere you are ware, you'll be so true to him
to be false to him. Do not you know of him, but
yet go fetch him hither: go.

Enter TROILUS.

Troil. How now, what's the matter?   60

Æneas. My lord, I scarce have leisure to salute you,
My matter is so rash: there is at hand
Paris your brother, and Deiphobus,
The Grecian Diomed, and our Antenor
Deliver'd to us; and for him forthwith,   65
Ere the first sacrifice, within this hour,
We must give up to Diomedes' hand
The Lady Cressida.

Troil.   Is it so concluded?

Æneas. By Priam and the general state of Troy.
They are at hand, and ready to effect it.   70

Troil. How my achievements mock me!
I will go meet them; and, my Lord Æneas,

47. there?] *Pope;* there *Q,F.*   Æneas?] *F; Æneas: | Q.*   53. It's] *Q* (its);
'tis *F.*   56. Ho,] *NCS, conj. Tannenbaum;* Who, *Q,F;* Pho! *Theobald;* Whoo!
Johnson.   57. you are] *Q;* y'are *F.*   59 S.D.] *F; not in Q.*   65. us] *F;*
him *Q.*   for him] *F; not in Q.*   67. Diomedes'] *Pope; Diomedes | Q;*
Diomeds | F.   68. so concluded] *Q;* concluded so *F.*

53. *It's*] Rare in Shakespeare's time,
and more usually '*Tis* (as in F); cf.
Abbott §228.

56. *Ho*] = whoa! (OED who *int.* =
Ho *int.*²). It seems clear that Æneas,

having called Pandarus to draw rein
(= whoa), goes on to talk him down
in a parody of his own style.

62. *rash*] sudden, hasty: cf. *Rom.*
II.ii.118.

We met by chance: you did not find me here.
Æneas. Good, good, my lord: the secrets of nature
Have not more gift in taciturnity.   75

Exeunt [Troilus and Æneas].

Pand. Is't possible? No sooner got but lost? The devil
take Antenor! The young prince will go mad. A
plague upon Antenor! I would they had broke's
neck!

Enter CRESSIDA.

Cress. How now? What's the matter? Who was here?   80
Pand. Ah, ah!
Cress. Why sigh you so profoundly? Where's my lord?
Gone?
Tell me, sweet uncle, what's the matter?
Pand. Would I were as deep under the earth as I am   85
above.
Cress. O the gods, what's the matter?
Pand. Pray thee get thee in: would thou hadst ne'er
been born! I knew thou wouldst be his death.

---

74. nature] *F;* neighbour *Pandar Q.*   75 S.D.] *Capell; Exeunt | Q; Exeunt. |*
Enter Pandarus and Cressid | F.   76. lost?] *Hanmer;* lost, *Q;* lost: *F.*   79 S.D.]
Enter Cress. How *Q; Cres.* How *F.*   81. ah!] *Q;* ha! *F.*   88. Pray thee] *Q;*
Prythee *F.*   89. wouldst] *F* (would'st); wouldest *Q.*

73.] Troilus is instructing Æneas in
his part.

74. *secrets of nature*] Whether one
follows F or Q, the line remains
metrically faulty: there is no evidence
that *secrets* could be pronounced as a
trisyllable. Walker (NCS) rightly
argues that *nature* and *neighbour* ought
to represent readings of the same word
in the MS copy (she suggests *nabor*),
but she may be wrong in saying that
secrets of nature is 'too abstract'. It is,
after all, no more so than Troilus'
How my achievements mock me! (l. 71),
and Æneas' language is frequently
high-flown (cf. I.iii.234–43, IV.i.20–
5). To argue that *secrets of neighbour
Pandar* refers to ll. 47–54 would hardly
help; Troilus, at least, had not heard
that conversation. Besides, Æneas is

most unlikely to use the term 'neighbour' as a title. Shakespeare's practice
appears to be this: that the merchant
class and lesser gentry will use the
term among themselves, or to their
inferiors (e.g. Leonato to Dogberry,
even Menenius to the Citizens), and
those inferiors will use it among
themselves (Mistress Quickly in *2H4;*
the Carriers in *1H4;* Dogberry to his
fellows); but that no nobleman will
use it to anybody—with the exception
of Cerimon (a Lord) to two Gentle-
men (*Per.* III.ii.110) whom he calls
'my gentle neighbours' (and thereby,
perhaps, distinguishes their propin-
quity from their title). The notion of
Æneas, high-flown and goddess-born,
referring to Pandarus in this way, is
most implausible.

O poor gentleman! A plague upon Antenor!   90

Cress. Good uncle, I beseech you, on my knees I
  beseech you, what's the matter?

Pand. Thou must be gone, wench, thou must be gone:
  thou art changed for Antenor. Thou must to thy
  father, and be gone from Troilus: 'twill be his   95
  death, 'twill be his bane; he cannot bear it.

Cress. O you immortal gods! I will not go.

Pand. Thou must.

Cress. I will not, uncle. I have forgot my father;
  I know no touch of consanguinity,   100
  No kin, no love, no blood, no soul so near me
  As the sweet Troilus! O you gods divine,
  Make Cressid's name the very crown of falsehood
  If ever she leave Troilus! Time, force, and death,
  Do to this body what extremes you can;   105
  But the strong base and building of my love
  Is as the very centre of the earth,
  Drawing all things to it. I'll go in and weep—

Pand. Do, do.

Cress. —Tear my bright hair, and scratch my praised cheeks,
  Crack my clear voice with sobs, and break my heart   111
  With sounding 'Troilus'. I will not go from Troy. *Exeunt.*

91–2. knees . . . you] *F;* knees *Q*.   105. extremes] *Q;* extremitie *F.*
108. I'll] *Q;* I will *F.*   weep—] *Theobald (subst.);* weepe. *Q,F.*   112 S.D.]
F; not in *Q*.

91–2. *on . . . you*] *Q*, I think, is more
likely to have omitted an *I beseech you*
than F to have repeated one.

96. *bane*] destruction, ruin; cf. *Mac.*
v. iii. 59: 'I will not be afraid of death
and bane'.

cannot] will not be able to.

99–102. *I have . . . Troilus*] Noble
cites Matthew xix. 5; Baldwin (*Vario-*

rum) adds 1 Esdras iv. 20–1.

100. *touch of consanguinity*] sense of
kinship.

104. *force*] compulsion, violence.

110–12. *Tear . . . 'Troilus'*] Conventional (but not therefore insincere)
signs of grief: perhaps with some
recollection of Chaucer, *Troilus and
Criseyde*, iv. 736–41, 814–17.

[SCENE III]

Enter PARIS *and* TROILUS, *with* ÆNEAS,
DEIPHOBUS, ANTENOR, *and* DIOMEDES.

Paris. It is great morning; and the hour prefix'd
    For her delivery to this valiant Greek
    Comes fast upon.—Good my brother Troilus,
    Tell you the lady what she is to do,
    And haste her to the purpose.
Troil.   Walk into her house.   5
    I'll bring her to the Grecian presently;
    And to his hand when I deliver her,
    Think it an altar, and thy brother Troilus
    A priest, there off'ring to it his own heart.   *[Exit.]*
Paris. I know what 'tis to love,   10
    And would, as I shall pity, I could help.
    Please you walk in, my lords?   *Exeunt.*

[SCENE IV]

Enter PANDARUS *and* CRESSIDA.

Pand. Be moderate, be moderate.
Cress. Why tell you me of moderation?

Scene III

S.D.] *NCS* (*subst.*); *Enter Paris, Troyl. Æneas, Deiphob. Anth. Diomedes.* | *Q,F*
(*subst.*).   3. upon] *Q,F;* upon us *Pope.*   9. own] *Q; not in F.*   9 S.D.]
Capell (*subst.*); *not in Q,F.*   12. lords?] *Q;* Lords. *F.*

Scene III

S.D.] Paris and Troilus must of
necessity be apart from the rest: their
conversation (ll. 1–11) is largely
private; and one can hardly have a
full entry *en masse* only to begin the
scene with a series of asides.

  1. *great morning*] full day (= *grand
jour*).

3. *Comes . . . upon*] Cf. Abbott §192.
5. *her house*] The house belongs to
Calchas (cf. IV.i.38), despite the
occasional assumption of editors that
it belongs to Pandarus. Here, Shakespeare thinks of the person most
immediately concerned, in order to
identify the place.
8–9.] Troilus reverts to Petrarchan
imagery when moved.

The grief is fine, full, perfect, that I taste,
And violenteth in a sense as strong
As that which causeth it: how can I moderate it?		5
If I could temporize with my affection,
Or brew it to a weak and colder palate,
The like allayment could I give my grief.
My love admits no qualifying dross,
No more my grief, in such a precious loss.		10

Enter TROILUS.

Pand. Here, here, here he comes. Ah, sweet ducks!
Cress. O Troilus, Troilus!		[*Embraces him.*]
Pand. What a pair of spectacles is here! Let me embrace,
    too. 'O heart', as the goodly saying is,
        O heart, heavy heart,		15
        Why sigh'st thou without breaking?

Scene IV

3. full,] *Q;* full *F.*		4. violenteth] *Q;* no lesse *F;* violenceth *Keightley.*
6. affection] *F;* affections *Q.*		9. dross] *Q;* crosse *F*		10 S.D.] *As Q; after*
9, F.		11. Ah, . . . ducks!] *Capell* (*subst.*)*;* a . . . ducks. *Q;* a . . . ducke. *F;*
ah, . . . duck! *Johnson.*		12 S.D.] *Malone; not in Q,F.*		14–19.] *As Pope*
(*subst.*)*; as prose, Q,F.*		16. sigh'st] *Q* (sighst)*;* sighest *F.*

Scene IV

4. *violenteth*] rages (a rare image).
OED gives this as the *intransitive* use;
but it is just possible that the object
might be understood (Cressida being
wholly impelled by her grief) and, in
that case, the sense would be 'forces',
'coerces'. F's *no lesse* it is difficult to
see as a misreading of *violenteth*, even
from MS; and why should the compositor be consulting MS here, if
violenteth were what he could not
decipher, and that word stood in print
in Q? (Did the F collator set down
violents me?)
		in a sense] in a manner, to a degree.
		6. *temporize*] come to terms with.
		affection] propensity, bent.
		7. *palate*] taste. Cressida sees grief
in the same terms as Troilus sees love
(III. ii. 17–20).

8. *allayment*] dilution; cf. *Cor.*
II. i. 48.
		11. *ducks*] An endearment, perhaps
childish, then as now. There seems to
be something old-fashioned or affected in it: the other Shakespearean
characters who use it are Pistol (*H5*
II. iii. 53), Bottom (*MND* v. i. 270)
and Autolycus (*Wint.* IV. iv. 318).
		13. *pair of spectacles*] A deliberate
facetiousness.
		14.] The *goodly saying* has not been
traced (although Shakespeare would
have been quite capable of composing
his own doggerel), but popular songs
are easily lost.
		15.] Pope's emendation *O heavy* is
certainly more metrical; but the
verses are meant to be *sung*, and music
sets right much that, on paper, looks
halting. (One might therefore argue
that this was a genuine ballad, and

where he answers again
    Because thou canst not ease thy smart
    By friendship nor by speaking.
There was never a truer rhyme. Let us cast away   20
nothing, for we may live to have need of such a
verse: we see it, we see it. How now, lambs?

Troil. Cressid, I love thee in so strain'd a purity
    That the blest gods, as angry with my fancy,
    More bright in zeal than the devotion which   25
    Cold lips blow to their deities, take thee from me.

Cress. Have the gods envy?

Pand. Ay, ay, ay, ay, 'tis too plain a case.

Cress. And is it true that I must go from Troy?

Troil. A hateful truth.

Cress.   What, and from Troilus too?   30

Troil. From Troy and Troilus.

Cress.   Is't possible?

Troil. And suddenly; where injury of chance
    Puts back leave-taking, jostles roughly by
    All time of pause, rudely beguiles our lips
    Of all rejoindure, forcibly prevents   35
    Our lock'd embrasures, strangles our dear vows

---

23. strain'd] *Q;* strange *F.*   26. deities,] *Q;* Deities: *F.*   31. Is't] *Q,F;*
Is it *Rowe.*   33. back] *Q;* by *F.*   36. embrasures] *Q,F;* embraces *Pope;*
embraceures *White.*

---

not something composed for the occasion; but it is easy to make words to
known tunes, and it has always been
done.)

17.] Cf. *Ham.* iv.v.64. Again, the
musical form (supposing the song to
exist, and to be sung in full) would
probably make clear the parts in the
dialogue.

19. *friendship*] Collier's suggestion
of *silence* has the virtue of maintaining
the balance with *speaking*, but simple
antonyms may not be in question: if
the ballad *be* genuine, we do not know
the dramatic context of the lines.
Besides, Pandarus may be enjoying
wordplay—*friend* could = lover, par-
amour.

23. *strain'd*] clarified, refined.

24. *fancy*] love; sometimes with the
implication fancy+fantasy (love+the
imaginative power it engenders).

33. *Puts back*] rejects, says 'no' to.
(*Puts by* (F) means much the same;
but it looks as if *by* were caught up
from the end of the line.)

35. *rejoindure*] reunion (or perhaps
merely union); no other instance
known, but cf. *Tw.N.* v.i.155:
'Confirm'd by mutual joinder of your
hands'.

36. *embrasures*] The QF reading
normally = windows. Plainly a word
with the root [*em*]*brace* is needed, and
Shakespeare is not much given to
French borrowings (e.g. *embrassure* or
White's suggestion *embraceure*). We
might read *embraces* (with Pope),

Even in the birth of our own labouring breath.
We two, that with so many thousand sighs
Did buy each other, must poorly sell ourselves
With the rude brevity and discharge of one.   40
Injurious Time now with a robber's haste
Crams his rich thiev'ry up, he knows not how;
As many farewells as be stars in heaven,
With distinct breath and consign'd kisses to them,
He fumbles up into a loose adieu,   45
And scants us with a single famish'd kiss
Distasted with the salt of broken tears.
Æneas. (*Within.*) My lord, is the lady ready?
Troil. Hark, you are call'd. Some say the Genius
Cries so to him that instantly must die.   50
Bid them have patience: she shall come anon.

40. one.] *Pope;* one, *Q;* our *F.*   41. Time] *Q (subst.);* time; *F.*   42. thiev'ry]
Q; theeuerie *F.*   47. Distasted] *Q;* Distasting *F.*   tears.] *Q;* teares. *Enter*
Æneus. / *F.*   48 S.D.] *Q,F.*   49–50. Genius / Cries so] *Q;* genius so / Cries,
come *F.*

supposing that the compositor's eye
caught *-ure* from *rejoindure*, above; but
since both *rejoindure* and *embrasures* (in
this context) are apparently nonce-
words, it might be improper to argue
that either was right in order to prove
the other corrupt. Perhaps *rejoindure*
should be *rejoinder* (although *that* =
response, reply; often in a legal sense):
perhaps *embrasures* should be *embra-*
ceures. I doubt whether we ought to
read *embraces*.

37. *labouring*] giving birth.

40. *discharge*] (a) exhalation of
breath (in sighing); (b) payment (in
selling).

one] F's *our* can surely derive only
from the misreading of MS, and not
of print? (F makes no sense here.)

44. *distinct breath*] Each farewell is
thought of as leisurely, and distinguished from the rest.

consign'd] Perhaps for 'consigning'
(= ratifying) (cf. Abbott §374):
otherwise, 'added as ratification'
(NCS).

45. *fumbles up*] *fumble* = (primarily)
handle awkwardly; but *fumble up* (cf.
OED *fumble* 5 b) is used of indistinct,
imperfect speech: hence, (a) clumsily
gathers up (what has been stolen);
(b) confusedly utters (the *loose adieu*).

46. *scants*] grudgingly allows, limits.

47. *Distasted*] made distasteful.

broken] Probably = breaking: i.e.
tears which interrupt the farewell and
the kiss (cf. again Abbott §374):
otherwise, interrupted, not allowed
to flow freely.

49. *Genius*] guardian or tutelary
spirit, which has oversight of a man
until his death (and which, perhaps,
conducts him from the world).

49–50. *Genius . . . so*] Q and F are
indifferent here. The Genius may, or
may not, say 'Come': it certainly
does not speak as Æneas has done
(which is what both texts seem to
imply). Troilus, of course, means that
it interrupts a man in some desired
action.

Pand. Where are my tears? Rain, to lay this wind, or
    my heart will be blown up by th'root.   [*Exit.*]
Cress. I must then to the Grecians?
Troil.   No remedy.
Cress. A woeful Cressid 'mongst the merry Greeks: 55
    When shall we see again?
Troil. Hear me, my love: be thou but true of heart—
Cress. I, true? How now, what wicked deem is this?
Troil. Nay, we must use expostulation kindly,
    For it is parting from us.   60
    I speak not 'Be thou true' as fearing thee—
    For I will throw my glove to Death himself
    That there's no maculation in thy heart—
    But 'Be thou true' say I to fashion in
    My sequent protestation: be thou true,   65
    And I will see thee.
Cress. O you shall be expos'd, my lord, to dangers
    As infinite as imminent! But I'll be true.
Troil. And I'll grow friend with danger: wear this sleeve.

---

53. th'root] *NCS;* the root *F;* my throate *Q* .   53 S.D.] *Dyce; Exit Pandarus /*
Theobald; not in Q,F.   55–6. Greeks: / When] *Q (subst.);* Greekes. / *Troy.*
When *F.*   57. my love] *F;* loue *Q.*   heart—] *Rowe (subst.);* heart. *Q,F.*
63. there's] *F;* there is *Q.*   65–6.] As *F; as one line Q .*

---

52. *Rain . . . wind*] tears, to stop my
sighs (from the common but erroneous belief that wind decreased
because rain began to fall—*post hoc,
ergo propter hoc*). The figure is inten-
tionally absurd: cf. *Ant.* 1.ii.145–8:
'We cannot call her winds and waters
sighs and tears; they are greater
storms and tempests than almanacs
can report'.

53. *th'root*] Q's *my throat* is perhaps
an attempt at correction (*th'root* read
as *throot/throat*, and *my* inserted).

55. *merry Greeks*] roisterers, loose
fellows. (Cressida plays on the literal
sense, and on the familiar, contemptuous name: cf. also her remark at
1.ii.110.)

56. *see*] meet; cf. *H8* 1.i.2.

58. *deem*] opinion, judgement.

60.] i.e. we shall soon have no
opportunity to speak *at all* (let alone
leisure for expostulation). Expostulation is personified as a guest departing.

62. *throw . . . to*] challenge formally.

63. *maculation*] spot or stain. OED
cites the Coventry Mystery Plays for
two examples before this.

64. *fashion in*] form; *fashion* = contrive, arrange; but *fashion in* here
comes near to meaning 'introduce'.

67–8. *O . . . imminent*] It will be
infinitely dangerous to attempt to visit
the Greek camp unobserved.

69. *sleeve*] Detachable, in the dress
of both men and women. Cf. Chaucer,
Troilus and Criseyde, v.1043: 'She
made hym were a pencel [= token]
of hire sleve'.

Cress. And you this glove: when shall I see you?   70
Troil. I will corrupt the Grecian sentinels
　　　To give thee nightly visitation.
　　　But yet be true.
Cress.　　　　　　　O heavens—'be true' again?
Troil. Hear why I speak it, love.
　　　The Grecian youths are full of quality,   75
　　　Their loving well compos'd, with gift of nature flowing,
　　　And swelling o'er with arts and exercise.
　　　How novelty may move, and parts with person,
　　　Alas, a kind of godly jealousy—
　　　Which I beseech you call a virtuous sin—   80
　　　Makes me afeard.
Cress.　　　　　　　O heavens, you love me not!
Troil. Die I a villain then!
　　　In this I do not call your faith in question
　　　So mainly as my merit: I cannot sing,
　　　Nor heel the high lavolt, nor sweeten talk,   85

72–3. To . . . true] *As F; as one line,* Q.   73. 'be true'] *As Hanmer;* be true
Q,F.   74. it, love.] *F3 (subst.);* it loue, Q; it; Loue: *F.*   76.] Their . . .
nature, / Flowing *F;* They're . . . nature, / Flowing *Rowe; not in* Q.
76–7. flowing, / And swelling] *F (subst.);* And flowing *Staunton;* And swelling Q.
78. novelty] *Q;* nouelties *F.*   person] *F;* portion Q.   81. afeard] *Q;*
affraid *F.*

70. *glove*] Like the sleeve, often
worn as a token in the hat or the
helmet, but not invariably as a sign
of love; cf. *H5* IV.i.217–22.

72. *nightly*] by night.

76.] F's line must imply simple
omission by Q, but in that case it is
l. 76, and not l. 77, that must be converted to an Alexandrine by the
addition of *flowing.* Shakespeare seems,
admittedly, never to have used *swell
o'er* elsewhere; but since he has only
once used *flows over* (*Ant.* v.ii.24), one
cannot safely emend on that basis. I
prefer to read *Their* (as in F) and not
They're (as Rowe, etc.): Troilus is
explaining the *quality* that particularly engages his attention. The
Greeks are accomplished and courtly
lovers, and their love-making is
nature improved by art.

78. *novelty*] Shakespeare seems to

use only the singular: cf. *Meas.*
III.ii.217; *All's W.* II.iii.20.

parts] natural gifts or endowments.

person] Q's *portion* is probably
affected (semantically) by *parts.*
Troilus implies that the young Greeks
are personable, handsome fellows.

79. *godly jealousy*] Echoing 2 Corinthians xi.2 (as Theobald noted).

81. *afeard*] The usual form until
c. 1700, when it was finally superseded
by *afraid* (cf. F's *affraid*).

83–4. *faith . . . merit*] Troilus puns:
faith = (a) fidelity, (b) belief, or
creed; *merit* = (a) deserts, (b) works
deserving Divine reward. That is, he
continues to use the language of
religious belief and practice that he
had already employed at IV.iii.7–9.

84. *mainly*] strongly; cf. *main*
(II.iii.273).

85. *lavolt*] = lavolta: a dance for

Nor play at subtle games—fair virtues all,
To which the Grecians are most prompt and pregnant;
But I can tell that in each grace of these
There lurks a still and dumb-discoursive devil
That tempts most cunningly. But be not tempted.   90
Cress. Do you think I will?
Troil.   No.
But something may be done that we will not;
And sometimes we are devils to ourselves,
When we will tempt the frailty of our powers,
Presuming on their changeful potency.   95
Æneas. (*Within.*) Nay, good my lord!
Troil.   Come, kiss, and let us part.
Paris. (*Within.*) Brother Troilus!
Troil. [*Aloud.*]   Good brother, come you hither,
And bring Æneas and the Grecian with you.
Cress. My lord, will you be true?
Troil. Who, I?—alas, it is my vice, my fault.   100
Whiles others fish with craft for great opinion,

91–2. No. / But] *As Pope;* No, but *Q,F.*   97 S.D. *Troil.* [*Aloud.*]] *This edn;*
Troy. / *Q,F.*   99. true?] *Q;* true? *Exit.* / *F.*

two persons, consisting much of high
leaps and bounds. Queen Elizabeth I
was thought to perform it well.

86. *subtle*] (a) requiring dexterity
or skill; (b) deceptive, delusive.
Exactly what games Troilus has in
mind it is hard to guess—perhaps a
bluffing game, like Poker—but since
card-games, at least, tended to employ
terms such as 'hand' and 'five-fingers'
(quite apart from the latent sexual
sense of the word 'play'), precision
may not be necessary.

87. *pregnant*] ready, inclined.

92. *will not*] Emphatic (= do not
will). Troilus picks up Cressida's *Do
you think I will?* (= do you suppose me
likely to be tempted?) and restores to
it its original sense (= Do you think I
would do so willingly?).

95. *Presuming . . . potency*] Literally,
this looks as if it should mean 'taking
it for granted that they are changeable', although the context seems to

require the opposite—'supposing that
they have power *not* to change'. The
temptation of l. 94 appears to suppose
that we presume on (put too much
faith in) a potency which *then* turns
out to be changeable; but I suspect
that the emphasis ought rather to be
on *devils* and *will*: we insist upon
testing ourselves, and we are *devils to
ourselves* in expecting that our powers
may well prove changeable (i.e.
devils goes with l. 95: it is the 'dia-
bolic' part in us which has confidence
in our tendency to change).

101.] Cf. Gratiano's judgement:
'But fish not with this melancholy
bait / For this fool gudgeon, this
opinion' (*Mer. V.* i.i. 101–2).

101–4.] Troilus plays with the two
senses of simplicity, developing the
paradox that truth is a vice or fault
(ll. 99–100). Others, he appears to
say, seek great reputation (*opinion*) by
deceit or hypocrisy: he, by being true,

I with great truth catch mere simplicity;
Whilst some with cunning gild their copper crowns,
With truth and plainness I do wear mine bare.

     Enter [ÆNEAS, PARIS, ANTENOR,
       DEIPHOBUS, *and* DIOMEDES.]

Fear not my truth: the moral of my wit   105
Is 'Plain and true'; there's all the reach of it.
Welcome, Sir Diomed: here is the lady
Which for Antenor we deliver you.
At the port, lord, I'll give her to thy hand,
And by the way possess thee what she is.   110
Entreat her fair, and by my soul, fair Greek,
If e'er thou stand at mercy of my sword,
Name Cressid, and thy life shall be as safe
As Priam is in Ilion.

Diom.   Fair Lady Cressid,
So please you, save the thanks this prince expects.   115
The lustre in your eye, heaven in your cheek,
Pleads your fair usage; and to Diomed
You shall be mistress, and command him wholly.

Troil. Grecian, thou dost not use me courteously,
To shame the zeal of my petition to thee   120
In praising her. I tell thee, lord of Greece,

104 S.D.] *Malone (after 106); Enter the Greekes. | F; not in Q.*   106. 'Plain and
true'] *Johnson;* plaine and true *Q,F.*   117. usage] *Q* (vsage); visage *F.*
120. zeal] *Theobald;* seale *Q,F.*   to thee] *Q;* towards *F;* towards thee *Rowe.*
121. In] *Q;* I *F;* By *Rowe.*

gets a reputation for rusticity; but
what he really means is that the
others get reputation alone by their
skill in deception, whereas he, being
true, is free from all artifice, and
being straightforward, is pure sincerity. The same kind of paradox
holds for ll. 103–4: the others *look*
golden, and *are* copper-gilt; he *looks*
merely bare, but *is* what he is.

103–4.] Truth and plainness do not
prevent a play upon words: *copper
crowns* = copper coins gilded to
appear as French crowns; but *wear*
leads at once to *crown* as top of the
head.

109. *port*] gate (of town). Troy was,
of course, a walled city: cf. Prologue,
ll. 8, 15.

110. *possess*] inform, instruct.

111. *Entreat*] treat, use.

115.] Cressida need not thank
Troilus for the treatment Diomedes
will accord her: her own merit is
cause enough.

117. *usage*] F's *visage* is a simple
misreading of *printed* copy (since Q,
of course, reads *vsage*).

118. *mistress*] Diomedes uses the
language of courtly love. Troilus
refers to him as *servant* at l. 123.

She is as far high-soaring o'er thy praises
As thou unworthy to be call'd her servant.
I charge thee use her well, even for my charge;
For, by the dreadful Pluto, if thou dost not,   125
Though the great bulk Achilles be thy guard,
I'll cut thy throat.
Diom.   O, be not mov'd, Prince Troilus.
Let me be privileg'd by my place and message
To be a speaker free. When I am hence
I'll answer to my lust. And know you, lord,   130
I'll nothing do on charge: to her own worth
She shall be priz'd. But that you say 'Be't so'—
I'll speak it in my spirit and honour, 'No!'
Troil. Come, to the port. I'll tell thee, Diomed,
This brave shall oft make thee to hide thy head.   135
Lady, give me your hand, and, as we walk,
To our own selves bend we our needful talk.
                    [*Exeunt Troilus, Cressida, and Diomedes.*]
                    Sound trumpet.
Paris. Hark, Hector's trumpet!
Æneas.   How have we spent this morning!
The prince must think me tardy and remiss,
That swore to ride before him to the field.   140

---

130. you, lord] *Q* (you Lord); my Lord *F.*   134. Come,] *Theobald;* Come
Q,F.   137 S.D. *Exeunt . . . Diomedes] Rann, conj. Ritson; Exeunt* Tro. *and* Cre. /
Capell; not in *Q,F.*   *Sound trumpet.*] *F;* not in *Q.*

124. *even . . . charge*] simply because I command it. Diomedes has discourteously ignored a polite request.

125. *by . . . Pluto*] Apparently a favourite oath with Troilus: cf. v.ii.102.

126. *bulk*] massive carcass, ('body of great proportions', OED). Bulk could refer *both* to trunk/body and to the mass or size of it: here, the senses combine.

128–30.] Diomedes, being upon a diplomatic errand (to exchange prisoners) is immune from assault. He introduces this speech by a reminder of his diplomatic privilege; and then begins to exploit that privilege by saying that he will respond to Troilus' threat (sc. on the field of battle) exactly as he chooses. Shakespeare may have remembered that, on the first embassy after the Greeks had landed (cf. IV.v.213-15), Diomedes had deliberately insulted the Trojans (Caxton, pp. 560-1).

130. *to my lust*] at my good pleasure (OED 2c). Cf. *Lucr.*, l. 1384: 'Gazing upon the Greeks with little lust'.

132. *But . . . so'—*] 'But as far as your command to me is concerned.'

134. *I'll tell thee*] I tell you (emphatic).

135. *brave*] defiance, boast.

Paris. 'Tis Troilus' fault: come, come, to field with him.
Deiph. Let us make ready straight.
Æneas. Yea, with a bridegroom's fresh alacrity
          Let us address to tend on Hector's heels.
          The glory of our Troy doth this day lie   145
          On his fair worth and single chivalry.   *Exeunt.*

[SCENE V]

Enter AJAX *armed,* AGAMEMNON, ACHILLES, PATROCLUS,
          MENELAUS, ULYSSES, NESTOR, *and* Others.

Agam. Here art thou in appointment fresh and fair
          Anticipating time with starting courage.
          Give with thy trumpet a loud note to Troy,
          Thou dreadful Ajax, that the appalled air
          May pierce the head of the great combatant,   5
          And hale him hither.

141. him.] *Rowe;* him. *Exeunt.* | *Q,F (subst.).*   142–6.] *F; not in Q.*
142. *Deiph.* Let] *Malone; Dio.* Let *F.*   146 S.D.] *Rowe; not in F.*

Scene v

S.D.] *As Capell; Enter Aiax armed, Achilles, Patroclus, Agam., Menelaus, Vlisses,*
Nestor, Calcas, &c. | *Q,F (subst.).*   2. time . . . courage.] *Theobald;* time.
With . . . courage, *Q,F.*   5–6. May . . . hither] *As F; one line, Q.*

142–6.] Certainly authorial (and not an actor's interpolation, as Malone believed), but perhaps equally certain to be a first shot, wisely omitted by the time Q (or its copy) was prepared, and injudiciously recovered by F. (Notice that F has an *Exeunt* at l. 141, but no S.D. at the end of the scene.) It is not exactly that the lines are botched; but they betray a loss of direction, an uncertain grasp of the dramatic moment, which shows in the awkward wordiness of l. 144, and its sharp contrast with the high-flown airs of l. 143, which, after all, are also misplaced. One may *encounter darkness like a bride,* or *be a bridegroom* in one's death; but does one really show *a bridegroom's fresh alacrity* merely in attending on Hector?

Scene v

1. *appointment*] accoutrement.

2.] Rhythmically, it feels very odd to begin a scene so pat with the second line end-stopped, but editors have generally followed Theobald, and no doubt rightly: it is hard to accept the alternative notion that the *starting courage* of Ajax is shown by having his trumpet sound.

starting courage] bounding spirit: cf. *R2* 1.iii.91 (*my dancing soul*), where Mowbray rejoices in *This feast of battle with mine adversary.* The situations are closely comparable.

4–6. *that . . . hither*] If air may be a bond to tie the ears of the Greeks to the tongue of Nestor (1.iii.66), then (when *appalled* by loud noise) it may

Ajax.   Thou, trumpet, there's my purse.
　Now, crack thy lungs, and split thy brazen pipe;
　Blow, villain, till thy sphered bias cheek
　Out-swell the colic of puff'd Aquilon. *N. Wind.*
　Come, stretch thy chest, and let thy eyes spout blood:　10
　Thou blowest for Hector.   [*Flourish.*]
Ulyss. No trumpet answers.
Achill.   'Tis but early days.
Agam. Is not yond Diomed, with Calchas' daughter?
Ulyss. 'Tis he, I ken the manner of his gait:
　He rises on the toe; that spirit of his   15
　In aspiration lifts him from the earth.

[*Enter* DIOMEDES *and* CRESSIDA.]

Agam. Is this the Lady Cressid?
Diom.   Even she.

---

9. colic] *Q,F;* choler *conj. anon (Delius);* choller *NCS.*　　11 S.D.] *This edn;*
Trumpet sounds. | Hanmer; not in Q,F.　13. yond] *Q;* yong *F.*　　16 S.D.] F2
(*subst.; after 12*); *not in Q,F.*

perhaps be allowed to bring Hector to combat. The air is at once the medium through which sound moves, and a kind of extension of the sound itself (*pierce the head*) as well as an extension of what the sound signifies (*hale him hither*).

6. *trumpet*] i.e. trumpeter.

8–9.] The trumpeter's cheek is swollen by pressure of air: hence, *bias* (like a wood at bowls) and *sphered*. It also resembles the round-cheeked representations of the winds at the four corners of early maps.

9. *colic*] Sometimes emended: most ingeniously by Walker in NCS (*choller* = jaw, chaps). But emendation is unnecessary: Shakespeare clearly associated the term with imprisoned wind (cf. *1H4* III.i.25–8: 'oft the teeming earth / Is with a kind of colic pinch'd and vex'd / By the imprisoning of unruly wind / Within her womb'), and Hotspur's mocking speech at that place is not so far in tone from the almost burlesque exaggeration found here in Ajax. Colic

was not merely a constriction of the gut (as OED implies); there was also wind-colic (*tormina ventris: flatus hypochondriacus*). The image in l. 10 is far more absurd.

9. *Aquilon*] the North wind.

10. *thy eyes*] Cf. Abbott §237, on *thy* before a vowel.

12. *No trumpet answers*] Perhaps cf. Ezekiel vii. 14 ('They have blown the trumpet, even to make all ready, but none goeth to the battle').

early days] early in the day; *days* represents the old genitive singular, as in *now-a-days*.

13. *yond*] Probably adverbial (= yonder), but possibly the demonstrative pronoun. The distinction was not always kept.

14. *ken*] recognize. Not (at this time) a word predominantly Scottish; it is, of course, common in Chaucer, but also in Spenser and Malory.

15. *He ... toe*] *Variorum* quotes from Greene, *Planetomachia*, to show that those subservient to Venus go 'stalking on their tiptoes'.

Agam. Most dearly welcome to the Greeks, sweet lady.

[*Kisses her.*]

Nest. Our general doth salute you with a kiss.

Ulyss. Yet is the kindness but particular;   20
  'Twere better she were kiss'd in general.

Nest. And very courtly counsel: I'll begin.   [*Kisses her.*]
  So much for Nestor.

Achill. I'll take that winter from your lips, fair lady:

[*Kisses her.*]

  Achilles bids you welcome.   25

Menel. I had good argument for kissing, once.

Patro. But that's no argument for kissing now;
  For thus popp'd Paris in his hardiment,   [*Steps between.*]
  And parted thus you and your argument.   [*Kisses her.*]

Ulyss. [*Aside.*] O deadly gall, and theme of all our
    scorns!   30
  For which we lose our heads to gild his horns.

Patro. The first was Menelaus' kiss: this, mine;

[*Kisses her again.*]

  Patroclus kisses you.

Menel.   O, this is trim.

Patro. Paris and I kiss evermore for him.

Menel. I'll have my kiss, sir. Lady, by your leave.   35

Cress. In kissing, do you render or receive?

18 S.D.] *Dyce (and at 22, 24, 29, 32); not in Q,F.*   28 S.D.] *Johnson (subst.);
not in Q,F.*   29.] *F; not in Q.*   30 S.D.] *Keightley; not in Q,F.*

20–1.] This sarcasm may be at the expense of either Cressida or the Greeks. The incident has been referred to *Faerie Queene*, iii.x.46, where Hellenore is kissed by all the Satyrs in turn.

20. *particular*] (a) single; (b) individual.

24.] Deighton saw this as a parallel to *Tim.* iv.iii.65–6, and as an allusion to the belief that disease was transferred by kissing; but Nestor is merely old and cold, an emblem of winter and the last age of man.

26.] Menelaus sounds unexpectedly like Sir Andrew Aguecheek (*Tw.N.* ii.iii.181: 'I was adored once too').

28. *hardiment*] act of daring; but I suspect Patroclus of an obscene allusion to tumescence (cf. *pop* = thrust in, or enter, suddenly and unexpectedly).

30. *theme ... scorns*] The theme is both Helen and her separation from Menelaus; this theme the Greeks mock (scorn) as they are doing here, but they also suffer scorns in being put at mortal risk for Helen's sake.

33. *trim*] fine. Usually, as here, sarcastic; cf. *Ado* iv.i.320.

36.] A traditional ambiguity; cf. Charles d'Orléans: 'My gostly fadir, y me confesse, / ffirst to god and then to yow / That at a wyndow (wot ye how) / I stale a cosse of gret swetnes, /

Menel. Both take and give.

Cress.   I'll make my match to live,
    The kiss you take is better than you give:
    Therefore, no kiss.

Menel. I'll give you boot, I'll give you three for one.   40

Cress. You are an odd man: give even or give none.

Menel. An <u>odd</u> man, lady?—Every man is <u>odd</u>.

Cress. No, Paris is not, for you know 'tis true
    That you are odd, and he is even with you.

Menel. You fillip me o'th'head.

Cress.   No, I'll be sworn.   45

Ulyss. It were no match, your nail against his horn.
    May I, sweet lady, beg a kiss of you?

Cress. You may.

Ulyss.   I do desire it.

Cress.   Why, beg two.

Ulyss. Why then, for Venus' sake, give me a kiss
    When Helen is a maid again, and his.   50

Cress. I am your debtor; claim it when 'tis due.

Ulyss. Never's my day, and then a kiss of you.

---

37. *Menel.*] *White, conj. Tyrwhitt; Patr.* / *Q,F.*   38, 39.] *As Pope; one line, Q,F.*
48. Why, beg two.] *This edn, conj. Johnson;* Why begge then. *Q;* Why begge
then? *F;* Why beg too. *conj. Ritson.*   50. his.] *Capell;* his—*Q,F.*

Which don was out avisynes; / But
hit is doon, not vndoon, now . . . / But
y restore it shall dowtles / Ageyn, if so
be that y mow' (*Secular Lyrics of the
XIVth and XVth Centuries,* ed. R. H.
Robbins, 1955, pp. 183–4). Perhaps
also see Tilley M 24: 'The maid
which takes, sells herself'.

37. *I'll . . . live*] I will wager my life
(knowing that I shall win).

40. *boot*] odds.

41. *odd*] unusual, strange.

42. *odd*] singular, unique.

44. *odd*] left over, wanting your
partner (cf. odd man out).

even] quits (and hence, not odd,
though perhaps still at odds).

45. *fillip*] flick, tap.

o' th' head] Reference to a cuckold's
head implied an allusion to his horns.

46.] Ulysses picks up the contrast
(*nail/horn*), alluding to the *fillip* (both
blow and witty sarcasm) and to the
similarity of material involved.

48. *two*] Johnson's conjecture suits
both Cressida's flippancy and her on-
coming disposition: besides, from l. 28
to l. 52, most lines rhyme. *I do desire* is
stronger than *May I . . . beg*, and therefore Cressida offers the suggestion of
two kisses (which fits *desire*), corrects
Ulysses, and proffers herself as willing.
QF *then* may have been caught from
the line below.

50.] Perhaps cf. the song in Hardy,
The Woodlanders, Ch. x, after Giles
Winterbourne's party: 'A maid again
I never shall be / Till apples grow on
an orange tree'.

Diom. Lady, a word: I'll bring you to your father.

Exeunt [Diomedes and Cressida].

Nest. A woman of quick sense.

Ulyss.   Fie, fie upon her!

There's language in her eye, her cheek, her lip—   55
Nay, her foot speaks; her wanton spirits look out
At every joint and motive of her body.
O, these encounterers, so glib of tongue,
That give accosting welcome ere it comes,
And wide unclasp the tables of their thoughts   60
To every ticklish reader: set them down
For sluttish spoils of opportunity
And daughters of the game.   *Flourish.*

All.   The Trojan's trumpet.

53 S.D.] *Capell (Exeunt* Dio *and* Cre.*); not in Q,F.*   55. There's] *Q;* Ther's a *F.*
59. accosting] *Hudson, conj. Theobald;* a coasting *Q,F.*   61. ticklish] *Q;*
tickling *F.*   63, 63 S.D. game. *Flourish.*] *Q;* game. *Exeunt. | Florish* [after
entry] *F;* game. *Trumpet within | Theobald.*   63. Trojan's] *This edn, conj.
Delius;* Troyans *Q,F (subst.);* Trojans' *Theobald.*

54. *A . . . sense*] Nestor's *quick*
(= (a) rapid; (b) lively) need not
imply that he sees Cressida as a
wanton.

Fie] Expressing 'contempt or dislike' (Schmidt), but also disgust.

55–6. *There's . . . speaks*] Cf. Proverbs vi. 12–13: 'A naughty person, a
wicked man, walketh with a froward
mouth. He winketh with his eyes, he
speaketh with his feet, he teacheth
with his fingers'. Steevens (*Variorum*
note) cites Burton, *Anatomy of Melancholy*, Pt III, Sect. 2, Mem. 2, Subs. 3:
'they speake in their gait, they speake
with their eyes, they speake in their
carriage of their bodies'.

57. *motive*] moving limb or organ
(OED 'only in Shaks.'): cf. *R2*
I.i.193.

58. *encounterers*] those who meet one
halfway.

59. *accosting*] addressing, making
advances: QF *a coasting* (= ? approach) is not found elsewhere. For
accost, cf. *Tw.N.* I.iii.51 and III.ii.19.

60. *tables*] tablets (for memoranda):
cf. *Ham.* I.v.98.

61. *ticklish*] easily aroused (especially sexually). Walker (NCS) prefers
F's *tickling*, because (a) *ticklish* was
probably affected by *sluttish* (next
line), and (b) Cressida is blatantly
open to encouragement. But since the
encounterers are as active as their
partners (cf. l. 59), and since *the tables
of their thoughts* may be presumed
rather to tickle the reader, than to be
tickled by him, I retain the Q reading.
It is the reader (as Johnson observed
of Lord Hailes) who is combustible
(Boswell, *Life*, ed. R. W. Chapman,
1953, p. 869).

62.] 'Corrupt wenches, of whose
chastity every opportunity may make
prey' (Johnson).

63. *game*] sexual play; cf. gamester
(= prostitute), *All's W.* v.iii.187.

The . . . trumpet] Delius is obviously
right: it is for Hector's trumpet that
the Greeks have been waiting.
A. P. Rossiter (*Angel with Horns*, 1961,

Agam. Yonder comes the troop.

    Enter HECTOR [*armed*], ÆNEAS, TROILUS, PARIS,
        DEIPHOBUS, *and* Attendants.

Æneas. Hail, all the state of Greece! What shall be done   65
    To him that victory commands? Or do you purpose
    A victor shall be known—will you the knights
    Shall to the edge of all extremity
    Pursue each other—or shall they be divided
    By any voice or order of the field?   70
    Hector bade ask.

Agam.   Which way would Hector have it?
Æneas. He cares not: he'll obey conditions.
Agam. 'Tis done like Hector.
Achill.   But securely done,
    A little proudly, and great deal misprizing *underrating*
    The knight oppos'd.

64 S.D.] *Enter all of Troy* | *Q* (*at 63, after Flourish*)*; F* (*after 63*).   HECTOR . . .
Attendants] *F; not in Q.*   65. the] *Q;* you *F.*   70–1. By . . . ask] *As Rowe*[3]*;*
as one line, Q,F.   73–4. *Agam.* . . . A little] *NCS; Aga* 'Tis . . . done. | *Achil.*
A little *conj. Theobald; Aga:* 'Tis . . . done, | A little *Q,F.*   74. misprizing]
Q; disprising *F.*

p. 133) suggested the 'knavish device'
of aural ambiguity—the cry could
certainly be heard as *The Trojan
strumpet*—but the trumpet call is what
modulates the scene, from facetious
comment and moral distaste, on the
one hand, to serious chivalric action,
on the other.

65–6. *What . . . him*] Steevens (cited
Variorum): 'This phrase is scriptural,
and signifies—"what honour shall he
receive?". So, in 1 Samuel xvii. 26:
"What shall be done to the man that
killeth this Philistine?"'.

66–70.] Æneas is *not* asking whether
the victors should receive honour, or
whether the Greeks would prefer no
victor to emerge. He asks (a) what
shall be done with the victor, and
then (b) should the victory be determined by battle *à l'outrance* (to the
edge of all extremity) or should the
combatants be separated by the
Marshal (and, presumably, judged on
'points')?

66–9. *Or . . . or*] The usual formula
for disjunctive questions, and found
as late as Pope.

70.] i.e. by the Marshal of the lists
and his officers (cf. *R2* I.iii throughout, but especially ll. 42–5).

73–5. *'Tis . . . oppos'd*] Theobald
came very near to solving the problem
here. Clearly, Achilles should speak at
least some of these lines, if Æneas is to
reply to him and correct him: hence,
Pope gave the whole speech to
Achilles, whereas Theobald divided
it, giving l. 73 to Agamemnon and the
remainder to Achilles. It seems preferable to make the simplest division,
and to allow to Agamemnon a
magnanimous absoluteness of compliment.

73. *securely*] 'carelessly', 'confidently' (Schmidt): (perhaps) over-
confidently.

74. *misprizing*] underrating, slighting.

Æneas.   If not Achilles, sir,   75
    What is your name?
Achill.   If not Achilles, nothing.
Æneas. Therefore Achilles. But whate'er, know this:
    In the extremity of great and little,
    Valour and pride excel themselves in Hector;
    The one almost as infinite as all,   80
    The other blank as nothing. Weigh him well,
    And that which looks like pride is courtesy.
    This Ajax is half made of Hector's blood;
    In love whereof, half Hector stays at home:
    Half heart, half hand, half Hector comes to seek   85
    This blended knight, half Trojan and half Greek.
Achill. A maiden battle, then? O, I perceive you.

    without blood   [*Enter* DIOMEDES.]

Agam. Here is Sir Diomed. Go, gentle knight,
    Stand by our Ajax. As you and Lord Æneas
    Consent upon the order of their fight,   90
    So be it: either to the uttermost,
    Or else a breath. The combatants being kin
    Half stints their strife before their strokes begin.
                                [*Ajax and Hector enter the lists.*]
Ulyss. They are oppos'd already.
Agam. What Trojan is that same that looks so heavy?   95
Ulyss. The youngest son of Priam, a true knight;

75-6.] *As Pope², conj. Theobald;* The knight oppos'd. | *Æne.* If... name? | ...
nothing. *Q,F.*   87 S.D.] *White¹; not in Q,F.*   92. breath] *Q;* breach *F.*
93 S.D.] *Malone; not in Q,F.*   94-5. *Ulyss. . . .* already. | *Agam.* What] *F;*
Vlisses: what *Q.*   96. Priam, ... knight] *Q; Priam;* | A true Knight; they
call him *Troylus* | *F.*

77. *But whate'er*] Æneas is adept at
polite snubs (cf. I.iii.222-31).
78-9.] Hector's valour is greater
than that of any other man, and his
pride less.
83.] Cf. l. 119, and note, below.
87. *maiden*] without bloodshed.
perceive] understand.
91. *to the uttermost*] à l'outrance (cf.
ll. 67-9 above).
92. *a breath*] a bout for exercise (cf.
II.iii.114).

93. *stints*] checks.
94. *oppos'd*] set face to face in the
lists.
95-6.] The omission of l. 94 from
Q may explain why that text dupli-
cated the name Ulysses (as vocative,
and as speech-heading) and omitted
the name Agamemnon; see Introduction, pp. 5-6.
96. *knight*] F's addition here of
They call him Troilus is an error, since
the words recur (metrically) at l. 108.

Not yet mature, yet matchless; firm of word,
Speaking in deeds, and deedless in his tongue;
Not soon provok'd, nor, being provok'd, soon calm'd;
His heart and hand both open and both free;   100
For what he has he gives, what thinks he shows,
Yet gives he not till judgement guide his bounty,
Nor dignifies an impare thought with breath;
Manly as Hector, but more dangerous;
For Hector in his blaze of wrath subscribes   105
To tender objects, but he in heat of action
Is more vindicative than jealous love.
They call him Troilus, and on him erect
A second hope as fairly built as Hector.

97. matchless; firm] *F* (matchlesse, firme); matchlesse firme *Q*; matchless-firm *NCS*.   98. Speaking in] *F*; Speaking *Q*.   103. impare] *Q*; impaire *F*; impar *Capell*; impure *conj. Johnson.*

There are two possible explanations for their presence here: (a) they represent a 'first shot', immediately cancelled (Chambers, 1.440); (b) they are a 'cue-in' for a cut: i.e. ll. 97–107 were to be deleted, and the speech to run on as from l. 108. Certainly, as it stands, the full set-piece 'character' is not highly dramatic, and serves to distract an audience's attention while the combat is prepared. Hence, the length of the implied cut in F is simply a clue to stage conditions in some early production.

97.] Walker's reading is attractive, but not wholly defensible. If Troilus is *not yet mature* and yet unexpectedly excellent in some way, it is unlikely that his excellence will be the moral virtue of keeping his word. Troilus is *matchless*: the whole speech says so, making him *Manly as Hector, but more dangerous*, and reaching a climax in *on him erect / A second hope as fairly built as Hector*.

98.] Cf. Tilley W 797: 'Few words and many deeds'.

100. *free*] (a) liberal, bountiful (applied to Troilus's *hand*); (b) noble,

blameless, generous (applied to *heart*).

101–2.] Troilus corresponds to Aristotle's description of the liberal man: *Ethics*, IV.I.

103. *impare*] unjust, unworthy (= Lat. *impar*); *impure* (Johnson's conjecture) is irrelevant to Ulysses' argument. Again, Aristotle may help us. Shakespeare combines here the qualities of the liberal man with those of the magnanimous man, and the latter seeks *honour*, in the same measure as the former exercises liberality. An *impare* thought is beneath him (*Ethics*, IV.3).

105. *subscribes*] What is needed is the sense 'gives quarter' (cf. v.iii.40–3, v.iv.26–30). Editors usually follow OED, and gloss as 'yields': Professor Jenkins suggests 'relents' (citing *Lr* III.vii.64: 'All cruels else subscribe').

107. *vindicative*] i.e. vindictive, revengeful.

108.] Cf. Lydgate, III.2800–2 (p. 646): '. . . he slowe Hectoris two: / First hym þat was lik [vn] to noon oþer, / And Troilus after, þat was his owne broþer.'

Thus says Æneas, one that knows the youth   110
Even to his inches, and with private soul
Did in great Ilion thus translate him to me.

Alarum. [Hector and Ajax fight.]

Agam. They are in action.

Nest.   Now, Ajax, hold thine own!

Troil. Hector, thou sleep'st: awake thee!

Agam. His blows are well dispos'd. There, Ajax!   115

Trumpets cease.

Diom. You must no more.

Æneas.   Princes, enough, so please you.

Ajax. I am not warm yet; let us fight again.

Diom. As Hector pleases.

Hect.   Why then, will I no more.
Thou art, great lord, my father's sister's son,
A cousin-german to great Priam's seed;   120
The obligation of our blood forbids
A gory emulation 'twixt us twain.
Were thy commixtion Greek and Trojan so
That thou could'st say 'This hand is Grecian all,
And this is Trojan: the sinews of this leg   125
All Greek, and this, all Troy: my mother's blood

---

112 S.D.] *Rowe; Alarum | Q,F.*   115. dispos'd. There,] *Theobald (subst.);*
dispo'd, there *Q;* dispos'd there *F.*   120. cousin-german] *Pope;* couzen german *Q,F (subst.).*

---

111. *Even . . . inches*] most intimately, with great exactness.

with . . . soul] as his personal judgement.

112. *translate . . . me*] explain his nature to me.

118.] By later conventions, one would expect Hector, as challenger, to have no say here: it would be for Ajax to decide.

119.] That Ajax was the son of Telamon by Hesione was the opinion expressed not only by Lydgate (III.2046–8) but also by Cooper's *Thesaurus* of 1565 (cf. *Variorum* note). Yet Shakespeare might have guessed at the relationship on other grounds: Ajax announces himself as the son of Telamon in *Metamorphoses* XIII (at the

beginning of his speech claiming the arms of Achilles); and Telamon is given Hesione for his wife in *Metamorphoses* XI, when he and Hercules capture Troy. (The incident immediately following this concerns Peleus and Thetis, and the birth of Achilles—a passage which Shakespeare certainly knew.)

120. *cousin-german*] first cousin.

123. *commixtion*] mingled descent.

124–8. 'This . . . father's'] Boyle cites *Antonio's Revenge*, III.i.161 (*Variorum* note): 'O that I knew which joint, which side, which limb, / Were father all, and had no mother in't, / That I might rip it vein by vein, and carve revenge / In bleeding races! But since 'tis mix'd together, / Have

Runs on the dexter cheek, and this sinister
Bounds in my father's'—by Jove multipotent,
Thou shouldst not bear from me a Greekish member
Wherein my sword had not impressure made   130
Of our rank feud; but the just gods gainsay
That any drop thou borrow'dst from thy mother,
My sacred aunt, should by my mortal sword
Be drain'd! Let me embrace thee, Ajax.
By him that thunders, thou hast lusty arms;   135
Hector would have them fall upon him thus.
Cousin, all honour to thee!
Ajax.   I thank thee, Hector.
Thou art too gentle and too free a man.
I came to kill thee, cousin, and bear hence
A great addition earned in thy death.   140
Hect. Not Neoptolemus so mirable,

131. Of . . . feud] *F; not in Q.*   132. drop] *F;* day *Q.*   134. drain'd]*F3;*
drained *Q,F;* drainéd *Dyce.*

at adventure, pell mell, no reverse.'
But the conceit is by no means as
fantastic as may at first appear.
Hector proposes two kinds of argument: (a) *heraldic*: the arms of a
husband and his (armigerous) wife
were divided *party-per-pale* (i.e. along
the vertical axis), with the husband's
achievement on the *dexter* side
(although Hector, jesting, has allowed
himself false heraldry in l. 127); (b)
anatomical and physiological: until at
least Burton's time, it was supposed
that certain parts of the body—bones,
gristle, ligaments, membranes, fibres
—developed in the foetal stage from
the father's seed (= spermatic parts),
whereas fat, flesh, and skin derived
from the blood of the mother (= san-
guine parts). (This division did not by
any means include *all* parts of the
body, but the distinction was fundamental, and formed the basis of
diagnosis.)

128. *multipotent*] all-powerful; perhaps the earliest vernacular use, but
a common Latin word.

130. *impressure*] impression (cf.

Tw.N. II.v.95). For the form cf.
expressure at III.iii.203. The sense of
impresa/impress (= emblem) may also
be present: Hector's sword would
leave its 'character', its own mark,
behind it (cf. *impress*, II.i.99).

132. *drop*] Q's *day* is a simple misreading of MS.

134.] A line metrically defective;
but the pause (as so often) is dramatically significant, and marks a shift
from stasis to action (*Let me embrace
thee*).

135. *him that thunders*] i.e. Jove.

136.] Cf. *Cor.* IV.v.106–9. Aufidius
uses similar terms, but with less
restraint.

138.] Troilus is of the same opinion
(v.iii.32–9).

138. *free*] generous, gracious.

140. *addition*] distinctive title.

141. *Neoptolemus*] Two explanations
are possible. (a) Achilles' son, Pyrrhus
Neoptolemus, was already the subject
of prophecy, in that, without him,
Troy could not be taken. By prophecy
and parentage, therefore, he was to
be a great soldier (l. 142 might, on

On whose bright crest Fame with her loud'st Oyes
Cries 'This is he', could promise to himself
A thought of added honour torn from Hector.

Æneas. There is expectance here from both the sides   145
What further you will do.

Hect.   We'll answer it:
The issue is embracement. Ajax, farewell.

Ajax. If I might in entreaties find success—
As seld I have the chance—I would desire
My famous cousin to our Grecian tents.   150

Diom. 'Tis Agamemnon's wish; and great Achilles
Doth long to see unarm'd the valiant Hector.

Hect. Æneas, call my brother Troilus to me,
And signify this loving interview
To the expecters of our Trojan part: 155
Desire them home. Give me thy hand, my cousin;
I will go eat with thee, and see your knights.

Agamemnon and the rest come forward.

142. Oyes] *Q,F* (O yes).   143. could] *Q; could'st F.*   157 S.D.] *After
Rowe (Agamemnon and the rest of the Greeks come forward); Enter Agamemnon and the
rest | F; not in Q.*

this interpretation, refer to the prophecy). (b) As many eighteenth-
century editors suggested, Shakespeare
may have considered Neoptolemus as
the name of Achilles himself, supposing it to be the '*nomen gentilitium*'
(Johnson). Since Ajax is, in most
versions of the Troy story, inferior
only to Achilles himself in strength
and valour (and cf. the contest for the
arms of Achilles, *Metamorphoses* XIII)
I incline to Johnson's opinion.

mirable] marvellous.

142. *Oyes*] The call or cry of a
public crier or court officer (Old
French *oiez, oyez* = hear ye!). Delius
noted the rhymes of *oyes/toys* in *Wiv.*
v.v.42–3, and editors have sometimes
followed him in reading them as
monosyllables, and have therefore
emended here to *loudest Oyes*. But (to
judge from OED's citations) most
fifteenth- to seventeenth-century usage

makes *Oyes* a disyllable: I retain
loud'st, and assume that the formal,
ritual rhymes of the Fairy Queen in
Wiv. affected an archaic pronunciation
(*Oyes/toyës*).

149. *As . . . chance*] Since I seldom
have the opportunity to meet Hector
in order to entreat him at all.

seld] (= seldom): only here in
Shakespeare (if we except *The
Passionate Pilgrim,* l. 175, and the
compound *seld-shown* in *Cor.* II.i.211),
but common elsewhere.

155.] To these Trojans who are
awaiting us and the outcome of this
meeting.

156. *Desire . . . home*] Ask them to
return home. For omission of the verb
of motion, cf. ll. 149–50.

157 S.D.] Some direction is necessary, and F is so far right; but a fresh
entry is supererogatory, since Agamemnon and the other Greeks are

Ajax. Great Agamemnon comes to meet us here.

Hect. The worthiest of them, tell me name by name;
　　But for Achilles, my own searching eyes   160
　　Shall find him by his large and portly size.

Agam. Worthy all arms! as welcome as to one
　　That would be rid of such an enemy—
　　But that's no welcome. Understand more clear:
　　What's past and what's to come is strew'd with husks
　　And formless ruin of oblivion;   166
　　But in this extant moment, faith and troth,
　　Strain'd purely from all hollow bias-drawing,
　　Bids thee with most divine integrity
　　From heart of very heart, great Hector, welcome.   170

160. my] *Q;* mine *F.*   162. all] *Q;* of *F.*   164–9.] *F; not in Q.*   168.
bias-drawing] *Theobald;* bias drawing *F.*   169. Bids] *F;* Bid *Hanmer.*

'on' already. Whereabouts on his own stage Shakespeare supposed the lists and the spectators to be, it is uncertain, unless we assume (as producers nowadays do for *R2*) that the spectators are on an upper stage and the lists on the platform. In that case, the Greeks would go off, and re-enter on the main stage. F would have been right in retaining *Enter*, but wrong in failing to give an *Exeunt* (or, indeed, any indication of *Above*). However, all this assumes that we know where (and how) the play as we have it was played; and we do not.

161. *portly*] stately, imposing.

162. *Worthy all arms!*] = worthy warrior! F's *of* gives a phrase which is idiomatic, but curiously weak in this context: Hector is *altogether* a warrior, at *all* points.

162–3. *as . . . enemy*] Either (a) as welcome as you can be (being such a formidable foe), or (b) as welcome as such a great man must be, to one who wishes that he were not an enemy. The second is difficult, the first grudging.

164–9.] Q's omission is regrettable. Not only does Agamemnon need to be able to retract an attempt at wit that failed of its effect: he insists (as the

rest of the play insists) upon the value implicit in things *in this extant moment*— i.e. things as they are, considered intrinsically, and not in respect of a context of Time. (Troilus also considers value irrespective of *what's past and what's to come* in his argument at II. ii. 62 ff.)

165–6. *husks . . . oblivion*] Strictly, only *what's past* should be subject to the depredations of oblivion (cf. III. ii. 183–7), but Agamemnon sees what is to come (and therefore unformed) as 'disfigured' equally with that which has gone (and therefore worn away).

husks] outer shells or cases of seed or grain: Shakespeare twice uses it (*AYL* I. i. 37; *1H4* IV. ii. 36), each time with an allusion to the parable of the Prodigal Son (in which, as here, two estranged men, against all expectation, greet each other, and feast and rejoice: cf. Luke xv. 11–32).

167–70.] Agamemnon speaks sincerely. Not only is he free from prejudice and deceit (*hollow bias-drawing*) but his utterance wholly and perfectly expresses his being (*with most divine integrity*): i.e. he is no more 'in two minds' than is the Deity. Cf. the observations of Aquinas: 'It is

Hect. I thank thee, most imperious Agamemnon.

Agam. [*To Troilus.*] My well-fam'd lord of Troy, no less to
  you.

Menel. Let me confirm my princely brother's greeting:
  You brace of warlike brothers, welcome hither.

Hect. Who must we answer?

Æneas.   The noble Menelaus.   175

Hect. O, you my lord: by Mars his gauntlet, thanks!
  Mock not that I affect th'untraded oath:
  Your quondam wife swears still by Venus' glove.
  She's well, but bade me not commend her to you.

Menel. Name her not now, sir; she's a deadly theme.   180

Hect. O, pardon: I offend.

Nest. I have, thou gallant Trojan, seen thee oft,
  Labouring for destiny, make cruel way
  Through ranks of Greekish youth; and I have seen thee,
  As hot as Perseus, spur thy Phrygian steed,   185
  Despising many forfeits and subduements,
  When thou hast hung thy advanced sword i'th'air,
  Not letting it decline on the declin'd,

---

172 S.D.] *Rowe; not in Q,F.*   176. thanks!] *Pope* (thanks.)*; thankes, Q,F*
(thanks).   177. that . . . oath] *F; thy affect, the vntraded earth Q.*   186.
Despising many] *Q; And seene thee scorning F.*

---

plain that God is altogether simple,
and nowise composite' (*Summa Theologiae*, 1 a. iii. 7); and again: ' "one"
signifies . . . that which is perfect'
(*Summa Theologiae*, 3 a. lxxiii. 2).

171. *imperious*] imperial.

177. *untraded*] unfamiliar; cf. *traded
pilots* = skilled or practised navigators
(ii. ii. 65). The point of Hector's
raillery is, of course, that if you take
War and Love (the two main topics
of poetry) as matters for swearing by,
you have not only *gauntlet* and *glove*
but also *Mars* and *Venus* (who were
taken in his net by Vulcan, the proto-
type of cuckolds: cf. *Metamorphoses* iv).

178. *quondam*] Usually affected,
satirical, or ludicrous, in Shakespeare:
cf. *Ado* v. ii. 31; *LLL* v. i. 6; and
especially *H5* ii. i. 78 ('the quondam
Quickly').

180. *deadly theme*] matter for a mortal quarrel.

183. *Labouring for destiny*] doing the
work of Fate (in slaughtering Greeks).

185. *As . . . Perseus*] Perseus rode the
winged horse Pegasus.

186.] Q rightly avoids *And seen . . .*;
Nestor's speech is built in *three* (not
four) developing sections, each beginning with *I have seen*, and a subsidiary
form of the phrase is not needed.

186. *forfeits*] men already in their
death-throes (= forfeit to death).

subduements] men conquered.

187–8.] Cf. Pyrrhus with his sword
poised (*Ham.* ii. ii. 510). The posture
is statuesque; and Milton (who knew
Troilus well) may have recalled it in
Paradise Lost, vi. 316–17.

188.] Not letting fall [your sword]
on the fallen [opponent].

That I have said to some my standers-by
'Lo, Jupiter is yonder, dealing life';   190
And I have seen thee pause, and take thy breath,
When that a ring of Greeks have shrap'd thee in,
Like an Olympian wrestling. This have I seen,
But this thy countenance, still lock'd in steel,
I never saw till now. I knew thy grandsire,   195
And once fought with him: he was a soldier good;
But by great Mars, the captain of us all,
Never like thee. O, let an old man embrace thee,
And, worthy warrior, welcome to our tents.
Æneas. 'Tis the old Nestor.   200
Hect. Let me embrace thee, good old chronicle,
    That hast so long walk'd hand in hand with Time;
    Most reverend Nestor, I am glad to clasp thee.
Nest. I would my arms could match thee in contention
    As they contend with thee in courtesy.   205
Hect. I would they could.
Nest. Ha?
    By this white beard, I'd fight with thee tomorrow.
    Well, welcome, welcome: I have seen the time.
Ulyss. I wonder now how yonder city stands   210
    When we have here her base and pillar by us?
Hect. I know your favour, Lord Ulysses, well.

---

189. to some] *Q;* vnto *F.*   192. shrap'd] *Sisson;* shrupd *Q;* shut *conj. Collier;* hem'd *F.*   198. O, let] *Q;* Let *F.*   205.] *F; not in Q.*   207–8. Ha? / By] *Capell;* Ha? by *Q,F.*   208–9.] *As Q; as prose, F.*   209. time.] *Q,F;* time—*F3.*

189. *some my standers-by*] followers of mine: an archaic formula, also found in *Compl.* 148; otherwise, OED gives no example later than this. Shakespeare may have tried to give Nestor an older fashion of speech.

192. *shrap'd*] encircled, trapped: Sisson's ingenious emendation of Q's *shrupd.* OED gives no such verb with appropriate sense, but notes *shrape* (sb) = (a) snare; (b) cockpit, where birds fight.

194. *still*] continually, invariably.

195. *grandsire*] Laomedon. The fight is described by Lydgate (1.4147–97), and occurred during the return jour-

ney of Jason from securing the Golden Fleece.

201. *good old chronicle*] A phrase which Dryden remembered, when translating Ovid, *Metamorphoses* XII (Dryden, XII. 711; Ovid, XII. 540).

204–8.] Nestor's delighted pugnacity may also be Ovidian: cf. *Metamorphoses* XII. 597–9 (Dryden).

209. *I . . . time*] A phrase typical of an old man, *laudator temporis acti,* but not therefore ridiculous: admittedly, Shallow uses something like it (*2H4* III.ii. 206–14), but *Lr* v.iii. 276–7, and *Oth.* v.ii. 262–5, are much closer.

212. *favour*] looks, appearance.

Ah, sir, there's many a Greek and Trojan dead,
Since first I saw yourself and Diomed
In Ilion on your Greekish embassy.   215

Ulyss. Sir, I foretold you then what would ensue.
My prophecy is but half his journey yet;
For yonder walls that pertly front your town,
Yon towers, whose wanton tops do buss the clouds,
Must kiss their own feet.

Hect.   I must not believe you.   220
There they stand yet; and modestly I think
The fall of every Phrygian stone will cost
A drop of Grecian blood. The end crowns all;
And that old common arbitrator, Time,
Will one day end it.

Ulyss.   So to him we leave it.   225
Most gentle and most valiant Hector, welcome.
After the general, I beseech you next
To feast with me, and see me at my tent.

Achill. I shall forestall thee, Lord Ulysses, thou!
Now, Hector, I have fed mine eyes on thee;   230
I have with exact view perus'd thee, Hector,

219. Yon] *Q*; Yond *F*.   224–5. And . . . it] *As F; as prose, Q*.   229. Ulysses,
thou!] *Theobald; Vlisses thou: Q; Vlysses, thou: F*.   231–2. I . . . joint] *As
F; one line, Q*.

214–20. *Since . . . feet*] The first
embassy of Diomedes and Ulysses
occurs in both Caxton (pp. 558–62)
and in Lydgate (II. 6722–7109); but
Lydgate alone includes the walls and
towers in Ulysses' prophecy (II.
6872–4).

218. *pertly*] boldly, over-confidently
(OED 4).

219. *wanton*] (a) playful; (b) reck-
less; (c) amorous. The last sense seems
to have been suggested by *buss/kiss*;
but that is not, I think, the primary
sense here. It is rather (cf. *pertly*) the
light-hearted irresponsibility of Troy
to which Ulysses objects.

221. *modestly*] in all modesty, without exaggeration.

223. *The . . . all*] A commonplace
and a proverb (*Finis coronat opus*); cf.

Tilley E 116.

224–5. *And . . . end it*] Cf. Tilley
T 336.

229–45.] According to Caxton
(p. 602), Achilles invited Hector unarmed to his tent, expressed his
delight at his presence, and looked
forward to the encounter in which he
would kill him (see note to ll. 241–5,
below).

229. *forestall . . . thou*] The second
person singular (*thee/thou*) is directly
insulting and contemptuous (cf.
Abbott §232–3). Achilles has already
been annoyed by the ceremony that
attends the duel of Ajax and Hector
(IV. v. 73 ff.), and he now wishes to
assert himself as second in place after
Agamemnon.

And quoted joint by joint.
Hect.   Is this Achilles?
Achill. I am Achilles.
Hect. Stand fair, I pray thee; let me look on thee.
Achill. Behold thy fill.
Hect.   Nay, I have done already.   235
Achill. Thou art too brief: I will the second time,
      As I would buy thee, view thee limb by limb.
Hect. O, like a book of sport thou'lt read me o'er;
      But there's more in me than thou understand'st.
      Why dost thou so oppress me with thine eye?   240
Achill. Tell me, you heavens, in which part of his body

234. pray thee] *Q;* prythee *F.*

232. *quoted*] scrutinized, taken note of.

joint] limb (cf. *LLL* v.i.120: 'his great limb or joint'); but it is hard (in view of Achilles' subsequent remarks) not to see an allusion to the process of butchering, or cutting up the quarry: cf. also l. 238.

234. *fair*] unobstructed, open to view (OED 16, 17).

235.] Had Hector known of Ulysses' project, he could hardly have played his part better: his laconic dismissal of Achilles is in beautiful contrast to Achilles' stately self-regard.

236–7.] Achilles returns the implied rebuke by faulting Hector's judgement (*Thou art too brief*), but only on the grounds that he himself is, by contrast, taking due care in the purchase of a beast—whether horse or bullock hardly matters.

238. *book of sport*] handbook for huntsmen and fowlers. Hector turns naturally to the idea of battle as the pursuit of game: cf. v.vi.30, and Troilus and Æneas at 1.i.113, 115. (It may be worth remarking that Homer, in describing Achilles' pursuit of Hector about the walls of Troy, compares it to a hound chasing a fawn in the hills: *Iliad* xxii.)

240. *oppress*] molest. However, there may be a play upon a further and

highly specialized sense. In heraldry, to *oppress* is to place an 'ordinary' (e.g. a fess, a pale, a bend) over or across an animal: hence, Hector continues to see himself as a beast of the chase, or an heraldic beast (cf. Æneas' remark at iv.i.21), but one now 'oppressed' (or 'debruised') by the weight of Achilles' eye, which passes across him. (Professor Jenkins points out the ominous effect of this line.)

241–5.] Knight suggested that Shakespeare had removed this incident, with brilliant effect, from the point in *Iliad* xxii at which Achilles surveys Hector before killing him. If it were so, then Shakespeare must have read the passage in one of the Latin versions of the *Iliad*, for Chapman had not yet translated Book xxii. But it is more likely that the source was Caxton (pp. 602–3): Hector, during the truce in which Cressida was sent to her father, visited Achilles in the Greek camp and Achilles expressed pleasure at seeing him, but yet more pleasure at the prospect of killing him. (Shakespeare has handled his chronology freely: he keeps the visit of Hector and the exchange of Cressida together, but ignores the fact that, according to Caxton, Patroclus is already dead and the Sagittary recently slain by Diomedes.)

Shall I destroy him—whether there, or there, or there—
That I may give the local wound a name,
And make distinct the very breach whereout
Hector's great spirit flew? Answer me, heavens! 245

Hect. It would discredit the blest gods, proud man,
To answer such a question. Stand again.
Think'st thou to catch my life so pleasantly
As to prenominate in nice conjecture
Where thou wilt hit me dead?

Achill.   I tell thee yea. 250

Hect. Wert thou an oracle to tell me so,
I'd not believe thee. Henceforth guard thee well;
For I'll not kill thee there, nor there, nor there;
But, by the forge that stithied Mars his helm,
I'll kill thee everywhere, yea, o'er and o'er. 255
You wisest Grecians, pardon me this brag:
His insolence draws folly from my lips;
But I'll endeavour deeds to match these words,
Or may I never—

Ajax.   Do not chafe thee, cousin;
And you, Achilles, let these threats alone 260
Till accident or purpose bring you to't.
You may have every day enough of Hector,

251. an] *Q;* the *F.*   262. have] *Q; not in F.*

246–7.] In *Iliad* xxii, the *blest gods* do indeed debate whether or not Achilles shall catch and slay Hector.
248. *pleasantly*] simply, straightforwardly. But Hector may also be glancing at the sense 'mockingly', which would agree with the sarcasm of l. 249.
249. *nice*] precise.
254. *stithied*] forged, wrought by smith-work. (A *stithy* is properly an anvil, but—apparently in dialect use —developed as an alternative to *smithy.*) Q's *stichied* is simple misreading of Secretary hand (*c*: *t*).
254. *Mars his*] See Abbott §217.
256. *brag*] boast. Hector's immediate apology, and qualification of

his remarks, suggests that he remembered the proverb (which Pistol also knew) 'Brag is a good dog, but Holdfast is a better' (Tilley B 589). In Caxton (p. 603) Hector challenges Achilles to single combat, but neither boasts nor needs to apologize.
259. *chafe thee*] anger yourself. (Notice that Ajax uses the familiar *thee* to his cousin Hector, but *you* to Achilles.) The word *chafe* may come directly from Caxton: after Hector made his challenge, 'Achilles achauffid hym sore with these wordes' (p. 603).
261.] Until you meet Hector in the field, whether by accident, or because you have at last been moved to seek him.

If you have stomach. The general state, I fear,
Can scarce entreat you to be odd with him.

Hect. I pray you, let us see you in the field;   265
We have had pelting wars since you refus'd
The Grecians' cause.

Achill.   Dost thou entreat me, Hector?
Tomorrow do I meet thee, fell as death;
Tonight, all friends.

Hect.   Thy hand upon that match.

Agam. First, all you peers of Greece, go to my tent;   270
There in the full convive we; afterwards,
As Hector's leisure and your bounties shall
Concur together, severally entreat him.
Beat loud the taborins, let the trumpets blow,
That this great soldier may his welcome know.   275
        [*Flourish, and drums.*] *Exeunt [all but Troilus and Ulysses].*

Troil. My Lord Ulysses, tell me I beseech you,
In what place of the field doth Calchas keep?

Ulyss. At Menelaus' tent, most princely Troilus.
There Diomed doth feast with him tonight,
Who neither looks upon the heaven nor earth,   280

266–7. We . . . cause] *As F; one line,* Q.   268–9. Tomorrow . . . friends] *As F; one line,* Q.   271. we] Q; you *F.*   273–4. him . . . taborins,] *F;* him / To taste your bounties Q.   275 S.D. *Flourish, and drums.*] *This edn; Flourish / Capell.*   *Exeunt* [. . . *Ulysses.*]] *Malone (subst.); Exeunt /* Q,F.   280. upon . . . nor] Q; on heaven nor on *F.*

263. *stomach*] inclination; (perhaps) courage.
general state] Agamemnon's military staff.
264. *Can . . . you*] can hardly succeed in persuading you by their entreaties.
be odd] be in contention; fight.
266. *pelting*] trivial, insignificant.
271. *in the full*] to the height: that is, Agamemnon's will be a complete and genial feast, with nothing wanting.
convive] feast. Apparently a rare word (either as noun or verb) and probably taken directly from Latin. The noun occurs in Caxton: *Golden Legend* (cf. OED citation).
273. *Concur*] fall (conveniently)

together.
severally] separately, individually.
entreat] Either (a) treat (as at IV.iv.111), or (b) entertain (though that usage appears, from OED, to be Northern or Scottish).
274. *taborins*] OED insists that a taborin is a small drum, with one stick, used for accompanying a pipe; but it is clear from *Ant.* IV.viii.37 that (as here) the taborin was a larger, military drum. Shakespeare seems effectually to have identified it with *tabor*, which was the early generic name for drum.
277. *keep*] dwell; cf. II.i.120–1: 'I will keep where there is wit stirring'.

But gives all gaze and bent of amorous view
    On the fair Cressid.
Troil. Shall I, sweet lord, be bound to you so much,
    After we part from Agamemnon's tent,
    To bring me thither?
Ulyss.   You shall command me, sir.   285
    As gentle tell me, of what honour was
    This Cressida in Troy? Had she no lover there
    That wails her absence?
Troil. O sir, to such as boasting show their scars
    A mock is due. Will you walk on, my lord?   290
    She was belov'd, she lov'd; she is, and doth;
    But still sweet love is food for fortune's tooth.   *Exeunt.*

283. you] *Q;* thee *F.*   286. As] *F;* But *Q.*   291. she lov'd] *F;* my Lord *Q.*

286. *As gentle*] as courteously.   291. *she lov'd*] *Q*'s *my lord* is pro-
honour] repute, credit.   bably caught from the line above.
                                            292.] Cf. Tilley T 420.

[ACT V]

[SCENE I]

Enter ACHILLES *and* PATROCLUS.

Achill. I'll heat his blood with Greekish wine tonight,
Which with my scimitar I'll cool tomorrow.
Patroclus, let us feast him to the height.

Enter THERSITES.

Patro. Here comes Thersites.
Achill.   How now, thou core of envy!
Thou crusty botch of nature, what's the news?   5
Thers. Why, thou picture of what thou seemest, and

ACT V

Scene I

4. core] *F;* curre *Q.*   5. botch] *Theobald¹;* batch *Q,F.*   6–7.] *As F;*
Why . . . Idoll, / Of . . . thee *Q.*   6. seemest] *Q;* seem'st *F.*

2. *scimitar*] (QF Cemitar). Shakespeare twice uses the word elsewhere:
the warriors concerned are Morocco
(*Mer. V.* II.i.24) and Aaron (*Tit.*
IV.ii.91): in each case, the oriental or
exotic nature of the weapon's owner
is emphasized. In the present instance,
however, he may have remembered
Spenser, *Faerie Queene,* V.v.3, where
the spelling (Cemitare) is almost the
same as here.

4. *core*] F is almost certainly right:
core looks forward to *botch* (l. 5); on
the other hand, Q's *cur* might allude
to 'dog in the manger' (with respect
to *envy*), and Professor Brooks draws
my attention to the etymological
connection of dogs and cynics (who
might be thought envious). Thersites
is elsewhere called dog, or cur (II.i.7,

42, 87; this scene l. 28).

5. *crusty botch*] botch = boil, sore,
tumour (cf. *core* l. 4); crusty = (a)
scabby, (b) short-tempered; *crusty* may
have suggested *batch* (= number of
loaves at a baking) to Q's scribe or
compositor, in which case F let the
error pass. But a *crusty batch* would be
a desirable thing, and Achilles is
paying no compliments.

6. *picture . . . seemest*] picture = reali-
zation, symbol (OED 5b): hence,
Achilles manifests indeed the qualities
that his appearance would suggest—
as Deighton put it, 'fool in looks, fool
in reality'. But *picture* could also mean
'statue, effigy', and Thersites glances
at that sense also: Achilles is a mere
hewn block, as befits an *idol of idiot-
worshippers.*

idol of idiot-worshippers, here's a letter for thee.
Achill. From whence, fragment?
Thers. Why, thou full dish of fool, from Troy.
Patro. Who keeps the tent now?   10
Thers. The surgeon's box or the patient's wound.
Patro. Well said, adversity! And what needs these tricks?
Thers. Prithee be silent, boy, I profit not by thy talk;
    thou art said to be Achilles' male varlet.
Patro. Male varlet, you rogue? What's that?   15
Thers. Why, his masculine whore. Now the rotten dis-
    eases of the south, the guts-griping, ruptures,
    catarrhs, loads o' gravel i'th'back, lethargies, cold
    palsies, raw eyes, dirt-rotten livers, whissing lungs,

---

12. said, adversity!] *Capell;* said aduersity, *Q,F.*   needs these] *Kittredge;* needs
this *Q;* need these *F.*   13–14.] *As F;* Prithee ... talke, / Thou ... varlot. *Q.*
13. boy] *F;* box *Q.*   14. said] *Q;* thought *F.*   17. the guts-griping, rup-
tures] *Capell;* the guts-griping ruptures. *Q;* guts-griping Ruptures *F;* Guts-
griping, Ruptures *F4.*   18. catarrhs] *F; not in Q.*   i'th'] *F;* in the *Q.*
19–22. raw ... tetter] *Q;* and the like *F.*   19. whissing] *Q;* wheezing *Pope.*

---

9. *fool*] Quibbling on 'a kinde of
clouted creame called a foole or a
trifle in English' (OED, citing Florio,
Mantiglia).

10. *tent*] the roll of gauze (or other
medicated material) used for searching, cleaning, or keeping open a
wound (as at II.ii.16). Thersites
makes the obvious quibble (l. 11).

12. *adversity*] 'contrariety' (Steevens).

what . . . tricks?] Certainly *tricks*
(pl.), because Thersites has been
several times perverse (and hence
these, as in F); but *needs* is quite
acceptable: the impersonal verb
sometimes drops, and sometimes
retains, the final *-s:* cf. Abbott §297.

13. *boy*] An insult; cf. *AYL* I.i.52,
and *Cor.* v.vi.101–16. Q's *box* is
caused, partly by proximity to *box* in
l. 11, partly by the general similarity
of *x* and *y* in Secretary hand.

14. *said*] F's *thought* may perhaps be
justified: *said* occurs in l. 12.

male varlet] There is no certainty
that Thersites' imputation, glossed at
l. 16, is correct: the point was debated

by scholars (see *Variorum* note) but
the case was not proven; and for most
readers, Achilles and Patroclus were a
commonplace example of close friends.
Varlet seems not to have a homosexual
sense elsewhere; but that it carried
sexual overtones of some kind is
apparent from the OED quotation
from Skelton (*Works,* II.429/1 [attri-
buted]: 'The helper of harlettes, /
And captayne of verlettes') and Tusser
(*Fiue Hundred Pointes of Good Husban-
drie,* ed. 1878, p. 144: 'Such Lords ill
example doth giue, where verlets and
drabs so may liue').

17. *the south*] southern Europe, but
especially Italy (and Naples above
all) whence syphilis came into
England: cf. *Neapolitan bone-ache*
(II.iii.19–20). Thersites' catalogue is
not however concerned merely with
sexual diseases.

guts-griping] colic.

18. *loads . . . back*] stone in the
kidney.

lethargies] apoplexies.

18–19. *cold palsies*] paralysis.

19. *dirt-rotten livers*] (probably)

bladders full of impostume, sciaticas, lime-kilns   20
i'th'palm, incurable bone-ache, and the rivelled
fee-simple of the tetter, take and take again such
preposterous discoveries!

Patro. Why, thou damnable box of envy, thou, what
means thou to curse thus?   25

Thers. Do I curse thee?

Patro. Why, no, you ruinous butt, you whoreson
indistinguishable cur, no.

Thers. No? Why art thou then exasperate, thou idle
immaterial skein of sleave silk, thou green sarse-   30

---

25. means] *Q;* mean'st *F.*   29. No?] *F;* No *Q.*   30. sleave] *Q* (sleiue);
Sley'd *F.*

---

chronic hepatitis, often caused by
syphilis.

whissing lungs] asthma; *whissing =*
whistling, wheezing.

20. *bladders . . . impostume*] cystitis.

20–1. *lime-kilns i'th'palm*] psoriasis.

21. *rivelled*] wrinkled.

22. *fee-simple*] absolute or entire
possession (of estate).

tetter] any pustular eruption (e.g.
impetigo, ringworm).

take . . . again] plague twice over.

23. *preposterous discoveries*] manifesta-
tions of perversions (OED *discovery*
2c). For *preposterous*, cf. Dante,
Purgatorio, xxvi. 28–9 ('chè per lo
mezzo del cammino acceso / venia
gente col viso incontro a questa'),
where the poet discovers that the
penitents of natural and unnatural
lust run round their cornice in contrary directions.

24. *envy, thou*] For *thou*, cf. Abbott
§232–3.

25. *means*] F reads *mean'st* and may
be right; but I suspect that inversion
of subject and verb in the 2nd person
singular could produce omission or
elision of the final *-t* in any verb, and
not merely in those of which the root
ended with *-d* or *-t* (cf. Abbott §337):
one may see the alternative—the
assimilation of the *-t* to the pronoun—
often enough. Here, the pronoun is

iterated (*Why, thou . . . thou . . . thou
to curse . . .*) and assimilation is hardly
possible.

27. *ruinous butt*] damaged cask,
'leaky tub' (Professor Brooks's suggestion).

28. *indistinguishable cur*] mongrel dog
of no recognized kind or function.
Editors (and OED, a little doubtfully)
gloss *indistinguishable* as 'misshapen,
shapeless'; but the point is surely that
Thersites has (as a metaphorical dog)
no particular use but to snarl: cf.
Mac. iii. i. 94–8, where the 'valu'd
file / Distinguishes [each variety] /
According to the gift which boun-
teous Nature / Hath in him clos'd'.

29–33. *idle . . . nature*] 'Emblematically expressive of flexibility, com-
pliance, and mean officiousness'
(Johnson). Furthermore, all the
objects listed are either effeminate or
dependent.

30. *sleave silk*] 'silk thread capable
of being separated into smaller fila-
ments for use in embroidery etc.'
(OED).

sarsenet] fine silk cloth, used for
dress or lining. The term is used
contemptuously by Hotspur (= fitting a mercer's wife) in *1H4* iii. i. 245
('such sarsenet surety for thy oaths').
Linthicum (*Costume in the Drama of
Shakespeare*, pp. 121–2) notes that

net flap for a sore eye, thou tassel of a prodigal's
purse, thou: ah, how the poor world is pestered
with such water-flies, diminutives of nature!

Patro. Out, gall!

Thers. Finch egg!   35

Achill. My sweet Patroclus, I am thwarted quite
From my great purpose in tomorrow's battle.
Here is a letter from Queen Hecuba,
A token from her daughter, my fair love,
Both taxing me, and gaging me to keep   40
An oath that I have sworn. I will not break it.
Fall, Greeks: fail, fame: honour, or go or stay;
My major vow lies here, this I'll obey.
Come, come, Thersites, help to trim my tent;
This night in banqueting must all be spent.   45
Away, Patroclus!   *Exit [with Patroclus].*

Thers. With too much blood and too little brain these

---

32. purse, thou:] *Johnson* (purse, thou.)*;* purse-thou *Q;* purse thou: *F;* purse
thou? *F3;* Purse, thou? *F4.*   45–6.] *As F; one line, Q.*   46 S.D.] *Kittredge;
Exit | F; not in Q.*

---

sarsenet was made in taffeta weave,
both 'single and double' quality, and
thinks that the present passage implies
'contemptuous slightness'.

31. *tassel*] pendant decoration. OED
notes of *tossell* (which is the spelling
of Q) that it may be connected with
toss (vb), but does not explain how.

33. *waterflies*] Cf. *Ham.* v.ii.82–3:
'Dost know this waterfly?' (spoken of
Osric). In the present passage, the
image was obviously suggested by
sleave silk (l. 30), since that was the
material from which an angler made
his flies; cf. Donne, 'The Bait',
ll. 23–4: 'Or curious traitors, sleave-
silk flies / Bewitch poor fishes
wand'ring eyes'.

34. *gall*] bitter railer: perhaps with
a glance at oak-gall (a small excres-
cence upon natural growth).

35. *Finch egg*] Thersites' purpose is
abuse, and *egg* was apparently a
contemptuous term (cf. *Cor.* IV.iv.21,
Mac. IV.ii.82, *LLL* v.i.67), and

finches are small (though not the
smallest) birds.

40. *Both*] i.e. Hecuba and Polyxena
are both taxing Achilles.

taxing] charging, instructing.

gaging] binding by a formal promise. Either an aphetic form of *engage*,
or an independent derivative from Fr.
gager.

41. *oath*] Achilles promised Hecuba,
if he might win Polyxena, to make the
Greeks raise the siege and retire
(Caxton, p. 622); but he first saw
Polyxena on the anniversary of the
death of Hector, and not as early as
Shakespeare suggests.

44. *trim*] clean, put in order; cf.
Shr. IV.i.41, *Tp.* v.i.293.

47–9.] Thersites defines an impossibility. Achilles and Patroclus
may run mad from excess of *blood*
(= passion, 'humour'); but that they
should go mad from excess of *brain* is
as likely as that he should turn curer
of madmen.

two may run mad, but if with too much brain and
too little blood they do, I'll be a curer of madmen.
Here's Agamemnon: an honest fellow enough,   50
and one that loves quails, but he has not so much
brain as ear-wax; and the goodly transformation
of Jupiter there, his brother the bull, the primitive
statue and oblique memorial of cuckolds, a
thrifty shoeing-horn in a chain at his brother's   55
leg: to what form but that he is, should wit
larded with malice and malice forced with wit
turn him to? To an ass were nothing: he is both
ass and ox; to an ox were nothing: he is both ox

53. brother] *F;* be *Q.*   55. chain] *Q;* chaine, hanging *F.*   brother's] *F;*
bare *Q.*   57. forced] *F;* faced *Q;* farced *Pope.*

50. *honest*] A complex term (as
Empson showed: *The Structure of
Complex Words*, 2nd edn, 1952,
pp. 185–249) and OED does not
suggest the full range of meaning.
Here, *honest fellow* = man of the
world, broad-minded fellow, not
above a little excess in drinking and
wenching.

51. *quails*] whores. The quail
(*Coturnix coturnix*) was formerly thought
to be very amorous: it is a small,
plump, shy bird, and good eating (cf.
Exodus xvi. 12–13).

52–3. *the goodly . . . bull*] Jupiter
took the form of a white bull to seduce
Europa, the daughter of Agenor
(*Metamorphoses*, II. *ad fin.*). It is worth
noting that Ovid makes much play
with the appearance of the bull's
horns, saying how small they were,
but beautiful, polished and jewel-like,
and how Europa held one of them
when the bull swam away with her.

53. *brother the*] Q's *be the* is perhaps
a misreading of MS *bᵣ the*. It is just
possible that *brother bull* was intended
(with *brother* misdivided), and that the
text was miscorrected in F.

53–4. *the primitive . . . cuckolds*] As
bull, Menelaus is a representation of
the archetype of all horned beasts
(= cuckolds; cf. *Wiv.* v.v. 3–4:

'Remember, Jove, thou wast a bull
for thy Europa; love set on thy
horns'). But, as Baldwin pointed out
(*Variorum* note), Jove, in seducing
Europa, seduced a maid, cuckolded
nobody, and was not himself cuckolded: hence, the bull is an *oblique*
memorial—a glancing allusion.

55. *thrifty*] proper (sarcastically
spoken).

shoeing-horn] 'not-to-be-shaken off
hanger-on of his brother, like a
shoeing-horn hanging to a man's leg
by a chain.' (Deighton, who also
cited Dekker, *Match me in London*:
'You are held but as shoeing-horns to
wait on great lords' heels.')

brother's] Q's *bare* must again be a
misreading of MS (as at l. 53) and
here the copy is fairly certain to have
contained an abbreviation (e.g. *broˢ*).
Q's MS seems to have given the
compositor some trouble hereabouts:
cf. *faced* (for *forced/farced*: l. 57); *day*
(for *dog*: l. 60).

56–8. *to . . . to?*] i.e. Menelaus is
already beyond the reach of satirical
exaggeration; cf. Thersites' curse
upon Patroclus at II. iii. 28: '*thyself
upon thyself!*'

57. *forced*] stuffed; (like *larded*, a
culinary metaphor).

59. *ass and ox*] fool and cuckold.

and ass. To be a dog, a mule, a cat, a fitchook, a   60
toad, a lizard, an owl, a puttock, or a herring
without a roe, I would not care; but to be
Menelaus I would conspire against destiny. Ask
me not what I would be, if I were not Thersites;
for I care not to be the louse of a lazar, so I were   65
not Menelaus.—Hey-day! sprites and fires!

Enter HECTOR, [TROILUS,] AJAX, AGAMEMNON, ULYSSES,
NESTOR, [MENELAUS,] *and* DIOMEDES, *with lights.*

Agam. We go wrong, we go wrong.
Ajax.   No, yonder 'tis:
There, where we see the lights.
Hect.   I trouble you.
Ajax. No, not a whit.

Enter ACHILLES.

Ulyss.   Here comes himself to guide you.
Achill. Welcome, brave Hector; welcome, princes all.   70
Agam. So now, fair prince of Troy, I bid good night.

---

60. dog] F; day Q.   fitchook] Q; Fitchew F.   64. not what] F; what
Q.   66. Hey-day! sprites] Q; Hoy-day, spirits F.   66 S.D. TROILUS,]
Theobald; not in Q,F.   MENELAUS] *Capell; not in* Q,F.   67–8. No . . . lights]
As Capell; one line, Q,F.   68. lights] Q; light F.   69 S.D.] F; *not in* Q.
71. good] F; God Q.

---

60. *mule*] Q's *moyle* = dialect
variant.

fitchook] West Midland dialect
variant of *fitchew* (Q *Fichooke*) = pole-
cat (supposed to be very libidinous,
and notorious for its foul stench);
cf. *Lr* IV.vi.124, *Oth.* IV.i.144.

61. *puttock*] kite (probably the Red
Kite, *Milvus milvus*, i.e. a scavenging
bird, well-known in sixteenth-century
London, and feeding upon carrion,
as opposed to the nobler Falconidae,
which hunt game). For the significance of the kite in Shakespeare, see
E. A. Armstrong, *Shakespeare's Imagination* (rev. edn 1963).

61–2. *herring . . . roe*] shotten herring,

spent fish; cf. *1H4* II.iv.127, and
Tilley H 447.

62. *I . . . care*] I wouldn't mind; (so
at l. 65: *I care not*).

62–3. *to be . . . destiny*] (The threat
of) being Menelaus would be enough
to make me conspire against my fate.

65. *I care . . . be*] I wouldn't mind
being; cf. Abbott §356.

66. *Hey-day . . . fires*] A facetious
recognition of the approaching torches, supposed to be *ignes fatui*. Cf.
Lr III.iv: Gloucester's torch, variously
identified by the Fool and Edgar.

67.] Agamemnon seems to be a
little flown with wine.

Ajax commands the guard to tend on you.

Hect. Thanks and good night to the Greeks' general.

Menel. Good night, my lord.

Hect.   Good night, sweet Lord Menelaus.

Thers. [*Aside.*] Sweet draught! 'sweet', quoth a? Sweet   75
    sink, sweet sewer!

Achill. Good night and welcome both at once, to those
    That go or tarry.

Agam.   Good night.

                    Exeunt Agamemnon and Menelaus.

Achill. Old Nestor tarries; and you too, Diomed,
    Keep Hector company an hour or two.   80

Diom. I cannot, lord: I have important business,
    The tide whereof is now. Good night, great Hector.

Hect. Give me your hand.

Ulyss. [*Aside to Troilus.*] Follow his torch, he goes to Calchas'
    tent;

    I'll keep you company.

Troil. [*Aside to Ulysses.*]   Sweet sir, you honour me.   85

Hect. And so, good night.

                    [*Exit Diomedes; Ulysses and Troilus following.*]

Achill.   Come, come, enter my tent.

                    Exeunt [*all but Thersites*].

Thers. That same Diomed's a false-hearted rogue, a
    most unjust knave: I will no more trust him when
    he leers than I will a serpent when he hisses. He
    will spend his mouth and promise, like Brabbler   90

---

75 S.D.] *Staunton; not in Q,F.*   75. 'sweet'] *White²;* sweet *Q,F.*   77–8.] *As
Theobald;* Good night / And . . . tarry *Steevens; as prose, Q,F.*   78 S.D.] *Q
(Exeunt Agam: Menelaus); not in Q,F.*   84 S.D.] *Capell; not in Q,F.*   84–5.
Follow . . . company] *As F; as prose, Q;* Follow . . . goes / . . . company
Steevens.   85 S.D.] *Capell; not in Q,F.*   86 S.D. Exit . . . following.] *Capell
(subst.); not in Q,F.   Exeunt [. . . Thersites].] *Kittredge;* Exeunt / *Q,F.*

75. *draught*] cesspool, privy; (cf.
Matthew xv. 17); so also *sink.*

82. *tide*] full flood: i.e. time to use
one's opportunity: cf. *Caes.* iv. iii. 217.

84. *Calchas' tent*] Where Cressida
naturally lodged; cf. iv. v. 53.

88. *unjust*] perfidious, faithless.

89. *leers*] smiles (not in a pejorative
sense).

90. *spend his mouth*] be in full cry
(like a hound in pursuit).

Brabbler] hound that is always in
cry, though not on the scent; cf.
OED brabble = babble (which is the
more usual form with huntsmen).

the hound; but when he performs, astronomers foretell it, it is prodigious, there will come some change. The sun borrows of the moon when Diomed keeps his word. I will rather leave to see Hector than not to dog him; they say he keeps a   95 Trojan drab, and uses the traitor Calchas' tent. I'll after. Nothing but lechery: all incontinent varlets!   *Exit*

[SCENE II]

Enter DIOMEDES.

Diom. What, are you up here, ho? Speak.
Calch. [*Within.*] Who calls?
Diom. Diomed. Calchas, I think? Where's your daughter?
Calch. [*Within.*] She comes to you.

Enter TROILUS *and* ULYSSES [*at a distance; after them* THERSITES].

Ulyss. Stand where the torch may not discover us.   5

2 S.D.] *Hanmer; not in Q,F.*   3. your] *Q; you F.*   4 S.D. *Within*] *Hanmer; not in Q,F.*   at . . . THERSITES.] *Capell; not in Q,F.*

Scene II

2 S.D.] *Hanmer; not in Q,F.*   3. your] *Q; you F.*   4. *Within.*] *Hanmer; not in Q,F.*   S.D. *at . . .* THERSITES.] *Capell; not in Q,F.*

92. *prodigious*] ominous, portentous.

93–4. *The . . . word*] Diomedes is (always) as little to be trusted as Cressida expects a lover to be; cf. III.ii.82–7.

96. *uses*] Elliptically (= is accustomed to go to).

Scene II

4 S.D.] Since Cressida is to enter from the tent (which must be upstage centre, perhaps from behind a curtain —cf. Achilles, at III.iii.37 S.D.), she and Diomedes should play this scene as far upstage as possible. Troilus and Ulysses should be fairly well down-

stage and to one side (downstage of one of the great pillars, in the Elizabethan theatre: cf. l. 5), and Thersites is similarly placed on the other side. Shakespeare needs Thersites to provide a third, and very different, kind of comment on the wooing; and for most of the scene Thersites is not really concerned with Troilus and Ulysses. Exceptions occur at ll. 10–11, 134 and 176; but at those points he is less commentator than presenter; cf. Berowne, in *LLL* IV.iii.76–8.

5. *torch*] Where is this torch? Not, certainly, with the three spectators, nor in Diomedes' hand (or what

Enter CRESSIDA.

Troil. Cressid comes forth to him.
Diom.   How now, my charge.
Cress. Now, my sweet guardian. Hark, a word with you.
                                                          [*Whispers.*]
Troil. Yea, so familiar?
Ulyss. She will sing any man at first sight.
Thers. And any man may sing her, if he can take her   10
      clef: she's noted.
Diom. Will you remember?
Cress. Remember? Yes.
Diom. Nay, but do, then,
      And let your mind be coupled with your words.   15
Troil. What shall she remember?
Ulyss. List!
Cress. Sweet honey Greek, tempt me no more to folly.
Thers. Roguery.
Diom. Nay then—   20
Cress. I'll tell you what—
Diom. Fo, fo, come, tell a pin; you are forsworn.

6–8. How . . . familiar?] *As Q,F.;* How . . . Hark, / . . . familiar? *Capell.*
7 S.D.] *Rowe; not in Q ,F.*   10. sing] *Q;* finde *F.*   11. clef] *Q* (Cliff) *; life F.*
13. *Cress.*] *F*²; *Cal. / Q,F.*   14–15.] *As Capell; as prose, Q,F.*   16. shall] *Q ;*
should *F.*   20. then—] *Q* (then:) *;* then. *F.*   21. what—] *Q,F* (what.),
Collier.   22. come, tell] *Theobald*²; come tell *Q,F;* Come. Tell *Johnson.*   forsworn.] *Q;* a forsworne—*F.*

would he do when snatching the
sleeve?); and it seems unlikely that a
servant came to the assignation,
merely as a link-boy. Presumably one
must suppose that a cresset stood
before the tent. Was it that which
provoked Marston's pun in *Histriomastix* ('Come Cressida my Cresset
light')? (Yet Rowland had the same
pun in *The Letting of Humours Blood in
the Head-Vaine*, as early as 1600.)

9.] Ulysses remembers Cressida's
behaviour at IV.V.17–53.

11. *clef*] Q's spelling *Cliff* (= clift,
cleft) goes far to make the pun clear:
(a) *clef* (from Fr. *clef* = key) = sign
identifying the stave on which the
musical notes appear, and hence
fixing the pitch of the notes; (b) *cleft*
= female pudendum. F's *life* can
hardly be anything but a misreading
of MS.

noted] known: recognized for what
she is (i.e. of ill repute) (punning on
notes of music).

18. *folly*] whoredom.

22. *tell a pin*] = Don't trouble to tell
me of nothing. But *pin* (like *needle*, cf.
II.i.82n.) had sexual overtones: cf.
pincase in John Heywood's *The playe
called the foure PP*, ll. 242–52.

forsworn] Having been (effectually)
unfaithful already, Cressida can
hardly stand upon her honour.

Cress. In faith, I cannot: what would you have me do?
Thers. A juggling trick: to be secretly open.
Diom. What did you swear you would bestow on me?   25
Cress. I prithee, do not hold me to mine oath;
      Bid me do anything but that, sweet Greek.
Diom. Good night.
Troil. Hold, patience!
Ulyss. How now, Trojan?   30
Cress. Diomed.
Diom. No, no, good night; I'll be your fool no more.
Troil. Thy better must.
Cress. Hark, a word in your ear.
Troil. O plague and madness!   35
Ulyss. You are mov'd, prince: let us depart, I pray,
      Lest your displeasure should enlarge itself
      To wrathful terms. This place is dangerous,
      The time right deadly: I beseech you, go.
Troil. Behold, I pray you.
Ulyss.   Nay, good my lord, go off;   40
      You flow to great distraction: come, my lord.
Troil. I prithee, stay.
Ulyss.   You have not patience; come.
Troil. I pray you, stay: by hell and all hell's torments,
      I will not speak a word.
Diom.   And so, good night.
Cress. Nay, but you part in anger.
Troil.   Doth that grieve thee?   45
      O wither'd truth!
Ulyss.   How now, my lord?

27. do] *Q;* doe not *F.*   34. a] *Q;* one *F.*   36. pray] *Q;* pray you *F.*
40. Nay] *F;* Now *Q.*   41. distraction] *F;* distruction *Q;* destruction *Malone.*
43. all hell's] *Q;* hell *F.*   45–6.] *As Capell; as prose,Q,F.*   46. How now,
my] *Q;* Why, how now *F.*

23. *I cannot*] i.e. I cannot keep what-ever compact was agreed between us (referring back to *remember* at l. 12).
24. *juggling trick*] deception, feat of (almost impossible) skill.
      secretly open] (a) sexually accessible; (b) (at the literal level) privately public (or some such impossibility).

32. *fool*] gull, dupe.
41. *You . . . distraction*] 'Your heart is so full that it will overflow and vent itself in madness' (Schmidt).
      distraction] mental and emotional disorder; Q's *destruction* misses the point, that Troilus' rising passion is like a tide making, or a river in spate.

Troil.   By Jove,
  I will be patient.
Cress. Guardian! Why, Greek!
Diom.   Fo, fo, adieu, you palter.
Cress. In faith I do not. Come hither once again.
Ulysses. You shake, my lord, at something; will you go?   50
  You will break out.
Troil.   She strokes his cheek.
Ulyss.   Come, come.
Troil. Nay, stay: by Jove, I will not speak a word.
  There is between my will and all offences
  A guard of patience: stay a little while.
Thers. How the devil Luxury, with his fat rump and   55
  potato finger, tickles these together! Fry, lechery,
  fry.
Diom. But will you then?
Cress. In faith I will, la; never trust me else.
Diom. Give me some token for the surety of it.   60
Cress. I'll fetch you one.   *Exit.*
Ulyss. You have sworn patience.
Troil.   Fear me not, my lord;
  I will not be myself, nor have cognition
  Of what I feel: I am all patience.

Enter CRESSIDA.

Thers. Now the pledge: now, now, now!   65

48. adieu] *F ; not in Q.*   50–1. You . . . out] *As F2; as prose, Q,F.*   56.
these] *F ; not in Q.*   58. But] *F ; not in Q.*   59. la] *Theobald;* lo *Q,F;* goe
F2; lord *Collier.*   62. my] *Q ;* sweete *F.*

48. *palter*] shuffle, equivocate.

55. *Luxury*] = lechery. It is not clear
why the personification of this deadly
sin should have a *fat rump* (but perhaps cf. Pompey in *Meas.*, who had
one also: II.i.214–15).

56. *potato finger*] Potatoes (like other
unfamiliar foods) were thought of as
aphrodisiacs: cf. *Wiv.* v.v.18–19:
'Let the sky rain potatoes'. (A similar
assumption concerning passion-fruit
upset the digestion of the Eighth
Army in Italy, in 1943.)

Fry] burn with strong passion (OED
4c, 4d): a normal usage in the late
sixteenth century and without any
ludicrous overtones.

59. *la*] Emphasizing an asseveration.

63. *I . . . myself*] 'I will suppress my
true feelings.' But significantly, at the
moment of witnessing the duplicity
(and hence the dual nature, the two
persons) of Cressida, Troilus denies
his own individual identity.

65.] Thersites' responses in this

Cress. Here, Diomed, keep this sleeve.

Troil. O beauty, where is thy faith?

Ulyss.   My lord!

Troil. I will be patient; outwardly I will.

Cress. You look upon that sleeve; behold it well.

 He lov'd me—O false wench!—Give't me again!   70

           [*Takes the sleeve.*]

Diom. Whose was't?

Cress. It is no matter, now I ha't again.

 I will not meet with you tomorrow night;

 I prithee, Diomed, visit me no more.

Thers. Now she sharpens: well said, whetstone.   75

Diom. I shall have it.

Cress.   What, this?

Diom.   Ay, that.

Cress. O all you gods! O, pretty, pretty pledge!

 Thy master now lies thinking on his bed

 Of thee and me, and sighs, and takes my glove,

 And gives memorial dainty kisses to it,   80

 As I kiss thee—Nay, do not snatch it from me:

        [*Diomedes snatches the sleeve.*]

 He that takes that doth take my heart withal.

Diom. I had your heart before: this follows it.

68.] *F; not in Q*.   69. *Cress.*] *F; Troy: | Q*.   70 S.D.] *NCS; not in Q,F*. 72. ha't] *Q; haue't F*.   78. on] *Q; in F*.   80–1. And . . . thee] *As F; one line, Q*.   81–2. Nay . . . He] *Theobald, conj. Thirlby; Dio: Nay . . . me. | Cres:* He *Q,F*.   81 S.D.] *Theobald*[2] *(after* thee*); not in Q,F*.   82. doth take] *Q;* rakes *F*.

---

scene are not wholly those of a detached commentator: sometimes (as here) he seems to derive a kind of sexual excitement, like that of a voyeur, from what he sees. (For the iteration, and the emphasis upon the present moment, in a time of heightened sexual awareness, cf. Iago's words, in *Oth.* I.i.88–9: 'Even now, now, very now, an old black ram / Is tupping your white ewe').

67.] Cf. Luke viii. 25 (Noble).

75. *whetstone*] Cressida, by refusal, is sharpening Diomedes' desire (which

she well knew to be the best way: cf. I.ii.287–94). But cf. further Tilley W 296: 'A whet is no let' (i.e. an edge cuts all the better for the slight delay caused by whetting), and Tilley W 298: 'He lies for the whetstone' (i.e. the whetstone was the proverbial prize for extravagant lying).

80. *memorial . . . kisses*] 'tender kisses of remembrance' (Deighton).

81–2.] Thirlby's conjecture (adopted by Theobald) is necessary if the sleeve is not to change hands with ludicrous frequency.

Troil. I did swear patience.

Cress. You shall not have it, Diomed: faith, you shall not.   85
  I'll give you something else.

Diom. I will have this. Whose was it?

Cress.   It is no matter.

Diom. Come, tell me whose it was.

Cress. 'Twas one's that lov'd me better than you will.
  But now you have it, take it.

Diom.   Whose was it?   90

Cress. By all Diana's waiting-women yond,
  And by herself, I will not tell you whose.

Diom. Tomorrow will I wear it on my helm,
  And grieve his spirit that dares not challenge it.

Troil. Wert thou the devil, and wor'st it on thy horn,   95
  It should be challeng'd.

Cress. Well, well, 'tis done, 'tis past—and yet it is not:
  I will not keep my word.

Diom.   Why then, farewell:
  Thou never shalt mock Diomed again.

Cress. You shall not go; one cannot speak a word   100
  But it straight starts you.

Diom.   I do not like this fooling.

Troil. Nor I, by Pluto, but that that likes not you
  Pleases me best.

Diom.   What, shall I come? the hour?

Cress. Ay, come: O Jove, do come: I shall be plagu'd.

Diom. Farewell till then.

84–5. patience. / *Cress.* You] *F*; patience. / You *Q*.   89. one's] *Q* (on's); one
F.   91. By] *F*; And by *Q*.   98–101. Why . . . you] *As F; as prose*, *Q*.
102–3. Nor . . . best] *As Hanmer; as prose*, *Q,F*.   102. *Troil.*] *Hanmer; Ther: /*
Q,F.   you] *Q*; me *F*.   103. What,] *Rowe*; What *Q,F*.   hour?] *Pope;*
houre—*Q*; houre. *F*.   104. do] *Q*; doe, *F*.

---

91. *Diana's waiting-women*] the stars.
In the circumstances, no oath could be
less appropriate.

94. *grieve*] afflict.

102–3.] Hanmer was surely right
in giving this speech to Troilus. It is
dramatically appropriate, since he
rejoices in his rival's discomfiture, and

it is in his style: (for other allusions to
Pluto, cf. IV.iv.125 and V.ii.152, as
well as to Charon at III.ii.9–10, and
Styx at V.iv.19). If it is to be ascribed
to Troilus, then it should be divided
as verse: Q and F set it as prose.

104. *plagu'd*] vexed, teased.

Cress.   Good night; I prithee come.   105
                                        Exit Diomedes.
    Troilus, farewell! One eye yet looks on thee,
    But with my heart the other eye doth see.
    Ah, poor our sex! this fault in us I find:
    The error of our eye directs our mind.
    What error leads must err; O, then conclude,   110
    Minds sway'd by eyes are full of turpitude.   *Exit.*
Thers. A proof of strength she could not publish more,
    Unless she said 'My mind is now turn'd whore'.
Ulyss. All's done, my lord.
Troil.   It is.
Ulyss.   Why stay we then?
Troil. To make a recordation to my soul   115
    Of every syllable that here was spoke.
    But if I tell how these two did co-act,
    Shall I not lie, in publishing a truth?
    Sith yet there is a credence in my heart,
    An esperance so obstinately strong,   120
    That doth invert th'attest of eyes and ears,
    As if those organs had deceptious functions,
    Created only to calumniate.
    Was Cressid here?
Ulyss.   I cannot conjure, Trojan.
Troil. She was not, sure.

---

105 S.D.] *Capell (Exit* Dio.)*; Exit | F (after* then)*; not in Q.*   111. Minds] *F;*
Mindes *Q.*   113. said] *Q;* say *F.*   117. co-act] *F* (coact)*; Court Q.*
121. th'attest] *Q;* that test *F.*   122. had deceptious] *F;* were deceptions *Q.*
123–4. Created . . . here] *As F;* one line, *Q.*

106–7.] Cressida's pose is emblematic, like that of King Claudius (*Ham.* I.ii.11), or of Paulina (*Wint.* v.ii.72–3).

109.] Cressida alludes to the conventional notion of blind Cupid as well as to the moral implications of the figure.

112.] She could not better manifest a forceful proof.

115. *recordation*] commemorative account.

117. *co-act*] 'act together' (rare)

(OED).

119. *credence*] act of belief.

120. *esperance*] hope. Like *credence*, a word more obviously medieval than Shakespearean: it occurs also in *Lr* IV.i.4, and in *1H4* II.iii.72, v.ii.96 (as the motto of the Percies).

121. *attest*] testimony.

122.] Q's *deceptions* is an easy minim error (from the like ending of *functions*); *were* (for *had*) may have been conscious editing by scribe or compositor.

Ulyss.   Most sure she was.   125
Troil. Why, my negation hath no taste of madness.
Ulyss. Nor mine, my lord: Cressid was here but now.
Troil. Let it not be believ'd for womanhood.
        Think, we had mothers; do not give advantage
        To stubborn critics, apt, without a theme   130
        For depravation, to square the general sex
        By Cressid's rule: rather, think this not Cressid.
Ulyss. What hath she done, prince, that can soil our mothers?
Troil. Nothing at all, unless that this were she.
Thers. Will a swagger himself out on's own eyes?   135
Troil. This she?—No, this is Diomed's Cressida.

133. soil] *F;* spoile *Q.*   135. a] *Q;* he *F.*

125.] A defective line, but the pause can be made dramatically significant.

128. *for*] out of regard for (OED 21 c).

129–32. *do not . . . rule*] Troilus sees all destructive satirists as willing enough to abuse women, even when there is no cause for it whatever; and he wants to keep from calling Cressida a whore, because to do so would be to provide the classic case for defamation of the whole sex.

130. *critics*] satirists, fault-finders.

131. *depravation*] detraction, calumny.

131–2. *to . . . rule*] Punning on *rule* = (a) general principle of conduct, (b) carpenter's square, and on *square* = (a) regulate, adjust, (b) shape, cut.

132. *rather . . . Cressid*] Troilus has reverted in effect to the thesis which he advanced in II.ii, but the proposition is now reversed. There, he argued that the keeping of Helen had good consequences, and hence that Helen herself must be of value. Here, women (and especially Cressida) are valuable, and not matter for calumny: hence, this woman, being exceptional in having no value, is therefore neither Cressida nor any other proper representative of her sex.

133–4.] The opposition of two kinds of mind can hardly be more succinctly expressed. Ulysses will not extrapolate from Cressida's action in order to condemn women in general, for that would be irrational: at the same time, one is aware that he is drawn neither to attack nor to defend women. But Troilus, since he cares more for principles than for persons, cannot help seeing a whole sex *embodied* in one woman: to see her as woman is to see all perfections potentially within her; and hence he must turn to metaphysics, and to the whole question of identity, in order to help himself.

135.] 'Will he bring himself, by sheer bluster, to deny the evidence of his eyes?' To *swagger . . . out of* = to bully (someone) out of (a state).

136–59.] A supremely difficult speech, because, although it attempts to use the language of logic and the methods of rhetoric, it is primarily (though not of course wholly) concerned to give utterance to an intolerable state of feeling, and one, moreover, which, by virtue of Troilus' single-minded dedication, is indissolubly linked with his whole moral being. It is easy to mock Troilus (as, in their different ways, both Ulysses and Thersites do), but that is to assume that he is trying to be merely

> If beauty have a soul, this is not she;
> If souls guide vows, if vows be sanctimonies,
> If sanctimony be the gods' delight,
> If there be rule in unity itself,   140
> This is not she. O madness of discourse,
> That cause sets up with and against itself!
> Bifold authority! where reason can revolt

138. be sanctimonies] *Q;* are sanctimonie *F.*   141. is] *F;* was *Q.*   142. itself!] *Capell;* it selfe, *Q;* thy selfe *F.*   143. Bifold] *Q* (By-fould)*;* By foule *F.*

rational about something which lies without him: it is less easy to mock if one tries, as he does, to body forth the unbearable consequences of having pledged one's truth to what is now known to be false. (Cf. C. Williams, *English Poetic Mind,* 1932, pp. 60–2; cited *ad loc.* by *Variorum.*)

137.] *If . . . soul*] If Beauty be embodied in mortal woman (cf. the extravagant speech of the servant, at III.i.31–2). Troilus comes very close to speaking of Cressida in terms which Aquinas reserved for God (cf. *Summa Theologiae,* 1 a.xiii.5: 'Creatures are shaped to God as to their principle: their perfections surpassingly pre-exist in Him').

138. *If . . . vows*] Troilus affirms, in effect, that it is the very principle of one's being which directs one, when one performs a vow. To believe otherwise would be to commit himself to the merely opportunist world of Ulysses.

sanctimonies] things sacred.

139. *sanctimony*] sanctity, holiness (especially of life or character).

140. *rule*] law, principle; *rule in unity* means that unity is indivisible. As Aquinas points out, '*One* signifies, not only that which is indivisible or continuous, but also that which is perfect' (*Summa Theologiae,* 3 a.lxxiii.2). Troilus' difficulty arises because, if his concept of Cressida be divided, then *he himself must be divided also* (cf. *Summa Theologiae,* 1.lxxxvii.1. *ad.* 3: 'Knower and known are one—this is universally true').

141. *madness of discourse*] i.e. not a *rejection* of discourse (= logical argument, rational proceeding) but a paradoxical statement enforced by the nature of the facts—namely, that reasoning (which includes Troilus' premisses) appears to contradict the evidence before him (which depends upon the *traded pilots* eyes and ears; cf. II.ii.64–5). Hence, one *cause* (= case, plea) divides, and is both plaintiff and defendant.

143–5.] 'Where reasoning can proceed by contradiction, without confounding itself; and confusion (sc. *loss* of distinction of two separate persons —Cressida as she is and was) can take on all the appearance of reason without contradiction.' I think that the *loss* of l. 144 is the loss of the principle of individuation (without which there could be no reasoning). As long as Cressida appears to be two (contradictory) persons in one body—for she was there, and yet she could not have done what she did—Troilus is unable to make distinctions, and yet reason seems still to operate. (It may be worth noting that a pattern of paradox and chiasmus, dealing with loss, state, and confounding of state, and concluding with the final loss of love, is also to be found in Sonnet 64, ll. 5–13: 'When I have seen the hungry ocean gain / Advantage on the kingdom of the shore, / And the firm soil win of the wat'ry main, / Increasing store with loss, and loss with store; / When I have seen such interchange of state, / Or state itself

Without perdition, and loss assume all reason
Without revolt. This is, and is not, Cressid.   145
Within my soul there doth conduce a fight
Of this strange nature, that a thing inseparate
Divides more wider than the sky and earth;
And yet the spacious breadth of this division
Admits no orifex for a point as subtle   150
As Ariachne's broken woof to enter.
Instance, O instance! strong as Pluto's gates:
Cressid is mine, tied with the bonds of heaven.
Instance, O instance! strong as heaven itself:
The bonds of heaven are slipp'd, dissolv'd, and
    loos'd;   155
And with another knot, five-finger-tied,

---

151. Ariachne's] F (*Ariachnes*); *Ariachna's* / Q (*corrected*); *Ariathna's* / Q (*uncorrected*); Ariadne's *conj.* Steevens.   156. five-finger-tied] *Pope*; fiue finger tied F; finde finger tied Q.

---

confounded to decay; / Ruin hath taught me thus to ruminate— / That Time will come and take my love away. / This thought is as a death . . .')

146. *there . . . fight*] a fight is joined. A lame gloss; but see OED's comment: 'Of uncertain meaning: ?*intr.* (for *refl.*) "conducts itself, carries itself on, goes on".'

147–51. *a thing . . . enter*] 'There is infinite distance between the two persons of Cressida (whose being admits no division), yet the two persons, so distinct, cannot be separated by the finest of points.'

147. *inseparate*] inseparable, indivisible.

150. *orifex*] (erroneous form of) orifice; perhaps originating with Marlowe (*2 Tamburlaine*, III.iv.9).

151. *Ariachne's*] (erroneous form of) *Arachne's*, but the line requires four syllables. Q (uncorrected) reads *Ariathna's* (= Ariadne's), which suggests the reason for the conflation of the names: (a) Ariadne used a clue of thread to find a way for Theseus

through the Cretan Labyrinth (*Metamorphoses* VIII); (b) Arachne wove cloth as well as Pallas could, and was, for her presumption, changed into a spider (*Metamorphoses* VI).

broken woof] In jealousy, Pallas, after the contest, tore the web that Arachne had woven.

152. *Instance*] particular example as evidence of a general proposition.

155. *bonds*] legal, or moral, ties or obligations.

dissolv'd] untied.

156. *another . . . -tied*] 'A knot tied by giving her hand to Diomed' (Johnson). Such a knot would certainly be *five-finger-tied* (counting the thumb as a finger); but *five-finger* is also the name of several common plants (creeping tormentil, oxlip, bird's-foot-trefoil), and all three have leaves which, in outline, look like a complex love-knot. J. H. Walter points out (privately) that, in Chaucer's *Parson's Tale*, lechery in its five stages demonstrates the 'hand of the devel with fyve fyngres' (ll. 852–64).

The fractions of her faith, orts of her love,
The fragments, scraps, the bits, and greasy relics
Of her o'er-eaten faith are given to Diomed.
Ulyss. May worthy Troilus be half attach'd   160
  With that which here his passion doth express?
Troil. Ay, Greek; and that shall be divulged well
  In characters as red as Mars his heart
  Inflam'd with Venus. Never did young man fancy
  With so eternal and so fix'd a soul.   165
  Hark, Greek: as much as I do Cressid love,
  So much by weight hate I her Diomed.
  That sleeve is mine that he'll bear on his helm;

---

159. faith] *Q,F;* truth *S. Walker.*   given] *Q;* bound *F.*   166. much as] *F2;*
much *Q,F.*   Cressid] *Q; Cressida F.*   168. on] *Q;* in *F.*

---

157. *fractions*] fragments, broken
pieces.

orts] broken meats, refuse; cf.
Lucr., l. 985, where Lucrece begs that
Tarquin may 'have time a beggar's
orts to crave'. Cressida was a beggar
(*Tw.N.*iii.i.56), as Robert Henryson
had made clear (*Testament of Cresseid*).

158.] Cf. *remainder viands* (ii.ii.71).

159. *o'er-eaten*] begnawed and bit-
ten.

faith] S. Walker's conjecture is possible, in view of the repetition (ll. 157,
159), but Troilus' tirade is here
heavily emphatic, moving from *faith*
to *love*, and then back to *faith* (which
is the crucial concept).

given] F's *bound* continues what is
implied by *knot* (by contrast with
bonds, l. 153); Q's *given* shifts from
knots, by way of food fragments, to
the giving of alms: i.e. Troilus has
moved from a judgement upon
Cressida's act to a judgement (and,
in effect, a curse) upon his rival. (For
the giving of alms, and the possible
associations, in Shakespeare's mind,
with the later development of Cressida's story, cf. note to *orts,* l. 157.)

160. *Troilus be*] Walker's conjecture
(*Troilus be but*) preserves strict metre;
but I should be glad to be assured

(a) that Shakespeare never allowed
himself the licence of variable stress
and pronunciation; and (b) that
Ulysses is being merely dispassionate,
and not slightly sarcastic (dwelling
emphatically on *Troilus*). Indeed,
sarcasm seems to have been perceived
by Troilus himself; notice his shift
from *sweet lord, sir, sweet sir* (iv.v.283,
285, v.i.85) to *Ay, Greek* (l. 162)—cf.
Æneas, at i.iii.245. Ulysses' *Trojan* (*I
cannot conjure, Trojan,* l. 124) is not, it
seems, offensive, but merely dry and
formal (cf. *Grecian,* iv.iv.119). It is
the word *Greek* which may be potentially ironic or insulting.

160–1.] 'Can Troilus be half as
much moved as his speech suggests?'
attach'd/With] seized (upon) by,
affected by (OED 3).

164. *fancy*] love. (The other Shakespearean character to use the verb
absolutely in this way is, unfortunately, Malvolio; cf. *Tw.N.* ii.v.25).

165.] with a soul so eternally and
constantly devoted.

168–9. *helm . . . casque*] Mere
synonyms for helmet, head armour.
Strictly considered, the *helm* was a
heavy, padded, and almost cylindrical
helmet, with one small slit for vision,
and was used for tilting.

Were it a casque compos'd by Vulcan's skill
My sword should bite it. Not the dreadful spout   170
Which shipmen do the hurricano call,
Constring'd in mass by the almighty sun,
Shall dizzy with more clamour Neptune's ear
In his descent than shall my prompted sword
Falling on Diomed.   175
Thers. He'll tickle it for his concupy.
Troil. O Cressid! O false Cressid! false, false, false!
Let all untruths stand by thy stained name,
And they'll seem glorious.
Ulyss.   O, contain yourself:
Your passion draws ears hither.   180

Enter ÆNEAS.

Æneas. I have been seeking you this hour, my lord;
Hector by this is arming him in Troy.
Ajax your guard stays to conduct you home.
Troil. Have with you, prince. My courteous lord, adieu.

172. sun] Q (sunne); Fenne F.   173–5. ear . . . Diomed] *As F*; ear . . . discent, / . . . *Diomed* / Q.

169. *casque . . . skill*] It was for *Achilles* that Vulcan (= Hephaestos) fashioned armour.

170–1.] There is no doubt that Shakespeare thought of the *hurricano* as a waterspout, and not as a violent storm: cf. *Lr* III. ii. 2–3. (OED gives only Shakespeare and Drayton for this sense.)

170. *spout*] = waterspout (OED 6).

172. *Constring'd*] drawn together, compressed. *Constringe* (< Lat. *constringere*) was perhaps introduced by Shakespeare; it was retained as a conscious Latinism, in opposition to *constrain*, the French derivative from the same Latin verb.

sun] F's *Fenne* is an obvious error (presumably misreading MS *sunne*); why F should produce a MS misreading here is far from clear.

173–5.] The collocation of the Trojan War, an ear surprised by sudden noise, and a mighty blow, is

found also in *Ham.* II. ii. 469–78.

174. *prompted*] incited, eager.

176. *tickle it*] Either (a) *it* = Diomedes' helmet; in which case Troilus is going to bludgeon his rival about the head (OED *tickle* 6 b) (i.e. Thersites is merely rephrasing in burlesque style what Troilus has phrased heroically); or (b) *it* is impersonal; in which case *tickle it* = stir things up. If that be so, Thersites is saying that Troilus will really make a go of it: that he will give Diomedes the beating of his life (and enjoy doing it). The difference between the two interpretations is largely a matter of tone. I incline to think that (b) is right.

concupy] (QF *concupie*). OED suggests that this is a variant of *concuby* (= concubine).

180. *passion*] passionate speech or outburst; cf. *MND* v. i. 303: 'Here she comes, and her passion ends the play'; Sonnet 20, l. 2.

Farewell, revolted fair! and Diomed,   185
Stand fast, and wear a castle on thy head!
Ulyss. I'll bring you to the gates.
Troil.   Accept distracted thanks.
                    Exeunt Troilus, Æneas, and Ulysses.
Thers. Would I could meet that rogue Diomed!—I
would croak like a raven: I would bode, I would
bode. Patroclus will give me anything for the   190
intelligence of this whore; the parrot will not do
more for an almond than he for a commodious
drab. Lechery, lechery, still wars and lechery!
Nothing else holds fashion. A burning devil take
them!   *Exit.*

[SCENE III]

Enter HECTOR *and* ANDROMACHE.

Androm. When was my lord so much ungently temper'd
To stop his ears against admonishment?
Unarm, unarm, and do not fight today.
Hect. You train me to offend you; get you in.

195 S.D.] *Q; not in F.*

Scene III

4. in] *Q; gone F.*

186. *castle*] OED suggests 'close-fitting helmet . . . but perhaps *fig.*', citing Nares and Holinshed (context ambiguous). The normal sense of *castle* seems better fitted to Troilus' rather hectic rhetoric (cf. ll. 170–5).

189.] Cf. Tilley R 33: 'The croaking raven bodes misfortune'.

191. *intelligence of*] information concerning.

191–3. *parrot . . . drab*] Cf. Tilley A 220. 'An almond for parrot' seems to have implied a reward for speaking (though some citations suggest a reward for tactful silence). Not merely proverbial: see Skelton, *Speke Parrot*, 9, 86, not only for the phrase, but also for the suggestion that one 'parrot' at least was lecherous.

194. *burning devil*] Flames were often enough associated with devils, and with Hell at large; but there is a peculiar appropriateness in connecting them with the sin of lechery (cf. Marlowe, *Dr Faustus*, II.i.144, *hot whore*—referring to the devil with fire-works). *Variorum* argues that *burning* alludes to the symptoms of venereal disease, but the case is perhaps not proven.

Scene III

4. *train*] draw, induce.

By all the everlasting gods, I'll go.   5
Androm. My dreams will, sure, prove ominous to the day.
Hect. No more, I say.

Enter CASSANDRA.

Cass.   Where is my brother Hector?
Androm. Here, sister, arm'd, and bloody in intent.
 Consort with me in loud and dear petition,
 Pursue we him on knees; for I have dreamt   10
 Of bloody turbulence, and this whole night
 Hath nothing been but shapes and forms of slaughter.
Cass. O, 'tis true.
Hect.   Ho! Bid my trumpet sound!
Cass. No notes of sally, for the heavens, sweet brother.
Hect. Be gone, I say: the gods have heard me swear.   15
Cass. The gods are deaf to hot and peevish vows;
 They are polluted offerings, more abhorr'd
 Than spotted livers in the sacrifice.
Androm. O, be persuaded: do not count it holy
 To hurt by being just. It is as lawful,   20
 For we would give much, to use violent thefts,
 And rob in the behalf of charity.
Cass. It is the purpose that makes strong the vow;
 But vows to every purpose must not hold:
 Unarm, sweet Hector.
Hect.   Hold you still, I say.   25
 Mine honour keeps the weather of my fate:
 Life every man holds dear, but the dear man

---

5. all] *Q; not in F.*   14. *Cass.*] *F; Cres. / Q.*   20–3. To . . . *Cass.*] *F; not in Q.*
21. give . . . use] *Rann, conj. Tyrwhitt;* count give much to as *F.*

6. *ominous to*] prophetic in respect of.
9. *dear*] ardent, zealous.
14. *sally*] sortie (both French words).
16. *peevish*] headstrong, self-willed.
18. *spotted*] tainted, polluted (and, hence, of ill-omen).
20. *just*] firm to a purpose or vow.
21. *For*] because.
 use] Almost certainly, *count* is wrongly introduced from l. 19; Tyrwhitt's conjecture *use* is a good guess

for the compositor's *as* (and a glance at Schmidt, sv (c), will show how plausible a guess it was: cf. *use mercy, use expostulation, use our utmost studies*).
23–4.] An argument to which Shakespeare frequently reverts: cf. *John* III. i. 205–8; *LLL* IV. iii. 357–8.
26. *keeps the weather*] is upwind (= at a tactical advantage): hence, is above, or superior to.
27–8.] Every man would live if he could, but the man who is truly

Holds honour far more precious-dear than life.

Enter TROILUS.

How now, young man; mean'st thou to fight today?
Androm. Cassandra, call my father to persuade.   30

Exit Cassandra.

Hect. No, faith, young Troilus; doff thy harness, youth.
I am today i'th'vein of chivalry:
Let grow thy sinews till their knots be strong
And tempt not yet the brushes of the war.
Unarm thee, go; and doubt thou not, brave boy,   35
I'll stand today for thee and me and Troy.
Troil. Brother, you have a vice of mercy in you,
Which better fits a lion than a man.
Hect. What vice is that? Good Troilus, chide me for it.
Troil. When many times the captive Grecian falls   40
Even in the fan and wind of your fair sword,
You bid them rise, and live.
Hect.   O, 'tis fair play.

28. precious-dear] *F2;* precious deere *Q;* precious, deere *F.*   29. mean'st] *F;*
meanest *Q.*   31. No, faith,] *Theobald;* No faith *Q,F.*   40. Grecian falls]
Q,F; Grecians fall *Rowe.*   42. them] *Q,F;* him *anon. conj. apud Camb.*

worthy rates honour higher than life.

29. *young man*] Hector's modes of address to Troilus (cf. *young Troilus,* l. 31; *youth,* l. 31; *brave boy,* l. 35) are meant primarily as dramatic irony, since he has not watched, as we have, the painful scene in which Troilus emotionally matured—but they may also reflect on the violence which Troilus advocates in the next few lines.

30. *father*] = father-in-law (i.e. Priam).

33. *knots*] Either (a) the points at which the sinews joined bone and muscle; or (b) the nerve ganglia (since nerve and sinew were not properly distinguished).

34. *tempt*] make trial of, assay.
brushes] hostile encounters.

37–8.] Lions were traditionally clement, because of their inherent nobility. Shakespeare's sources pointed to a specific instance of Hector's clemency as the reason for the final overthrow of the Trojans: see Lydgate, III.2122–51 (where Hector, at the request of his cousin Ajax, prevents the Trojans from burning the Greek ships); Caxton, pp. 589–90, and especially p. 590 ('This was the cause wherfore the troians lost to haue the victorye / to the whiche they myght neuer after atteyne ne come for fortune was to them contrarye').

40. *captive*] miserable, wretched (OED 4; = caitiff).

41.] Editors have wished to emend *fair,* but the line as a whole corresponds so closely to *Ham.* II.ii.469 ('But with the whiff and wind of his fell sword') that one is tempted to let well alone: swords that can be *fell* could equally be *fair,* since both attributes

Troil. Fool's play, by heaven, Hector.
Hect.   How now, how now?
Troil. For th'love of all the gods,
    Let's leave the hermit pity with our mother;   45
    And when we have our armours buckled on
    The venom'd vengeance ride upon our swords,
    Spur them to ruthful work, rein them from ruth!
Hect. Fie, savage, fie.
Troil.   Hector, then 'tis wars.
Hect. Troilus, I would not have you fight today.   50
Troil. Who should withhold me?
    Not fate, obedience, nor the hand of Mars
    Beckoning with fiery truncheon my retire;
    Not Priamus and Hecuba on knees,
    Their eyes o'er-galled with recourse of tears;   55
    Nor you, my brother, with your true sword drawn,
    Oppos'd to hinder me, should stop my way,
    But by my ruin.

Enter PRIAM *and* CASSANDRA.

Cass. Lay hold upon him, Priam, hold him fast:

45. mother] *Q ;* Mothers *F.*   53. Beckoning] *Theobald;* Beckning *Q,F.*   58.
But . . . ruin] *F; not in Q.*

derive from the swordsman, and not from the weapon. *Fair* is, besides, a conventional term of approval, for both persons and objects, throughout Malory; and for the medieval and chivalric tone of the present passage, one may note *honour* (ll. 26, 28), *harness* (l. 31), *chivalry* (l. 32), *brushes* (l. 34), and *captive* (l. 40).

45. *mother*] F's *Mothers* probably came by attraction from *gods*, *armours* and *swords*.

47. *ride*] Subjunctive.

48. *ruthful*] 'lamentable, piteous, rueful' (OED).

ruth] compassion.

49. *Hector . . . wars*] Troilus naturally wishes to fight for himself, since he seeks vengeance, and not the exercise of mercy: perhaps Shakespeare recalled the allusion in Caxton (p. 590;

cf. note to ll. 37–8 above): 'And therfore virgile sayth / Non est misericordia in bello That is to saye ther is no mercy in bataille'.

53. *truncheon*] staff held by the marshal of a formal combat (Deighton compares the *warder* of *R2* I.iii.118); *fiery* is a transferred epithet. Classically, Mars had no truncheon.

55. *o'ergalled*] made excessively sore. *recourse*] repeated flow.

58.] Editors have generally accepted the half-line as genuine, and indeed the rhythm of Troilus' climax requires it. It is odd that Q should omit it: most odd, in that the compositor who set this page (L1ᵛ) was apparently trying to make space at this point, and left white space above and below the ensuing stage direction.

He is thy crutch. Now if thou lose thy stay,   60
Thou on him leaning, and all Troy on thee,
Fall all together.
Priam.   Come, Hector, come: go back.
Thy wife hath dreamt; thy mother hath had visions;
Cassandra doth foresee; and I myself
Am, like a prophet, suddenly enrapt   65
To tell thee that this day is ominous.
Therefore, come back.
Hect.   Æneas is afield,
And I do stand engag'd to many Greeks,
Even in the faith of valour, to appear
This morning to them.
Priam.   Ay, but thou shalt not go.   70
Hect. I must not break my faith.
You know me dutiful; therefore, dear sir,
Let me not shame respect, but give me leave
To take that course, by your consent and voice,
Which you do here forbid me, royal Priam.   75
Cass. O Priam, yield not to him.
Androm.   Do not, dear father.
Hect. Andromache, I am offended with you:
Upon the love you bear me, get you in. *Exit Andromache.*
Troil. This foolish, dreaming, superstitious girl
Makes all these bodements.
Cass.   O, farewell, dear Hector.   80
Look how thou diest: look how thy eye turns pale:
Look how thy wounds do bleed at many vents;
Hark how Troy roars, how Hecuba cries out,
How poor Andromache shrills her dolours forth;

82. do] *Q;* doth *F.*

60. *stay*] support, 'object of reliance' (OED).

65. *enrapt*] caught up in prophetic excitement. The word is usually *rapt* in Shakespeare.

69. *Even . . . valour*] 'by the honour of a brave man' (Deighton).

Even] Probably monosyllabic; cf. Abbott §466.

73. *shame respect*] deny my filial duty.

81–2. *Look how . . . Look how . . .*] *Not* a formal comparison, but an exclamation merely (cf. note to I.iii.79).

84. *dolours*] Usually singular (as in F), except in *Cym.* v.iv.80; *Lr* II.iv.54 and *Meas.* I.ii.46 are both quibbles, and hence unreliable evidence.

Behold! distraction, frenzy, and amazement   85
Like witless antics one another meet,
And all cry 'Hector! Hector's dead! O, Hector!'
Troil. Away, away!
Cass. Farewell—yet soft: Hector, I take my leave;
Thou dost thyself and all our Troy deceive.   *Exit.*   90
Hect. You are amaz'd, my liege, at her exclaim.
Go in and cheer the town: we'll forth and fight,
Do deeds worth praise, and tell you them at night.
Priam. Farewell: the gods with safety stand about thee.
          [*Exeunt severally Priam and Hector.*] *Alarums.*
Troil. They are at it, hark! Proud Diomed, believe   95
I come to lose my arm, or win my sleeve.

Enter PANDARUS.

Pand. Do you hear, my lord, do you hear?
Troil. What now?
Pand. Here's a letter come from yond poor girl.
Troil. Let me read.   100
Pand. A whoreson tisick, a whoreson rascally tisick, so
          troubles me, and the foolish fortune of this girl,
          and what one thing, what another, that I shall

85. distraction] *F;* destruction *Q.*   89. yet] *Q;* yes *F.*   90 S.D.] *F; not in
Q.*   93. worth] *Q;* of *F.*   94 S.D.] *As Malone; Alarum | Q,F.*   96 S.D.
PANDARUS.] *Q,F (Pandar), Rowe.*   102. me,] *Q;* me; *F.*   103. thing, what]
Q,F; thing, and what *Rowe.*

85. *distraction*] Q's *destruction* may
simply be deduced from context:
Hector's death involves the destruction of Troy.
86. *antics*] grotesque or ludicrous
actors.
91. *exclaim*] outcry. Both rare and
obsolete: found in Caxton. Most
examples (certainly, all others in
Shakespeare) are in the plural, so that
Tannenbaum wished to read *exclaims*
here; but those plurals are used for
generalizing argument: here, Cassandra has made one outcry only before
Priam.
96.] The two clauses are in an unexpected order (= hysteron proteron).

Troilus intends to win his sleeve, or
lose his arm in the attempt. Cf. the
sequence implied at v.vi.24–5, and in
John IV.iii.8.
97–112.] See Introduction, p. 6.
99.] The letter occurs also in
Chaucer, at great length, and plainly
'no matter from the heart'; see *Troilus
and Criseyde,* v. 1590–631.
101. *tisick*] = phthisic: i.e. pul-
monary consumption. Coughs (especially the chin-cough) were usually
the disease of usurers in the Elizabethan drama; but cf. v.i. 18–19
(*catarrhs . . . whissing lungs*). For the
significance of Pandarus' diseases, see
note to v.x. 56.

leave you one o'th's days; and I have a rheum in
mine eyes, too, and such an ache in my bones that   105
unless a man were cursed I cannot tell what to
think on't. What says she there?

Troil. Words, words, mere words, no matter from the heart;
Th'effect doth operate another way.   [*Tears the letter.*]
Go, wind, to wind: there turn and change together.   110
My love with words and errors still she feeds,
But edifies another with her deeds.   *Exeunt [severally].*

[SCENE IV]

Excursions. Enter THERSITES.

Thers. Now they are clapper-clawing one another, I'll
go look on. That dissembling abominable varlet
Diomed has got that same scurvy, doting, foolish
knave's sleeve of Troy there in his helm. I would

---

104. o'th's] *Q (subst.), F;* o' these *Rowe.*   109 S.D.] *Rowe (subst.); not in Q,F.*
112. deeds] *Q;* deedes. / *Pand.* Why, but heare you? / *Troy.* Hence brother
lackie; ignomie and shame / Pursue thy life, and liue aye with thy name. *F.*
112 S.D.] *As Malone; Exeunt. / Q; A Larum. Exeunt. / F.*

Scene IV

S.D.] *As Capell; Enter Thersites : excursions. / Q; Enter Thersites in excursion. / F.*
3. foolish] *Q;* foolish yong *F.*   4. Troy there] *Q;* Troy, there *F;* Troy there,
Steevens.

104–5. *rheum . . . bones*] Both
symptoms of venereal disease: cf.
II.iii.19–20.

109.] Her words and deeds contradict one another.

110. *wind*[1]] empty words.

111. *errors*] Editors do not comment,
but the usual sense will not serve:
something like 'falsehoods, deviations
from truth' is needed.

Scene IV

1. *clapper-clawing*] handling roughly,
drubbing; cf. Epistle, l. 3 (which
probably represents a memory of the
present passage), and *Wiv.* II.iii.64.
OED admits some uncertainty about

the exact sense: its first citation is
from Nashe (characteristically).

2–9.] Thersites' language is copious
rather than vituperative: he is concerned only to demean. The method
is typical of the theatrical clown—
suspense built up, and exploited, with
each new epithet—and the effect
depends largely upon aggregation and
timing.

3. *that same*] Usually sarcastic (as
Deighton saw); cf. Franz §317.

4. *knave's . . . Troy*] = sleeve of the
[foolish] knave of Troy. The locution
was already common in Middle
English: cf. John Ball's 'Letter to the
Peasants of Essex' (reprinted in K.

fain see them meet, that that same young Trojan   5
ass, that loves the whore there, might send that
Greekish whoremasterly villain with the sleeve
back to the dissembling luxurious drab of a sleeveless errand. O'th'other side, the policy of those crafty
swearing rascals—that stale old mouse-eaten dry   10
cheese Nestor, and that same dog-fox Ulysses—is
not proved worth a blackberry. They set me up in
policy that mongrel cur Ajax, against that dog of
as bad a kind Achilles; and now is the cur Ajax
prouder than the cur Achilles, and will not arm   15
today; whereupon the Grecians begin to proclaim
barbarism, and policy grows into an ill opinion.

Enter DIOMEDES, TROILUS *following.*

Soft: here comes sleeve, and t'other.
Troil. Fly not, for shouldst thou take the river Styx
     I would swim after.

10. stale] *Q*; stole *F*.   16. begin] *Rowe³*; began *Q,F*.   17 S.D.] *Capell*
(after 18); *Enter Diomed and Troylus | F; not in Q.*   18. t'other] *Q*; th'other *F*.
19–20. Fly . . . after] *As F; as prose, Q.*

Sisam, *Fourteenth Century Verse and
Prose*, 1944, p. 161, l. 10): 'þe Kynges
sone of heuene schal paye for al'.

8. *luxurious*] lustful.

8–9. *sleeveless errand*] fruitless journey (returning, of course, without the
sleeve; cf. Tilley E 180); *of* = on.

9. *policy*] scheming.

9–10. *crafty swearing*] *crafty* is an
adjective used as an adverb (cf.
Abbott §1), and as such may sometimes be hyphenated with the word
succeeding (cf. Abbott §2, and *2H4*
Ind. 37).

11. *dog-fox*] Alluding to the traditional cunning of Ulysses (which
became deceit and intrigue in later
poets: cf. Ovid, *Metamorphoses* XIII).
Comparison with a fox is appropriate:
apart from Æsop, one may cite Tilley
F 647 ('An old fox cannot be taken by
a snare') and F 648 ('An old fox need
learn no craft').

11–12. *is not . . . blackberry*] Cf. *1H4*
II.iv.234–5: 'If reasons [quibbling on
raisins] were as plentiful as black-
berries'. Also Tilley B 442.

12. *set me up*] For the dative pronoun, cf. Abbott §220.

13–15.] Thersites' *cur* and *dog*
substantiate Nestor's opinion (I.iii.
391–2).

16–17. *to proclaim . . . opinion*] 'To
set up the authority of ignorance, to
declare that they will be governed by
policy no longer' (Johnson). The
opposition of *Greeks* and *barbarism* is
of course deliberate.

17. *policy*] formal government,
polity.

19. *take*] enter (by way of escape,
and especially to kill scent): the usual
huntsman's term to describe a beast
fleeing into running water. War and
hunting are again analogues at
I.i.115, IV.i.18–21, and V.vi.30–1.

Diom.   Thou dost miscall retire: 20
     I do not fly; but advantageous care
     Withdrew me from the odds of multitude.
     Have at thee!

Thers. Hold thy whore, Grecian! Now for thy whore, Trojan!
     Now the sleeve, now the sleeve!   25

          Enter HECTOR. [*Exeunt Diomedes and Troilus, fighting.*]

Hect. What art thou, Greek? Art thou for Hector's match?
     Art thou of blood and honour?

Thers. No, no: I am a rascal, a scurvy railing knave:
     a very filthy rogue.

Hect. I do believe thee: live.   [*Exit.*]

Thers. God-a-mercy that thou wilt believe me, but a   31
     plague break thy neck for frighting me.—What's
     become of the wenching rogues? I think they have
     swallowed one another. I would laugh at that mir-
     acle; yet in a sort lechery eats itself. I'll seek them.   35
                                        Exit.

                         [SCENE V]

                Enter DIOMEDES *and* Servant.

Diom. Go, go, my servant, take thou Troilus' horse;
     Present the fair steed to my Lady Cressid.

22–3.] *As F; one line, Q.*   24–5.] *As Q; as prose, F.*   25 S.D. *Exeunt . . .*
fighting] *Capell; not in Q,F.*   30 S.D.] *Rowe; not in Q,F.*

                              Scene v

S.D. *Servant.*] *Q ; Servants | F.*

     20. *Thou . . . retire*] 'You have mis-
taken tactical withdrawal for flight.'
     26. *Art . . . match?*] 'Are you a man
honourable enough to be matched
with Hector?'
     30.] Hector's generosity and court-
esy shape, nevertheless, the perfect
insult.
     31. *God-a-mercy*] thank you.
     32. *plague . . . neck*] Why should
Thersites imagine that plagues can
break bones?

     35. *lechery eats itself*] Either (a)
lechery destroys its pleasure in en-
compassing its end (cf. Sonnet 129),
or (b) lechery consumes the lecher
(according to the common Renaissance notion that sexual intercourse
shortened life; cf. Donne, 'Farewell to
Love', ll. 24–5).

                              Scene v

     1. *Troilus' horse*] The incident is
found in Caxton (p. 608) and Lyd-

Fellow, commend my service to her beauty;
Tell her I have chastis'd the amorous Trojan,
And am her knight by proof.

Serv.   I go, my lord.   [*Exit.*]   5

Enter AGAMEMNON.

Agam. Renew, renew! The fierce Polydamas
Hath beat down Menon; bastard Margarelon
Hath Doreus prisoner,
And stands colossus-wise, waving his beam,
Upon the pashed corses of the kings   10
Epistrophus and Cedius. Polixenes is slain;
Amphimacus and Thoas deadly hurt;
Patroclus ta'en or slain; and Palamedes

5. *Serv.*] F; *Man.* | Q.   *Exit.*] *Dyce; not in* Q,F.   S.D. *Enter* AGAMEMNON]
As F; Q (*after* proof).   6. Polydamas] Q (*Polidamas*), *Pope; Polidamus* | F·
11. Epistrophus] *Var.* '73; *Epistropus* | Q,F.   12. Thoas] *Pope; Thous* | Q,F.

gate (III.4620–41). Diomedes' tone is
meant to be chivalric (and perhaps a
little strained).

6. *Renew*] sc. the fight: attack once
more.

Polydamas] a bastard son of Priam
(in Caxton, Polidamus).

7. *Menon*] According to Caxton,
cousin to Achilles, and ultimately
slain by Hector.

Margarelon] Margareton (Caxton),
Margariton (Lydgate). Q and F agree,
but a *t : l* error would be easy.

8. *Doreus*] Dorius (Caxton); one of
four earls who accompanied Ajax
(Thelamon ayax).

9. *colossus-wise*] resembling the great
bronze Apollo at Rhodes, which is
supposed to have stood astride the
harbour entrance, and was accounted
one of the seven wonders of the world;
cf. *Caes.* I.ii. 133–4, and *1H4* v.i. 123–4.

beam] spear (strictly, the shaft), so
called in respect of its colossal size.
This use of beam is not noted, but cf.
I Samuel xvii.7 (of Goliath): 'And
the staff of his spear was like a
weaver's beam'; and *Faerie Queene*,
III.vii.40: 'All were the beame in

bignes like a mast'.

10. *pashed*] battered (cf. II.iii.204).
OED notes that the verb was very
popular *c.* 1570–1630: apparently it
was suitable for heroic contexts.

11. *Epistrophus*] In Caxton, Epistropus; he was slain by Hector, after
speaking to him 'many vilayns wordes'
(p. 599). There is, in Caxton, a second
Epistropus, who fights for the Trojans: he it was who brought the
Sagittary to Troy (p. 567).

Cedius] Brother of the (Grecian)
Epistropus, and slain by Hector in
avenging his brother's death.

Polixenes] 'hector slewe Polixenes
the noble duc that fought sore ayenst
hym' (Caxton, p. 600).

12. *Amphimacus*] 'Duc' or 'erle' who,
with Doreus, attended on Ajax.

Thoas] cousin to Achilles; King of
Tholye (Caxton), or Duke of Athens
(Lydgate). Mentioned in *Metamor-
phoses* XIII.

13. *Palamedes*] A Duke, and a major
figure in Caxton's narrative; he killed
Sarpedon and Deiphobus, succeeded
Agamemnon as leader of the Greeks,
and was at last slain by Paris.

Sore hurt and bruis'd; the dreadful Sagittary
Appals our numbers. Haste we, Diomed,   15
To reinforcement, or we perish all.

Enter NESTOR [*and* Soldiers].

Nest. Go bear Patroclus' body to Achilles,
And bid the snail-pac'd Ajax arm, for shame.
There is a thousand Hectors in the field;
Now here he fights on Galathe his horse   20
And here lacks work: anon he's there afoot,
And there they fly, or die, like scaled sculls
Before the belching whale; then is he yonder,
And there the strawy Greeks, ripe for his edge,
Fall down before him like a mower's swath.   25
Here, there, and everywhere, he leaves and takes,
Dexterity so obeying appetite
That what he will he does, and does so much
That proof is call'd impossibility.

Enter ULYSSES.

Ulyss. O, courage, courage, princes: great Achilles   30
Is arming, weeping, cursing, vowing vengeance:

16 S.D.] *This edn; Enter Nestor* | *Q,F.*   21. here] *This edn; there Q,F.*
22. scaled] *F;* scaling *Q.*   sculls] *Q,F;* schools *anon conj. apud Camb.;* shoals
Pope.   24. strawy] *Q;* straying *F.*   25. a] *Q;* the *F.*   28. will] *Q;* will,
F; wills *conj. Capell.*

14. *Sagittary*] A centaur, noted as an
archer, and subsequently slain by
Diomedes. Caxton justifies the epithet
'dreadful', referring to 'the horrour of
the sagittarye' (p. 600).

16 S.D.] Somebody is needed here
to obey Nestor's commands.

20. *Galathe*] Known to both Caxton
and Lydgate: said to have been killed
under Hector (Caxton, p. 584), and
yet alive, to be taken by Achilles and
recaptured by the Trojans, after the
death of Polixenes (p. 600).

21. *here*] The emendation is neces-
sary: the pattern goes *here*|*here*:*there*|
there:*yonder*|*there*—summed up as *Here,
there, and everywhere*. *There* was pro-

bably caught up from the following
line: cf. *scaling*—for *scaled*—affected
by *belching* below.

22. *scaled sculls*] schools of fish;
scull is an older form of *school*, and
could be applied to almost any flock,
herd, or shoal of creatures.

23.] A libel on whales, which do
not belch but vent, and which consume only the smallest of marine
crustaceae—creatures which, nevertheless, do swim in shoals.

25.] Cf. *3H6* v. vii. 3–4.
swath] 'the quantity falling at one
sweep of the scythe' (OED 3).

26. *leaves and takes*] kills or spares at
inclination (cf. *Cor.* II. ii. 107–8).

Patroclus' wounds have rous'd his drowsy blood,
Together with his mangled Myrmidons
That noseless, handless, hack'd and chipp'd,
    come to him,
Crying on Hector. Ajax hath lost a friend,   35
And foams at mouth, and he is arm'd and at it,
Roaring for Troilus, who hath done today
Mad and fantastic execution,
Engaging and redeeming of himself
With such a careless force and forceless care   40
As if that lust, in very spite of cunning,
Bade him win all.

Enter AJAX.

Ajax. Troilus! thou coward Troilus!   *Exit.*
Diom.   Ay, there, there!   *Exit.*

41–2.] *As Rowe³; one line, Q,F.*   41. lust] *Q; luck F.*   42 S.D.–43. *Enter*
AJAX / *Ajax.* Troilus!] *F (subst.); Enter Aiax. Troylus / Q.*   43–4. there! . . .
together] *as NCS; there? / Nest . . . together. Exit / Q,F (subst.).*

32. *blood*] Less figurative (= temper, disposition) than literal: Achilles
has been sick (cf. II.iii.178ff.). (The
word *blood* is so complex, and its
senses so nicely balanced at this date
between physical and metaphorical,
that paraphrase is difficult.)

34.] Hector has been so dextrous
that he could maim or disfigure as he
would, rather than kill or wound as
he might. Each wound among the
Myrmidons is *a scar to scorn* (cf.
I.i.111).

noseless] The nose was frequently an
object of contemptuous and malevo-
lent attack: cf. *Oth.* IV.i.140–1 ('I see
that nose of yours, but not that dog I
shall throw't to'). Shakespeare may
have remembered that King Thoas
(l. 12 above) lost his nose in fighting
with Hector (Lydgate, III.3015–16).

35. *Crying on*] complaining of.

39. *Engaging and redeeming*] as if
drawing up and then cancelling or
paying off a bond (i.e. for his life);
engaging also = fighting at close
quarters.

40.] 'So effortless in attack, and so
unruffled in defence'. Despite Tatlock's suggestion, that *forceless* = reck-
less (because *no force* = never mind),
it seems clear that the two phrases
must correspond to the two verbs in
l. 39.

41–2.] 'As if his own desire for
conquest, despite any question of skill
in arms, were enough to ensure his
victory.' F's *luck* (Q *lust*) seems weak;
it is Troilus' passion for revenge (as
Ulysses had seen; and cf. v.ii), and
not mere chance, which is wholly
controlling him now.

43, 47 S.D.] Exits at this point are
difficult to determine. Agamemnon
and Ulysses have to leave; Diomedes,
who has been silent for thirty-eight
lines, may have a motive for pursuing
Troilus, but it is not wholly clear what
it may be—he has just defeated him,
and yet he wishes to 'correct' him a
few moments after this (v.vi.3).
Nestor seems to be a detached observer (l. 44), and hence, perhaps, is
unlikely to remove briskly, as Ajax

Nest. So, so, we draw together.

Enter ACHILLES.

Achill.   Where is this Hector?
Come, come, thou boy-queller, show thy face;   45
Know what it is to meet Achilles angry.
Hector! where's Hector? I will none but Hector. *Exeunt.*

[SCENE VI]

Enter AJAX.

Ajax. Troilus! thou coward Troilus! show thy head.

Enter DIOMEDES.

Diom. Troilus, I say! Where's Troilus?
Ajax.   What wouldst thou?
Diom. I would correct him.
Ajax. Were I the general, thou shouldst have my office
Ere that correction. Troilus, I say! What, Troilus!   5

Enter TROILUS.

Troil. O traitor Diomed! Turn thy false face, thou traitor,

47 S.D.] *Capell; Exit* | *Q,F.*

Scene VI

S.D.] *F; as speech-heading at 1, Q.*   1 S.D.] *F (Diomed); as speech-heading at 2,
Q.*

does. Achilles is plainly on reconnaissance. I have given an *Exit* where it seems unavoidable—especially to Diomedes, who sounds as excited as Ajax—and assume that the remnant goes off at l. 47, following Achilles.

44. *So . . . together*] Nestor means that the Greeks are in some measure co-operating (even though their motive is merely personal revenge, and not obedience to command).

45. *boy-queller*] murderer of boys. Apparently *hapax legomenon*, but *man-queller* was the formal term for homicide from the thirteenth century until

the seventeenth century (cf. *quell: Mac.* i.vii.73).

46. *Achilles angry*] Did Shakespeare remember the beginning of the *Iliad*? (But see Caxton, p. 637, where 'Achilles quoke for yre' on hearing of the slaughter of his Myrmidons by Troilus, in the eighteenth battle.)

Scene VI

3. *correct*] chastise (so also *correction* in l. 5); the usual sense in Shakespeare.

6.] To call a knight 'Traitor' compelled him to retaliate. Malory makes

And pay the life thou ow'st me for my horse.
Diom. Ha, art thou there?
Ajax. I'll fight with him alone: stand, Diomed.
Diom. He is my prize. I will not look upon.   10
Troil. Come, both you cogging Greeks: have at you both!
                    Exit Troilus [, *with Ajax and Diomedes, fighting*].

Enter HECTOR.

Hect. Yea, Troilus? O, well fought, my youngest brother!

Enter ACHILLES.

Achill. Now do I see thee—Ha! have at thee, Hector!
                                        [*They fight.*]
Hect. Pause, if thou wilt.
Achill. I do disdain thy courtesy, proud Trojan.   15
        Be happy that my arms are out of use:
        My rest and negligence befriends thee now,
        But thou anon shalt hear of me again;
        Till when, go seek thy fortune.   *Exit.*
Hect.   Fare thee well.

7. the] *Capell;* thy *Q,F.*   ow'st] *Capell;* owest *Q,F.*   11 S.D. *Exit . . .
fighting*] *This edn; Exeunt fighting | Rowe; Exit Troylus | F; not in Q.   Enter
HECTOR] F; not in Q.*   12 S.D.] *F; as speech-heading at 13, Q.*   13. thee—
Ha! have] *Q* (thee ha, haue); thee; ha! have *Camb.;* thee; haue *F.*   S.D.]
After Rowe (*Fight*); *dropping his sword | Capell; not in Q,F.*

it clear: 'Sir, now muste you deffende you lyke a knyght, othir ellis ye be shamed for ever, for now ye be called uppon treson, hit ys tyme for you to styrre!' (*Works,* ed. E. Vinaver, 1954, p. 855).

7. *the*] QF *thy* is caught from l. 6.

10. *look upon*] be a mere spectator; cf. *Wint.* v.iii. 100.

11. *cogging*] cheating, deceitful (especially with dice or cards). Hence, *Greeks* carries much of its sense of 'frauds' or 'confidence tricksters'. Juvenal (*Satires,* III) is informative: 'Ingenium velox, audacia perdita, sermo | Promptus . . . Grammaticus, rhetor, geometres, pictor, aliptes, |

Augur, schoenobates, medicus, magus; omnia novit | Graeculus esuriens, in coelum iusseris, ibit.' (ll. 73–4, 76–8). See also T. J. B. Spencer, *Fair Greece, Sad Relic* (1954), pp. 32–40.

13 S.D.] Unless the scene be mere slapstick (and I do not think it is) some fighting is necessary: the audience expected, and seems usually to have got, prolonged bouts. There is no need for Achilles to drop his sword (as Capell suggested): he is merely 'fat, and scant of breath', and Hector is behaving towards him with the same generous courtesy that he showed to Ajax.

I would have been much more a fresher man,   20
Had I expected thee.

Enter TROILUS.

How now, my brother?
Troil. Ajax hath ta'en Æneas: shall it be?
No! by the flame of yonder glorious heaven,
He shall not carry him! I'll be ta'en too
Or bring him off. Fate, hear me what I say: 25
I reck not, though thou end my life today.   *Exit.*

Enter One *in [sumptuous] armour.*

Hect. Stand, stand, thou Greek; thou art a goodly mark.
No? wilt thou not? I like thy armour well:
I'll frush it and unlock the rivets all
But I'll be master of it. Wilt thou not, beast, abide?   30
                                           [*Exit Greek.*]
Why then, fly on; I'll hunt thee for thy hide.   *Exit.*

21 S.D.] *As Camb.; after* brother, *Q,F.*   26. reck] *Pope;* wreake *Q,F.*   thou]
F; I Q.   26 S.D. *Enter . . . armour] Malone; Enter one in armour | Q,F.*   30.
not, beast,] *F4;* not beast *Q,F.*   30 S.D.] *After NCS (after* of it)*; not in Q,F.*
31 S.D.] *Q,F; Exeunt | Malone.*

20. *much . . . fresher*] For the transposed article, cf. Abbott §422; for the double comparative, §11.

24. *carry*] vanquish, conquer; cf. *All's W.* III.vii.19.

24–5. *I'll . . . off*] For the unexpected order of these alternatives, see note to v.iii.96.

25. *bring him off*] rescue him.

26. *thou*] It is more reasonable for Troilus to defy Fate (as in F) than merely to inform it (as in Q).

26 S.D. *sumptuous armour*] Lydgate and Caxton both make it clear how *rich* the armour was—a point not wholly plain from Shakespeare's text

(Lydgate, III.5332–43; Caxton, p. 613).

29. *frush*] beat violently (like an armourer or a smith); Caxton, p. 595 (Hector, attacking Achilles): 'he all to frusshid and brake his helme'.

30. *But*] Cf. Abbott §126.

abide] Not, apparently, a technical term from hunting, despite the context.

31. *hide*] i.e. the armour. Hector, contrary to his thesis in II.ii, is now dealing with 'outsides' only—with appearance, and not with intrinsic value. His comment at v.viii.2 therefore becomes an epitaph upon himself.

[SCENE VII]

Enter ACHILLES, *with* Myrmidons.

Achill. Come here about me, you my Myrmidons;
Mark what I say. Attend me where I wheel,
Strike not a stroke, but keep yourselves in breath;
And when I have the bloody Hector found,
Empale him with your weapons round about;   5
In fellest manner execute your arms.
Follow me, sirs, and my proceedings eye:
It is decreed Hector the great must die.   *Exeunt.*

Enter MENELAUS *and* PARIS, [*fighting;*] *then* THERSITES.

Thers. The cuckold and the cuckold-maker are at it.
Now, bull! Now, dog! 'Loo, Paris, 'loo!—Now,   10
my double-horned Spartan! 'Loo, Paris, 'loo! The
bull has the game: ware horns, ho!
                          Exeunt Paris and Menelaus.

Scene VII

1. *Achill.* Come] *F; Come Q.*   2. say.] *Johnson; say, Q; say; F; say,—Capell.*
6. arms] *Q; arme F.*   8. *Exeunt] Pope; Exit | Q,F.*   S.D. *Enter ...*
THERSITES.] *As Malone; Enter Thersites, Menelaus, and Paris | Q,F (subst.).*
10. dog! . . . 'loo!] *Rowe (subst.); dogge lowe, Paris lowe, Q; dogge, lowe; Paris*
lowe; *F.*   11. double-horned Spartan] *conj. Kellner;* double hen'd spartan *Q;*
double hen'd sparrow *F.*   12 S.D. *Exeunt] Hanmer; Exit | Q,F.*

1–8.] The procedure proposed here
by Achilles is that which (in both
Caxton and Lydgate) he employs in
killing Troilus. The fussy repetitions
in this speech may derive from Lydgate's account, which Shakespeare
follows fairly closely. Cowden Clarke
thought the language as flat and
stilted as that of *1H6* (see *Variorum*
note).

2. *wheel*] move in an arc (*not*, in this
context, to move a whole line of
troops as upon a pivot). The word
appears to have developed several
new senses as a military term,
c. 1579–1600.

5. *Empale*] surround or close in (as

with stakes).

6. *execute your arms*] Either (a)
manage your weapons (cf. *execution* at
I.iii.210), or (b) carry out this operation (in which case, *arms* = fighting,
warfare: cf. *2H4* IV.ii.118).

7. *proceedings*] actions; perhaps,
'advances'.

10–12.] Thersites sees the combat
as a bull-baiting.

10. *'Loo*] cry of encouragement to
dogs or hounds.

11. *double-horned Spartan*] Q's *double-*
henned is wrong—Menelaus has no
hens; but he has *horns* twice over, as
both bull and cuckold.

Enter MARGARELON.

Marg. Turn, slave, and fight.
Thers. What are thou?
Marg. A bastard son of Priam's.   15
Thers. I am a bastard, too: I love bastards. I am
　　bastard begot, bastard instructed, bastard in
　　mind, bastard in valour, in everything illegitimate.
　　One bear will not bite another, and wherefore
　　should one bastard? Take heed: the quarrel's most   20
　　ominous to us—if the son of a whore fight for a
　　whore, he tempts judgement. Farewell, bastard.   [*Exit.*]
Marg. The devil take thee, coward.   *Exit.*

[SCENE VIII]

Enter HECTOR.

Hect. Most putrefied core, so fair without,
　　Thy goodly armour thus hath cost thy life.
　　Now is my day's work done: I'll take my breath.
　　Rest, sword; thou hast thy fill of blood and death.
　　　　　　　　　　　　　　　　　　　　　　　 [*Disarms.*]

Enter ACHILLES *and* Myrmidons.

Achill. Look, Hector, how the sun begins to set,   5

12 S.D. *Enter* MARGARELON.] *Capell; Enter Bastard | Q,F.*   16–17. am bastard]
Q; am a Bastard *F.*   22 S.D.] *Capell; not in Q,F.*   23 S.D.] *Q; Exeunt | F.*

Scene VIII

3. take my] *Q;* take good *F.*   4 S.D. *Disarms.*] *Kittredge; not in Q,F.*
S.D. *and*] *Q; and his | F.*

16–17. *I am bastard begot*] I follow
Q. Since every phrase elsewhere in
Thersites' list omits the article, it
should be omitted here.
　19. *One . . . another*] Theobald
referred to Juvenal, *Satires*, xv.164
('saevis inter se convenit ursis'; cited
in *Variorum*). But cf. also *Ado* iii.ii.69–
70.

Scene VIII

1. *putrefied core*] It is sometimes suggested that the Greek was syphilitic,
but what evidence supports it? The
source is more likely to be Matthew
xxiii.27 ('Ye are like unto whited
sepulchres, which indeed appear
beautiful outward, but are within
full of dead men's bones, and of all
uncleanness'). The *symbolic* function
of the dead Greek is not in doubt.
　core] Perhaps half punning on *corse*
(= corpse).

How ugly night comes breathing at his heels;
Even with the vail and dark'ning of the sun
To close the day up, Hector's life is done.
Hect. I am unarm'd: forego this vantage, Greek.
Achill. Strike, fellows, strike: this is the man I seek.   10
                                        [*Hector falls.*]
So, Ilion, fall thou next! Come, Troy, sink down!
Here lies thy heart, thy sinews, and thy bone.
On, Myrmidons, and cry you all amain
'Achilles hath the mighty Hector slain'.   *Retreat.*
Hark: a retire upon our Grecian part.   15
Myrm. The Trojan trumpets sound the like, my lord.
Achill. The dragon wing of night o'er-spreads the earth
And, stickler-like, the armies separates.
My half-supp'd sword, that frankly would have fed,
Pleas'd with this dainty bait, thus goes to bed.   20
Come: tie his body to my horse's tail;
Along the field I will the Trojan trail.   *Exeunt. Retreat.*

6–7. heels; . . . sun] *Rowe (subst.); heeles | . . . darkning . . . Sunne, Q;
heeles, | . . . darking . . . Sunne. F.*   10 S.D.] *Capell; not in Q,F.*   11. thou
next! Come] *Q; thou: now F; thou next. Now Pope.*   13. and cry] *Q; cry F.*
15. retire] *Q; retreat F.*   16. Trojan trumpets] *F; Troyans trumpet Q.*
sound] *Q; sounds F.*   18. separates.] *Q; separates F.*   20. bait] *Q; bed
F.*   22 S.D.] *NCS (subst.); Exeunt: | Q; Exeunt. | Sound Retreat. Shout. | F.*

7. *vail*] setting. It is notable that
almost all senses of the verb imply
that something is lowered (or doffed:
e.g. a sail, a hat) in token of respect or
of submission.

13. *amain*] aloud, with full voice.

16.] How many trumpets or Trojans there may be, an editor must
choose for himself.

17.] Cf. *MND* iii.ii.379, and *Cym.*
ii.ii.48. Shakespeare is perhaps con-
flating two passages in Ovid: (a)
Medea's journey in the dragon-drawn
chariot (*Metamorphoses* vii); (b) the
horses of the night from *Amores*,
i.xiii.40 (cited by Marlowe in *Dr
Faustus*, v ii.145: 'O lente lente
currite noctis equi'; and alluded to in
Dido, ll. 25–7). Nosworthy (*Cym.*,
Arden edn) suggests a connection
with *Hero and Leander*, ll. 107–8, but

the dragons of that poem belong to
the Moon. Classical scholarship seems
to know of no connection between
dragons and night.

18. *stickler-like*] like a moderator or
umpire, 'to see fair play, and to part
the combatants when they have
fought enough' (OED); cf. Æneas and
Diomedes, at iv.v.88–118.

19. *frankly*] freely, fully.

20. *bait*] light meal, or refreshment
between meals. Shakespeare uses *bait*
elsewhere only in the primary modern
sense (= food to lure) but that is no
good reason for emending to *bit* (F2).

thus . . . bed] is thus sheathed.

21–2.] Caxton and Lydgate both
record this detail (although referring
it to the death of Troilus), and both
reproach Achilles for so barbarous a
deed.

[SCENE IX]

Enter AGAMEMNON, AJAX, MENELAUS, NESTOR, DIOMEDES,
and the Rest, *marching. Shouts within.*

Agam. Hark, hark: what shout is that?
Nest. Peace, drums.　　　　　　　　　　　[*Drums cease.*]
Soldiers. [*Within.*] Achilles! Achilles! Hector's slain! Achilles!
Diom. The bruit is, Hector's slain, and by Achilles.
Ajax. If it be so, yet bragless let it be:　　　　　　　　5
　　Great Hector was as good a man as he.
Agam. March patiently along. Let one be sent
　　To pray Achilles see us at our tent.
　　If in his death the gods have us befriended,
　　Great Troy is ours, and our sharp wars are ended.　　10
　　　　　　　　　　　　　　　　　　　Exeunt.

[SCENE X]

Enter ÆNEAS, PARIS, ANTENOR, *and* DEIPHOBUS.

Æneas. Stand, ho! yet are we masters of the field.
　　Never go home: here starve we out the night.

Enter TROILUS.

Troil. Hector is slain.
All.　　　　　　　　Hector? The gods forbid.

Scene IX

S.D. *Shouts within.*] *Capell; not in* Q,F.　　1. shout is that?] *F;* is this? *Q.*
2 S.D.] *This edn; not in* Q,F.　　3. *Soldiers* [*Within.*]] *Q; Sold. | F.*　　slain!
Achilles!] *Pope²; slaine, Achilles. | F;* slaine *Achilles. | Q.*　　6. as . . . man]
Q; a man as good *F.*

Scene X

2. Never] *F; Troy.* Neuer *Q.*　　2 S.D.] *As F; after* 1, *Q.*　　3. *Troil.* Hector]
F; Hector | Q.　　Hector?] *F; Hector! | Q.*

Scene IX

S.D. *marching*] i.e. with drums to
give the step (something very difficult
to keep, in a long file, without some
form of aural assistance).

4. *bruit*] report, rumour.

5. *bragless*] without vain boasting.

7. *patiently*] quietly; 'calmly, tran-
quilly' (Schmidt). OED does not
notice this sense.

7–8. *Let . . . tent*] Evidently Agamemnon has learned nothing in the
course of the play: he is still without
effective authority.

Scene X

2.] I am not wholly convinced that
Q reads wrongly here, in giving l. 2
to Troilus, since his point at ll. 15–21
is precisely that the Trojans must
'never go home' because of the news
they will bear. (However, Troilus
changes his mind almost at once.)

starve we out] 'let us endure in

Troil. He's dead, and at the murderer's horse's tail
　　　In beastly sort dragg'd through the shameful field.   5
　　　Frown on, you heavens: effect your rage with speed;
　　　Sit, gods, upon your thrones, and smile at Troy.
　　　I say at once let your brief plagues be mercy,
　　　And linger not our sure destructions on.
Æneas. My lord, you do discomfort all the host.   10
Troil. You understand me not that tell me so.
　　　I do not speak of flight, of fear, of death,
　　　But dare all imminence that gods and men
　　　Address their dangers in. Hector is gone.
　　　Who shall tell Priam so, or Hecuba?   15
　　　Let him that will a screech-owl aye be call'd
　　　Go into Troy, and say there 'Hector's dead'.
　　　There is a word will Priam turn to stone,
　　　Make wells and Niobes of the maids and wives,
　　　Cold statues of the youth, and, in a word,   20
　　　Scare Troy out of itself. But march away.
　　　Hector is dead: there is no more to say.—
　　　Stay yet: you vile abominable tents,
　　　Thus proudly pight upon our Phrygian plains,

6. on, you] *F4;* on you *Q,F.*   7. smile at Troy.] *Q,F;* smite all Troy *Hanmer;* smite all Troy! *Dyce;* smite at Troy, *Warburton.*   12. fear, of] *F;* feare of *Q.*   17. into] *Q;* in to *F.*   there] *F;* their *Q.*   20. Cold] *Q* (Could); Coole *F.*   21–2. But . . . dead] *F; not in Q.*   23. yet: you] *F;* yet you *Q.*   vile] *F;* proud *Q.*   24. pight] *F;* pitcht *Q.*

perishing cold' (OED *starve* 5 b; but possibly 'let us keep watch as the night withers away'.

　5. *beastly sort*] brutal manner (Caxton terms it *vylonnye*).

　9. *linger . . . on*] Do not protract our inevitable destruction. Cf. *H5* II. Chorus. 31: ('Linger your patience on') and *2H4* I. ii. 238 ('lingers it out'), where the same pattern (verb-object-adverb) occurs.

　10. *discomfort*] dismay, discourage.

　13. *imminence*] impending danger. A rare word, both as abstraction and (as here) implied concrete. No earlier occurrence noted.

　14. *Address*] prepare; (perhaps) direct.

　19. *Niobes*] Alluding to the story of Niobe, wife of Amphion (*Metamorphoses* VI), who was punished for blasphemy by the death of all her children (and the consequent suicide of her husband), and who was converted by grief to a weeping figure of stone; cf. *Ham.* I. ii. 149.

　23. *vile*] Q's *proud* was picked up from l. 24.

　24. *pight*] Old form of p. part. of *pitch*. Shakespeare uses this form nowhere else, and *pitched* only of battles. Caxton uses *pight* in a passage following upon the deaths of Ajax and Paris: it occurs four pages after the death of Troilus (which Shakespeare certainly read: cf. note to v. viii. 21–2),

Let Titan rise as early as he dare,   25
I'll through and through you! and thou great-siz'd
    coward,
No space of earth shall sunder our two hates:
I'll haunt thee like a wicked conscience still,
That mouldeth goblins swift as frenzy's thoughts.
Strike a free march to Troy! With comfort go: 30
Hope of revenge shall hide our inward woe.

Exeunt [all but Troilus].

Enter PANDARUS.

Pand. But hear you, hear you!
Troil. Hence, broker-lackey! Ignomy and shame

26. and thou] *Q,F;* And, thou *Collier;* and thou, *Pope.*   29. frenzy's] *Q*
(frienzes), *F* (frensies), *Pope;* frenzy *Capell.*   30. march to Troy!] *F* (march to
Troy,); march, to Troy *Q.*   31 S.D. *Exeunt . . . Troilus.] Exeunt* Æneas *and*
Trojans *Malone; not in Q,F.   Enter* PANDARUS.] *Q,F; As* Troilus *is going out,*
enter, from the other side, Pandarus. *Malone.*   33. broker-lackey] *Dyce;* broker,
lacky *Q,F (subst.);* brothel, lacky *F3;* brothel-lacquy *Theobald.*   ignomy and]
F (subst.); ignomyny, *Q.*

and the context emphasizes the grief
and final despair of the Trojans: 'The
next nyght folowyng Agamenon
made the ooste to aproche ner to the
cyte And there pyght her tentes And
the troians kepte the wallys day and
nyght / Than had the troians no more
esperance ne hope of theyr lyues /
whan they sawe that alle the sones of
kynge pryant were dede And ther is no
tonge that can expresse the lamenta-
cions that the kynge pryant made and
his wyf and his doughters.'

25. *Titan*] Hyperion, the sun god.
It may be coincidence that Lydgate
refers to Titan, when mentioning
sunset on the day of Hector's death
('whan Titan went doun': III. 5416).

26. *great-siz'd coward*] i.e. Achilles.

27. *sunder*] 'separate by intervening
space or barrier' (OED, which thinks
this sense a rarity, and gives this as its
first example). Not found in Shakespeare after *c.* 1603.

28. *haunt*] stick to, dog, follow
closely (cf. IV.i.11 n.). Shakespeare

uses the verb both of men in pursuit
on the battlefield (e.g. *1H4* v.iii.4),
and of vexatious thoughts (e.g. *3H6*
v.vi.11, *R3* IV.i.73): here, the two
contexts coincide. The modern sense
(as applied to ghosts walking) may
also be present: cf. *goblins* in the next
line.

29. *goblins*] malicious spirits; cf.
Ham. I.iv.40 ('spirit of health or
goblin damn'd'), and Milton, *Paradise
Lost,* II.688 ('the goblin full of wrath'
= Death).

30. *free march*] Sense uncertain; but
cf. Abbott §4 ('Adjectives signifying
effect were often used to signify the
cause'), and OED sv 20b (ready,
prompt); a *free march* would therefore
take the Trojans briskly back to the
city.

33. *broker-lackey*] pander. It seems
best to follow Dyce, and to combine
the terms, in order to emphasize the
contempt latent in each.

ignomy and shame] Professor T. W.
Craik points out (privately) that this

Pursue thy life, and live aye with thy name!   *Exit.*
Pand. A goodly medicine for my aching bones! O   35
world, world, world! Thus is the poor agent
despised. O traitors and bawds, how earnestly are
you set awork, and how ill requited. Why should
our endeavour be so loved and the performance so
loathed? What verse for it, what instance for it?—   40
Let me see:

Full merrily the humble-bee doth sing
Till he hath lost his honey and his sting;
And being once subdu'd in armed tail,
Sweet honey and sweet notes together fail.   45
Good traders in the flesh, set this in your painted
cloths:

34 S.D.] *Rann; Exeunt all but Pandarus.* | *Q; Exeunt* | *F.*   36. world, world,
world] *F;* world, world—*Q.*   37. traitors] *Q,F;* traders *Deighton, conj. W.J.
Craig.*   39. loved] *Q;* desir'd *F.*   40. loathed? What] *F;* loathed, what *Q.*
47. cloths] *Rowe;* cloathes *Q.F.*

phrase occurs also in *Cambises* (l. 280),
'It will redound to my ignomy and
shame.' (The form *ignomy*, for igno-
miny, is common: it occurs at
v. iii. 112+2 [F only].)

35. *aching bones*] i.e. the *Neapolitan
bone-ache* of ii. iii. 19–20 and v. iii. 105.

37. *traitors*] W. J. Craig's conjecture
is very plausible (despite the possibility of contamination from l. 46):
cf. *broker-lackey* (l. 33) and *poor agent*
(l. 36), as well as *this sailing Pandar*
(i. i. 103). Yet *traitors* is not an impossible reading: cf. the opinion of
Touchstone ('to be bawd to a bell-
wether, and to betray a she-lamb of a
twelve-month to a crooked-pated old
cuckoldy ram, out of all reasonable
match': *AYL* iii. ii. 78–81). But Pandarus is what you make him: he is a
trader from the point of view of
Troilus, a traitor from that of Cressida.

40. *instance*] proverbial or traditional saying or rhyme, to support
one's argument. Pandarus is curiously
rich in them.

42–5.] Pandarus means, apparently,
that the happiness of the pander is lost
when he is no longer effective (song
ceases with honey and sting). His
argument in ll. 37–40 says (a) that
the employer of panders comes to
detest the agent who procured for
him, and (b) that the rejected pander,
once so desirable, becomes impotent
(something which belongs with his
aching bones). He appeals, in effect, to
the sexual pattern—expectation,
attainment, revulsion—as Cressida
did (i. ii. 295–6): 'That she was never
yet that ever knew / Love got so sweet
as when desire did sue'.

46–7. *painted cloths*] painted hang-
ings for rooms (less elaborate than
tapestries), often containing moral
commonplaces as well as moral
exempla: cf. *AYL* iii. ii. 269 ('I answer
you right painted cloth') and *1H4*
iv. ii. 25 ('Lazarus in the painted
cloth'). The contemptuous tone is
most apparent in *Lucr.*, ll. 244–5.

As many as be here of Pandar's hall,
Your eyes, half out, weep out at Pandar's fall;
Or if you cannot weep, yet give some groans,   50
Though not for me, yet for your aching bones.
Brethren and sisters of the hold-door trade,
Some two months hence my will shall here be made.
It should be now, but that my fear is this:
Some galled goose of Winchester would hiss.   55
Till then I'll sweat and seek about for eases,
And at that time bequeath you my diseases.   *Exit.*

48. Pandar's] *Rowe; Pandars | Q;* Panders *F;* Panders' *Kittredge.*   51. your]
F; my *Q.*   57 S.D.] *Rowe; Exeunt | F; not in Q.*

48. *of . . . hall*] i.e. members of the
guild of panders.

49. *eyes, half out*] eyes affected by
venereal disease.

51.] Cf. note to l. 35.

52.] Bawds and panders (and *not*
prostitutes lounging at doors, as
Partridge suggests: *Shakespeare's
Bawdy,* rev. edn, 1955, p. 217); cf.
Oth. IV.ii.27–30, 91–5, and *Per.*
IV.vi.118, 164–5.

53. *Some . . . hence*] i.e. by Shrove
Tuesday, reckoning from Twelfth
Night. (See Introduction, pp. 21–2.)
here] We can only guess where
Pandarus was speaking this line.

55. *galled . . . Winchester*] an infected
prostitute from the Southwark stews,
who is offended (by Pandarus). A
Winchester goose was both a prostitute and a sore from venereal infection: the two were quite likely to go
together. The brothels of Southwark
stood on land under the jurisdiction
of the bishops of Winchester. (Cf.
1H6 I.iii.53.)

56. *sweat*] The 'sweating tub' was
the usual treatment for venereal
diseases (cf. *powdering-tub of infamy,
H5* II.i.75).
eases] 'means of relieving pain or
discomfort' (OED 10).

57. *bequeath . . . diseases*] Rather
'wish my diseases upon you' than
'transmit my diseases to you'. There
is no natural reason why a pander
should become infected by his trade;
but Pandarus is a kind of surrogate for
Cressida (who, according to tradition,
became a leprous beggar), and he
bears symbolic diseases with him.
Further, the heirs of Pandarus are
hard to identify. No normal audience
would be composed of *brethren and
sisters of the hold-door trade* (and it is
difficult to imagine one which was):
one must therefore posit an audience
which would find amusing such
scurrilous abuse; and, to that extent,
Alexander's theory of performance at
an Inn of Court is very plausible.

APPENDIX I

DISTURBANCES IN SHEET F

There is some evidence to suggest that the printing of the Quarto of *Troilus and Cressida* was disturbed during the setting of sheet F, and that the disturbance can be traced to the acquisition of fresh copy. On F2^r and F2^v, Cressida speaks the same speech twice (the distance between the speeches being roughly one quarto page: namely 35 lines of type from III.ii.60—'Will you walk in, my lord?'—to III.ii.97).[1] Sheet F is already known to have been printed with a new (third) skeleton; there is evidence that it was set by a third compositor; there is more proof-correction in sheet F than in any other sheet in Q (more indeed than has been noticed); and there is evidence from type-shortages to suggest that, whereas F1^r was set while outer E was being wrought-off, yet the remainder of sheet F was set while sheets G and H were also in type. Furthermore, while most play-quartos printed by Eld run to an exact number of complete sheets, the Quarto of *Troilus* runs to an extra half-sheet.[2] I append the details of the evidence below.

The printing of the Quarto is untidy and irregular by comparison with most Eld play-quartos of 1607–11.[3] *Troilus* is spoiled by signs of haste, by casual misprints, by a mixture of compositorial conventions, and by the irregular occurrence of crowding and space-wasting that indicate careless and inaccurate casting-off. There are fourteen instances of proof-correction in outer F, of which two (not hitherto noticed) occur on F1^r of the Malone (Bodleian) copy, and involve two proper names (III.i.131, *Deipholus, Helenes* [uncorrected]: *Deiphobus, Helenus* [corrected]): either the copy was very hard to decipher, or the compositor was unfamiliar with the names. From the evidence of running titles, the Quarto was set by formes, and one would therefore expect

1. The Quarto averages 38 lines to a page, though 36 occur on L1^v, and 37 on L2, where a compositor was trying to waste space.
2. Sheet M consists of one leaf (two pages) of type, and one blank leaf.
3. Middleton's *Trick to Catch the Old One* (1608) is agreeably set: Chapman's two *Byron* plays, printed together in one volume, are positively elegant.

accurate casting-off. In fact, apart from the white space and crowding referred to above,[1] the collation itself suggests either inaccuracy, or a change in the calculation. The collation for the first state of the Quarto is A–L⁴, M² (last leaf blank). Other Eld quartos go thus: *The Puritan* (1607) A–H⁴; *What You Will* (1607) A–H⁴; *Revenger's Tragedy* (1607/8) A–I⁴; *Devil's Charter* (1607/8) A–M⁴; *Trick to Catch the Old One* (1608) A–H⁴; *Your Five Gallants* (1608) A–I⁴; *Byron* plays (1608) A²B–R⁴.[2]

The presence of a third compositor is not difficult to demonstrate. To refine on the spellings used by Philip Williams and Alice Walker[3] by adding five others (ticle, bucle/tickle, buckle: himself &c./him-self &c.: -y/-ie: -'d [in preterite]/-d: *Cress., Vlyss.* [speech-headings]/*Cres., Vlys.*) will still not allow allocation of sheet F to Compositors A or B. Sheet F is full of anomalies ('shall bee' occurs with *Cressid*, for example): it tries to spell *Cressid(a)*, but corrects 'Cressed' to *Cressed* (F4ᵛ); it yields *Pryam* (unique in Q), and 'alasse' (for 'alas'), which is frequent elsewhere in Eld, but not found elsewhere in *Troilus*. And further, it twice uses as catchword the ensuing speech-heading with the first word of dialogue (*Hell.* Com-/*Cres*: blinde)—again, known elsewhere in Eld but not in Q *Troilus*[4]—and it signs page F4, whereas Eld quartos, like most others, sign 'one-beyond-the-middle'.

Shortage of sorts allows one to deduce something of the order of setting sheet F. On F1ʳ (III.i. 137, 141) *Queene* is set with a swash italic Q, and the implied shortage of roman Q may be traced to sheet E (E4 has four roman Qs and E4ᵛ nine).[5] On the other hand, whatever compositor set sheet F tried to spell Cressid(a) as *Cressid(a)* (with two exceptions), and was frequently driven to use italic *s* and *si* (ligature), in place of italic *ssi* (ligature). Eld had three, perhaps four, such ligatures: two (one certainly recognizable from uneven tails to the *ss*) occur on E4 (inner E): two on F4 (inner F) and one on F4ᵛ (outer F). After that, there is one on G4ᵛ (outer G), and four in sheet H (H3, H3ᵛ, and twice

1. For crowding, consider D1ʳ, E1ᵛ, K1ᵛ–K3ʳ; for white space and wasting space by turning over needlessly, paragraphing prose speeches, using VV for W, setting speech-headings in full, see F2ᵛ, L1ᵛ.

2. *Ram Alley* (1611) is exceptional and irregular—A²B⁴2B²C–I⁴—but may have been altered to include material of topical interest.

3. Williams and Walker used Cressid(a)/Cresseid(a): Hellen/Helen: shalbe, wilbe/shall be, will be: ritch/rich: els/else.

4. Speech-heading alone for catchword is found twenty-eight times.

5. I remember D. F. Mackenzie's caveat, in 'Printers of the Mind', *SB*, XXII (1969): another text might have been in type at the same time as *Troilus*. But if *Troilus* made a 'scape', Eld might well have concentrated on that, and not on the other volume.

on H4^v—that is, one on inner H, and three on outer H): the irregular ligature is that on H3^v. It is reasonable to assume, though not certain, that sheets G and H together combined to cause the shortage of italic ligatures in sheet F.[1] If so, then F stood in type from the point at which E was being distributed until sheet H was at any rate being set (and possibly until H was distributed).

It seems to me that evidence of this kind does not support Walker's theory (NCS, p. 130) that a third skeleton was required because two compositors 'could set sheets faster than two presses could print them off'. I prefer to see the disturbances in printing sheet F as an indication that at least one passage (III.ii.60–97) was inserted into the text.[2] Whatever was done was, I think, sufficient to upset Eld's calculations in casting-off, and force him to use the half-sheet of M for his text: an accident which he turned to good account, by using the other half-sheet to impose his second title-page, and the Epistle.[3]

1. The italic ligatures do not occur in sheets B, C or D, and only one is to be found in sheet E.

2. There *may* have been more—perhaps a little more in the part of Pandarus, to account for the 'conceited wooing' referred to on the second title-page—but there is no sure evidence for that.

3. I do not therefore assume that, if Eld had not acquired new copy, he would have let the first title-page stand. The King's Men, or the Stationers' Company, might well have compelled him to cancel it. But things fell out better for him as they did.

APPENDIX II

THE INNS OF COURT THEORY

In 1928–9 Peter Alexander first propounded the theory that *Troilus and Cressida* was written for performance at one of the Inns of Court.[1] It ought to be said at once that there is no direct evidence to support the theory, but that at the same time it has received cautious approval from scholars as conservative as Greg. It is unlikely that the theory would have been born at all, if *Troilus* had not made its 'scape' in Quarto in 1609, since otherwise it would have appeared first in the Folio, with only the entry to Roberts in the *Stationers' Register* to provide more information about the play than could be deduced from the text itself. But as it is, we have the Quarto in its two states, and can speculate about the implications of two different title-pages together with an anonymous epistle.[2]

The theory rests upon the following supports:

1. the implications of the Roberts entry;
2. the contradiction of the first title-page by the second;
3. the argument of the Epistle;
4. the consonance of these three with the play;

and I shall discuss them in turn.

1. It is generally agreed that the entry to Roberts was a 'blocking entry', intended by the Lord Chamberlain's Men to prevent unauthorized publication of the play. As a stay on publication it succeeded for six years, and we do not know why it failed; but, from 1600 onwards, four Shakespeare plays were published in Quarto; and 1609 was an unusual year, in that

---

1. *Library*, ix (1928–9), pp. 267–86.

2. I should add that I believe that there may be a connection between the statements of the second title-page and the Epistle, on the one hand, and the disturbance which occurred in printing sheet F of the Quarto, on the other (see Appendix I). However, there is no possibility of demonstrating such a connection with any certainty; and it would be improper to erect *that* hypothesis upon the one propounded by Peter Alexander.

it saw the printing of both *Troilus* and *Pericles*, as well as the Sonnets.[1]

The Roberts entry refers to 'the booke', which may well mean the prompt-book (though that cannot be proved); and it adds 'as yt is acted by my lo: Chamberlens Men'. No theatre is mentioned—it was not necessary: title lay with the Company—and one may regret it; but the ambiguity lies in the phrase 'as yt is acted'. All that one can properly deduce is that by 7 February 1603 *Troilus* had been acted at least once: where, or how often, cannot be known.

2. The first title-page of the Quarto corresponds to the second entry in the *Stationers' Register* (28 January 1609) which was made preparatory to publication, and which calls the play 'The history of Troylus and Cressida'. Greg thought that it had 'an authoritative appearance' (Shakespeare Quarto Facsimile). The title-page also says that the play printed is 'As it was acted by the Kings Maiesties seruants at the Globe'. The Chamberlain's Men became the King's Men after James's accession, and the Globe was their theatre: on the other hand, a publisher guessing at the facts (knowing that here was a Shakespeare play, and that Shakespeare was a member of the King's Men) might easily supply company and theatre to the title-page without further evidence.

'As it was acted' cannot be pressed to bear much significance: it tells us nothing about date (or dates) of performance.

The second title-page says nothing of company or theatre; though it may be going too far to say (as Alice Walker does in NCS) that the first title-page 'was cancelled in order to withdraw the statement' that the King's Men had played *Troilus* at the Globe. Its use of the phrase 'Famous Historie', and its reference to 'the conceited wooing of Pandarus', reads like advertisement.

3. The Epistle also advertises, and claims that the play is a witty comedy. It also says that the play has made a 'scape', since the 'grand possessors' (presumably the King's Men) would prevent Shakespeare's plays from being printed if they could; and further, that the play has never been 'stal'd with the Stage' (which may imply the *public* stage) nor 'sullied with the smoky breath of the multitude' (which almost certainly

---

1. *Hamlet* was licensed in 1602, and *Othello* in 1621. *Antony and Cleopatra* and *Pericles* were protected by blocking entries in 1608

refers to the audience of the public theatres). How far this can be pressed is again uncertain: if the Epistle belongs to 1609, it may be a poor witness to the playing of plays in 1603; but as an advertisement it is ambiguous. If it is addressed to the reading public (the 'Eternall reader') in general, then it is trying to emphasize a 'new play' which has escaped. If it is written by—shall we say, a lawyer? (and the Epistle is full of legal facetiousness)[1]—then its points may be different, for it seems to be mocking not only the King's Men but also certain grave seniors ('grand censors'). From what is known of feasts at Gray's Inn, at least, the Benchers might well fit that part. In sum, whoever wrote the Epistle was in some sense connected with lawyers: he knew that the play ought not to have been printed: he asserted that the play had never been performed *publicly*: and he praised it in terms that would please an audience that enjoyed comedy and satire. If that implies that certain lawyers had already enjoyed a performance at an Inn of Court, then the Epistle is inviting them to repeat their enjoyment; but it is also tempting a wider public simply to profit by the 'scape' the play has made. Denial of public performance tempts one to assume, but does not confirm, private performance.

All this, if it should be true, implies that the Inns of Court could afford to have a play performed (as we know they could) and perhaps that they could commission a new play for themselves. Had they done so, such a play must have been written in the expectation that it would serve subsequently (perhaps slightly cut) at the Globe. The Epistle denies that it was so played. It may have been in error.

4. The play itself is less difficult to interpret. It is not necessary to label it a comical satire in order to see that it would suit what we know of the taste of an Inn of Court: it is intelligent, complex, and full of devices for ironic reduction. It also contains some of Shakespeare's most accomplished oratory, two full-dress debates, discussion of topics (as in Hector's arguments) that would directly interest a lawyer, and much matter that is potentially ironic—that is to say, the better-read the audience, the more irony would it see in (shall we say) Shakespeare's handling of Antenor. The few legal puns and allusions (which seem to be confined to Pandarus' part,

---

1. E.g. pleas/plays; titles; Commentaries; actions; power of wit (by analogy with power of attorney); judgement.

in III.ii and the Epilogue) may help to confirm the implications of the rest, but are of little weight.[1]

One would like to know how *Troilus* escaped, and when the Epistle was written; whether the first title-page told the truth or not; and whether, if the play *were* ever performed at the Globe, it was before or after 1603, and seldom or often played. We are unlikely to know. Alexander's theory remains a theory, but plausible.

1. '. . . swear the oaths now to her that you have sworn to me' (III.ii.40–1); 'a kiss in fee-farm' (49–50); 'Words pay no debts, give her deeds' (55); 'Here's "In witness whereof the parties interchangeably—"' (57–8); 'Go to, a bargain made: seal it, seal it, I'll be the witness' (195–6); 'my will shall here be made' (v.x.53); 'bequeath you my diseases' (57).

APPENDIX III

ARISTOTLE, *ETHICS*

Shakespeare does not normally allude to his sources. Certainly he does not document his plays, as Jonson did, to provide authority for what his characters do and say; and it is, therefore, strange to find Aristotle explicitly cited by Hector at II.ii. 167–8. In other places Shakespeare alludes to an ancient writer only in passing—obliquely, to Virgil (*Ham.* II.ii.440 ff.), directly, to Caesar (*2H6* IV.vii.57–8), and with a comment on Ovid, by contrast with Aristotle (*Shr.* I.i.32–3), that makes him a surrogate for both light reading and frivolous behaviour; but the point to be made is that these were all school authors—something that any grammar-school boy with a good sprag memory would be familiar with. With *Troilus and Cressida* the case is different. Here, in a play held to be learned and sophisticated, in the middle of a serious debate on a matter of moral and legal principle, a major speaker cites a major philosopher. It is a matter that deserves further investigation, and I wish to argue that Shakespeare was fairly familiar with at least the first half of the *Nicomachean Ethics*.[1]

It is fortunate that Hector's citation is itself characteristic of his author, in that it makes the connection between a psychological condition (the passionate and unstable nature of youth) and an ethical problem (the relationship of justice and natural law to the question 'Should one return Helen?'). Hector's argument runs, in summary, like this.

1. Paris and Troilus are both arguing as young men do, who are unfit for moral (political) philosophy, and who deal in passions rather than just judgements on right and wrong.

1. Two caveats ought to be entered at once. First, it is most unlikely, in a question concerning abstract ideas, that it would ever be possible to demonstrate with certainty that a writer is deriving from any given source; the best to be hoped for is a strong preponderance of possibilities. Secondly, since Aristotle had for so long been a major influence on European thought, it is difficult to be sure, in determining derivation, that an idea comes directly from Aristotle, and not from (say) Hooker, whose method and arguments are so largely Aristotelian.

2. In such judgements pleasure and revenge are deaf to right reason.
3. It is natural justice for debts to be paid. The nearest debt is that of wife to husband.
4. All nations have a law to curb uncontrolled appetites (implying that unruly appetite led to the rape of Helen).
5. Helen is Menelaus' wife. Both natural law and the law of nations require that she should be returned to him.

These propositions are supported by the following passages from the *Ethics*.[1]

1a. Political science is not a proper study for the young. The young man is not versed in the practical business of life . . . He is swayed by his feelings; he will . . . derive no benefit from a study the end of which is not *knowing* but *doing*. [He lives] the kind of life which is a succession of unrelated emotional experiences. (I.3: p. 28)
1b. Acts which are the effects of passion are surely the very last that can be called acts of deliberate choice. (III.2: p. 83)
2. When Pleasure is at the bar, the jury is not impartial. So it will be best for us if we feel towards her as the Trojan elders felt towards Helen . . . If we are for packing her off, as they were with Helen, we shall be the less likely to go wrong.[2]
   (II.9: p. 74)
3. Justice between husband and wife comes nearer true justice than does that between master and slaves . . . It is in fact justice between husband and wife that is the true form of domestic justice. (v.6: p. 157)
4. [Legislators] inflict pains and penalties for misbehaviour . . . Their motive . . . is to stop evil practices. (III.5: p. 90)
5a. Now of political justice. There are two forms of it, the natural and the conventional. It is natural when it has the same validity everywhere, and is unaffected by any view we may take about the justice of it. It is conventional when there is no original reason why it should take one form rather than another, and the rule it imposes is reached by agreement, after which it holds good. (v.7: p. 157)
5b. [Cf. 3, above.]

1. References are to the translation by J. A. K. Thomson (Penguin Classics, 1955).
2. It is significant that, in discounting pleasure when trying to reach a just decision, Aristotle should use as an analogy the very topic which Hector is discussing.

5c. The law never looks beyond the question 'What damage
     was done?' . . . What the judge seeks to do is to redress the
     inequality . . . whereby he takes from the aggressor any
     gain he may have secured.   (v.4: p. 148)

But there is more to the question than Hector's allusion and
argument. A number of passages in Books II, III and IV of the
Ethics suggest that an Aristotelian pattern in handling moral and
psychological material may be seen also in *Troilus*: character
types correspond to persons of the play; and a number of topics—
courage, honour, moral responsibility, the nature of choice, and
so on—occur with sufficient frequency in both works to suggest
more connections between them. Let us take our examination
further.

Aristotle's analysis of virtues and vices in terms of his formula
of the mean is conducted in a way with which modern readers are
more familiar in the work of Theophrastus: that is, he isolates in
each instance the mean and its two related extremes in terms of a
'character'. Hence we find the boaster, the buffoon, the braggart
and the ironist all introduced briefly in II.7 (p. 70). Some of
them are developed in more detail in IV.7 (p. 133); the man
who claims qualifications better than he truly possesses, for
example, is very like the Ajax of the end of III.iii (and Ajax in
Metamorphoses XIII), whereas the man who is ironical in moderation is close to Ulysses as he appears in the medicinal mocking of
Achilles, and in his handling of Troilus in Act v. There is something of Ajax to be found in the boor; whereas the buffoon, who
'never can resist a joke, sparing neither himself, nor anyone else,
provided he can raise a laugh' has obviously gone into the make-
up of Thersites.[1] But these figures, although suggestive, are not
certainly to be identified with persons in the play. Far more
persuasive are the two characters of the liberal man and the
magnanimous man, for they can be found in Ulysses' 'character'
of Troilus (IV.v.96–112) and in the behaviour of Hector. Not all
the details of that account of Troilus come from Aristotle, for
some are Renaissance commonplaces; but the form of his
generosity derives from the *Ethics*. Consider:

The liberal man will not give to the wrong persons, nor at the

1. One can find Thersites in Book II also: 'The malicious man . . . is so far
from being pained by the misfortunes of another that he is actually tickled by
them' (p. 135). (Aristotle allows some overlapping of the buffoon and the wit;
but since the wit is a man 'whose pleasantries do not go too far', it is clear that
Thersites comes closer to being the man 'who would rather venture on risqué
jokes and hurt the feelings of his victims than fail to raise a laugh'.)

wrong time, nor in any wrong way, since if he did, he would no longer be sustaining his character of liberal man.

. . . It is, however, eminently characteristic of the liberal man to give rather too much . . .   (IV. I: pp. 112, 111)

and compare it with

> His heart and hand both open and both free;
> For what he has he gives, what thinks he shows,
> Yet gives he not till judgement guide his bounty,
> Nor dignifies an impare thought with breath; . . .
>
> (IV. v. 100–3)

There is little obvious *dramatic* point in attributing this quality to Troilus: his liberality, strictly considered, has nowhere to act in the play,[1] and it establishes no contrast with the behaviour of other characters; so that it looks as if Shakespeare's portrait was influenced by his reading of the *Ethics*, and Troilus emerged as, in part, the Liberal Man.[2]

Hector is in many respects the Magnanimous Man. He seeks honour (though not at any price):

> For honour is the greatest of external goods   (IV. 3: p. 121)
> The gentleman . . . [identifies] the good with honour
>
> (I. 5: p. 30)
> The superior man, then, has the right attitude to honour and dishonour.   (IV. 3: p. 121)

He also sees honour, and danger, in their proper proportion:

> Mine honour keeps the weather of my fate:
> Life every man holds dear, but the dear man
> Holds honour far more precious-dear than life.
>
> (v. iii. 26–8)

Compare this with Aristotle:

> The superior man will not run petty risks, nor indeed risks of any kind if he can help it . . . but he rises to meet a crisis and, so long as that lasts, he will put his life in peril for that cause.
>
> (IV. 3: p. 123)

Hector bears himself in the Greek camp with modest confidence and courtesy, with two exceptions: first, when he teases Menelaus and at once apologizes for it (IV. v. 176–81), and secondly, when

1. Unless, by any chance, Shakespeare's imagination was triggered by a memory of Henryson's *Testament*, so that he made Troilus liberal because (in the *Testament*) he had given generous alms to Cressida and the other lepers.

2. I cannot decide whether or not an audience was expected to *recognize* the Liberal Man.

having been directly insulted by Achilles, he allows himself a brief and irascible 'brag', and then (recalled to self-control by his cousin) offers a prompt reconciliation. The quick loss and recovery of temper is characteristic of the 'gentle' man (IV.5: p. 127), but it is the magnanimous man (who embodies all the virtues) who is otherwise sketched here; consider, for example, this passage from the *Ethics*:

> He stands on his dignity with people who are high in public esteem or favourites of fortune . . . He is not given to recriminations, even against his ill-wishers, unless he means to be deliberately insulting . . . He does not nurse resentment, for it is not like a superior man to remember things against people.
>
> (IV.3: pp. 124–5)

Even the first moves towards the quarrel with Achilles can be found in Aristotle, for Hector, having identified Achilles, refuses to be impressed by what he sees:

> *Hect.* Stand fair, I pray thee; let me look on thee.
> *Achill.* Behold thy fill.
> *Hect.* Nay, I have done already.
>
> (IV.v.234–5)

This is very close to

> He is not a gushing person, because nothing strikes him as a subject of mighty admiration. (IV.3: pp. 124–5)

In the duel with Ajax, Hector does not exert himself, and seems indeed to be not fully involved: a trait which is explained, in context, by his kinship with Ajax, but which is also a sign of magnanimity. Troilus' encouragement to him—

> Hector, thou sleep'st: awake thee! (l. 114)

—suggests his easy half-engagement; Æneas' comment upon Hector's indifference to the rules to be chosen for the combat—

> He cares not: he'll obey conditions (l. 72)

—implies another aspect of the same thing: compare it with *Ethics*, IV.3 (p. 124)

> It is his way to make no effort, or to hang back, except when some really great honour or achievement is open to him.

And his easy dismissal of the cowardly Thersites is also part of the pattern of magnanimity:

> *Hect.*   What art thou, Greek? Art thou for Hector's match?
>   Art thou of blood and honour?
> *Thers.* No, no: I am a rascal, a scurvy railing knave: a
>   very filthy rogue.
> *Hect.*   I do believe thee: live.   (v. iv. 26–30)

This seems to correspond to two observations of Aristotle:

> [He] does not assume airs in his dealings with persons of no
> great distinction . . . He will not enter the lists against ordinary
> competitors for distinction.   (IV. 3: p. 124)

Indeed, Hector comes near enough to the Aristotelian model for
Aristotle's own summary to be applied to him:

> Greatness in all the virtues is surely what stamps him for what
> he is . . . It would be totally out of character for such a man to
> run away helter-skelter, or to be guilty of cheating . . . Greatness
> of soul is the beautiful completion of the virtues, for it adds to
> them its own greatness, and is inseparable from them. And this
> makes it hard for a man to be truly great in soul; without a fine
> moral sense it is impossible.   (IV. 3: pp. 121–2)

We need not suppose, however, that Hector's conduct is con-
sistently good by the standards of Aristotle. On the contrary, the
Ethics twice points to venial errors of which Hector is guilty. In
the first place, despite his acute arguments in the Trojan debate,
he should not be classified as a philosopher—that is, as one
capable of recognizing the ultimate good at all times. Rather, he
can be classified with 'the gentleman . . . and the man of affairs
[who] identify the good with honour' (I. 5: p. 30): that is, he
pursues at times a secondary and not a primary good. And since
he twice lapses from that conduct which his better judgement
would approve—when, in the debate, he leaves the question of
Helen, and turns to his challenge; and when, further, he pursues
a Greek because of his rich armour, *and because he flees*—we can
judge him by Aristotle's psychological argument. Aristotle
assumes two principles in the soul, one rational, and one in
opposition to reason. The irrational principle sometimes operates
to produce unexpected, and even unintended, consequences, just
as, in a case of paralysis, a man may intend to move a limb to the
right and it moves to the left. We see the limb but not the erratic
impulse. That impulse however is not wholly irrational, and it is
normally amenable to reason in the continent man, and especially
so in the temperate and the brave man. The irrational principle
is most easily seen in the man whom Aristotle calls incontinent:

hence, perhaps, some of the force of Thersites' sneer—'All incontinent varlets'.[1]

It is perhaps not necessary to take the argument further: the evidence I have hitherto cited should be enough to determine whether or not Shakespeare had the *Ethics*[2] in mind when he wrote the play; but it may help to append a brief list of passages from the *Ethics* which also suggest a connection with *Troilus*.[3]

Ethics	*Troilus*
I. I:	I. iii. 206–8:
The master arts are to be preferred to those of the subordinate skills, for it is the former that provide the motive for pursuing the latter.	So that the ram that batters down the wall, For the great swinge and rudeness of his poise, They place before his hand that made the engine, ...
I. 3:	[The whole drift of Ulysses'
The end [of political science] is not knowing but doing.	thesis presented to Achilles, but especially III. iii. 183–4:]
I. 8:	... things in motion sooner
Honour and rewards fall to those who show their good qualities in action.	catch the eye Than what stirs not.
I. 5:	I. iii. 352–3:
Why do men seek honour? surely, in order to confirm the favourable opinion they have formed of themselves.	What heart receives from hence a conquering part To steel a strong opinion to themselves?
I. 6:	I. i. 74–7:
A thing may be called good in three ways; in itself, in some quality it has, in some relation it bears to something else. But the essence of a thing—what it is in itself—is by its very nature prior to any relation it may have.	Because she's kin to me, therefore she's not so fair as Helen. And she were not kin to me, she would be as fair o' Friday as Helen is o' Sunday. I. ii. 67: Well, I say Troilus is Troilus.
	II. ii. 53: What's aught but as 'tis valued?

1. The discussion of incontinence occurs first in I. 13 (pp. 52–3).
2. Or, more specifically, the first five Books of the *Ethics*: I find little in Books VI–X to suggest any connection with *Troilus*, and what there is has already been discussed in some form in the earlier Books.
3. Such passages are not in themselves persuasive evidence, but they 'speak ... with the other proofs'.

Ethics

Troilus

II.ii. 59–61:
And the will dotes that is
    attributive
To what infectiously itself
    affects,
Without some image of
    th'affected merit.

II.iii. 118–19:
Much attribute he hath, and
    much the reason
Why we ascribe it to him; . . .

III.iii. 5–12:
I have abandon'd Troy, . . .
    sequestering from me all
That time, acquaintance,
    custom, and condition
Made tame and most familiar
    to my nature;
And here, to do you service,
    am become
As new into the world, strange,
    unacquainted.

v.ii. 145:
This is, and is not, Cressid.

I.9:
We do not naturally speak of a
cow or a horse or other beast as
'happy', for none of the brute
creation can take part in moral
activities.

[Much of the speech of
Thersites yields examples of
men compared with brutes for
the purpose of depreciation—
though Ulysses can use such
terms as well: e.g. 'A very
horse, that has he knows not
what!' (III.iii. 126)]

II.2:
Children and animals are as
capable of voluntary action as
adult men; but they have not
the same capacity for deliberate
choice.

II.i.96–9:
Thers. I serve here voluntary.
Achill. Your last service was
suff'rance—'twas not
voluntary, no man is beaten
voluntary: Ajax was here the
voluntary, and you as under an
impress.

III. 1:
[This chapter, introducing the
subject of moral responsibility,
discusses at length the
distinction of voluntary and
involuntary acts.]

Ethics

III. 2 :

Deliberate choice [affords] a
better test of character than is
supplied by actions. [The
concept is usually called
electio/election.]

III. 8 :

Of the moods which resemble
courage, this which has a high
spirit for its driving force seems
the most natural; indeed,
when it includes deliberate
choice and purpose, it is hard
to distinguish from courage.
We must not forget that it is
human to be painfully affected
by anger and to find revenge
sweet. But the most one can
say of those who fight from no
higher motive than anger is
that they are good fighters: one
cannot call them brave. For
they are not moved by honour
or guided by principle; simply
they are swayed by their
feelings.

III. 12 :

Our word for 'intemperance'
is also applied to the
naughtiness of children, which
has a certain resemblance to
the wantonness of their
errors . . . For the life of
children, as much as that of
intemperate men, is wholly
governed by desires, and it is in
them that the craving for
pleasant things is strongest.

Troilus

I. iii. 348–9:

And choice, being mutual act
  of all our souls,
Makes merit her election, . . .

II. ii. 62–3:

I take today a wife, and my
  election
Is led on in the conduct of my
  will: . . .

II. ii. 66–8:

—how may I avoid,
Although my will distaste what
  it elected,
The wife I choose?

[Quotation is irrelevant here—
it is more convenient to
indicate examples, e.g. Hector
(I. ii) angry at defeat: Ajax
(II. i) beating Thersites when
frustrated: Troilus (IV. iv)
insulted by Diomedes: Troilus
(V. ii) betrayed by Cressida:
Troilus (V. iii) urging Hector to
abandon mercy in fight ('The
venom'd vengeance ride upon
our swords'): Achilles (V. v and
afterwards) avenging
Patroclus: Ajax, Diomedes and
Troilus (V. vi) all intent on
revenge.]

II. ii. 169–72:

The reasons you allege do
  more conduce
To the hot passion of
  distemper'd blood
Than to make up a free
  determination
'Twixt right and wrong: . . .

Ethics

III. 9:
The end at which courage aims
is a source of pleasure, but we
are blinded to this by the pains
incident to its exercise.

V. I:
The unjust man grasps at more
than his fair share . . .;
of evils . . . he in fact chooses the
lesser portion.

IV. 5:
Evil destroys even itself.

Troilus

II. ii. 143–6:
    Paris, you speak
Like one besotted on your
    sweet delights.
You have the honey still, but
    these the gall:
So to be valiant is no praise
    at all.

I. iii. 121–4:
And appetite, an universal
    wolf,
So doubly seconded with will
    and power,
Must make perforce an
    universal prey,
And last eat up himself.
II. iii. 156:
He that is proud eats up
    himself: . . .
V. iv. 32–5:
What's become of the wenching
rogues? I think they have
swallowed one another. I
would laugh at that miracle;
yet in a sort lechery eats itself.

APPENDIX IV

DEGREE

Ulysses' speech on degree is notable for two things: it is a *tour de force* of forensic rhetoric, and it is a tissue of commonplaces. By it, and by Hector's appeal to the 'laws of nature and of nations', the audience is meant to judge the action of the play. Because it is full of commonplaces, it is difficult to trace its ideas to their sources, for any civilized community depends upon order and degree, and will exalt them in any discussion of political principles (although the precise sense given to the terms, like the context in which they are to operate, and the reasons why they may seem to be more important at one time than another—all these will vary from state to state, from age to age). For this reason, commentators have tried to find sources for the speech in Plato, especially in *Republic* VIII, which deals with the shortcomings of democracy; in Elyot's *Gouernour*, which develops Plato's argument specifically for early Tudor society; in the *Iliad* itself, when Odysseus rebukes Greek disorder and Agamemnon admits that, were they united, the Greeks would conquer Troy at once (*Iliad* II): in Hooker (*Ecclesiastical Polity*, I.iii.2); in Ovid's description of creation from Chaos (*Metamorphoses* I), which appears to have been an important influence on sixteenth-century political theorizing; and in the Homily *Of Obedience*, which Shakespeare must have known, because he could not avoid hearing it read from the pulpit. To these, because he used similar commonplaces elsewhere in his works, we may add Shakespeare himself: the image of the bee as an emblem of ordered commonwealth is found in *Henry V*, at least as eloquently expressed as in the *Gouernour*; and the plays are full of images of disorder expressed as chaotic intermingling of the elements (as one finds also in the emblem books). The distinctions to be drawn between these possible sources must depend on two things: first, whether the emphasis may be on the beauty of order, or upon the hideousness of chaos; and secondly, whether the principle of control is law, or justice, or order itself, or degree (that is, hierarchy) or even love (as in that cosmic order that Chaucer learned from Boethius, and which ultimately goes back to the Platonic figures of music and planetary order which Shakespeare draws on in *The Merchant of Venice*, v.i).

What likelihood there may be that one might trace a source for Shakespeare, I do not know. Ultimately, his ideas might have been stimulated by the *Iliad*, and the debate there. His *emotions*, on the other hand, were likely to express themselves in concepts that he learned from Ovid, who provided him with images both of Chaos and of flux, and whose Jove is himself in a position very like Agamemnon's, uncertain how to contain disorder (*Metamorphoses*, 1.208–18). Other texts ultimately go back to Plato in principle, though not in detail; but since the purpose of each is different from Plato's, it is hard to know whether that purpose itself influenced Shakespeare's response or not. The Homily, for example, uses traditional arguments for the necessity of order and hierarchy, but its purpose is to support the sovereign as both absolute monarch and religious leader: hence, it derives from the fear of sacrilege part of its force as argument.[1] Hooker, on the other hand, appeals to cosmic order and natural law, although his purpose is ultimately to justify human order in divine worship. I think that on the whole Shakespeare took his ideas where he found them, irrespective of possible agreements in other doctrines with the writer from whom he drew. I think also that, like most poets, he wrote eloquently of order and the threat of disorder[2] because order is a condition of their music-making (as it was for Plato); and that therefore he found even more help in the poets, especially Ovid, than ever he could in the most learned writer on political theory.

1. If we assume—and I believe it—that Shakespeare wrote the 'three pages' of the *Play of Sir Thomas More*, then it is certain that he was prepared to use that argument: 'And 'twere no error if I told you all / You were in arms 'gainst God.' But the *More* pages invoke apostolic doctrine, as well as the fear of disorder and cannibalism; those *topoi* were out of place in the Greek debate in *Troilus*.

2. Remember especially Pope's *Dunciad* iv.

APPENDIX V

SOURCE MATERIALS

1. Geoffrey Chaucer, *Troilus and Criseyde.*

Geoffrey Chaucer, *Troilus and Criseyde*, in *Works*, ed. F. N. Robinson, 2nd edn, 1957; Book I, ll. 624–721, 750–60, 876–89, 981–7; Book II, ll. 610–51, 1247–74; Book III, ll. 1422–42, 1555–68; Book IV, ll. 736–41, 1485–91.

[Pandarus consoles Troilus.]

'Ye, Troilus, now herke,' quod Pandare;   [624]
'Though I be nyce, it happeth often so,
That oon that excesse doth ful yvele fare
By good counseil kan kepe his frend therfro.
I have myself ek seyn a blynd man goo
Ther as he fel that couthe loken wide;
A fool may ek a wis-man ofte gide.   630

'A wheston is no kervyng instrument.
But yet it maketh sharppe kervyng tolis.
And there thow woost that I have aught myswent,
Eschuw thow that, for swich thing to the scole is;
Thus often wise men ben war by foolys.
If thow do so, thi wit is wel bewared;
By his contrarie is every thyng declared.

'For how myghte evere swetnesse han ben knowe
To him that nevere tasted bitternesse?
Ne no man may ben inly glad, I trowe,   640
That nevere was in sorwe or som destresse.
Eke whit by blak, by shame ek worthinesse,
Ech set by other, more for other semeth,
As men may se, and so the wyse it demeth.

'Sith thus of two contraries is o lore,
I, that have in love so ofte assayed
Grevances, oughte konne, and wel the more,
Counseillen the of that thow art amayed.
Ek the ne aughte nat ben yvel appayed,
Though I desyre with the for to bere   650
Thyn hevy charge; it shal the lasse dere.

'I woot wel that it fareth thus be me
As to thi brother, Paris, an herdesse,
Which that icleped was Oënone,
Wrot in a compleynte of hir hevynesse.
Yee say the lettre that she wrot, I gesse.'
'Nay nevere yet, ywys,' quod Troilus.
'Now,' quod Pandare, 'herkne, it was thus:

'"Phebus, that first fond art of medicyne,"
Quod she, "and couthe in every wightes care   660
Remedye and reed, by herbes he knew fyne,
Yet to hymself his konnyng was ful bare;
For love hadde hym so bounden in a snare,
Al for the doughter of the kynge Amete,
That al his craft ne koude his sorwes bete."

'Right so fare I, unhappily for me.
I love oon best, and that me smerteth sore;
And yet, peraunter, kan I reden the,
And nat myself; repreve me na more.
I have no cause, I woot wel, for to sore   670
As doth an hauk that listeth for to pleye;
But to thin help yet somwhat kan I seye.

'And of o thyng right siker maistow be,
That certein, for to dyen in the peyne,
That I shal nevere mo discoveren the;
Ne, by my trouthe, I kepe nat restreyne
The fro thi love, theigh that it were Eleyne
That is thi brother wif, if ich it wiste:
Be what she be, and love hire as the liste!

'Therfore, as frend, fullich in me assure,   680
And telle me plat now what is th'enchesoun
And final cause of wo that ye endure;
For douteth nothyng, myn entencioun
Nis nat to yow of reprehencioun,
To speke as now, for no wight may byreve
A man to love, tyl that hym list to leve.

'And witteth wel that bothe two ben vices,
Mistrusten alle, or elles alle leve.
But wel I woot, the mene of it no vice is,
For for to trusten som wight is a preve   690
Of trouth, and forthi wolde I fayn remeve
Thi wronge conseyte, and do the som wyght triste
Thi wo to telle; and tel me, if the liste.

'The wise seith, "Wo hym that is allone,
For, and he falle, he hath non helpe to ryse";
And sith thow hast a felawe, tel thi mone;
For this nys naught, certein, the nexte wyse
To wynnen love, as techen us the wyse,
To walwe and wepe as Nyobe the queene,
Whos teres yet in marble ben yseene.   700

'Lat be thy wepyng and thi drerynesse,
And lat us lissen wo with oother speche;
So may thy woful tyme seme lesse.
Delyte nat in wo thi wo to seche,
As don thise foles that hire sorwes eche
With sorwe, whan thei han mysaventure,
And listen naught to seche hem other cure.

'Men seyn, "to wrecche is consolacioun
To have another felawe in hys peyne."
That owghte wel ben oure opynyoun,   710
For, bothe thow and I, of love we pleyne.
So ful of sorwe am I, soth for to seyne,
That certeinly namore harde grace
May sitte on me, for-why ther is no space.

'If God wol, thow art nat agast of me,
Lest I wolde of thi lady the bygyle!
Thow woost thyself whom that I love, parde,
As I best kan, gon sithen longe while.
And sith thow woost I do it for no wyle,
And seyst I am he that thow trustest moost,   720
Telle me somwhat, syn al my wo thow woost.'

[*Troilus rejects Pandarus' comfort.*]

But natheles, whan he hadde herd hym crye   750
'Awake!' he gan to syken wonder soore,
And seyde, 'Frend, though that I stylle lye,
I am nat deef. Now pees, and crye namore,
For I have herd thi wordes and thi lore;
But suffre me my meschief to bywaille,
For thi proverbes may me naught availle.

'Nor other cure kanstow non for me.
Ek I nyl nat ben cured; I wol deye.
What knowe I of the queene Nyobe?
Lat be thyne olde ensaumples, I the preye.'   760

[*Pandarus praises Criseyde.*]

And whan that Pandare herde hire name nevene,   [876]
Lord, he was glad, and seyde, 'Frend so deere,
Now far aright, for Joves name in hevene.
Love hath byset the wel; be of good cheere!
For of good name and wisdom and manere   880
She hath ynough, and ek of gentilesse.
If she be fayr, thow woost thyself, I gesse.

'Ne I nevere saugh a more bountevous
Of hire estat, n'a gladder, ne of speche
A frendlyer, n'a more gracious
For to do wel, ne lasse hadde nede to seche
What for to don; and al this bet to eche,
In honour, to as fer as she may strecche,
A kynges herte semeth by hyrs a wrecche.

'And for to speke of hire in specyal,   [981]
Hire beaute to bithynken and hire youthe,
It sit hire naught to ben celestial
As yet, though that hire liste bothe and kowthe;
But trewely, it sate hire wel right nowthe
A worthi knyght to loven and cherice,
And but she do, I holde it for a vice.

[*Criseyde watches Troilus returning from the field.*]

But as she sat allone and thoughte thus,   610
Ascry aros at scarmuch al withoute,
And men cride in the strete, 'Se, Troilus
Hath right now put to flighte the Grekes route!'
With that gan al hire meyne for to shoute,
'A, go we se! cast up the yates wyde!
For thorwgh this strete he moot to paleys ride;

'For other wey is fro the yate noon
Of Dardanus, there opyn is the cheyne.'
With that com he and al his folk anoon
An esy pas rydyng, in routes tweyne,   620
Right as his happy day was, sooth to seyne,
For which, men seyn, may nought destourbed be
That shal bityden of necessitee.

This Troilus sat on his baye steede,
Al armed, save his hed, ful richely;
And wownded was his hors, and gan to blede,
On which he rood a pas ful softely.
But swich a knyghtly sighte, trewely,
As was on hym, was nought, withouten faille,
To loke on Mars, that god is of bataille.   630

So lik a man of armes and a knyght
He was to seen, fulfilled of heigh prowesse;
For bothe he hadde a body and a myght
To don that thing, as wel as hardynesse;
And ek to seen hym in his gere hym dresse,
So fressh, so yong, so weldy semed he,
It was an heven upon hym for to see.

His helm tohewen was in twenty places,
That by a tyssew heng his bak byhynde;
His sheeld todasshed was with swerdes and maces,   640
In which men myght many an arwe fynde
That thirled hadde horn and nerf and rynde;
And ay the peple cryde, 'Here cometh oure joye,
And, next his brother, holder up of Troye!'

For which he wex a litel reed for shame,
Whan he the peple upon hym herde cryen,
That to byholde it was a noble game,
How sobrelich he caste down his yën.
Criseÿda gan al his chere aspien,
And leet it so softe in hire herte synke,   650
That to hireself she seyde, 'Who yaf me drynke?'

[*Pandarus shows Troilus to Criseyde.*]

And right as they declamed this matere,   [1247]
Lo, Troilus, right at the stretes ende,
Com rydyng with his tenthe som yfere,
Al softely, and thiderward gan bende   1250
Ther as they sete, as was his way to wende
To paleis-ward; and Pandarus hym aspide,
And seyde, 'Nece, ysee who comth here ride!

'O fle naught in (he seeth us, I suppose),
Lest he may thynken that ye hym eschuwe.'
'Nay, nay,' quod she, and wex as red as rose.
With that he gan hire humbly to saluwe,
With dredful chere, and oft his hewes muwe;
And up his look debonairly he caste,
And bekked on Pandare, and forth he paste.   1260

God woot if he sat on his hors aright,
Or goodly was biseyn, that ilke day!
God woot wher he was lik a manly knyght!
What sholde I drecche, or telle of his aray?
Criseyde, which that alle thise thynges say,
To telle in short, hire liked al in-fere,
His person, his aray, his look, his chere,

His goodly manere, and his gentilesse,
So wel that nevere, sith that she was born,
Ne hadde she swych routh of his destresse;   1270
And how so she hath hard ben here-byforn,
To God hope I, she hath now kaught a thorn,
She shal nat pulle it out this nexte wyke.
God sende mo swich thornes on to pike!

[*Troilus' aubade, lamenting the shortness of night.*]

'Myn hertes lif, my trist, and my plesaunce,   [1422]
That I was born, allas, what me is wo,
That day of us moot make disseveraunce!
For tyme it is to ryse and hennes go,
Or ellis I am lost for evere mo!
O nyght, allas! why nyltow over us hove,
As longe as whan Almena lay by Jove?

'O blake nyght, as folk in bokes rede,
That shapen art by God this world to hide   1430
At certeyn tymes wyth thi derke wede,
That under that men myghte in reste abide,
Wel oughten bestes pleyne, and folk the chide,
That there as day wyth labour wolde us breste,
That thow thus fleest, and deynest us nought reste.

'Thow doost, allas, to shortly thyn office,
. Thow rakle nyght, ther God, maker of kynde,
The, for thyn haste and thyn unkynde vice,
So faste ay to oure hemysperie bynde,
That nevere more under the ground thow wynde!   1440
For now, for thow so hiest out of Troie,
Have I forgon thus hastili my joie!'

[*Pandarus teases Criseyde.*]

Pandare, o-morwe which that comen was   [1555]
Unto his nece and gan hire faire grete,
Seyde, 'Al this nyght so reyned it, allas,
That al my drede is that ye, nece swete,
Han litel laiser had to slepe and mete.
Al nyght,' quod he, 'hath reyn so do me wake,   1560
That som of us, I trowe, hire hedes ake.'

And ner he com, and seyde, 'How stant it now
This mury morwe? Nece, how kan ye fare?'
Criseyde answerde, 'Nevere the bet for yow,
Fox that ye ben! God yeve youre herte kare!
God help me so, ye caused al this fare,
Trowe I,' quod she, 'for al youre wordes white.
O, whoso seeth yow, knoweth yow ful lite.'

[*Criseyde laments her departure.*]

    Hire ownded heer, that sonnyssh was of hewe,   [736]
    She rente, and ek hire fyngeres longe and smale
    She wrong ful ofte, and bad God on hire rewe,
    And with the deth to doon boote on hire bale.
    Hire hewe, whilom bright, that tho was pale,   740
    Bar witnesse of hire wo and hire constreynte;

[*Troilus fears the Greeks as suitors.*]

    'Ye shal ek seen so many a lusty knyght   [1485]
    Among the Grekis, ful of worthynesse,
    And ech of hem with herte, wit, and myght
    To plesen yow don al his bisynesse,
    That ye shul dullen of the rudenesse
    Of us sely Troians, but if routhe   1490
    Remorde yow, or vertu of youre trouthe.

2.   William Caxton, *The Recuyell of the Historyes of Troye*.

William Caxton, *The Recuyell of the Historyes of Troye. Written in French by Raoul Lefevre. Translated and Printed by William Caxton*, ed. H. Oskar Sommer, 1894; pp. 590, 608, 638–9.

[*Ajax meets Hector in fight, and persuades him to withdraw for that day.*]

And than hector for curtoifye enbraced hym in his armes and made hym grete chiere And offryd to hym to do all his playfir yf he defired ony thynge of hym / And prayd hym that he wolde come to troye with hym for to fee his lignage of hys moder fyde / But the fayd Thelamon that entended no thynge but to his auauntage fayde that he wolde not goo at thys tyme / But prayd to hector fayng / that yf he louyd hym fo moche as he fayde / that he wolde for his fake and at his Inftance do ceffe the bataill for that day / and that the troians fhold leue the grekes in pees / The vnhappy hector accorded to hym his requefte. And blewe an horn & made alle his peple to withdrawe in to the cyte Than had the troians begonne to putte fyre in the fhippes of the grekes and had alle brente hem / Ne had hector callyd them fro thens / whereof the troians were fory of the rapeell This was the caufe wherfore the troians loft to haue the victorye / to the whiche they myght neuer after atteyne ne come for fortune was to them contrarye And therfore virgile fayth / Non eft mifericordia in bello That is to faye ther is no mercy in bataill A man ought not to take mifericorde / But take the victorye who may gete hit.

[*Diomedes takes Troilus' horse, and presents it to* [*Criseyde*].]

[Diomedes] fought with troillous at his comyng and fmote hym

doun and toke hys horſe / and ſente hit to breſeyda. And dyde
do ſaye to her by his ſeruant / that hit was troyllus horſe her
loue / that he had beten hym by his proweſſe / and prayd her fro
than forth on that ſhe wold holde hym for her loue and frende.

[*Achilles with his Myrmidons kills Troilus. (Shakespeare uses the details
of this incident for the slaying of Hector).*]

And afore that Achilles entryd in to the bataylle he aſſemblid
his myrondones / And prayd hem that they wolde entende to
none other thynge but to encloſe troyllus and to holde hym wyth
oute ſleynge tyll he cam And that he wolde not be ſer fro hem /
And they promyſid hym that they ſo do wolde / And he ſmote
in to the bataylle / And of that other ſyde cam troyllus that
began to ſlee and bete doun / alle them that he raughte. And
dyde ſo moche that aboute mydday he put the grekes to flight /
Than the myrondones that were well two thouſand fyghtyng
men and had not forgete the comandement of theyr lord /
threſtid in amonge the troians and recouerid the ſelde / And as
they helde hem to geder & ſought no man but troyllus / they
fonde hym þᵗ he foughte ſtrongly & was encloſid on all parties /
but he ſlewe & wounded many. And as he was all allone amonge
hem and had no man to ſocoure hym / they ſlewe his horſe / And
hurte hym in many places / And araced of his heed his helme /
And his coyffe of yron / And he deffended hym the beſte wyſe he
cowde / Than cam on Achilles whan he ſawe troyllus alle naked /
And ran vpon hym in a rage / And ſmote of his heed And caſte
hit vnder the feet of the horſe / And toke the body and bonde
hit to the taylle of his horſe And ſo drewe hit after hym thurgh
oute the ooſte / O what vylonnye was hit to drawe ſo the ſone of
ſo noble a kynge / that was ſo worthy and ſo hardy / Certes yf
ony nobleſſe had ben in Achilles / he wold not haue done this
vylonye.

3. John Lydgate, *Lydgate's Troy Book*.
    John Lydgate, *Lydgate's Troy Book*, ed. Henry Bergen,
    E.E.T.S., 1906–35 (e.s. 97, 103, 106, 126); Book III, ll. 4620–
    41, 4934–49, 4987–99, 5325–72, 4417–37.

[*Diomedes takes Troilus' horse, and presents it to Criseyde.*]

Dyomede cam with his meyne,   4620
And many worþi, ridyng hym aboute,
And Troylus met, among[es] al þe route,
Al sodeynly, of hap or auenture,
And hym vnhorsith, as it was his evre;
And after þat, anoon he hent his stede,
And bad a squier þat he shuld it lede
Vn-to Cryseyde, only for hir sake,

Beseching hir þat she wolde it take
As for a gyfte of hir owne man,
Sith he þat day for hir loue it wan   4630
Amyd þe feld, þoruȝ his grete myȝt,
Of hym þat was whilom hir owne knyȝt.
And he in haste on his weie is went,
And þer-of made vn-to hir present,
Preying hir, in ful humble wyse,
Þis litel gifte þat she nat dispise,
But it receive for a remembraunce,
And with al þis, þat it be plesaunce,
Of verray pite and of wommanhede
On hir seruaunt, callid Diomede,   4640
To remembre, þat was be-come her knyȝt.

[*Andromache pleads with Hector to refrain from battle.*]

And specially on þe woful morwe,   [4934]
Whan þat she sawe þis stok of worþines,
As he was wont, manfully him dresse
To armyn hym in stele bornyd briȝt,
Þis Troyan wal, Hector, þis worþi knyȝt,
She can no more, but at his fet fil doun,
Lowly declarynge hir avisioun,   4940
With quakynge herte of verray wommanhede.
Where-of, God wote, he toke litil hede,
But þer-of hadde indignacioun,
Platly affermyng, þat no discrecioun
Was to trest in swiche fantasies,
In dremys shewid, gladly meynt with lyes,
Ful of iapis and illusiouns,
Of whiche, pleynly, þe conclusiouns
Be nat ellis but folkis to delude, . . .

[*Andromache begs Hecuba and Priam to help restrain Hector.*]

And seide, 'allas!' with a ful pale chere, [4987]
'Helpe in þis cas, myn owne moder dere,
Of wommanhed and routh[e] doþ me grace,
Þat my lord in-to þe feld ne pace;   4990
And doth ȝour deuer, of moderly pite
Benignely and goodly for to se
To his knyȝthod and his hiȝe prowes,
For to restreyne his renomed noblesse,
Þilke day to handle spere nor shelde,
Nor þat he go armyd in-to þe felde.'
And boþe tweyne assent[e] for þe beste,
And condescende vn-to hir requeste,
Finally accordynge in-to oon.

[*Hector pursues and kills a Greek king, in rich armour; and his covetousness
is his downfall.*]

But al þis tyme, Hector, vp & doun,   [5325]
As he was wont, pleieþ þe lyoun
Amonge Grekis in many sondri place,
And with his swerd gan hem so to enchase,
Þat as þe deth, where þei myȝt hym sen,
Þei fledde a-forn hym like a swarm of ben: 5330
For noon so hardy was hym to with-sette.
And, in þis while, a Grekysh kyng he mette,
Were it of hap or of auenture,
Þe whiche, in soth, on his cotearmvre
Enbroudid had ful many riche stoon,
Þat ȝaf a liȝt, whan þe sonne shoon,
Ful briȝt and clere, þat Ioie was to sene:
For perlis white and emeraudis grene,
Ful many oon, were þere-Inne set,
And on þe cercle of his basenet,   5340
And rounde enviroun of his aventaille,
In velwet fret, al aboue þe maille,
Safirs ynde and oþer stonys rede,
Of whos array, whan Hector takeþ hede,
Towardis hym faste gan hym drawe.
And firste, I fynd, how he haþ him slawe;
And after þat, by force of his manhede,
He rent hym vp a-forn him on his stede,
And faste gan wiþ hym for to ride
From þe wardis a litel oute a-side,   5350
At good leiser, pleynly, ȝif he may,
To spoillen hym of his riche array,
Ful glad & liȝt of his newe emprise.
But out! allas! on fals couetyse!
Whos gredy fret,—þe whiche is gret pite,—
In hertis may nat liȝtly staunchid be;
Þe etyk gnaweþ be so gret distresse,
Þat it diffaceth þe hiȝe worþines,
Ful ofte sythe, of þies conquerours,
And of her fame rent aweie þe flours.   5360
Desyre of hauynge, in a gredy þouȝt,
To hiȝe noblesse sothly longeth nouȝt,
No[r] swiche pelfre, spoillynge, nor robberie
Apartene to worþi chiualrye:
For couetyse and knyȝthod, as I lere,
In o cheyne may nat be knet y-fere;
For kouþe it is, þat ofte swiche ravyne
Hath cause ben and rote of þe ruyne
Of many worþi—who-so liste take hede—

Like as ȝe may now of Hector rede,
Þat sodeinly was brouȝt to his endynge
Only for spoillynge of þis riche kyng.

[*Criseyde comes to the Greek camp, and yields on the same night to Diomedes.*]

skippeth ouer wher ȝe list nat rede,   [4417]
Til ȝe come where þat Dyomede
For hir was sent in-to Troye toun,
Where ceriously is maked mencioun,   4420
First, how þat she to hym delyuered was
For Anthenor and for kyng Thoas,
And how Troilus gan hir to conveie,
With many oþer, to bringe hir on þe weie;
And after þis, how þat Dyomede,
By þe weie gan hir bridel lede
Til he hir brouȝt to hir fadres tent;
And how Calchas, in ful good entent,
Received hir, logged þer he lay,
And of hir speche duryng al þat day,   4430
And al þe manner hool and euerydel—
Al is rehersid ceriously and wel
In Troylus boke, as ȝe han herd me seyn—
To write it efte, I holde it wer but veyn.
But Guydo seith, longe or it was nyȝt,
How Cryseyde for-soke hir owne knyȝt,
And ȝaf hir herte vn-to Dyomede.

4.   Ovid, *Metamorphoses*.

Shakespeare's Ovid, being Arthur Golding's translation of the Metamorphoses, ed. W. H. D. Rouse, 1904; Book I, ll. 141–72, 257–79; Book XIII, ll. 12–14, 27–34, 261–7, 390–8, 437–47, 525–51; Book XII, ll. 486–91.

[*Disorders of the Iron Age.*]

Next after this succeeded streight, the third and brazen
    age: [141]
More hard of nature, somewhat bent to cruell warres and
    rage,
But yet not wholy past all grace. Of yron is the last
In no part good and tractable as former ages past.
For when that of this wicked age once opened was the veyne
Therein all mischief rushed forth, then Fayth and Truth were
    faine
And honest shame to hide their heades: for whom stept stoutly in,

Craft, Treason, Violence, Envie, Pryde and wicked Lust to win.
The shipman hoyst his sailes to wind, whose names he did not
    knowe:
And shippes thet erst in toppes of hilles and mountaines had
    ygrowe,   150
Did leape and daunce on uncouth waves: and men began to
    bound,
With dowles and diches drawen in length the free and fertile
    ground.
Which was as common as the Ayre and light of Sunne before.
Not onely corne and other fruites, for sustnance and for store,
Were now exacted of the earth: but eft they gan to digge
And in the bowels of the ground unsaciably to rigge,
For Riches coucht and hidden deepe in places nere to Hell,
The spurres and stirrers unto vice, and foes to doing well.
Then hurtfull yron came abrode, then came forth yellow golde
More hurtfull than the yron farre, then came forth battle
    bolde   160
That feightes with both, and shakes his sword in cruell bloudy
    hand.
Men live by ravine and by stelth: the wandring guest doth stand
In daunger of his host: the host in daunger of his guest:
And fathers of their sonne in laws: yea seldome time doth rest
Betweene borne brothers such accord and love as ought to bee,
The goodman seekes the goodwives death, and his againe seekes
    shee.
The stepdames fell their husbands sonnes with poyson do assayle.
To see their fathers live so long the children doe bewayle.
All godlynesse lyes under foote. And Ladie *Astrey* last
Of heavenly vertues from this earth in slaughter drownèd
    past.   170
    And to thintent the earth alone thus should not be opprest,
    And heaven above in slouthfull ease and carelesse quiet rest.

[*Lycaon is punished for his enormities by becoming a wolf.*]

I gave a signe that God was come, and streight the common
    sort   [257]
Devoutly prayde, whereat *Lycaon* first did make a sport
And after said: by open proufe ere long I minde to see,
If that this wight a mighty God or mortall creature bee.   260
The truth shall trie it selfe: he ment (the sequele did declare)
To steale upon me in the night and kyll me unbeware.
And yet he was not so content: but went and cut the throte,
Of one that laye in hostage there which was an *Epyrote*:
And part of him he did to rost, and part he did to stew.
Which when it came upon the borde, forthwith I overthrew
The House with just revenging fire upon the owners hed,

Whoo seeing that, slipt out of doores amazde for feare, and fled
Into the wild and desert woods, where being all alone,
As he endevorde (but in vaine) to speake and make his mone,   270
He fell a howling: wherewithall for verie rage and moode
He ran me quite out of his wits and waxed furious woode,
Still practising his wonted lust of slaughter on the poore
And sielie cattle, thirsting still for bleud as heretofore.
His garments turnde to shackie heare, his armes to rugged pawes:
So is he made a ravening Woolf: whose shape expressely drawes
To that the which he was before: his skinne is horie graye,
His looke still grim with glaring eyes, and every kinde of waye
His cruell hart in outward shape dooth well it self bewraye.

[*The contest for the armour of Achilles: Ajax pleads his military prowess
and his birth.*]

                For looke how farre I him excell   [12]
In battell and in feates of armes: so farre beares hee the bell
From mee in talking.

            I of *Telamon* am knowne the sonne too bee   [27]
Who under valeant *Hercules* the walles of *Troy* did scale,
And in the shippe of *Pagasa* too *Colchos* land did sayle.
His father was that *Aeäcus* whoo executeth ryght   30
Among the ghostes where *Sisyphus* heaves up with all his myght
The massye stone ay tumbling downe. The hyghest *Jove* of all
Acknowledgeth this *Aeäcus*, and dooth his sonne him call.
Thus am I *Ajax* third from *Jove*.

[*Ulysses pleads his wisdom and policy.*]

             For if thou my deedes seeke,   [261]
I practysd sundry pollycies too trappe our foes unware:
I fortifyde our Camp with trench which heretoofore lay bare:
I hartned our companions with a quiet mynd too beare
The longnesse of the weery warre: I taught us how wee were
Bothe too bee fed and furnished: and too and fro I went
Too places where the Counsell thought most meete I should bee
    sent.

[*Ulysses' sarcasm at the expense of Ajax' wit and diplomacy.*]

            Appoynt not mee thertoo: 390
But let sir *Ajax* rather go. For he with eloquence
Or by some suttle pollycie, shall bring the man[1] fro thence
And pacyfie him raging through disease, and wrathfull ire.
Nay, first the river *Simois* shall too his spring retyre,
And mountaine *Ida* shall thereon have stonding never a tree,
Yea and the faythlesse towne of *Troy* by Greekes shall reskewd bee,

1. i.e. Philoctetes.

Before that *Ajax* blockish wit shall aught at all avayle
When my attempts and practyses in your affayres doo fayle.

[*The active man is controlled by the intelligent.*]

             Thou hast a hand that serveth well in fyght,   [437]
Thou hast a wit that stands in neede of my direction ryght.
Thy force is witlesse: I have care of that that may ensew.
Thou well canst fyght: the king dooth choose the tymes for
      fyghting dew   440
By myne advyce. Thou only with thy body canst avayle,
But I with bodye and with mynd too profite doo not fayle.
And looke how much the mayster dooth excell the gally slave,
Or looke how much preheminence the Capteine ought too have
Above his souldyer: even so much excell I also thee.
A wit farre passing strength of hand inclosed is in mee.
In wit rests cheefly all my force.

[*Neoptolemus sacrifices Polyxena to the ghost of his father Achilles.*]

             It happened by the way,   [525]
That *Agamemnon* was compeld with all his fleete too stay
Uppon the coast of *Thrace*, untill the sea were wexen calme,
And till the hideous stormes did cease, and furious wynds were
      falne.
Heere rysing gastly from the ground which farre about him brake,
Achilles with a threatning looke did like resemblance make,   530
As when at *Agamemnon* he his wrongfull swoord did shake,
And sayd: Unmyndfull part yee hence of mee O Greekes? and
      must
My merits thanklesse thus with mee be buryed in the dust?
Nay, doo not so. But too thentent my death dew honour have
Let *Polyxene* in sacrifyse bee slayne uppon my grave.
Thus much he sayd: and shortly his companions dooing as
By vision of his cruell ghost commaundment given them was,
Did fetch her from her mothers lappe, whom at that tyme, well
      neere,
In that most great adversitie alonly shee did cheere.
The haultye and unhappye mayd, and rather too bee
      thought   540
A man than woman, too the tumb with cruell hands was brought,
Too make a cursed sacrifyse. Whoo mynding constantly
Her honour, when shee standing at the Altar prest too dye,
Perceyvd the savage ceremonies in making ready, and
The cruell *Neöptolemus* with naked swoord in hand,
Stand staring with ungentle eyes uppon her gentle face,
    Shee sayd: Now use thou when thou wilt my gentle blood.
      The cace
Requyres no more delay. Bestow thy weapon in my chest,

Or in my throte: (in saying so shee profered bare her brest,
And eeke her throte). Assure your selves it never shalbee
    seene,   550
That any wyght shall (by my will) have slave of *Polyxeene*.

[*Nestor regrets his lost youth and vigour, and laments that he can no longer
be reckoned equal with Hector.*]

                Then was the tyme that I   [486]
Should sent have beene too conquer *Troy*. Then was the tyme
    that I
Myght through my force and prowesse, if not vanquish *Hector*
    stout,
Yit at the least have hilld him wag, I put you out of Dout.
But then was *Hector* no body: or but a babe. And now   490
Am I forspent and worne with yeeres.

Ulysses of Time
P. 215
note 174